A·N·N·U·A·L E·D·I·T·I·O·N·S

Geography 02/03

Seventeenth Edition

EDITOR

Gerald R. Pitzl

Macalester College

Gerald R. Pitzl, professor of geography at Macalester College, received his bachelor's degree in secondary social science education from the University of Minnesota in 1964 and his M.A. (1971) and Ph.D. (1974) in geography from the same institution. He teaches a wide array of geography courses and is the author of a number of articles on geography, the developing world, and the use of the Harvard case method.

McGraw-Hill/Dushkin

530 Old Whitfield Street, Guilford, Connecticut 06437

Visit us on the Internet

http://www.dushkin.com

Credits

1. **Geography in a Changing World**
   Unit photo—© 2002 by PhotoDisc, Inc.
2. **Human-Environment Relationships**
   Unit photo—© United Nations by Rick Grunbaum.
3. **The Region**
   Unit photo—© United Nations by Chen.
4. **Spatial Interaction and Mapping**
   Unit photo—Courtesy of Digital Stock.
5. **Population, Resources, and Socioeconomic Development**
   Unit photo—© United Nations by J. K. Isaac.

Copyright

Cataloging in Publication Data
Main entry under title: Annual Editions: Geography. 2002/2003.
1. Geography—Periodicals. I. Anthropo-geography—Periodicals. 3. Natural resources—Periodicals.
I. Pitzl, Gerald R., *comp.* I. Title: Geography.
ISBN 0–07–250658–X 658'.05 ISSN 1091–9937

Seventeenth Edition

Printed in the United States of America 1234567890BAHBAH5432 Printed on Recycled Paper

Editors/Advisory Board

Members of the Advisory Board are instrumental in the final selection of articles for each edition of ANNUAL EDITIONS. Their review of articles for content, level, currentness, and appropriateness provides critical direction to the editor and staff. We think that you will find their careful consideration well reflected in this volume.

Staff

To the Reader

In publishing ANNUAL EDITIONS we recognize the enormous role played by the magazines, newspapers, and journals of the public press in providing current, first-rate educational information in a broad spectrum of interest areas. Many of these articles are appropriate for students, researchers, and professionals seeking accurate, current material to help bridge the gap between principles and theories and the real world. These articles, however, become more useful for study when those of lasting value are carefully collected, organized, indexed, and reproduced in a low-cost format, which provides easy and permanent access when the material is needed. That is the role played by ANNUAL EDITIONS.

The articles in this seventeenth edition of *Annual Editions: Geography* represent the wide range of topics associated with the discipline of geography. The major themes of spatial relationships, regional development, the population explosion, and socioeconomic inequalities exemplify the diversity of research areas within geography.

The book is organized into five units, each containing articles relating to geographical themes. Selections address the conceptual nature of geography and the global and regional problems in the world today. This latter theme reflects the geographer's concern with finding solutions to these serious issues. Regional problems, such as food shortages in the Sahel and the greenhouse effect, concern not only geographers but also researchers from other disciplines.

The association of geography with other fields is important, because expertise from related research will be necessary in finding solutions to some difficult problems. Input from the focus of geography is vital in our common search for solutions. This discipline has always been integrative. That is, geography uses evidence from many sources to answer the basic questions, "Where is it?" "Why is it there?" and "What is its relevance?" The first group of articles emphasizes the interconnectedness not only of places and regions in the world but of efforts toward solutions to problems as well. No single discipline can have all of the answers to the problems facing us today; the complexity of the issues is simply too great.

The writings in unit 1 discuss particular aspects of geography as a discipline and provide examples of the topics presented in the remaining four sections. Units 2, 3, and 4 represent major themes in geography. Unit 5 addresses important problems faced by geographers and others.

Annual Editions: Geography 02/03 will be useful to both teachers and students in their study of geography. The anthology is designed to provide detail and case study material to supplement the standard textbook treatment of geography. The goals of this anthology are to introduce students to the richness and diversity of topics relating to places and regions on Earth's surface, to pay heed to the serious problems facing humankind, and to stimulate the search for more information on topics of interest.

I would like to express my gratitude to Barbara Wells-Howe for her continued help in preparing this material for publication. Her typing, organization of materials, and many helpful suggestions are greatly appreciated. Without her diligence and professional efforts, this undertaking could not have been completed. Special thanks are also extended to Ian Nielsen for his continued encouragement during the preparation of this new edition, and to the rest of the editorial staff for coordinating the production of the reader. A word of thanks must go as well to all those who recommended articles for inclusion in this volume and who commented on its overall organization. Peter O. Muller, Tom Paradise, Eileen Starr, Wayne J. Strickland, and Randy W. Widdis were especially helpful in that regard.

In order to improve the next edition of *Annual Editions: Geography,* we need your help. Please share your opinions by filling out and returning to us the postage-paid *article rating form* on the last page of this book. We will give serious consideration to all your comments.

Gerald R. Pitzl
Editor

Contents

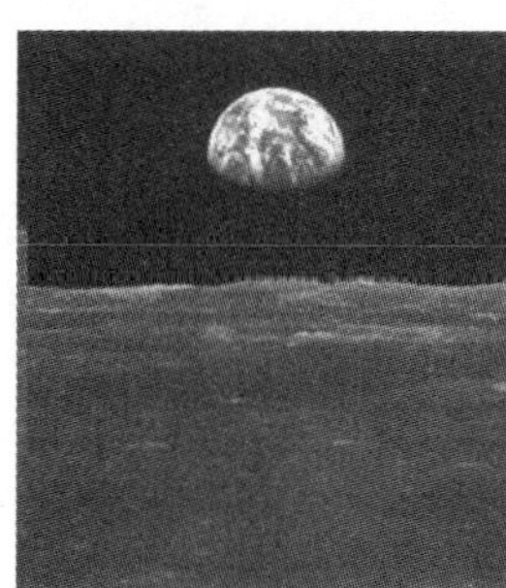

UNIT 1
Geography in a Changing World

Nine articles discuss the discipline of geography and the extremely varied and wideranging themes that define geography today.

The concepts in bold italics are developed in the article. For further expansion, please refer to the Topic Guide and the Index.

UNIT 2
Human-Environment Relationships

Ten articles examine the relationship between humans and the land on which we live. Topics include global warming, water management, urban sprawl, pollution, and the effects of human society on the global environment.

The concepts in bold italics are developed in the article. For further expansion, please refer to the Topic Guide and the Index.

UNIT 3
The Region

Ten selections review the importance of the region as a concept in geography and as an organizing framework for research. A number of world regional trends, as well as the patterns of areas relationships, are examined.

The concepts in bold italics are developed in the article. For further expansion, please refer to the Topic Guide and the Index.

UNIT 4
Spatial Interaction and Mapping

Eight articles discuss the key theme in geographical analysis: place-to-place spatial interaction. Human diffusion, transportation systems, and cartography are some of the themes examined.

The concepts in bold italics are developed in the article. For further expansion, please refer to the Topic Guide and the Index.

UNIT 5
Population, Resources, and Socioeconomic Development

Nine articles examine the effects of population growth on natural resources and the resulting socioeconomic level of development.

The concepts in bold italics are developed in the article. For further expansion, please refer to the Topic Guide and the Index.

The concepts in bold italics are developed in the article. For further expansion, please refer to the Topic Guide and the Index.

Topic Guide

This topic guide suggests how the selections in this book relate to the subjects covered in your course. You may want to use the topics listed on these pages to search the Web more easily.

On the following pages a number of Web sites have been gathered specifically for this book. They are arranged to reflect the units of this *Annual Edition.* You can link to these sites by going to the DUSHKIN ONLINE support site at *http://www.dushkin.com/online/.*

ALL THE ARTICLES THAT RELATE TO EACH TOPIC ARE LISTED BELOW THE BOLD-FACED TERM.

World Wide Web Sites

The following World Wide Web sites have been carefully researched and selected to support the articles found in this reader. The easiest way to access these selected sites is to go to our DUSHKIN ONLINE support site at *http://www.dushkin.com/online/*.

AE: Geography 02/03

The following sites were available at the time of publication. Visit our Web site—we update DUSHKIN ONLINE regularly to reflect any changes.

General Sources

About: Geography
http://geography.about.com
This Web site, created by the About network, contains hyperlinks to many specific areas of geography including cartography, population, country facts, historic maps, physical geography, topographic maps, and many others.

The Association of American Geographers (AAG)
http://www.aag.org
Surf this site of the Association of American Geographers to learn about AAG projects and publications, careers in geography, and information about related organizations.

Geography Network
http://www.geographynetwork.com
The Geography Network is an online resource to discover and access geographical content, including live maps and data, from many of the world's leading providers.

National Geographic Society
http://www.nationalgeographic.com
This site provides links to National Geographic's huge archive of maps, articles, and other documents. Search the site for information about worldwide expeditions of interest to geographers.

The New York Times
http://www.nytimes.com
Browsing through the archives of the *New York Times* will provide you with a wide array of articles and information related to the different subfields of geography.

Social Science Internet Resources
http://www.wcsu.ctstateu.edu/library/ss_geography.html
This site is a definitive source for geography-related links to universities, browsers, cartography, associations, and discussion groups.

U.S. Geological Survey (USGS)
http://www.usgs.gov
This site and its many links are replete with information and resources for geographers, from explanations of El Niño, to mapping, to geography education, to water resources. No geographer's resource list would be complete without frequent mention of the USGS.

UNIT 1: Geography in a Changing World

Alternative Energy Institute (AEI)
http://www.altenergy.org
The AEI will continue to monitor the transition from today's energy forms to the future in a "surprising journey of twists and turns." This site is the beginning of an incredible journey.

Geological Survey of Sweden: Other Geological Surveys
http://www.sgu.se/index_e.htm
This site provides links to the national geographical surveys of many countries in Europe and elsewhere, including Brazil, South Africa, and the United States, for very interesting and informative browsing.

Mission to Planet Earth
http://www.earth.nasa.gov
This site will direct you to information about NASA's Mission to Planet Earth program and its Science of the Earth System. Surf here to learn about satellites, El Niño, and even "strategic visions" of interest to geographers.

Nuclear Power Introduction
http://library.thinkquest.org/17658/nuc/nucintroht.html?tqskip1=1&tqtime=0125
Here you will find information regarding alternative energy forms. There is a brief introduction to nuclear power and a link to the geography of nuclear power--maps that show where nuclear power plants exist.

Poverty Mapping
http://www.povertymap.net
Poverty maps can quickly provide information on the spatial distribution of poverty. Here you will find maps, graphics, data, publications, news, and links that provide the public with poverty mapping from the global to the subnational level.

Santa Fe Institute
http://acoma.santafe.edu/sfi/research/
This home page of the Santa Fe Institute—a nonprofit, multidisciplinary research and education center—will lead you to a plethora of valuable links related to its primary goal: to create a new kind of scientific research community, pursuing emerging science. Such links as Evolution of Language, Ecology, and Local Rules for Global Problems are offered.

Solstice: Documents and Databases
http://solstice.crest.org/docndata.shtml
In this online source for sustainable energy information, the Center for Renewable Energy and Sustainable Technology (CREST) offers documents and databases on renewable energy, energy efficiency, and sustainable living. The site also offers related Web sites, case studies, and policy issues. Solstice also connects to CREST's Web presence.

UNIT 2: Human-Environment Relationships

Alliance for Global Sustainability (AGS)
http://www.global-sustainability.org
The AGS is a cooperative venture seeking solutions to today's urgent and complex environmental problems. Research teams from four research universities study large-scale, multidisciplinary environmental problems that are faced by the world's ecosystems, economies, and societies.

Environment News Service: Global Warming Could Make Water a Scarce Resource

http://ens.lycos.com/ens/dec2000/2000L-12-15-06.html

This article, by Lazaroff, makes interesting reading. Lazaroff reports the results of a 2-year study of the potential impacts of climate change on the nation's fresh and salt water systems. One of the conclusions: "Humans are changing the climate."

Human Geography

http://www.geog.le.ac.uk/cti/hum.html

The CTI Centre for Geography, Geology and Meteorology provides this site, which contains links to human geography in relation to agriculture, anthropology, archaeology, development geography, economic geography, geography of gender, and many others.

The North-South Institute

http://www.nsi-ins.ca/ensi/index.html

Searching this site of the North-South Institute—which works to strengthen international development cooperation and enhance gender and social equity—will help you find information on a variety of development issues.

United Nations Environment Programme (UNEP)

http://www.unep.ch

Consult this home page of UNEP for links to critical topics of concern to geographers, including desertification and the impact of trade on the environment. The site will direct you to useful databases and global resource information.

World Health Organization

http://www.who.int

This home page of the World Health Organization will provide you with links to a wealth of statistical and analytical information about health in the developing world.

UNIT 3: The Region

AS at UVA Yellow Pages: Regional Studies

http://xroads.virginia.edu/~YP/regional/regional.html

Those interested in American regional studies will find this site a gold mine. Links to periodicals and other informational resources about the Midwest/Central, Northeast, South, and West regions are provided here.

Can Cities Save the Future?

http://www.huduser.org/publications/econdev/habitat/prep2.html

This press release about the second session of the Preparatory Committee for Habitat II is an excellent discussion of the question of global urbanization.

IISDnet

http://iisd.ca

The International Institute for Sustainable Development, a Canadian organization, presents information through gateways entitled Business and Sustainable Development, Developing Ideas, and Hot Topics. Linkages is its multimedia resource for environment and development policymakers.

NewsPage

http://www.individual.com

Individual, Inc., maintains this business-oriented Web site. Geographers will find links to much valuable information about such fields as energy, environmental services, media and communications, and health care.

Telecommuting as an Investment: The Big Picture—John Wolf

http://www.svi.org/telework/forums/messages5/48.html

This page deals with the many issues related to telecommuting,including its potential role in reducing environmental pollution. The site discusses such topics as employment law and the impact of telecommuting on businesses and employees.

The Urban Environment

http://www.geocities.com/RainForest/Vines/6723/urb/index.html

Global urbanization is discussed fully at this site, which also includes the original 1992 Treaty on Urbanization.

Virtual Seminar in Global Political Economy/Global Cities & Social Movements

http://csf.colorado.edu/gpe/gpe95b/resources.html

This Web site is rich in links to subjects of interest in regional studies, such as sustainable cities, megacities, and urban planning. Links to many international nongovernmental organizations are included.

World Regions & Nation States

http://www.worldcapitalforum.com/worregstat.html

This site provides strategic and competitive intelligence on regions and individual states, geopolitical analyses, geopolitical factors of globalization factors, geopolitics of production, and much more.

UNIT 4: Spatial Interaction and Mapping

Edinburgh Geographical Information Systems

http://www.geo.ed.ac.uk/home/gishome.html

This valuable site, hosted by the Department of Geography at the University of Edinburgh, provides information on all aspects of Geographic Information Systems and provides links to other servers worldwide. A GIS reference database as well as a major GIS bibliography is included.

Geography for GIS

http://www.ncgia.ucsb.edu/cctp/units/geog_for_GIS/GC_index.html

This hyperlinked table of contents was created by Robert Slobodian of Malaspina University. Here you will find information regarding GIS technology.

GIS Frequently Asked Questions and General Information

http://www.census.gov/ftp/pub/geo/www/faq-index.html

Browse through this site to get answers to FAQs about Geographic Information Systems. It can direct you to general information about GIS as well as guidelines on such specific questions as how to order U.S. Geological Survey maps. Other sources of information are also noted.

International Map Trade Association

http://www.maptrade.org

The International Map Trade Association offers this site for those interested in information on maps, geography, and mapping technology. Lists of map retailers and publishers as well as upcoming IMTA conferences and trade shows are noted.

PSC Publications

http://www.psc.lsa.umich.edu/pubs/abs/abs94-319.html

Use this site and its links from the Population Studies Center of the University of Michigan for spatial patterns of immigration and discussion of white and black flight from high immigration metropolitan areas in the United States.

U.S. Geological Survey

http://www.usgs.gov/research/gis/title.html

This site discusses the uses for Geographic Information Systems and explains how GIS works, addressing such topics as data integration, data modeling, and relating information from different sources.

UNIT 5: Population, Resources, and Socioeconomic Development

African Studies WWW (U.Penn)

http://www.sas.upenn.edu/African_Studies/AS.html

Access to rich and varied resources that cover such topics as demographics, migration, family planning, and health and nutrition is available at this site.

Geography and Socioeconomic Development

http://www.ksg.harvard.edu/cid/andes/Documents/Background%20Papers/Geography&Socioeconomic%20Development.pdf

John L. Gallup wrote this 19 page background paper examining the state of the Andean region. He explains the strong and pervasive effects geography has on economic and social development.

Human Rights and Humanitarian Assistance

http://www.pitt.edu/~ian/resource/human.htm

Through this site, part of the World Wide Web Virtual Library, you can conduct research into a number of human-rights topics in order to gain a greater understanding of the issues affecting indigenous peoples in the modern era.

Hypertext and Ethnography

http://www.umanitoba.ca/faculties/arts/anthropology/tutor/aaa_presentation.new.html

This site, presented by Brian Schwimmer of the University of Manitoba, will be of great value to people who are interested in culture and communication. He addresses such topics as multivocality and complex symbolization, among many others.

Research and Reference (Library of Congress)

http://lcweb.loc.gov/rr/

This research and reference site of the Library of Congress will lead you to invaluable information on different countries. It provides links to numerous publications, bibliographies, and guides in area studies that can be of great help to geographers.

Space Research Institute

http://arc.iki.rssi.ru/Welcome.html

Browse through this home page of Russia's Space Research Institute for information on its Environment Monitoring Information Systems, the IKI Satellite Situation Center, and its Data Archive.

World Population and Demographic Data

http://geography.about.com/cs/worldpopulation/

On this site you will find information about world population and additional demographic data for all the countries of the world.

We highly recommend that you review our Web site for expanded information and our other product lines. We are continually updating and adding links to our Web site in order to offer you the most usable and useful information that will support and expand the value of your Annual Editions. You can reach us at: *http://www.dushkin.com/annualeditions/*.

World Map

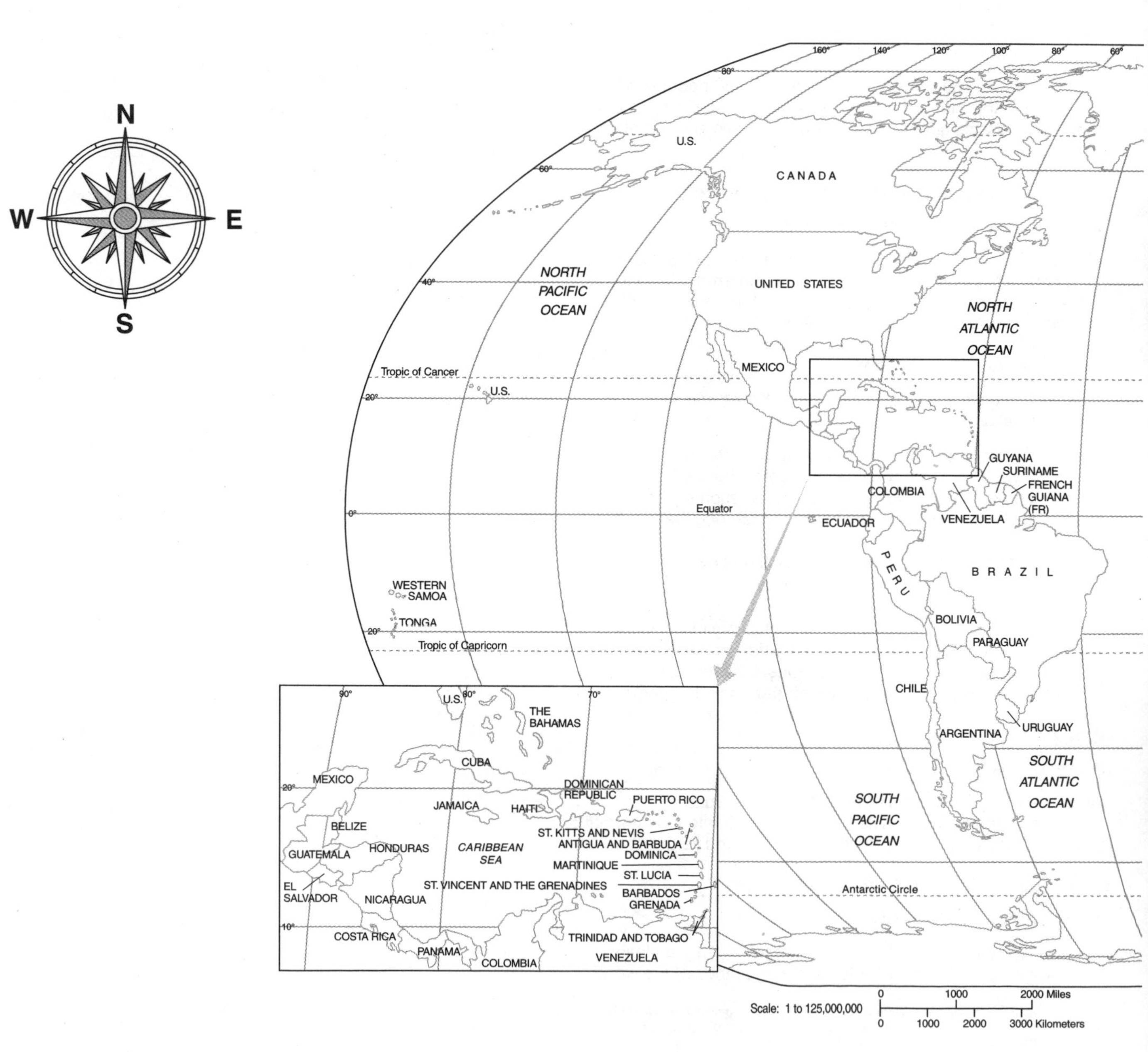

N
W
E
S
160°
140°
120°
100°
80°
60°
80°
60°
40°
20°
0°
20°
U.S.
CANADA
NORTH
PACIFIC
OCEAN
UNITED STATES
NORTH
ATLANTIC
OCEAN
MEXICO
Tropic of Cancer
U.S.
GUYANA
SURINAME
FRENCH
GUIANA
(FR)
COLOMBIA
VENEZUELA
Equator
ECUADOR
PERU
BRAZIL
WESTERN
SAMOA
TONGA
BOLIVIA
PARAGUAY
Tropic of Capricorn
CHILE
ARGENTINA
URUGUAY
SOUTH
ATLANTIC
OCEAN
SOUTH
PACIFIC
OCEAN
Antarctic Circle
90°
U.S.
80°
70°
THE
BAHAMAS
CUBA
MEXICO
DOMINICAN
REPUBLIC
JAMAICA
HAITI
PUERTO RICO
BELIZE
ST. KITTS AND NEVIS
ANTIGUA AND BARBUDA
GUATEMALA
HONDURAS
CARIBBEAN
SEA
DOMINICA
MARTINIQUE
ST. LUCIA
ST. VINCENT AND THE GRENADINES
BARBADOS
EL
SALVADOR
NICARAGUA
GRENADA
10°
COSTA RICA
TRINIDAD AND TOBAGO
PANAMA
COLOMBIA
VENEZUELA
Scale: 1 to 125,000,000
0
1000
2000 Miles
0
1000
2000
3000 Kilometers

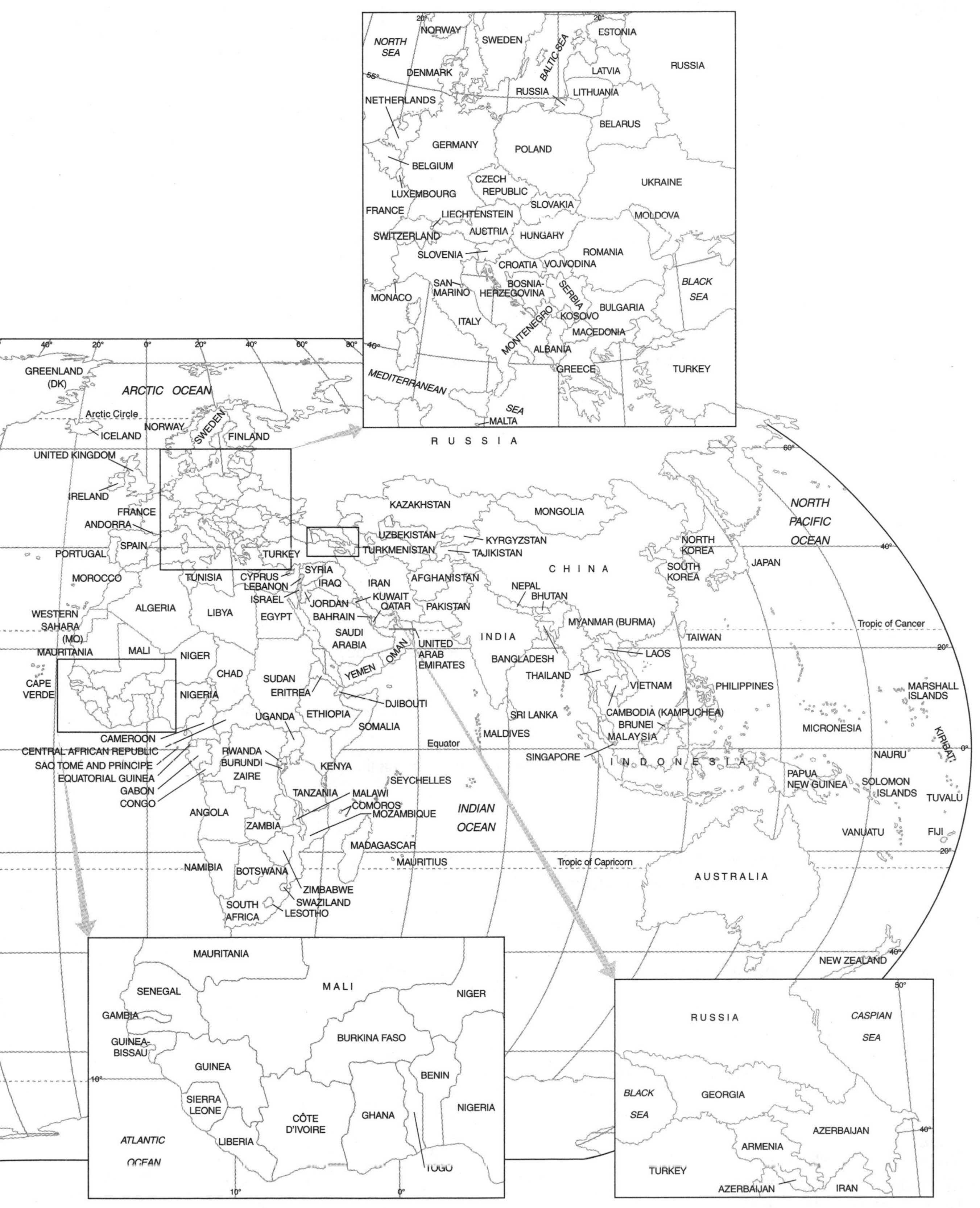

NORTH SEA
NORWAY
SWEDEN
BALTIC SEA
ESTONIA
RUSSIA
DENMARK
LATVIA
RUSSIA
LITHUANIA
NETHERLANDS
BELARUS
GERMANY
POLAND
BELGIUM
CZECH REPUBLIC
UKRAINE
LUXEMBOURG
SLOVAKIA
FRANCE
LIECHTENSTEIN
MOLDOVA
SWITZERLAND
AUSTRIA
HUNGARY
SLOVENIA
ROMANIA
CROATIA
VOJVODINA
SAN MARINO
BOSNIA-HERZEGOVINA
SERBIA
BLACK SEA
MONACO
BULGARIA
KOSOVO
ITALY
MONTENEGRO
MACEDONIA
ALBANIA
GREECE
TURKEY
MEDITERRANEAN SEA
MALTA
GREENLAND (DK)
ARCTIC OCEAN
Arctic Circle
ICELAND
NORWAY
SWEDEN
FINLAND
R U S S I A
UNITED KINGDOM
IRELAND
FRANCE
ANDORRA
SPAIN
PORTUGAL
KAZAKHSTAN
MONGOLIA
NORTH PACIFIC OCEAN
UZBEKISTAN
KYRGYZSTAN
TURKMENISTAN
TAJIKISTAN
NORTH KOREA
SOUTH KOREA
JAPAN
TURKEY
MOROCCO
TUNISIA
CYPRUS
LEBANON
ISRAEL
SYRIA
IRAQ
IRAN
AFGHANISTAN
C H I N A
NEPAL
BHUTAN
ALGERIA
LIBYA
EGYPT
JORDAN
KUWAIT
QATAR
BAHRAIN
PAKISTAN
WESTERN SAHARA (MO)
SAUDI ARABIA
UNITED ARAB EMIRATES
I N D I A
MYANMAR (BURMA)
Tropic of Cancer
TAIWAN
MAURITANIA
MALI
NIGER
CHAD
SUDAN
YEMEN
OMAN
BANGLADESH
LAOS
THAILAND
VIETNAM
PHILIPPINES
MARSHALL ISLANDS
CAPE VERDE
NIGERIA
ERITREA
DJIBOUTI
ETHIOPIA
UGANDA
SOMALIA
SRI LANKA
CAMBODIA (KAMPUCHEA)
BRUNEI
MALAYSIA
MICRONESIA
KIRIBATI
CAMEROON
CENTRAL AFRICAN REPUBLIC
SAO TOMÉ AND PRINCIPE
EQUATORIAL GUINEA
GABON
CONGO
RWANDA
BURUNDI
ZAIRE
KENYA
MALDIVES
Equator
SINGAPORE
I N D O N E S I A
NAURU
SEYCHELLES
PAPUA NEW GUINEA
SOLOMON ISLANDS
TUVALU
TANZANIA
MALAWI
COMOROS
MOZAMBIQUE
ANGOLA
ZAMBIA
INDIAN OCEAN
VANUATU
FIJI
MADAGASCAR
MAURITIUS
Tropic of Capricorn
NAMIBIA
BOTSWANA
ZIMBABWE
SWAZILAND
SOUTH AFRICA
LESOTHO
AUSTRALIA
NEW ZEALAND
MAURITANIA
MALI
NIGER
SENEGAL
GAMBIA
GUINEA-BISSAU
BURKINA FASO
GUINEA
BENIN
SIERRA LEONE
CÔTE D'IVOIRE
GHANA
NIGERIA
LIBERIA
ATLANTIC OCEAN
TOGO
RUSSIA
CASPIAN SEA
BLACK SEA
GEORGIA
AZERBAIJAN
ARMENIA
TURKEY
AZERBAIJAN
IRAN

UNIT 1

Geography in a Changing World

Unit Selections

1. **Rediscovering the Importance of Geography**, Alexander B. Murphy
2. **The Geography of Poverty and Wealth**, Jeffrey D. Sachs, Andrew D. Mellinger, and John L. Gallup
3. **The Four Traditions of Geography**, William D. Pattison
4. **Teaching Geography's Four Traditions With Poetry**, Daniel P. Donaldson
5. **The American Geographies**, Barry Lopez
6. **Human Domination of Earth's Ecosystems**, Peter M. Vitousek, Harold A. Mooney, Jane Lubchenco, and Jerry M. Melillo
7. **Sculpting the Earth From Inside Out**, Michael Gurnis
8. **Nuclear Power: A Renaissance That May Not Come**, *The Economist*
9. **A Broken Heartland**, Jeff Glasser

Key Points to Consider

- Why is geography called an integrating discipline?
- How is geography related to earth science? Give some examples of these relationships.
- What are area studies? Why is the spatial concept so important in geography? What is your definition of geography?
- Discuss whether or not change is a good thing. Why is it important to anticipate change?
- Will nuclear power generation increase?
- What does interconnectedness mean in terms of places? Give examples of how you as an individual interact with people in other places. How are you "connected" to the rest of the world?
- What will the world be like in the year 2010? Tell why you are pessimistic or optimistic about the future. What, if anything, can you do about the future?

Links: www.dushkin.com/online/
These sites are annotated in the World Wide Web pages.

Alternative Energy Institute (AEI)
http://www.altenergy.org

Geological Survey of Sweden: Other Geological Surveys
http://www.sgu.se/index_e.htm

Mission to Planet Earth
http://www.earth.nasa.gov

Nuclear Power Introduction
http://library.thinkquest.org/17658/nuc/nucintroht.html?tqskip1=1& tqtime=0125

Poverty Mapping
http://www.povertymap.net

Santa Fe Institute
http://acoma.santafe.edu/sfi/research/

Solstice: Documents and Databases
http://solstice.crest.org/docndata.shtml

What is geography? This question has been asked innumerable times, but it has not elicited a universally accepted answer, even from those who are considered to be members of the geography profession. The reason lies in the very nature of geography as it has evolved through time. Geography is an extremely wide-ranging discipline, one that examines appropriate sets of events or circumstances occurring at specific places. Its goal is to answer certain basic questions.

The first question—Where is it?—establishes the location of the subject under investigation. The concept of location is very important in geography, and its meaning extends beyond the common notion of a specific address or the determination of the latitude and longitude of a place. Geographers are more concerned with the relative location of a place and how that place interacts with other places both far and near. Spatial interaction and the determination of the connections between places are important themes in geography.

Once a place is "located," in the geographer's sense of the word, the next question is, Why is it here? For example, why are people concentrated in high numbers on the North China plain, in the Ganges River Valley in India, and along the eastern seaboard in the United States? Conversely, why are there so few people in the Amazon basin and the Central Siberian lowlands? Generally, the geographer wants to find out why particular distribution patterns occur and why these patterns change over time.

The element of time is another extremely important ingredient in the geographical mix. Geography is most concerned with the activities of human beings, and human beings bring about change. As changes occur, new adjustments and modifications are made in the distribution patterns previously established. Patterns change, for instance, as new technology brings about new forms of communication and transportation and as once-desirable locations decline in favor of new ones. For example, people migrate from once-productive regions such as the Sahel when a disaster such as drought visits the land. Geography, then, is greatly concerned with discovering the underlying processes that can explain the transformation of distribution patterns and interaction forms over time. Geography itself is dynamic, adjusting as a discipline to handle new situations in a changing world.

Geography is truly an integrating discipline. The geographer assembles evidence from many sources in order to explain a particular pattern or ongoing process of change. Some of this evidence may even be in the form of concepts or theories borrowed from other disciplines. The first article of this unit stresses the importance of geography as a discipline and proclaims its "rediscovery." The next article emphasizes the critical importance of geographical concepts in a study of global wealth and poverty.

Throughout its history, four main themes have been the focus of research work in geography. These themes or traditions, according to William Pattison in "The Four Traditions of Geography," link geography with earth science, establish it as a field that studies land-human relationships, engage it in area studies, and give it a spatial focus. Although Pattison's article first appeared over 30 years ago, it is still referred to and cited frequently today. Much of the geographical research and analysis engaged in today would fall within one or more of Pattison's traditional areas, but new areas are also opening for geographers. Daniel Donaldson's invocation of poetry to gain new insights to Pattison's traditions is intriguing. In a particularly thought-provoking essay, the eminent author Barry Lopez discusses local geographies and the importance of a sense of place. In "Human Domination of the Earth's Ecosystems," we see how human activity is significantly altering the globe. The surface of the earth is subject to geological processes, the focus of the next article. The question of nuclear power plant expansion in the United States is raised next. The last article considers the continued depopulation of the vast Great Plains.

Article 1

POINT OF VIEW

Rediscovering the Importance of Geography

By Alexander B. Murphy

As AMERICANS STRUGGLE to understand their place in a world characterized by instant global communications, shifting geopolitical relationships, and growing evidence of environmental change, it is not surprising that the venerable discipline of geography is experiencing a renaissance in the United States. More elementary and secondary schools now require courses in geography, and the College Board is adding the subject to its Advanced Placement program. In higher education, students are enrolling in geography courses in unprecedented numbers. Between 1985–86 and 1994–95, the number of bachelor's degrees awarded in geography increased from 3,056 to 4,295. Not coincidentally, more businesses are looking for employees with expertise in geographical analysis, to help them analyze possible new markets or environmental issues.

In light of these developments, institutions of higher education cannot afford simply to ignore geography, as some of them have, or to assume that existing programs are adequate. College administrators should recognize the academic and practical advantages of enhancing their offerings in geography, particularly if they are going to meet the demand for more and better geography instruction in primary and secondary schools. We cannot afford to know so little about the other countries and peoples with which we now interact with such frequency, or about the dramatic environmental changes unfolding around us.

From the 1960s through the 1980s, most academics in the United States considered geography a marginal discipline, although it remained a core subject in most other countries. The familiar academic divide in the United States between the physical sciences, on one hand, and the social sciences and humanities, on the other, left little room for a discipline concerned with how things are organized and relate to one another on the surface of the earth—a concern that necessarily bridges the physical and cultural spheres. Moreover, beginning in the 1960s, the U.S. social-science agenda came to be dominated by pursuit of more-scientific explanations for human phenomena, based on assumptions about global similarities in human institutions, motivations, and actions. Accordingly, regional differences often were seen as idiosyncrasies of declining significance.

Although academic administrators and scholars in other disciplines might have marginalized geography, they could not kill it, for any attempt to make sense of the world must be based on some understanding of the changing human and physical patterns that shape its evolution—be they shifting vegetation zones or expanding economic contacts across international boundaries. Hence, some U.S. colleges and universities continued to teach geography, and the discipline was often in the background of many policy issues—for example, the need to assess the risks associated with foreign investment in various parts of the world.

By the late 1980s, Americans' general ignorance of geography had become too widespread to ignore. Newspapers regularly published reports of surveys demonstrating that many Americans could not identify major countries or oceans on a map. The real problem, of course, was not the inability to answer simple questions that might be asked on *Jeopardy!*; instead, it was what that inability demonstrated about our collective understanding of the globe.

Geography's renaissance in the United States is due to the growing recognition that physical and human processes such as soil erosion and ethnic unrest are inextricably tied to their geographical context. To understand modern Iraq, it is not enough to know who is in power and how the political system functions. We also need to know something about the country's ethnic groups and their settlement patterns, the different physical environments and resources within the country, and its ties to surrounding countries and trading partners.

Those matters are sometimes addressed by practitioners of other disciplines, of course, but they are rarely central to the analysis. Instead, generalizations are often made at the level of the state, and little attention is given to spatial patterns and practices that play out on local levels or across international boundaries. Such preoccupations help to explain why many scholars were caught off guard by the explosion of ethnic unrest in Eastern Europe following the fall of the Iron Curtain.

Similarly, comprehending the dynamics of El Niño requires more than knowledge of the behavior of ocean and air currents; it is also important to understand how those currents are situated with respect to land masses and how they relate to other climatic patterns, some of which have been altered by the burning of fossil fuels and other human activities. And any attempt to understand the nature and extent of humans' impact on the environment requires consideration of the relationship between human and physical contributions to environmental change. The factories and cars in a city produce smog, but surrounding mountains may trap it, increasing air pollution significantly.

TODAY, academics in fields including history, economics, and conservation biology are turning to geographers for help with some of their concerns. Paul Krugman, a noted economist at the Massachusetts Institute of Technology, for example, has turned conventional wisdom on its head by pointing out the role of historically rooted regional inequities in how international trade is structured.

Geographers work on issues ranging from climate change to ethnic conflict to urban sprawl. What unites their work is its focus on the shifting organization and character of the earth's surface. Geographers examine changing patterns of vegetation to study global warming; they analyze where ethnic groups live in Bosnia to help understand the pros and cons of competing administrative solutions to the civil war there; they map AIDS cases in Africa to learn how to reduce the spread of the disease.

Geography is reclaiming attention because it addresses such questions in their relevant spatial and environmental contexts. A growing number of scholars in other disciplines are realizing that it is a mistake to treat all places as if they were essentially the same (think of the assumptions in most economic models), or to undertake research on the environment that does not include consideration of the relationships between human and physical processes in particular regions.

Still, the challenges to the discipline are great. Only a small number of primary- and secondary-school teachers have enough training in geography to offer students an exciting introduction to the subject. At the college level, many geography departments are small; they are absent altogether at some high-profile universities.

Perhaps the greatest challenge is to overcome the public's view of geography as a simple exercise in place-name recognition. Much of geography's power lies in the insights it sheds on the nature and meaning of the evolving spatial arrangements and landscapes that make up our world. The importance of those insights should not be underestimated at a time of changing political boundaries, accelerated human alteration of the environment, and rapidly shifting patterns of human interaction.

Alexander B. Murphy is a professor and head of the geography department at the University of Oregon, and a vice-president of the American Geographical Society.

Article 2

The Geography of Poverty and Wealth

Tropical climate and lack of access to sea trade have hurt the poorest nations. But new aid programs can point the way to prosperity

by Jeffrey D. Sachs, Andrew D. Mellinger and John L. Gallup

Why are some countries stupendously rich and others horrendously poor? Social theorists have been captivated by this question since the late 18th century, when Scottish economist Adam Smith addressed the issue in his magisterial work *The Wealth of Nations.* Smith argued that the best prescription for prosperity is a free-market economy in which the government allows businesses substantial freedom to pursue profits. Over the past two centuries, Smith's hypothesis has been vindicated by the striking success of capitalist economies in North America, western Europe and East Asia and by the dismal failure of socialist planning in eastern Europe and the former Soviet Union.

Smith, however, made a second notable hypothesis: that the physical geography of a region can influence its economic performance. He contended that the economies of coastal regions, with their easy access to sea trade, usually outperform the economies of inland areas. Although most economists today follow Smith in linking prosperity with free markets, they have tended to neglect the role of geography. They implicitly assume that all parts of the world have the same prospects for economic growth and long-term development and that differences in performance are the result of differences in institutions. Our findings, based on newly available data and research methods, suggest otherwise. We have found strong evidence that geography plays an important role in shaping the distribution of world income and economic growth.

Coastal regions and those near navigable waterways are indeed far richer and more densely settled than interior regions, just as Smith predicted. Moreover, an area's climate can also affect its economic development. Nations in tropical climate zones generally face higher rates of infectious disease and lower agricultural productivity (especially for staple foods) than do nations in temperate zones. Similar burdens apply to the desert zones. The very poorest regions in the world are those saddled with both handicaps: distance from sea trade and a tropical or desert ecology.

A skeptical reader with a basic understanding of geography might comment at this point, "Fine, but isn't all of this familiar?" We have three responses. First, we go far beyond the basics by systematically quantifying the contributions of geography, economic policy and other factors in determining a nation's performance. We have combined the research tools used by geographers—including new software that can create detailed maps of global population density—with the techniques and equations of macroeconomics. Second, the basic lessons of geography are worth repeating, because most economists have ignored them. In the past decade the vast majority of papers on economic development have neglected even the most obvious geographical realities. Third, if our findings are true, the policy implications are significant. Aid programs for developing countries will have to be revamped to specifically address the problems imposed by geography. In particular, we have tried to formulate new strategies that would help nations in tropical zones raise their agricultural productivity and reduce the prevalence of diseases such as malaria.

The Geographical Divide

The best single indicator of prosperity is gross national product (GNP) per capita—the total value of a country's economic output, divided by its population. A map showing the world distribution of GNP per capita immediately reveals the vast gap between rich and poor nations

GNP per Capita

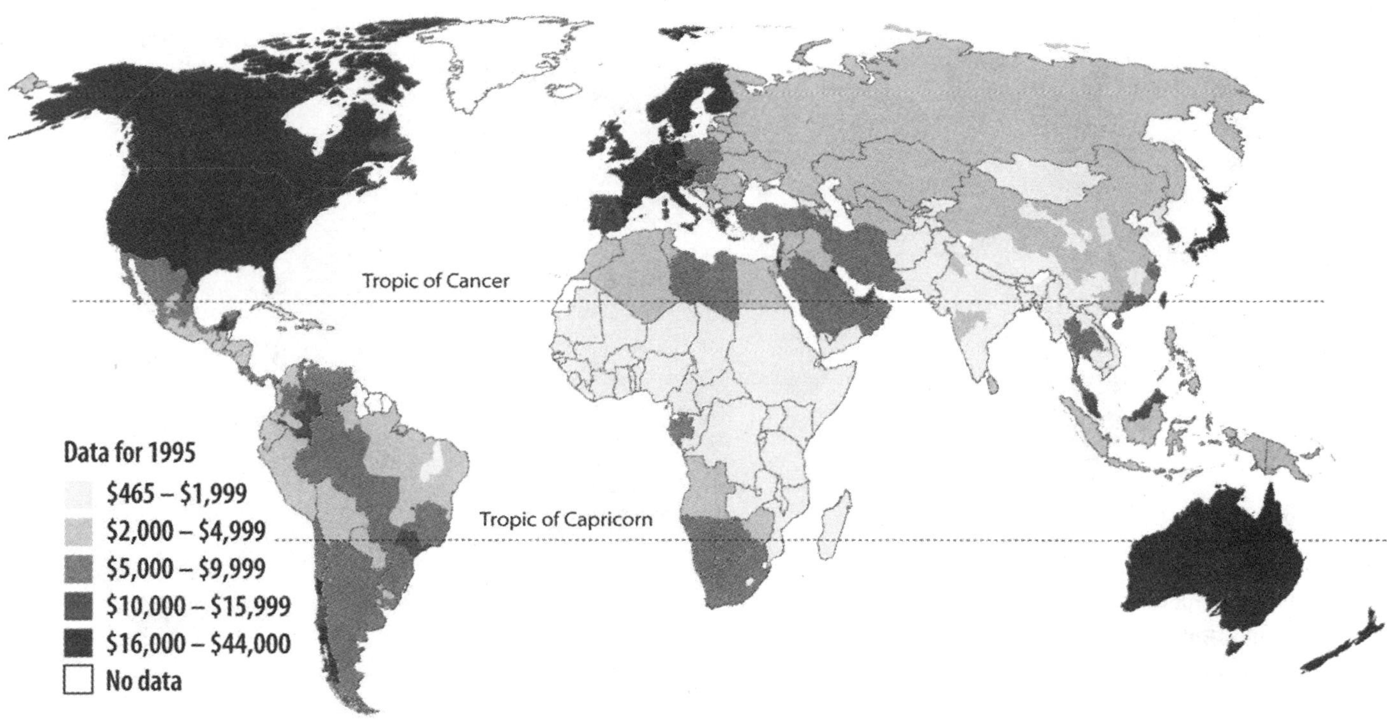

Wealth and climate are inextricably linked. By comparing world maps showing GNP per capita and climate zones, one notices that temperate-zone countries are generally much more prosperous than tropical-zone nations. And in each climate zone, the regions near the seacoasts and waterways are richer than the hinterlands.

[*see map GNP per capita.*] Notice that the great majority of the poorest countries lie in the geographical tropics—the area between the tropic of Cancer and the tropic of Capricorn. In contrast, most of the richest countries lie in the temperate zones.

A more precise picture of this geographical divide can be obtained by defining tropical regions by climate rather than by latitude. The map Climate Zones divides the world into five broad climate zones based on a classification scheme developed by German climatologist Wladimir P. Köppen and Rudolph Geiger. The five zones are tropical-subtropical (hereafter referred to as tropical), desert-steppe (desert), temperate-snow (temperature), highland and polar. The zones are defined by measurements of temperature and precipitation. We excluded the polar zone from our analysis because it is largely uninhabited.

Among the 28 economies categorized as high income by the World Bank (with populations of at least one million), only Hong Kong, Singapore and part of Taiwan are in the tropical zone, representing a mere 2 percent of the combined population of the high-income regions. Almost all the temperate-zone countries have either high-income economies (as in the cases of North America, western Europe, Korea and Japan) or middle-income economies burdened by socialist policies in the past (as in the cases of eastern Europe, the former Soviet Union and China). In addition, there is a strong temperate-tropical divide within countries that straddle both types of climates. Most of Brazil, for example, lies within the tropical zone, but the richest part of the nation—the southernmost states—is in the temperate zone.

The importance of access to sea trade is also evident in the world map of GNP per capita. Regions far from the sea, such as the landlocked countries of South America, Africa and Asia, tend to be considerably poorer than their coastal counterparts. The differences between coastal and interior areas show up even more strongly in a world map delineating GNP density—that is, the amount of economic output per square kilometer... Geographic information system software is used to divide the world's land area into five-minute-by-five-minute sections (about 100 square kilometers at the equator). One can estimate the GNP density for each section by multiplying its population density and its GNP per capita. Researchers must use national averages of GNP per capita when regional estimates are not available.

To make sense of the data, we have classified the world's regions in broad categories defined by climate and proximity to the sea. We call a region "near" if it lies within 100 kilometers of a seacoast or a sea-navigable waterway (a river, lake or canal in which oceangoing vessels can operate) and "far" otherwise. Regions in each of the four climate zones we analyzed can be either near or far, resulting in a total of eight categories. The table on the next page shows how the

Climate Zones

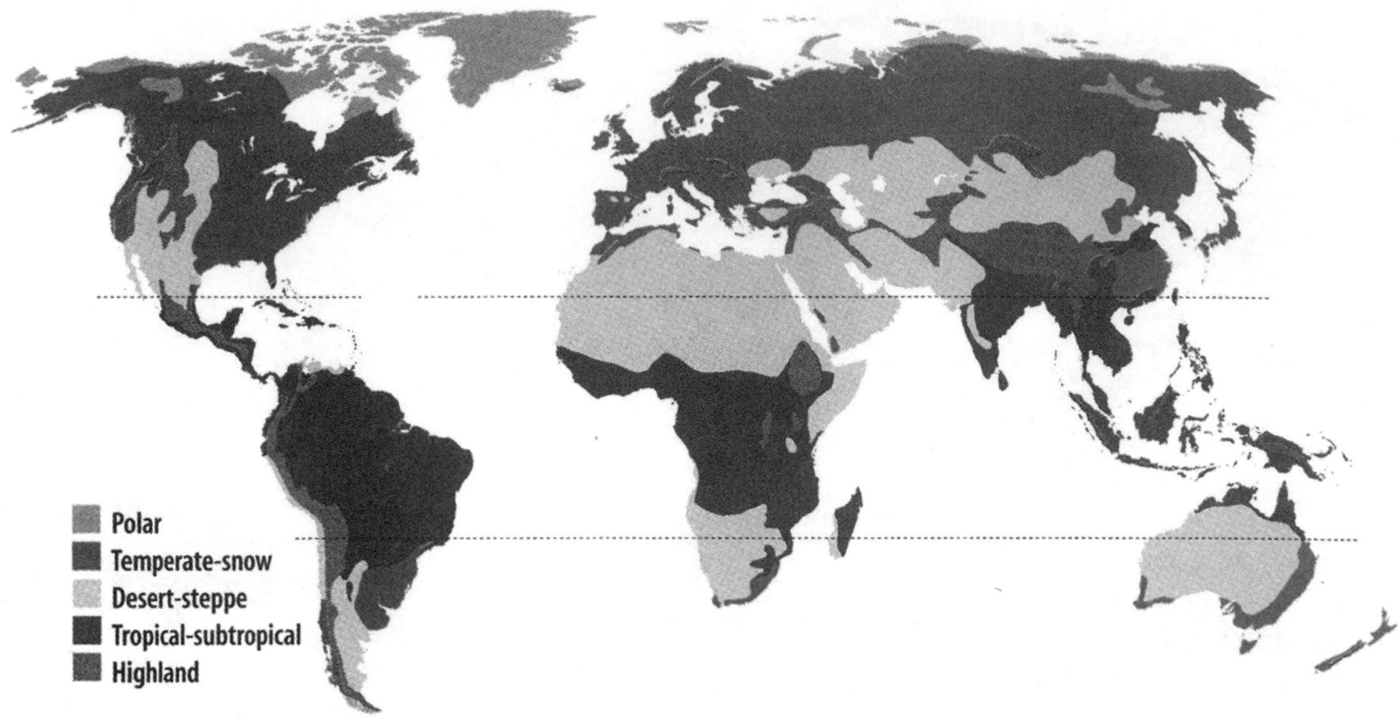

world's population, income and land area are divided among these regions.

The breakdown reveals some striking patterns. Global production is highly concentrated in the coastal regions of temperate climate zones. Regions in the "temperate-near" category constitute a mere 8.4 percent of the world's inhabited land area, but they hold 22.8 percent of the world's population and produce 52.9 percent of the world's GNP. Per capita income in these regions is 2.3 times greater than the global average, and population density is 2.7 times greater. In contrast, the "tropical-far" category is the poorest, with a per capita GNP only about one third of the world average.

Interpreting the Patterns

In our research we have examined three major ways in which geography affects economic development. First, as Adam Smith noted, economies differ in their ease of transporting goods, people and ideas. Because sea trade is less costly than land- or air-based trade, economies near coastlines have a great advantage over hinterland economies. The per-kilometer costs of overland trade within Africa, for example, are often an order of magnitude greater than the costs of sea trade to an African port. Here are some figures we found recently: The cost of shipping a six-meter-long container from Rotterdam, the Netherlands, to Dar-es-Salaam, Tanzania—an air distance of 7,300 kilometers—was about $1,400. But transporting the same container overland from Dar-es-Salaam to Kigali, Rwanda—a distance of 1,280 kilometers by road—cost about $2,500, or nearly twice as much.

Second, geography affects the prevalence of disease. Many kinds of infectious diseases are endemic to the tropical and subtropical zones. This tends to be true of diseases in which the pathogen spends part of its life cycle outside the human host: for instance, malaria (carried by mosquitoes) and helminthic infections (caused by parasitic worms). Although epidemics of malaria have occurred sporadically as far north as Boston in the past century, the disease has never gained a lasting foothold in the temperate zones, because the cold winters naturally control the mosquito-based transmission of the disease. (Winter could be considered the world's most effective public health intervention.) It is much more difficult to control malaria in tropical regions, where transmission takes place year-round and affects a large part of the population.

According to the World Health Organization, 300 million to 500 million new cases of malaria occur every year, almost entirely concentrated in the tropics. The disease is so common in these areas that no one really knows how many people it kills annually—at least one million and perhaps as many as 2.3 million. Widespread illness and early deaths obviously hold back a nation's economic performance by significantly reducing worker productivity. But there are also long-term effects that may be amplified over time through various social feedbacks.

For example, a high incidence of disease can alter the age structure of a country's population. Societies with high levels of child mortality tend to have high levels of fertility: mothers bear many children to guarantee that at least some will survive to adulthood. Young children will therefore constitute a large proportion of that country's population. With so many children, poor families cannot invest much in each child's education. High fertility also constrains the role of women in society, because child rearing takes up so much of their adult lives.

Third, geography affects agricultural productivity. Of the major food grains—wheat, maize and rice—wheat grows only in temperate climates, and maize and rice crops are generally more productive in temperate and subtropical climates than in tropical zones. On average, a hectare of land in the tropics yields 2.3 metric tons of maize, whereas a hectare in the temperate zone yields 6.4 tons. Farming in tropical rain-forest environments is hampered by the fragility of the soil: high temperatures mineralize the organic materials, and the intense rainfall leaches them out of the soil. In tropical environment that have wet and dry seasons—such as the African savanna—farmers must contend with the rapid loss of soil moisture resulting from high temperatures, the great variability of precipitation, and the ever present risk of drought. Moreover, tropical environments are plagued with diverse infestations of pests and parasites that can devastate both crops and livestock.

Many of the efforts to improve food output in tropical regions—attempted first by the colonial powers and then in recent decades by donor agencies—have ended in failure. Typically the agricultural experts blithely tried to transfer temperate-zone farming practices to the tropics, only to watch livestock and crops succumb to pests, disease and climate barriers. What makes the problem even more complex is that food productivity in tropical regions is also influenced by geologic and topographic conditions that vary greatly from place to place. The island of Java, for example, can support highly productive farms because the volcanic soil there suffers less nutrient depletion than the nonvolcanic soil of the neighboring islands of Indonesia.

Moderate advantages or disadvantages in geography can lead to big differences in long-term economic performance. For example, favorable agricultural or health conditions may boost per capita income in temperate-zone nations and hence increase the size of their economies. This growth encourages inventors in those nations to create products and services to sell into the larger and richer markets. The resulting inventions further raise economic output, spurring yet more inventive activity. The moderate geographical advantage is thus amplified through innovation.

In contrast, the low food output per farm worker in tropical regions tends to diminish the size of cities, which depend on the agricultural hinterland for their sustenance. With a smaller proportion of the population in urban areas, the rate of technological advance is usually slower. The tropical regions therefore remain more rural than the temperate regions, with most of their economic activity concentrated in low-technology agriculture rather than in high-technology manufacturing and services.

The Wealth of Regions

Climate Zone (percent of world total)		Near*	Far*
Tropical			
Land area	19.9%	5.5%	14.4%
Population	40.3%	21.8%	18.5%
GNP	17.4%	10.5%	6.9%
Desert			
Land area	29.6%	3.0%	26.6%
Population	18.0%	4.4%	13.6%
GNP	10.1%	3.2%	6.8%
Highland			
Land area	7.3%	0.4%	6.9%
Population	6.8%	0.9%	5.9%
GNP	5.3%	0.9%	4.4%
Temperate			
Land area	39.2%	8.4%	30.9%
Population	34.9%	22.8%	12.1%
GNP	67.2%	52.9%	14.3%

Source: Andrew D. Mellinger
* "Near" means within 100 kilometers of seacoast or sea-navigable waterway; "far" means otherwise.

We must stress, however, that geographical factors are only part of the story. Social and economic institutions are critical to long-term economic performance. It is particularly instructive to compare the post-World War II performance of free-market and socialist economies in neighboring countries that share the same geographical characteristics: North and South Korea, East and West Germany, the Czech Republic and Austria, and Estonia and Finland. In each case we find that free-market institutions vastly outperformed socialist ones.

The main implication of our findings is that policymakers should pay more attention to the developmental barriers associated with geography—specifically, poor health, low agricultural productivity and high transportation costs. For example, tropical economies should strive to diversify production into manufacturing and service sectors that are not hindered by climate conditions. The successful countries of tropical southeast Asia, most notably Malaysia, have achieved stunning advances in the past 30 years, in part by addressing public health problems and in part by moving their economies away from climate-dependent commodity exports (rubber, palm oil and so on) to electronics, semiconductors and other industrial sectors. They were helped by the high concentration of their populations in coastal areas near international sea lanes and by the relatively tractable conditions for the control of malaria and other tropical diseases. Sub-Saharan Africa is not so fortunate: most of its population is located far from the coasts, and its ecological conditions are harsher on human health and agriculture.

The World Bank and the International Monetary Fund, the two international agencies that are most influential in advising developing countries, currently place more emphasis on institutional reforms—for instance, overhauling a nation's civil service or its tax administration—than on the technologies needed to fight tropical diseases and low agricultural productivity. One formidable obstacle is that pharmaceutical companies have no market incentive to address the health problems of the world's poor. Therefore, wealthier nations should adopt policies to increase the companies' motivation to work on vaccines for tropical diseases. In one of our own initiatives, we called on the governments of wealthy nations to foster greater research and development by pledging to buy vaccines for malaria, HIV/AIDS and tuberculosis from the pharmaceutical companies at a reasonable price. Similarly, biotechnology and agricultural research companies need more incentive to study how to improve farm output in tropical regions.

The poorest countries in the world surely lack the resources to relive their geographical burdens on their own. Sub-Saharan African countries have per capita income levels of around $1 a day. Even when such countries invest as much as 3 or 4 percent of their GNP in public health—a large proportion of national income for a very poor country—the result is only about $10 to $15 per year per person. This is certainly not enough to control endemic malaria, much less to fight other rampant diseases such as HIV/AIDS, tuberculosis and helminthic infections.

A serious effort at global development will require not just better economic policies in the poor countries but far more financial support from the rich countries to help overcome the special problems imposed by geography. A preliminary estimate suggests that even a modest increase in donor financing of about $25 billion per year—only 0.1 percent of the total GNP of the wealthy nations, or about $28 per person—could make a tremendous difference in reducing disease and increasing food productivity in the world's poorest countries.

Further Information

AN INQUIRY INTO THE NATURE AND CAUSES OF THE WEALTH OF NATIONS. Adam Smith. Reprint. Modern Library, 1994.

GUNS, GERMS, AND STEEL: THE FATES OF HUMAN SOCIETIES. Jared Diamond. W. W. Norton, 1997.

THE WEALTH AND POVERTY OF NATIONS: WHY SOME ARE SO RICH AND SOME SO POOR. David S. Landes. W. W. Norton, 1998.

Additional data and research papers are available at www.cid.harvard.edu and sedac.ciesin.org on the Web.

JEFFREY D. SACHS, ANDREW D. MELLINGER and JOHN L. GALLUP conducted the research for this article under the auspices of Harvard University's Center for International Development (CID). Sachs is CID's director and serves as an economic adviser to governments in eastern Europe, the former Soviet Union, Latin America, Africa and Asia. Mellinger is a research associate at CID specializing in the multidisciplinary application of geographic information systems. Gallup is founder of developIT.org, which provides free technical support for information technology users and e-commerce in developing countries, and was recently a research fellow at CID.

The Four Traditions of Geography

William D. Pattison

Late Summer, 1990

To Readers of the *Journal of Geography:*

I am honored to be introducing, for a return to the pages of the *Journal* after more than 25 years, "The Four Traditions of Geography," an article which circulated widely, in this country and others, long after its initial appearance—in reprint, in xerographic copy, and in translation. A second round of life at a level of general interest even approaching that of the first may be too much to expect, but I want you to know in any event that I presented the paper in the beginning as my gift to the geographic community, not as a personal property, and that I re-offer it now in the same spirit.

In my judgment, the article continues to deserve serious attention—perhaps especially so, let me add, among persons aware of the specific problem it was intended to resolve. The background for the paper was my experience as first director of the High School Geography Project (1961–63)—not all of that experience but only the part that found me listening, during numerous conference sessions and associated interviews, to academic geographers as they responded to the project's invitation to locate "basic ideas" representative of them all. I came away with the conclusion that I had been witnessing not a search for consensus but rather a blind struggle for supremacy among honest persons of contrary intellectual commitment. In their dialogue, two or more different terms had been used, often unknowingly, with a single reference, and no less disturbingly, a single term had been used, again often unknowingly, with two or more different references. The article was my attempt to stabilize the discourse. I was proposing a basic nomenclature (with explicitly associated ideas) that would, I trusted, permit the development of mutual comprehension **and** confront all parties concerned with the pluralism inherent in geographic thought.

This intention alone could not have justified my turning to the NCGE as a forum, of course. The fact is that from the onset of my discomfiting realization I had looked forward to larger consequences of a kind consistent with NCGE goals. As finally formulated, my wish was that the article would serve "to greatly expedite the task of maintaining an alliance between professional geography and pedagogical geography and at the same time to promote communication with laymen" (see my fourth paragraph). I must tell you that I have doubts, in 1990, about the acceptability of my word choice, in saying "professional," "pedagogical," and "layman" in this context, but the message otherwise is as expressive of my hope now as it was then.

I can report to you that twice since its appearance in the *Journal*, my interpretation has received more or less official acceptance—both times, as it happens, at the expense of the earth science tradition. The first occasion was Edward Taaffe's delivery of his presidential address at the 1973 meeting of the Association of American Geographers (see *Annals AAG*, March 1974, pp. 1–16). Taaffe's working-through of aspects of an interrelation among the spatial, area studies, and man-land traditions is by far the most thoughtful and thorough of any of which I am aware. Rather than fault him for omission of the fourth tradition, I compliment him on the grace with which he set it aside in conformity to a meta-epistemology of the American university which decrees the integrity of the social sciences as a consortium in their own right. He was sacrificing such holistic claims as geography might be able to muster for a freedom to argue the case for geography as a social science.

The second occasion was the publication in 1984 of *Guidelines for Geographic Education: Elementary and Secondary Schools*, authored by a committee jointly representing the AAG and the NCGE. Thanks to a recently published letter (see *Journal of Geography*, March-April 1990, pp. 85–86), we know that, of five themes commended to teachers in this source,

> The committee lifted the human environmental interaction theme directly from Pattison. The themes of place and location are based on Pattison's spatial or geometric geography, and the theme of region comes from Pattison's area studies or regional geography.

Having thus drawn on my spatial, area studies, and man-land traditions for four of the five themes, the committee could have found the remaining theme, movement, there too—in the spatial tradition (see my sixth paragraph). However that may be, they did not avail themselves of the earth science tradition, their reasons being readily surmised. Peculiar to the elementary and secondary schools is a curriculum category framed as much by theory of citizenship as by theory of knowledge: the social studies. With admiration, I see already in the committee members' adoption of the theme idea a strategy for assimilation of their program to the established repertoire of social studies practice. I see in their exclusion of the earth science tradition an intelligent respect for social studies' purpose.

Here's to the future of education in geography: may it prosper as never before.

W. D. P., 1990

Reprinted from the Journal of Geography, 1964, pp. 211–216.

In 1905, one year after professional geography in this country achieved full social identity through the founding of the Association of American Geographers, William Morris Davis responded to a familiar suspicion that geography is simply an undisciplined "omnium-gatherum" by describing an approach that as he saw it imparts a "geographical quality" to some knowledge and accounts for the absence of the quality elsewhere.[1] Davis spoke as president of the AAG. He set an example that was followed by more than one president of that organization. An enduring official concern led the AAG to publish, in 1939 and in 1959, monographs exclusively devoted to a critical review of definitions and their implications.[2]

Every one of the well-known definitions of geography advanced since the founding of the AAG has had its measure of success. Tending to displace one another by turns, each definition has said something true of geography.[3] But from the vantage point of 1964, one can see that each one has also failed. All of them adopted in one way or another a monistic view, a singleness of preference, certain to omit if not to alienate numerous professionals who were in good conscience continuing to participate creatively in the broad geographic enterprise.

The thesis of the present paper is that the work of American geographers, although not conforming to the restrictions implied by any one of these definitions, has exhibited a broad consistency, and that this essential unity has been attributable to a small number of distinct but affiliated traditions, operant as binders in the minds of members of the profession. These traditions are all of great age and have passed into American geography as parts of a general legacy of Western thought. They are shared today by geographers of other nations.

There are four traditions whose identification provides an alternative to the competing monistic definitions that have been the geographer's lot. The resulting pluralistic basis for judgment promises, by full accommodation of what geographers do and by plain-spoken representation thereof, to greatly expedite the task of maintaining an alliance between professional geography and pedagogical geography and at the same time to promote communication with laymen. The following discussion treats the traditions in this order: (1) a spatial tradition, (2) an area studies tradition, (3) a man-land tradition and (4) an earth science tradition.

Spatial Tradition

Entrenched in Western thought is a belief in the importance of spatial analysis, of the act of separating from the happenings of experience such aspects as distance, form, direction and position. It was not until the 17th century that philosophers concentrated attention on these aspects by asking whether or not they were properties of things-in-themselves. Later, when the 18th century writings of Immanuel Kant had become generally circulated, the notion of space as a category including all of these aspects came into widespread use. However, it is evident that particular spatial questions were the subject of highly organized answering attempts long before the time of any of these cogitations. To confirm this point, one need only be reminded of the compilation of elaborate records concerning the location of things in ancient Greece. These were records of sailing distances, of coastlines and of landmarks that grew until they formed the raw material for the great *Geographia* of Claudius Ptolemy in the 2nd century A.D.

A review of American professional geography from the time of its formal organization shows that the spatial tradition of thought had made a deep penetration from the very beginning. For Davis, for Henry Gannett and for most if not all of the 44 other men of the original AAG, the determination and display of spatial aspects of reality through mapping were of undoubted importance, whether contemporary definitions of geography happened to acknowledge this fact or not. One can go further and, by probing beneath the art of mapping, recognize in the behavior of geographers of that time an active interest in the true essentials of the spatial tradition—*geometry* and *movement*. One can trace a basic favoring of movement as a subject of study from the turn-of-the-century work of Emory R. Johnson, writing as professor of transportation at the University of Pennsylvania, through the highly influential theoretical and substantive work of Edward L. Ullman during the past 20 years and thence to an article by a younger geographer on railroad freight traffic in the U.S. and Canada in the *Annals* of the AAG for September 1963.[4]

One can trace a deep attachment to geometry, or positioning-and-layout, from articles on boundaries and population densities in early 20th century volumes of the *Bulletin of the American Geographical Society*, through a controversial pronouncement by Joseph Schaefer in 1953 that granted geographical legitimacy only to studies of spatial patterns[5] and so onward to a recent *Annals* report on electronic scanning of cropland patterns in Pennsylvania.[6]

One might inquire, is discussion of the spatial tradition, after the manner of the remarks just made, likely to bring people within geography closer to an understanding of one another and people outside geography closer to an understanding of geographers? There seem to be at least two reasons for being hopeful. First, an appreciation of this tradition allows one to see a bond of fellowship uniting the elementary school teacher, who attempts the most rudimentary instruction in directions and mapping, with the contemporary research geographer, who dedicates himself to an exploration of central-place theory. One cannot only open the eyes of many teachers to the potentialities of their own instruction, through proper exposition of the spatial tradition, but one can also "hang a bell" on research quantifiers in geography, who are often thought to have wandered so far in their intellectual adventures as to have become lost from the rest. Looking outside geography, one may anticipate benefits from the readiness of countless persons to associate the name "geography" with maps. Latent within this readiness is a willingness to recognize as geography, too, what maps are about—and that is the geometry of and the movement of what is mapped.

Area Studies Tradition

The area studies tradition, like the spatial tradition, is quite strikingly represented in classical antiquity by a practitioner to whose surviving work we can point. He is Strabo, celebrated for his *Geography* which is a massive production addressed to the statesmen of Augustan Rome and intended to sum up and regularize knowledge not of the location of places and associated cartographic facts, as in the somewhat later case of Ptolemy, but of the nature of places, their character and their differentiation. Strabo exhibits interesting attributes of the area-studies tradition that can hardly be overemphasized. They are a pronounced tendency toward subscription primarily to literary standards, an almost omnivorous appetite for information and a self-conscious companionship with history.

It is an extreme good fortune to have in the ranks of modern American geography the scholar Richard Hartshorne, who has pondered the meaning of the area-studies tradition with a legal acuteness that few persons would challenge. In his *Nature of Geography*, his 1939 monograph already cited,[7] he scrutinizes exhaustively the implications of the "interesting attributes" identified in connection with Strabo, even though his concern is with quite other and much later authors, largely German. The major literary problem of unities or wholes he considers from every angle. The Gargantuan appetite for miscellaneous information he accepts and rationalizes. The companionship between area studies and history he clarifies by appraising the so-called idiographic content of both and by affirming the tie of both to what he and Sauer have called "naively given reality."

The area-studies tradition (otherwise known as the chorographic tradition) tended to be excluded from early American professional geography. Today it is beset by certain champions of the spatial tradition who would have one believe that somehow the area-studies way of organizing knowledge is only a subdepartment of spatialism. Still, area-studies as a method of presentation lives and prospers in its own right. One can turn today for reassurance on this score to practically any issue of the *Geographical Review*, just as earlier readers could turn at the opening of the century to that magazine's forerunner.

What is gained by singling out this tradition? It helps toward restoring the faith of many teachers who, being accustomed to administering learning in the area-studies style, have begun to wonder if by doing so they really were keeping in touch with professional geography. (Their doubts are owed all too much to the obscuring effect of technical words attributable to the very professionals who have been intent, ironically, upon protecting that tradition.) Among persons outside the classroom the geographer stands to gain greatly in intelligibility. The title "area-studies" itself carries an understood message in the United States today wherever there is contact with the usages of the academic community. The purpose of characterizing a place, be it neighborhood or nation-state, is readily grasped. Furthermore, recognition of the right of a geographer to be unspecialized may be expected to be forthcoming from people generally, if application for such recognition is made on the merits of this tradition, explicitly.

Man-Land Tradition

That geographers are much given to exploring man-land questions is especially evident to anyone who examines geographic output, not only in this country but also abroad. O. H. K. Spate, taking an international view, has felt justified by his observations in nominating as the most significant ancient precursor of today's geography neither Ptolemy nor Strabo nor writers typified in their outlook by the geographies of either of these two men, but rather Hippocrates, Greek physician of the 5th century B.C. who left to posterity an extended essay, *On Airs, Waters and Places*.[8] In this work made up of reflections on human health and conditions of external nature, the questions asked are such as to confine thought almost altogether to presumed influence passing from the latter to the former, questions largely about the effects of winds, drinking water and seasonal changes upon man. Understandable though this uni-directional concern may have been for Hippocrates as medical commentator, and defensible as may be the attraction that this same approach held for students of the condition of man for many, many centuries thereafter, one can only regret that this narrowed version of the man-land tradition, combining all too easily with social Darwinism of the late 19th century, practically overpowered American professional geography in the first generation of its history.[9] The premises of this version governed scores of studies by American geographers in interpreting the rise and fall of nations, the strategy of battles and the construction of public improvements. Eventually this special bias, known as environmentalism, came to be confused with the whole of the man-land tradition in the minds of many people. One can see now, looking back to the years after the ascendancy of environmentalism, that although the spatial tradition was asserting itself with varying degrees of forwardness, and that although the area-studies tradition was also making itself felt, perhaps the most interesting chapters in the story of American professional geography were being written by academicians who were reacting against environmentalism while deliberately remaining within the broad man-land tradition. The rise of culture historians during the last 30 years has meant the dropping of a curtain of culture between land and man, through which it is asserted all influence must pass. Furthermore work of both culture historians and other geographers has exhibited a reversal of the direction of the effects in Hippocrates, man appearing as an independent agent, and the land as a sufferer from action. This trend as presented in published research has reached a high point in the collection of papers titled *Man's Role in Changing the Face of the Earth*. Finally, books and articles can be called to mind that have addressed themselves to the most difficult task of all, a balanced tracing out of interaction between man and environment. Some chapters in the book mentioned above undertake just this. In fact the separateness of this approach is discerned only with difficulty in many places; however, its significance as a general research design that rises above environmentalism, while refusing to abandon the man-land tradition, cannot be mistaken.

The NCGE seems to have associated itself with the man-land tradition, from the time of founding to the present day, more than with any other tradition, although all four of the traditions are amply represented in its official magazine, *The Journal of Geography* and in the proceedings of its annual meetings. This apparent preference on the part of the NCGE members *for defining geography in terms of the man-land tradition* is strong evidence of the appeal that man-land ideas, separately stated, have for persons whose main job is teaching. It should be noted, too, that this inclination reflects a proven acceptance by the general public of learning that centers on resource use and conservation.

Earth Science Tradition

The earth science tradition, embracing study of the earth, the waters of the earth, the atmosphere surrounding the earth and the association between earth and sun, confronts one with a paradox. On the one hand one is assured by professional geographers that their participation in this tradition has declined precipitously in the course of the past few decades, while on the other one knows that college departments of geography across the nation rely substantially, for justification of their role in general education, upon curricular content springing directly from this tradition. From all the reasons that combine to account for this state of affairs, one may, by selecting only two, go far toward achieving an understanding of this tradition. First, there is the fact that American college geography, growing out of departments of geology in many crucial instances, was at one time greatly overweighted in favor of earth science, thus rendering the field unusually liable to a sense of loss as better balance came into being. (This one-time disproportion found reciprocate support for many years in the narrowed, environmentalistic interpretation of the man-land tradition.) Second, here alone in earth science does one encounter subject matter in the normal sense of the term as one reviews geographic traditions. The spatial tradition abstracts certain aspects of reality; area studies is distinguished by a point of view; the man-land tradition dwells upon relationships; but earth science is identifiable through concrete objects. Historians, sociologists and other academicians tend not only to accept but also to ask for help from this part of geography. They readily appreciate earth science as something physically associated with their subjects of study, yet generally beyond their competence to treat. From this appreciation comes strength for geography-as-earth-science in the curriculum.

Only by granting full stature to the earth science tradition can one make sense out of the oft-repeated addage, "Geography is the mother of sciences." This is the tradition that emerged in ancient Greece, most clearly in the work of Aristotle, as a wide-ranging study of natural processes in and near the surface of the earth. This is the tradition that was rejuvenated by Varenius in the 17th century as "Geographia Generalis." This is the tradition that has been subjected to subdivision as the development of science has approached the present day, yielding mineralogy, paleontology, glaciology, meterology and other specialized fields of learning.

Readers who are acquainted with American junior high schools may want to make a challenge at this point, being aware that a current revival of earth sciences is being sponsored in those schools by the field of geology. Belatedly, geography has joined in support of this revival.[10] It may be said that in this connection and in others, American professional geography may have faltered in its adherence to the earth science tradition but not given it up.

In describing geography, there would appear to be some advantages attached to isolating this final tradition. Separation improves the geographer's chances of successfully explaining to educators why geography has extreme difficulty in accommodating itself to social studies programs. Again, separate attention allows one to make understanding contact with members of the American public for whom surrounding nature is known as the geographic environment. And finally, specific reference to the geographer's earth science tradition brings into the open the basis of what is, almost without a doubt, morally the most significant concept in the entire geographic heritage, that of the earth as a unity, the single common habitat of man.

An Overview

The four traditions though distinct in logic are joined in action. One can say of geography that it pursues concurrently all four of them. Taking the traditions in varying combinations, the geographer can explain the conventional divisions of the field. Human or cultural geography turns out to consist of the first three traditions applied to human societies; physical geography, it becomes evident, is the fourth tradition prosecuted under constraints from the first and second traditions. Going further, one can uncover the meanings of "systematic geography," "regional geography," "urban geography," "industrial geography," etc.

It is to be hoped that through a widened willingness to conceive of and discuss the field in terms of these traditions, geography will be better able to secure the inner unity and outer intelligibility to which reference was made at the opening of this paper, and that thereby the effectiveness of geography's contribution to American education and to the general American welfare will be appreciably increased.

Notes

1. William Morris Davis, "An Inductive Study of the Content of Geography," *Bulletin of the American Geographical Society*, Vol. 38, No. 1 (1906), 71.
2. Richard Hartshorne, *The Nature of Geography*, Association of American Geographers (1939), and idem., *Perspective on the Nature of Geography*, Association of American Geographers (1959).
3. The essentials of several of these definitions appear in Barry N. Floyd, "Putting Geography in Its Place," *The Journal of Geography*, Vol. 62, No. 3 (March, 1963), 117–120.
4. William H. Wallace, "Freight Traffic Functions of Anglo-American Railroads," *Annals of the Association of American Geographers*, Vol. 53, No. 3 (September, 1963), 312–331.
5. Fred K. Schaefer, "Exceptionalism in Geography: A Methodological Examination," *Annals of the Association of American Geographers*, Vol. 43, No. 3 (September, 1953), 226–249.
6. James P. Latham, "Methodology for an Instrumental Geographic Analysis," *Annals of the Association of American Geographers*, Vol. 53, No. 2 (June, 1963), 194–209.
7. Hartshorne's 1959 monograph, *Perspective on the Nature of Geography*, was also cited earlier. In this later work, he responds to dissents from geographers whose preferred primary commitment lies outside the area studies tradition.
8. O. H. K. Spate, "Quantity and Quality in Geography," *Annals of the Association of American Geographers*, Vol. 50, No. 4 (December, 1960), 379.
9. Evidence of this dominance may be found in Davis's 1905 declaration: "Any statement is of geographical quality if it contains... some relation between an element of inorganic control and one of organic response" (Davis, *loc. cit.*).
10. Geography is represented on both the Steering Committee and Advisory Board of the Earth Science Curriculum Project, potentially the most influential organization acting on behalf of earth science in the schools.

Teaching Geography's Four Traditions with Poetry

ABSTRACT

Poetry is a powerful form of writing that has received relatively little attention from geography educators. However, most poetry is imbued with explicit and vivid references to physical and human phenomena over space, and is thus a source of information that may help illustrate a variety of geographic concepts. This article uses William Pattison's four traditions of geography as a framework for illustrating the explicitly spatial concepts present in selected poetry. Through the poetry of authors like Walt Whitman, Robert Frost, and Maya Angelou, this work introduces a new perspective from which to teach and to learn familiar geographic themes.

Key Words: *poetry, geographic education*

Daniel P. Donaldson

Present in much geographic and non-geographic research alike is the assertion that fiction and non-fiction literature offers educators a rich body of information of illustrating geographic concepts (see Machetti 1993, Chamberlain 1995, Kong and Tay 1998). Specifically, in a recent volume of Journal of Geography, Marra (1996) offers insight into this value of literary resources as she details ways in which children's picture books can be used to teach the national geography standards. She reminds us of the excitement reading can elicit. At all grade levels, reading can spark deep emotions and foster deep understandings. This research focuses on poetry, a form of literature that has great promise for supplementing geography learning, but one that has received little recent attention as an information source from professional geographers (Wang 1990 and Parsons 1996 are notable exceptions)....

In this case, William Pattison's four traditions (first published in 1964 and reprinted in the Journal of Geography in 1990) have been chosen for the framework of this study because they succinctly illustrate the content of more recent geography education paradigms. With few exceptions, while the "Five Themes of Geography" of 1984 and the "National Geography Standards" (Geography Education Standards Project 1994) break down the fundamental ideas of geography into smaller and often more specific units, they ultimately illustrate the simpler framework that Pattison identified in 1964 and geography education materials still use today (see Getis et al. 1999). Thus, a many K–12 educators are aware, Pattison's categorization can be expanded to include more completely and specifically the content of newer geography standards projects. For example, the "Spatial Tradition," which will be discussed in subsequent pages, also includes of the theme "Location" and "The World in Spatial Terms" found in the "Five Themes of Geography" and the "National Geography Standards" respectively. My intent is not to illustrate through poetry every tenet of any standards project. Rather, this paper focuses on the ways in which poetry often intersects and illuminates spatial patterns and processes. In that way, educators have great latitude in applying this literary source to any level of geography education framework.

The poetry selections included in this paper are an eclectic collection of diverse topics and authors. While much can be learned about the poet by reading his or her work, this paper does not showcase any one type of poetry or poet. The criteria for choosing poetry contained in this discussion is a particular poem's ability to illustrate spatial patterns and processes. Moreover, poems have been chosen based on their accessibility to students and teachers who have not necessarily had a great deal of training in the interpretation of literature and poetry. This selection is not exhaustive, and each selection may, at once, illustrate a variety of geographic concepts. It is hoped that the poems used here will act as a catalyst for further exploration into this rich source of geographic information.

Geography Through Poetic Expression

The use of poetry to illustrate geographic concepts has a long tradition. For example, many teachers in Celtic monastic schools in Ireland wrote educational poems that students would use to supplement their learning of geographic concepts. As the following verses illustrate, these poems contained much of what was known about the universe and the geography of the world as they new it (Fahy 1974, 36).

i

In the body of the firm world are known five equal zones marked out;
Two frigid of bright aspect; two temperate around a fiery.

ii

The fiery across the middle of the world; (there is) fire in its solid mass;
Two frigid at the border north and south; two temperate round the great heat.

iii

The north temperate zone under heaven, there is the abode of mankind;
It is that which God divided for ever, in thirds from the Torrian Sea.

iv

(There are) three parts of the world west and east, three parts in which are Adam's seed;
Three parts which God divided, Europe, Africa, and Asia.

While few modern geographers have been concerned with the use of poetry to illustrate geographic concepts, recent interdisciplinary literature is replete with work that focuses on the value of poetry as a learning tool. From poetic depictions of the Vietnam War and its aftermath (Mahony 1998), poetry of the last Korean dynasty (Contogenis and Choe 1997), and the wide range of perspectives illustrated in poetry of China (Hutcheon 1996), to more empirical work on the relationships between learning and poetry (Sedgwick 1997; Meyers 1998), it is clear that there is excitement about the prospects of using poetry to understand the world.

According to Thomas Arp, renowned teacher and scholar of poetic expression, poetry is often regarded as something central and essential to human existence—something that we are better off for having, and without which we are in many ways impoverished (Arp 1997: 3). But why set poetry apart from the larger body of literature, especially when exploring its merits as a teaching and learning resource? Arp (1997, 3) suggests, "Poetry is a form of language that says more and says it more intensely than does ordinary language." This medium offers unique insight into the often "highly-charged" moments that elicit detailed description of one's environment (Tuan 1977). One could perceive this medium as an expression that, for the sake of space, has been condensed to include the most essential spirit, and descriptive nature of the element(s) being described. Poems (and other written art forms such as novels and plays) are not written simply to communicate information. They exist to allow humans to expand their sense and perception of life, and to widen and sharpen their connections with the world around them. "Poets create significant new expressions for their readers—significant because focused and formed—in which readers can participate and from which they may gain a greater understanding and awareness of their world" (Arp 1997, 4). Thus, it is reasonable to expect that poetry represents a tool that will allow students (whether in geography class or elsewhere) to increase their range of geographic experience, as well as a glass through which students might clarify their view of the world.

Suppose, for example, one were interested in learning about winter. If one desired to simply inquire about the winter season, he or she might turn to an encyclopedia or a climatology text. There, one might find information pertaining to the cycle of the seasons, the yearly fluctuation of the angle of the sun, the average temperatures of winter in various places on the Earth, and types of winter precipitation experienced worldwide. But, unless one seeks this information for exclusively practical purposes, he or she is likely to be less than completely educated about the subject. While the empirical elements of the winter season might be reasonably clear, a deeper comprehension of the sensory nature of "winterness" would often be absent. Poetry can add significantly to one's understanding of winter. How is winter a mosaic of elements in which humans exist rather than simply a season of cold and a collection of meteorological measurements? To illustrate an answer to this question, consider the following song from William Shakespeare's, "Love's Labor Lost" (Art 1997, 6).

Winter

When icicles hang by the wall,
And Dick the shepherd blows his nail,
And Tom bears logs into the hall,
And milk comes frozen home in pail,
When blood is nipped and ways be foul,
Then mighty sings the staring owl,
"Tu-whit, Tu-who!"
A merry note,
While greasy John doth keel the pot.

When all aloud the wind doth blow,
And coughing drowns the parson's saw,
And birds sit brooding in the snow,
And Marian's nose looks red and raw,

When roasted crabs hiss in the bowl,
Then nightly sings the staring owl,
"Tu-whit, Tu-who!"
A merry note,
While greasy John doth keel the pot.
(William Shakespeare, 1564–1616)

This poem depicts the qualities of winter life at a country home in sixteenth-century England. Rather than explicitly outlining temperature variation, or any other encyclopedic description of the environmental conditions, Shakespeare suggests these qualities as he allows the reader to imagine and experience the winter landscape for him- or herself. One can, through the poet's language, not only learn something about the way of life and the experiences of the poet himself, but also of the realities and feelings associated with winter in rural England.

I do not introduce this example as an alternative to more objective inquiry about winter. Rather, my objective is to illustrate the value of using such media as an important supplement to traditional forms of geography education. When taught with the aid of poetry, the geographic principles outlined here can take on greater significance. Following is a discussion of how the geography "traditions" outlined by Pattison (1990), and discussed in upcoming pages, can be applied through familiar poetry sources.

Poetry and the Four Traditions of Geography

In their attempt to outline the history of geographic thought in America, Martin and James (1972, 433) continually underscore the importance of "seeking what is new and place it in balance with what is traditional." Forward progress for geography education must borrow from the tenets of past geographic theory, and inform that knowledge with current theoretical and practical research (Pattison 1990).

Many geographers have realized the value of such retrospection. Forged out of his experiences as the first director of the High School Geography Project from 1961 to 1963, William Pattison "re-offers" to the geography community an outline for considering the value of geographic inquiry. His perspective on the world and its phenomena is as applicable outside the walls of academic as it is to professional geographers. His four traditions of geography represent the fundamental core of geographic inquiry, although numerous other frameworks have been constructed since (e.g., Joint Committee on Geographic Education 1984 and Geographic Education Standards Project 1994). The four traditions represent the backdrop against which this research will be examined. These traditions are (1) the spatial tradition, (2) the area studies tradition, (3) the human-environment interaction tradition, and (4) the earth science tradition.

Poetry and the Spatial Tradition

Common to all sub-disciplines of geography is the axiom that "space matters." Fundamental to understanding the complex interworkings of the world's phenomena is the ability to extract from those phenomena such aspects as distance, location, movement and position (Pattison 1990). While this tradition remains important in geographic research today, it is not new to the discipline. In fact, people's concern for the explicitly spatial nature of the world can be formally linked to the early work of Claudius Ptolemy. His second-century *Geographia* was a monumental work for its time and was based on spatial tenets such as sailing distances, coastline features, and landmarks noted by Roman soldiers and merchants. Since the inauguration of American professional geography, researchers have continued this interest in the true essentials of the spatial tradition—geometry, "the language of spatial form" (Couclelis 1992, 218), and positioning and layout (Pattison 1990, 11). Those themes have provided the theoretical structure for myriad geographic examinations ranging from the empirical study of diffusion (Morrill, Gaile and Thrall 1988), to attempts at objectively measuring subjective and experiential space (Sack 1980) or space that is socially and/or historically constructed (Pred 1984; 1986).

Walt Whitman was greatly impressed with three great engineering achievements: the opening of the Suez Canal in 1869, the laying of the transatlantic undersea cable in 1866, and the joining of the Union Pacific and Central Pacific railroads in 1869 (Shahane 1972). He believed that technological objects were significant creations of humans and were thus fitting subjects for poetry. In "Passage to India" (Applebaum 1991, 103–111), Whitman ponders how "the great achievements of the present... our modern marvels" resulted in improved communication and travel—thus making possible a shorter passage to India. Whether through description of the way the Suez Canal was "initiated, open'd" by a "procession of steamships" or description of railway cars winding along the Platte River and the nation's first transcontinental railroad, the reader is often reminded that these transportation innovations are concrete manifestations of Columbus's dream of "tying the Eastern to the Western sea." Whitman's illustration of engineering marvels is meant to express humankind's progress in space and time. Throughout this work he suggests that while the present is significant, it is but an extension of the past (Shahane 1972, 55), and that when examining the transportation and communications marvels of the present, one must remain ever aware of how the present is "impell'd by the past." As spatial patterns and processes are illustrated in the classroom, those phenomena are often examined in relation to the complex picture of how the movement of people and other elements is facilitated by technological and transportation innovations. Whitman offers either an introduction to this subject matter or an example of those processes fit for further examination as students do more empirical work on spatial relationships.

"Prayer of Columbus" (Applebaum 1991, 111–113) continues Whitman's exposition on the marvels of exploration. Through subjective and sensory account of the journeys of Columbus, "A batter'd wrecke'd old man," one intent on converting "the unknown to the known," Whitman illustrates the difficulties of exploration and discovery through vivid description of a man "Pent by the sea... twelve dreary months," one "Sore, stiff with many toils, sicken'd and nigh to death." He also illustrates the importance of such an endeavor to human knowledge of the world and the wealth sought (in this case, by colonial expansion). He asks, Why else would one "take his way along the island's edge" along a "course disputed, lost" and endure such hardship in the process? In both cases illustrated above, Whitman offers additional content and context to historical events with which most students are already familiar, but information that might illustrate those concepts of space, exploration, navigation, and mapping in a way that elicits further inquiry.

Finally, Alfred, Lord Tennyson's, "Charge of the Light Brigade" (Smith 1995, 62–63) offers insight into the importance of relative location and distance. In geographic terms, this poem discusses the price that humans often pay to capture and retain world resources. Indeed, more so than many poems mentioned thus far, this work must be placed into context before it can be properly examined in the classroom. The Crimean War (1854–1856) pitted Britain against Russia, not for the acquisition of territory (as was the end result of the efforts described in the previous poem), but to guarantee Britain's naval supremacy in the Mediterranean. That action would indirectly forestall any threat to India that might have followed Russia replacing Britain as the dominant power in the Middle East (James 1994, 182). Tennyson's descriptions illustrate the micro-scale processes that must take place before territory is delineated on a map and before resource exploitation can commence. "All the world wonder'd" at the "wild charge made" by the might six-hundred of the "Noble Light Brigade." But in these verses, readers are reminded of the difference between the often romanticized notions of war and the realities of a small group of warriors as "Cannons behind them volley'd and thundered," and "stormed [them] with shot and shell." A geography class would be sorely lacking without illustrations of the importance of relative location. This work offers an often unfamiliar historical backdrop to inquiry about the ramifications of world conflict and resource protection.

Poetry and the Area Studies Tradition

Ptolemy's *Geographia* is a collection of the location of places and associated cartographic facts. Modern geographers may consult a source of similar antiquity as they trace the roots of the area-studies tradition. Strabo's *Geography* not only represents locational and cartographic tenets of places of the known world, but also of the nature of those places: their character and their differentiation (Pattison 1990). The American geographer Richard Hartshorne spent a great deal of time and effort pondering the meaning and application of the area-studies tradition. Hartshorne (1939, 242) attempted to come to terms with the masses of information that must be synthesized in order to gain a clear understanding of "the areal differentiation of the world." While this tradition has historically (and still does today) struggled to find a niche in American professional geography (Pattison 1990), it is nevertheless fueled by the humans' inherent curiosity about the earth (Tuan 1977) and the "phenomena that give character to particular places, and with likeness and differences among places" (James and Jones 1954, 6). Whether in the form of academic geographic research such as examinations of giant American bamboo in the architecture of Colombia and Ecuador (Parsons 1991), the geography of the Intifada (Noble and Efrat 1990), or illustration of the uniqueness of the Louisiana Purchase through the eyes of Lewis and Clark (Fisher 1998), the area-studies tradition remains a legitimate impetus for geographic inquiry.

Walt Whitman has been described as "a kind of genius of the American landscape" (Conron 1974, 302). His work, as well as others described here, move beyond the explicitly spatial nature of the world to describe the nature of places and the unique human and physical character of those places. "Starting from Paumanok" (Applebaum 1991, 1–11) is Whitman's account of his travels throughout the United States, a description of the intricate mosaic of the quality of life in the many physical and human regions he encounters. His description of the "dweller in Mannahatta city," "a miner in California," "the Dakota woods... far from the clank of crowds," or "the buffalo herds grazing in the plains" are among the hundreds of images charged with explicitly spatial character. As students study this work, they will have many opportunities to explore the varied landscapes that constitute often very different human and physical regions of the United States.

To supplement students' understanding of the physical and human characteristics of places further, Maya Angelou offers "Africa" (Bain, Beaty and Hunter 1986, 787). In this poem, Africa is made analogous to a woman. Africa's physical and human landscape is illustrated in the description of a continent that is "sugar cane sweet," "deserts her hair," "mountains her breasts," and "two Niles her tears" "Thus, she has lain, Black through the years." Angelou goes on to describe a continent that remembers the horrors of much of its history while it is striving to rise to prominence once again. Even today, much of the focus of American films and documentaries have done little to counter the idea that Africa must be a strangely unreal land—a "dark continent" (McCarthy 1983, xvi). "Africa" may be used to illustrate the mystery, as well as the true nature of this ill-understood land as it should elicit further inquiry about a region of the world that receives far too little attention.

Walt Whitman hears the "varied carols" of all the people that comprise the life and culture of America (United States) in "I Hear America Singing" (Applebaum 1991, 1). The mechanic, the boatman, the shoemaker, the carpenter, the mother, and the daughter all join in the chorus of the nation. Each person sings of "what belongs to him or her and to none else," and thus illustrates his or her joy of contributing to the vast and varied mosaic of a unique American culture—one that fosters numerous tangible artifacts and ideologies that must be considered if one is to appreciate and interpret the many cultural regions of the United States properly.

Merwin's "Burning Mountain," set in Pennsylvania, the state where he was raised, evokes a landscape "fissured" by a smouldering coal mine (Conron 1974, 40). "The hushed snow never arrives on that slope" and thus "betrays what the mount has at heart." "Here and there, popping in and out of their holes like ground-hogs gone nocturnal, the shy flames." Numerous areas in Pennsylvania are dominated by the relics of a century-long frenzy of coal mining. Most of the coal that was mined from the ground was cut and loaded by immigrants and their sons working deep in the ground (Marsh 1987, 337). In many instances, coal resources would be completely consumed—a situation that would thrust towns into a state of entropy from which they would never recover. However, at their peak, those towns represented a region of the United States that was vital to the nation's industrial complex and its place in the global economy. Merwin's work offers students an initial glimpse into the experience of living in a region dominated by coal extraction and the price some pay for the national good.

Poetry and the Human-Environment Interaction Tradition

Relationships between human and physical environments has been the focus of myriad geographic studies (Pattison 1990). In search of the roots of this tradition, Spate (1960) submits that "On Airs, Waters and Places" by Hippocrates, a Greek physician of the fifth century B.C., represents one of the first written contributions to the human-environment interaction tradition. His work is based on questions about the relationships between human health and the natural environment. Through the years, Hippocrates' ideas have been subject to many reinterpretations by American geographers. From environmental determinism to possibilism and probabilism, researchers have searched for the most appropriate paradigm for perceiving the relationship between humans and the natural environment. In 1906 W. M. Davis proclaimed, "Any statement is of geographic quality if it contains... some relation between an element of inorganic control and one of organic response" (Martin and James 1972, 432) Since then, geographers have taken up this line of geographic inquiry in a variety of spatial and ideological contexts. Whether a concern for the relationships between the "medicine men" and the flora of Brazilian Candomble (Voeks, 1990) or the clarification of the relationship between native Americans and the environment prior to European contact (Denevan 1992), geographers have continually acknowledged the importance of this tradition in geographic explanation.

A concern for the nature of interrelationships between humans and the natural environment is the cornerstone of geographic inquiry (Knight 1992). Indeed, the need to understanding this dynamic has existed from the beginning of time and is the subject of much consideration and contemplation. Meinig (1979) is one of many geographers who have devoted much effort to illustrating that places and regions are both "mold and mirror" (p. 188) of the society that creates them. Human beings exist in vastly different environments on the earth's surface and interact with those places in unique ways. Concurrently, the same people will be significantly affected by the modification of those places. The following poems may be used to illustrate the interconnectedness of humans and the natural environment.

"A Brook in the City" (Frost 1963, 285) is Robert Frost's artful description of the qualitative characteristics of rural-to-urban transformation. He muses about the fate of a brook that he had once known well but that now exists only on "ancient maps." Rather, the brook and the meadow grasses and the apple trees that marked its course are "cemented down" and "all for nothing it had ever done." In this case, the author seems to question the tradeoff that confronts us more and more every year: Are the benefits derived from increased urbanization outweighed by the destruction of natural areas? He reminds readers throughout this work that landscapes are works in progress, with explicit ties to the past and to the future. In reading this poem, students may reflect on the reasons for the way things were, for the way they exist at present, and for the way things appear to be progressing.

Perhaps nowhere in American history are human-environment interactions illustrated on such a large scale as in those years that saw massive waves of initial Anglo westward migration. Fascinated as he was with innovation and marches toward progress, Whitman wrote "Pioneers! O Pioneers!" (Applebaum 1991, 70–73) as an anthem dedicated to those who, by tremendous toil, succeeded in transforming wilderness into civilization (Shahane 1972). "Come my tan-faced children... get your weapons ready." "Have you your pistols? Have you your sharp-edged axes?" This poem typifies the impetus and subsequent actions of a new group of migrants, "So impatient, full of action, full of manly pride" and interacting with each other, as well as with tremendous environmental variety they would encounter on their way west. But to those who study this work carefully, it becomes apparent that Whitman, whether intentionally or not, also points to a paradox inherent in westward expansion through North America. In many cases, acquisition and successful use of new land necessarily involved the displacement and exploitation of indigenous peoples and environments (Takaki 1993). This poem may also lead to further inquiry into the worldwide implications of colonial expansion.

Appreciating the significance of the movements described in the previous work, it is appropriate to end this section with a poem through which Whitman intended to "idealize our great Pacific half of America" (Conron 1974, 310), "Song of the Redwood-Tree" (Applebaum 1991, 54–58). While Whitman is ecstatic about the discovery of the westward lands, he remains cognizant of the implications of the "swarming and busy race settling and organizing everywhere" (Conron 1974, 310). Set in coastal northern California and its mystical redwood forest stands, this poem takes the point of view of "a mighty dying tree in the redwood forest dense." The tone of the poem implies that the fate of a natural giant, "two hundred feet high," is sealed given the fervor with which waves of settlement crashed into the shore, "clearing the ground for broad humanity."

Poetry and the Earth Science Tradition

The earth science tradition was particularly prominent in the thinking of researches shortly before the founding of the profession (Martin and James 1972, 432). Indeed, the enthusiasm for this tradition was founded on Chamberlin's premise that, "Discernment of the meaning of surface features gives soul and sense to that too often soulless and senseless study, geography, for there is significance in every cape and every estuary, in every cataract and every delta" (Martin and James 1972, 432). It is commonly held that this tradition hangs on, however precariously, in almost all departments of geography because of its clear and concrete subject matter and subsequent respect afforded it by academics in other disciplines. The earth science tradition in geography has precipitated mineralogy, paleontology, meteorology, and other specialized fields of learning (Pattison 1990); yet, it has remained a distinct and important element of the modern geographic tradition. Geographers' work on topics ranging from alpine peri-glacial landforms (Clark and Schmidlin 1992) to rapids in canyon rivers (Graf 1979) offers valuable insight into geographic phenomena. Perceiving the natural environment as more than a collection of benign physical features, but rather an integral component of human-environment relationships, the earth science tradition is a subject matter that must be given due attention.

Poetry has many references to the physical landscape. Many would agree that some of the most contemplative moments are those where one is simply enjoying the splendor of a mountain meadow or pondering the creation and location of a mountain range and his or her relation to it. Robert Frost recalls the splendor of the "Birches" (Applebaum 1993, 15–17) as their branches "bent to the left and right" under the weight of a recent ice storm. He writes, "I like to think some boy's been swinging them. But swinging doesn't bend them down to stay as ice storms do." "They click on themselves as the breeze rises, and turn many-colored as the stir cracks and crazes their enamel." Those of us who have lived in parts of the world that experience ice storms and the juxtaposition of the horror of a slick road and the wonderment of the sun glistening off the branches of trees and the sound of ice beginning to crack away ("You'd think the inner dome of heaven had fallen") should appreciate such description. Especially for those who have not experienced such an event, this work can add much to the qualitative nature (recall Shakespeare's, "Winter" discussed earlier) of the physical world.

In "Storm Warnings"(Bain, Beaty and Hunter 1986, 721), Adrienne Rich begins by alerting us to the fact that "the glass has been falling all afternoon," and a "gray unrest is moving across the land." She describes in detail the sensory nature of the moments before a storm. She ponders the black sky, the wind, and the seeming insignificance of herself in the face of this weather event as she muses "time in the hand is not control of time." As Shakespeare does in "Winter," Rich places the reader into a rather fearful and wonderful situation. Understanding the forces that account for the particular weather and climate of a place or region requires a concentrated book learning. But to grasp the influence of these powerful forces on the perceptions of people, on their levels of preparedness, for example, is wonderfully illustrated in poets' recollection of those elements of nature that clocks and weatherglass cannot alter." Similarly, Emerson (Arp 1997, 171) described "The Snowstorm," "Announced by all the trumpets of the sky," as a phenomenon that proceeds without regard for human presence or intervention. This work nicely illustrates the qualitative nature of the snowstorm, as well as the vulnerability of humans in the face of weather. "Delayed, all friends shut out, the housemates sit around the radiant fireplace, enclosed," Emerson paints a picture of the vulnerability of his subjects; to be released from the grip of winter only as it ordains.

Set in a small fishing village on the coast of Wales, Dylan Thomas's "Poem in October" (Arp 1997, 220) traces the poet's walk in relation to the village, the weather, and the time of day. The poet's first name in Welsh means "water" (Arp 1997, 229). This begins to illustrate the prominence of natural features in the minds of the Welsh people. As well, it adds context to Thomas's work, one replete with descriptions of the natural environment in this part of the world in the fall of the year. As the poet makes his way through the village, he informs us of the way he feels in "rainy autumn," as the "winds blow cold" and "the town below lay leaved with October blood." Indeed, as with the other works previously described, this poem will not reveal to students all of the intricacies inherent in a study of the phenomena around which it is based. However, as with all the poems described here, if students are allowed to read, interpret, and reflect on the subjective and qualitative qualities of the spatial phenomena inherent in each work, they will have a valuable opportunity to move beyond the boundaries of strictly encyclopedic empirical learning.

Classroom Application

Much of the fundamental content, as well as the excitement of geography education revolves around the illustration and study of the uniqueness of place. In fact, regardless of the geography education structure consulted ("Four Traditions," "Five Themes of Geography," or the "Geography of Life"), prominent in each is a concern for the fact that regions the world over are unique, and that uniqueness is largely the result of geography. In that spirit, teachers might attempt the following exercises (and hopefully variations thereof) to integrate poetry into the geography education process.

Immediately following the classroom discussion of world or United States regions, assign groups of students to research the person and writing of a known poet whose work focuses on physical and/or human processes in the United States (e.g., Walt Whitman, Robert Frost, Ralph Waldo Emerson, or Herman Melville). Groups will scour paper and Internet sources (a list of which may be supplied by the teacher) about the poetry of their assigned author. Each group member will then choose a unique poem, examine its content, and prepare a short talk about how it contributes to an understanding of the human and/or physical geography of the United States. On an assigned day, each group will present its "alternative" geography of the uniqueness of their place as illustrated through selected poetry sources. A United States map with excerpts of poems attached to particular points representing the poem's setting will represent a lasting image of this project that will likely elicit much conversation.

In addition to using poetry to report and otherwise illustrate the uniqueness of place, students should also be encouraged to contribute to the body of that poetry. For example, students might be encouraged to write their own verse about the uniqueness of places, whether far off or in their own backyard. Indeed, results of this exercise are beginning to emerge as classes throughout the world are using the World Wide Web as a forum for posting and sharing poems that describe their corner of the world (see www.mecca.org/~graham/Poetry_Post.html, for example).

The preceding examples are but a hint of the myriad applications of using poetry to illustrate geographic concepts. They should be used as starting points or guidelines upon which to base the integration of poetry in geography education.

Conclusion

Clearly, the poems described in the preceding pages are but a small sampling of the wonderful verse available. Furthermore, as much of the language and context used by poets is often abstract, it is advisable to make use of the many poetry commentaries available (see Appendix A).

This article is intended as a springboard, a beginning rather than an end. My selection was intended to illustrate the ways in which this form of expression could form a framework for deeper, more qualitative understandings of spatial phenomena. These selections are also intended for a more mature high school audience, but doubtless, the ideas outlined here may be applied using poetry written at a more elementary level as well.

Regardless of the great esteem afforded many poets, it is true that they are merely humans laying bare their feelings about all manner of things. Some poems remain and are placed in bound volumes of poetry, countless others lay unseen. Yet all are valuable in that they illustrate the very nature of humans, the natural (or supernatural) world, and the interplay between the two. In this way, educators using poetry might consider allowing students to "contribute a verse" (Whitman 1928, 235) to the body of poetry. One of the most poignant aspects of poetry is that not only do poets reveal much about their perceptions of the world and its inhabitants, but that they also reflect the ways in which their environment affects what they write and how they write it. What will students' verses be? How will their environment influence what they write? Answers to these questions may add even more to the benefits derived from reading popular selections and prove a powerful addition to teaching and learning about the world and its inhabitants.

APPENDIX A: Sources of Poems Discussed in This Article

Applebaum, S. 1993. *Robert Frost: The Road Not Taken and Other Poems.* New York: Dover Publications, Inc.

Applebaum, S. 1991. *Walt Whitman: Selected Poems.* New York: Dover Publications, Inc.

Arp, T. 1997. *Perrine's Sound and Sense: An Introduction to Poetry,* 9th ed. Fort Worth, TX: Hardcourt Brace College Publishers.

Bain, C., Beaty, J., and Hunter J. 1986. *Norton Introduction to Literature.* New York and London: W. W. Norton and Company.

Conron, J. 1974. *The American Landscape: A Critical Anthology of Prose and Poetry.* Oxford: Oxford University Press.

Frost, R. 1963. *Complete Poems of Robert Frost.* New York: Holt, Rinehart, and Winston.

Smith, P. 1995. *100 Best-Loved Poems.* New York: Dover Publications, Inc.

Van Doren, M. 1951. *Introduction to Poetry.* New York: William Sloane Associates, Inc.

Wells, S., and Taylor, G. 1986. *William Shakespeare: The Complete Works.* Oxford: Clarendon Press.

Whitman, W. 1928. *Leaves of Grass.* New York: Macmillan Co.

References

Applebaum, S. 1991. *Walt Whitman: Selected Poems.* New York: Dover Publications, Inc.

Arp, T. 1997. *Perrine's Sound and Sense: An Introduction to Poetry.* 9th ed. Fort Worth, TX: Hardcourt Brace College Publishers.

Bain, C., J. Beaty and J. Hunter. 1986. *Norton Introduction to Literature.* New York and London: W. W. Norton and Company.

Chamberlain, P. 1995. *Metaphorical vision in the literary landscape of William Shakespeare,* Canadian Geographer 39(4): 306–322.

Clark, C., and T. Schmidlin. 1992. *Alpine periglacial landforms of eastern North America: A review. Permafrost and Periglacial Processes* 3: 225–230.

Conron, J. 1974. *The American Landscape: A Critical Anthology of Prose and Poetry.* Oxford: Oxford University Press.

Contogenis, C., and W. Choe. 1997. *Songs of the Kisaeng: Courtesan Poetry of the Last Korean Dynasty.* Rochester, NY: BOA Editions.

Couclelis, H. 1992. Location, place, region, and space. In R. Abler, M. Marcus and J. Olson (eds.), *Geography's Inner Worlds: Pervasive Themes in Contemporary American Geography.* New Brunswick, NJ: Rutgers University Press, 215–233.

Denevan, W. M. 1992. The pristine myth: The landscape of the Americas in 1492. *Annals of the Association of American Geographers* 82(3): 369–385.

Fahy, G. 1974. Geography in the early Irish monastic schools: A brief review of Airbheartach MacCosse's geographical poems, *Geographical Viewpoint* 3(1): 31–33.

Fisher, R. 1998. Lewis and Clark: Naturalist-explorers, *National Geographic* 194(4): 76–93.

Frost, R. 1963. *Complete Poems of Robert Frost.* New York: Holt, Rinehart, and Winston.

Graf, W. 1979. Rapids in canyon rivers. *Journal of Geology 87:* 533–551.

Geography Education Standards Project. 1994. *Geography for Life: National Geography Standards 1994.* Washington, DC: National Geographic Society.

Getis, A., J. Getis, and J. Fellmann. 1999. *Introduction to Geography.* Boston: McGraw-Hill.

Hartshorne, R. 1939. *The Nature of Geography: A Critical Survey of Current Thought in the Light of the Past.* Lancaster, PA: Association of American Geographers.

Hutcheon, R. 1996. *China-Yellow.* Hong Kong: The Chinese University Press.

James, P., and c. Jones. 1954. *American Geography, Inventory and Prospect.* Syracuse, NY: Syracuse University Press.

James, L. 1994. *Rise and Fall of the British Empire.* New York: St. Martin's Griffin.

Joint Committee of Geographic Education. 1984. *Guidelines for Geographic Education: Elementary and Secondary Schools.* Washington, DC, and Macomb, IL: Association of American Geographers and National Council for Geographic Education.

Knight, C. 1992. *Geography's worlds.* In R. Abler, M. Marcus and J. Olson (eds.), *Geography's Inner Worlds.* New Brunswick, NJ: Rutgers University Press, 9–26.

Kong, L., and L. Tay. 1998. *Exalting the past: Nostalgia and the construction of heritage in children's literature,* Area 30(2): 133–143.

Machetti, B. 1993. Japan's landscape in literature, *Journal of Geography* 92(4): 194–200.

Mahony, P. 1998. *From Both Sides Now, The Poetry of the Vietnam War and Its Aftermath.* New York: Scribner.

Marra, D. 1996. Teaching to the National Geography Standards through children's picture books, *Journal of Geography* 95(4): 148–153.

Marsh, B. 1987. Continuity and decline in the anthracite towns of Pennsylvania, *Annals of the Association of American geographers 77*(3): 337–352.

Martin, G., and P. James. 1972. *All Possible Worlds: A History of Geographical Ideas.* New York: John Wiley and Sons, Inc.

McCarthy, M. 1983. *Dark Continent: Africa as Seen by Americans.* Westport, CT: Greenwood Press.

Meinig, D. 1979. *Symbolic landscapes: Models of American community.* In D. Meinig (ed.), *Interpretation of Ordinary Landscapes.* Oxford University Press, 164–194.

Meyers, M. 1998. Passion for poetry, *Journal of Adolescent and Adult Literary* 41 (4): 262–271.

Morrill, R., G. Gaile and G. Thrall. 1988. *Spatial Diffusion. Scientific Geography Series 10.* Newbury Park, CA: Sage.

Nellis, M. 1994. Technology in geography education: Reflections and future directions, *Journal of Geography* 93(1): 36–39.

Noble, A., and E. Efrat. 1990. Geography of the Intifada, *Geographical Review* 80(3): 288–307.

Parsons, J. 1991. Giant American bamboo in the vernacular architecture of Colombia and Ecuador, *Geographical Review* 81(2): 131–154.

____, 1996. "Mr. Sauer" and the writers, *Geographical Review* 86(1): 22–41.

Pattison, W. 1990. The four traditions of geography, *Journal of Geography* 89 (5): 202–206 (first published 1964).

Pred, A. 1984. Place as historically contingent process: Structuration and the time-geography of becoming places, *Annals of the Association of American Geographers* 74(2): 279–297.

____, 1986. *Place, Practice and Structure: Social and Spatial Transformation in Southern Sweden 1750–1850.* Cambridge: Polity.

Sack, R. 1980. *Conceptions of Space in Social Thought: A Geographic Perspective.* Minneapolis: University of Minnesota Press.

Salter, K., and C. Salter. 1996. Keeping the geography education reform process in motion, *Journal of Geography* 95(4): 146–147.

Sedgwick, F. 1997. Read my Mind: Young Children, *Poetry and Learning.* London: New York: Routledge.

Shahane, V. 1972. *Whitman's Leaves of Grass.* Lincoln, NE: Cliffs Notes, Inc.

Smith, P. 1995, 100 *Best-Loved Poems.* New York: Dover Publications, Inc.

Spate, O. H. K. 1960. Quantity and quality in Geography, *Annals of the Association of American Geographers* 50(4): 379.

Takaki, R. 1993. *A Different Mirror: A History of Multicultural America.* Boston: Little, Brown and Company.

Tuan, Y. 1977. *Space and Place.* Minneapolis: University of Minnesota Press.

Voeks, R. 1990. Sacred leaves of Brazilian candomble, *Geographical Review* 80(2): 118–131.

Wang, X. 1990. Geography and Chinese Poetry, *Geographical Review* 80(1): 43–55.

Whitman, W. 1928. *Leaves of Grass.* New York: Macmillan Co.

Daniel P. Donaldson is an assistant professor in the Department of History and Geography at the University of Central Oklahoma, Edmond, OK 73034, USA. His major research interests include innovations in geography education.

The American Geographies

Americans are fast becoming strangers in a strange land, where one roiling river, one scarred patch of desert, is as good as another. America the beautiful exists—a select few still know it intimately—but many of us are settling for a homogenized national geography.

Barry Lopez

It has become commonplace to observe that Americans know little of the geography of their country, that they are innocent of it as a landscape of rivers, mountains, and towns. They do not know, supposedly, the location of the Delaware Water Gap, the Olympic Mountains, or the Piedmont Plateau; and, the indictment continues, they have little conception of the way the individual components of this landscape are imperiled, from a human perspective, by modern farming practices or industrial pollution.

I do not know how true this is, but it is easy to believe that it is truer than most of us would wish. A recent Gallup Organization and National Geographic Society survey found Americans woefully ignorant of world geography. Three out of four couldn't locate the Persian Gulf. The implication was that we knew no more about our own homeland, and that this ignorance undermined the integrity of our political processes and the efficiency of our business enterprises.

As Americans, we profess a sincere and fierce love for the American landscape, for our rolling prairies, free-flowing rivers, and "purple mountains' majesty"; but it is hard to imagine, actually, where this particular landscape is. It is not just that a nostalgic landscape has passed away—Mark Twain's Mississippi is now dammed from Minnesota to Missouri and the prairies have all been sold and fenced. It is that it has always been a romantic's landscape. In the attenuated form in which it is presented on television today, in magazine articles and in calendar photographs, the essential wildness of the American landscape is reduced to attractive scenery. We look out on a familiar, memorized landscape that portends adventure and promises enrichment. There are no distracting people in it and few artifacts of human life. The animals are all beautiful, diligent, one might even say well-behaved. Nature's unruliness, the power of rivers and skies to intimidate, and any evidence of disastrous human land management practices are all but invisible. It is, in short, a magnificent garden, a colonial vision of paradise imposed on a real place that is, at best, only selectively known.

To truly understand geography requires not only time but a kind of local expertise, an intimacy with place few of us ever develop.

The real American landscape is a face of almost incomprehensible depth and complexity. If one were to sit for a few days, for example, among the ponderosa pine forests and black lava fields of the Cascade Mountains in western Oregon, inhaling the pines' sweet balm on an evening breeze from some point on the barren rock, and then were to step off to the Olympic Peninsula in Washington, to those rain forests with sphagnum moss floors soft as fleece underfoot and Douglas firs too big around for five people to hug, and then head south to walk the ephemeral creeks and sun-blistered playas of the Mojave Desert in southern California, one would be reeling under the sensations. The contrast is not only one of plants and soils, a different array say, of brilliantly colored beetles. The shock to the senses comes from a different shape to the silence, a difference in the very quality of light, in the weight of the air. And this relatively short journey down the West Coast would still leave the traveler with all that lay to the east to explore—the anomalous sand hills of Nebraska, the heat and frog voices of Okefenokee Swamp, the fetch of Chesapeake Bay, the hardwood copses and black bears of the Ozark Mountains.

No one of these places, of course, can be entirely fathomed, biologically or aesthetically. They are mysteries upon which we impose names. Enchantments. We tick the names off glibly but lovingly. We mean no disrespect. Our genuine desire, though we might be skeptical about the time it would take and uncertain of its practical value to us, is to actually know these places. As deeply ingrained in the American psyche as the desire to conquer and control the land is the desire to sojourn in it, to sail up and down Pamlico Sound, to paddle a canoe through Minnesota's boundary waters, to walk on the desert of the Great Salt Lake, to camp in the stony hardwood valleys of Vermont.

To do this well, to really come to an understanding of a specific American geography, requires not only time but a kind of local expertise, an intimacy with place few of us ever develop. There is no way around the former requirement: If you want to know you must take the time. It is not in books. A specific geographical understanding, however, can be sought out and borrowed. It resides with men and women more or less sworn to a place, who abide there, who have a feel for the soil and history, for the turn of leaves and night sounds. Often they are glad to take the outlander in tow.

These local geniuses of American landscape, in my experience, are people in whom geography thrives. They are the antithesis of geographical ignorance. Rarely known outside their own communities, they often seem, at the first encounter, unremarkable and anonymous. They may not be able to recall the name of a particular wildflower—or they may have given it a name known only to them. They might have forgotten the precise circumstances of a local historical event. Or they can't say for certain when the last of the Canada geese passed through in the fall, or can't differentiate between two kinds of trout in the same creek. Like all of us, they have fallen prey to the fallacies of memory and are burdened with ignorance; but they are nearly flawless in the respect they bear these places they love. Their knowledge is intimate rather than encyclopedic, human but not necessarily scholarly. It rings with the concrete details of experience.

America, I believe, teems with such people. The paradox here, between a faulty grasp of geographical knowledge for which Americans are indicted and the intimate, apparently contradictory familiarity of a group of largely anonymous people, is not solely a matter of confused scale. (The local landscape is easier to know than a national geography.) And it is not simply ironic. The paradox is dark. To be succinct: The politics and advertising that seek a national audience must project a national geography; to be broadly useful that geography must, inevitably, be generalized and it is often romantic. It is therefore frequently misleading and imprecise. The same holds true with the entertainment industry, but here the problem might be clearer. The same films, magazines, and television features that honor an imaginary American landscape also tout the worth of the anonymous men and women who interpret it. Their affinity for the land is lauded, their local allegiance admired. But the rigor of their local geographies, taken as a whole, contradicts a patriotic, national vision of unspoiled, untroubled land. These men and women are ultimately forgotten, along with the details of the landscapes they speak for, in the face of more pressing national matters. It is the chilling nature of modern society to find an ignorance of geography, local or national, as excusable as an ignorance of hand tools; and to find the commitment of people to their home places only momentarily entertaining. And finally naive.

If one were to pass time among Basawara people in the Kalahari Desert, or with Kreen-Akrora in the Amazon Basin, or with Pitjantjatjara Aborigines in Australia, the most salient impression they might leave is of an absolutely stunning knowledge of their local geography—geology, hydrology, biology, and weather. In short, the extensive particulars of their intercourse with it.

In 40,000 years of human history, it has only been in the last few hundred years or so that a people could afford to ignore their local geographies as completely as we do and still survive. Technological innovations from refrigerated trucks to artificial fertilizers, from sophisticated cost accounting to mass air transportation, have utterly changed concepts of season, distance, soil productivity, and the real cost of drawing sustenance from the land. It is now possible for a resident of Boston to bite into a fresh strawberry in the dead of winter; for someone in San Francisco to travel to Atlanta in a few hours with no worry of how formidable might be crossing of the Great Basin Desert or the Mississippi River; for an absentee farmer to gain a tax advantage from a farm that leaches poisons into its water table and on which crops are left to rot. The Pitjantjatjara might shake their heads in bewilderment and bemusement, not because they are primitive or ignorant people, not because they have no sense of irony or are incapable of marveling, but because they have not (many would say not yet) realized a world in which such manipulation of the land—surmounting the imperatives of distance it imposes, for example, or turning the large-scale destruction of forests and arable land in wealth—is desirable or plausible.

In the years I have traveled through America, in cars and on horseback, on foot and by raft, I have repeatedly been brought to a sudden state of awe by some gracile or savage movement of animal, some odd wrapping of tree's foliage by the wind, an unimpeded run of dew-laden prairie stretching to a horizon flat as a coin where a pin-dot sun pales the dawn sky pink. I know these things are beyond intellection, that they are the vivid edges of a world that includes but also transcends the human world. In memory, when I dwell on these things, I know that in a truly national literature there should be odes to the Triassic reds of the Colorado Plateau, to the sharp and ghostly light of the Florida Keys, to the aeolian soils of southern Minnesota, and the Palouse in Washington, though the modern mind abjures the literary potential of such subjects. (If the sand and flood water farmers of Arizona and New Mexico were to take the black loams of Louisiana in their hands they would be flabbergasted, and that is the beginning of literature.) I know there should be eloquent evocations of the cobbled beaches of Maine, the plutonic walls of the Sierra Nevada, the orange canyons of the Kaibab Plateau. I have no doubt, in fact, that there are. They are as numerous and diverse as the eyes and fingers that ponder the country—it is that only a handful of them are known. The great majority are to be found in drawers and boxes, in the letters and private journals of millions of workaday people who have regarded their encounters with the land as an engagement bordering on the spiritual, as being fundamentally linked to their state of health.

One cannot acknowledge the extent and the history of this kind of testimony without being forced to the realization that something strange, if not dangerous, is afoot. Year by year, the number of people with firsthand experience in the land dwindles. Rural populations continue to shift to the cities. The family farm is in a state of demise, and government and industry continue to apply pressure on the native peoples of North America to sever their ties with the land. In the wake of this loss of personal and local knowledge from which a real geography is derived, the knowledge on which a country must ultimately stand, has [be]come something hard to define but I think sinister and unsettling—the packaging and marketing of land as a form of entertainment. An incipient industry, capitalizing on the nostalgia Americans feel for the imagined virgin landscapes of their fathers, and on a desire for adventure, now offers people a convenient though sometimes incomplete or even spurious geography as an inducement to purchase a unique experience. But the line between authentic experience and a superficial exposure to the elements of experience is blurred. And the real landscape, in all its complexity, is distorted even further in the public imagination. No longer innately mysterious and dignified, a ground from which experience grows, it becomes a curiously generic backdrop on which experience is imposed.

In theme parks the profound, subtle, and protracted experience of running a river is reduced to a loud, quick, safe equivalence, a pleasant distraction. People only able to venture into the countryside on annual vacations are, increasingly, schooled in the belief that wild land will, and should, provide thrills and exceptional scenery on a timely basis. If it does not, something is wrong, either with the land itself or possibly with the company outfitting the trip.

People in America, then, face a convoluted situation. The land itself, vast and differentiated, defies the notion of a national geography. If applied at all it must be applied lightly and it must grow out of the concrete detail of local geographies. Yet Americans are daily presented with, and have become accustomed to talking about, a homogenized national geography. One that seems to operate independently of the land, a collection of objects rather than a continuous bolt of fabric. It appears in advertisements, as a background in movies, and in patriotic calendars. The suggestion is that there can be national geography because the constituent parts are interchangeable and can be treated as commodities. In day-to-day affairs, in other words, one place serves as well as another to convey one's point. On reflection, this is an appalling condescension and a terrible imprecision, the very antithesis of knowledge. The idea that either the Green River in Utah or the Salmon River in Idaho will do, or that the valleys of Kentucky and West Virginia are virtually interchangeable, is not just misleading. For people still dependent on the soil for their sustenance, or for people whose memories tie them to those places, it betrays a numbing casualness, utilitarian, expedient, and commercial frame of mind. It heralds a society in which it is no longer necessary for human beings to know where they live, except as those places are described and fixed by numbers. The truly difficult and lifelong task of discovering where one lives is finally disdained.

If a society forgets or no longer cares where it lives, then anyone with the political power and the will to do so can manipulate the landscape to conform to certain social ideals or nostalgic visions. People may hardly notice that anything has happened, or assume that whatever happens—a mountain stripped of timber and eroding into its creeks—is for the common good. The more superficial a society's knowledge of the real dimensions of the land it occupies becomes, the more vulnerable the land is to exploitation, to manipulation for short-term gain. The land, virtually powerless before political and commercial entities, finds itself finally with no defenders. It finds itself bereft of intimates with indispensable, concrete knowledge. (Oddly, or perhaps not oddly, while American society continues to value local knowledge as a quaint part of its heritage, it continues to cut such people off from any real political power. This is as true for small farmers and illiterate cowboys as it is for American Indians, native Hawaiians, and Eskimos.)

The intense pressure of imagery in America, and the manipulation of images necessary to a society with specific goals, means the land will inevitably be treated like a commodity; and voices that tend to contradict the proffered image will, one way or another, be silenced or discredited by those in power. This is not new to America; the promulgation in America of a false or imposed geography has been the case from the beginning. All local geographies, as they were defined by hundreds of separate, independent native traditions, were denied in the beginning in favor of an imported and unifying vision of America's natural history. The country, the landscape itself, was eventually defined according to dictates of Progress like Manifest Destiny, and laws like the Homestead Act which reflected a poor understanding of the physical lay of the land.

When I was growing up in southern California, I formed the rudiments of a local geography—eucalyptus trees, February rains, Santa Ana winds. I lost much of it when my family moved to New York City, a move typical of the modern, peripatetic style of American life, responding to the exigencies of divorce and employment. As a boy I felt a hunger to know the American landscape that was extreme; when I was finally able to travel on my own, I did so. Eventually I visited most of the United States, living for brief periods of time in Arizona, Indiana, Alabama, Georgia, Wyoming, New Jersey, and Montana before settling 20 years ago in western Oregon.

The astonishing level of my ignorance confronted me everywhere I went. I knew early on that the country could not be held together in a few phrases, that its geography was magnificent and incomprehensible, that a man or woman could devote a lifetime to its elucidation and still feel in the end that he had but sailed many thousands of miles over the surface of the ocean. So I came into the habit of traversing landscapes I wanted to know with local tutors and reading what had previously been written about, and in, those places. I came to value exceedingly novels and essays and works of nonfiction that connected human enterprise to real and specific places, and I grew to be mildly distrustful of work that occurred in no particular place, work so cerebral and detached as to be refutable only in an argument of ideas.

These sojourns in various corners of the country infused me, somewhat to my surprise on thinking about it, with a great sense of hope. Whatever despair I had come to feel at a waning sense of the real land and the emergence of false geographies—elements of the land being manipulated, for example, to create erroneous but useful patterns in advertising—was dispelled by the depth of a single person's local knowledge, by the serenity that seemed to come with that intelligence. Any harm that might be done by people who cared nothing for the land, to whom it was not innately worthy but only something ultimately for sale, I thought, would one day have to meet this kind of integrity, people with the same dignity and transcendence as the land they occupied. So when I traveled, when I rolled my sleeping bag out on the shores of the Beaufort Sea, or in the high pastures of the Absaroka Range in Wyoming, or at the bottom of the Grand Canyon, I absorbed those particular testaments to life, the indigenous color and songbird song, the smell of sun-bleached rock, damp earth, and wild honey, with some crude appreciation of the singular magnificence of each of those places. And the reassurance I felt expanded in the knowledge that there were, and would likely always be, people speaking out whenever they felt the dignity of the Earth imperiled in those places.

The promulgation of false geographies, which threaten the fundamental notion of what it means to live somewhere, is a current with a stable and perhaps growing countercurrent. People living in New York City are familiar with the stone basements, the cratonic geology, of that island and have a feeling for birds migrating through in the fall, their sequence and number. They do not find the city alien but human, its attenuated natural history merely different from that of rural Georgia or Kansas. I find the countermeasure, too, among Eskimos who cannot read but who might engage you for days on the subtleties of sea-ice topography. And among men and women who, though they have followed in the footsteps of their parents, have come to the conclusion that they cannot farm or fish or log in the way their ancestors did; the finite boundaries to this sort of wealth have appeared in their lifetime. Or among young men and women who have taken several decades of book-learned agronomy, zoology, silviculture and horticulture, ecology, ethnobotany, and fluvial geomorphology and turned it into a new kind of local knowledge, who have taken up residence in a place and sought, both because of and in spite of their education, to develop a deep intimacy with it. Or they have gone to work, idealistically, for the National Park Service or the fish and wildlife services or for a private institution like the Nature Conservancy. They are people to whom the land is more than politics and economics. These are people for whom the land is alive. It feeds them, directly, and that is how and why they learn its geography.

In the end, then, if one begins among the blue crabs of Chesapeake Bay and wanders for several years, down through the Smoky Mountains and back to the bluegrass hills, along the drainages of the Ohio and into the hill country of Missouri, where in summer a chorus of cicadas might drown out human conversation, then up the Missouri itself, reading on the way the entries of Meriwether Lewis and William Clark and musing on the demise of the plains grizzly and the sturgeon, crosses west into the drainage of the Platte and spends the evenings with Gene Weltfish's *The Lost Universe*, her book about the Pawnee who once thrived there, then drops south to the Palo Duro Canyon and the irrigated farms of the Llano Estacado in Texas, turns west across the Sangre de Cristo, southernmost of the Rocky Mountain ranges, and moves north and west up onto the slickrock mesas of Utah, those browns and oranges, the ocherous hues reverberating in the deep canyons, then goes north, swinging west to the insular ranges that sit like battleships in the pelagic space of Nevada, camps at the steaming edge of the sulfur springs in the Black Rock desert, where alkaline pans are glazed with a ferocious light, a heat to melt iron, then crosses the northern Sierra Nevada, waist-deep in summer snow in the passes, to descend to the valley of the Sacramento, and rises through groves of the elephantine redwoods in the Coast Range, to arrive at Cape Mendocino, before Balboa's Pacific, cormorants and gulls, gray whales headed north for Unimak Pass in the Aleutians, the winds crashing down on you, facing the ocean over the blue ocean that gives the scene its true vastness, making this crossing, having been so often astonished at the line and the color of the land, the ingenious lives of its plants and animals, the varieties of its darknesses, the intensity of the stars overhead, you would be ashamed to discover, then, in yourself, any capacity to focus on ravages in the land that left you unsettled. You would have seen so much, breathtaking, startling, and outsize, that you might not be able for a long time to break the spell, the sense, especially finishing your journey in the West, that the land had not been as rearranged or quite as compromised as you had first imagined.

After you had slept some nights on the beach, however, with that finite line of the ocean before you and the land stretching out behind you, the wind first battering then cradling you, you would be compelled by memory, obligated by your own involvement, to speak of what left you troubled. To find the rivers dammed and shrunken, the soil washed away, the land fenced, a tracery of pipes and wires and roads laid down everywhere and animals, cutting the eye off repeatedly and confining it—you had expected this. It troubles you no more than your despair over the ruthlessness, the insensitivity, the impetuousness of modern life. What underlies this obvious change, however, is a less noticeable pattern of disruption: acidic lakes, the skies empty of birds, fouled beaches, the poisonous slags of industry, the sun burning like a molten coin in ruined air.

It is a tenet of certain ideologies that man is responsible for all that is ugly, that everything nature creates is beautiful. Nature's darkness goes partly unreported, of course, and human brilliance is often perversely ignored. What is true is that man has a power, literally beyond his comprehension, to destroy. The lethality of some of what he manufactures, the incompetence with which he stores it or seeks to dispose of it, the cavalier way in which he employs in his daily living substances that threaten his health, the leniency of the courts in these matters (as though products as well as people enjoyed the protection of the Fifth Amendment), and the treatment of open land, rivers, and the atmosphere as if, in some medieval way they could still be regarded as disposal sinks of infinite capacity, would make you wonder, standing face to in the wind at Cape Mendocino, if we weren't bent on an errant of madness.

The geographies of North America, the myriad small landscapes that make up the national fabric, are threatened—by ignorance of what makes them unique, by utilitarian attitudes, by failure to include them in the moral universe, and by brutal disregard. A testament of minor voices can clear away an ignorance of any place, can inform us of its special qualities; but no voice, by merely telling a story, can cause the poisonous wastes that saturate some parts of the land to decompose, to evaporate. This responsibility falls ultimately to the national community, a vague and fragile entity to be sure, but one that, in America, can be ferocious in exerting its will.

Geography, the formal way in which we grapple with this areal mystery, is finally knowledge that calls up something in the land we recognize and respond to. It gives us a sense of place and a sense of community. Both are indispensable to a state of well-being, an individual's and a country's.

One afternoon on the Siuslaw River in the Coast Range of Oregon, in January, I hooked a steelhead, a sea-run trout, that told me, through the muscles of my hands and arms and shoulders, something of the nature of the thing I was calling "the Siuslaw River." Years ago I had stood under a pecan tree in Upson Country, Georgia, idly eating the nuts, when slowly it occurred to me that these nuts would taste different from pecans growing somewhere up in South Carolina. I didn't need a sharp sense of taste to know this, only to pay attention at a level no one had ever told me was necessary. One November dawn, long before the sun rose, I began a vigil at the Dumont Dunes in the Mojave Desert in California, which I kept until a few minutes after the sun broke the horizon. During that time I named to myself the colors by which the sky changed and by which the sand itself flowed like a rising tide through grays and silvers and blues into yellows, pinks, washed duns, and fallow beiges.

It is through the power of observation, the gifts of eye and ear, of tongue and nose and finger, that a place first rises up in our mind; afterward, it is memory that carries the place, that allows it to grow in depth and complexity. For as long as our records go back we have held these two things dear, landscape and memory. Each infuses us with a different kind of life. The one feeds us, figuratively and literally. The other protects us from lies and tyranny. To keep landscapes intact and the memory of them, our history in them, alive, seems as imperative a task in modern time as finding the extent to which individual expression can be accommodated, before it threatens to destroy the fabric of society.

If I were now to visit another country, I would ask my local companion, before I saw any museum or library, any factory or fabled town, to walk me in the country of his or her youth, to tell me the names of things and how, traditionally, they have been fitted together in a community. I would ask for the stories, the voice of memory over the land. I would ask about the history of storms there, the age of the trees, the winter color of the hills. Only then would I ask to see the museum. I would want first the sense of a real place, to know that I was not inhabiting an idea. I would want to know the lay of the land first, the real geography, and take some measure of the love of it in my companion before [having] stood before the painting or read works of scholarship. I would want to have something real and remembered against which I might hope to measure their truth.

Barry Lopez has written The Rediscovery of North America (*Vintage*), *and his most recent book is* Field Notes (*Knopf*).

Human Domination of Earth's Ecosystems

Human alteration of Earth is substantial and growing. Between one-third and one-half of the land surface has been transformed by human action; the carbon dioxide concentration in the atmosphere has increased by nearly 30 percent since the beginning of the Industrial Revolution; more atmospheric nitrogen is fixed by humanity than by all natural terrestrial sources combined; more than half of all accessible surface fresh water is put to use by humanity; and about one-quarter of the bird species on Earth have been driven to extinction. By these and other standards, it is clear that we live on a human-dominated planet.

Peter M. Vitousek, Harold A. Mooney, Jane Lubchenco, Jerry M. Melillo

All organisms modify their environment, and humans are no exception. As the human population has grown and the power of technology has expanded, the scope and nature of this modification has changed drastically. Until recently, the term "human-dominated ecosystems" would have elicited images of agricultural fields, pastures, or urban landscapes; now it applies with greater or lesser force to all of Earth. Many ecosystems are dominated directly by humanity, and no ecosystem on Earth's surface is free of pervasive human influence.

This article provides an overview of human effects on Earth's ecosystems. It is not intended as a litany of environmental disasters, though some disastrous situations are described; nor is it intended either to downplay or to celebrate environmental successes, of which there have been many. Rather, we explore how large humanity looms as a presence on the globe—how, even on the grandest scale, most aspects of the structure and functioning of Earth's ecosystems cannot be understood without accounting for the strong, often dominant influence of humanity.

We view human alterations to the Earth system as operating through the interacting processes summarized in Fig. 1. The growth of the human population, and growth in the resource base used by humanity, is maintained by a suite of human enterprises such as agriculture, industry, fishing, and international commerce. These enterprises transform the land surface (through cropping, forestry, and urbanization), alter the major biogeochemical cycles, and add or remove species and genetically distinct populations in most of Earth's ecosystems. Many of these changes are substantial and reasonably well quantified; all are ongoing. These relatively well-documented changes in turn entrain further alterations to the functioning of the Earth system, most notably by driving global climatic change (*1*) and causing irreversible losses of biological diversity (*2*).

Land Transformation

The use of land to yield goods and services represents the most substantial human alteration of the Earth system. Human use of land alters the structure and functioning of ecosystems, and it alters how ecosystems interact with the atmosphere, with aquatic systems, and with surrounding land. Moreover, land transformation interacts strongly with most other components of global environmental change.

The measurement of land transformation on a global scale is challenging; changes can be measured more or less straightforwardly at a given site, but it is difficult to aggregate these changes regionally and globally. In contrast to analyses of human alteration of the global carbon cycle, we cannot install instruments on a tropical mountain to collect evidence of land transformation. Remote sensing is a most useful technique, but only recently has there been a serious scientific effort to use high-resolution civilian satellite imagery to evaluate even the more visible forms of land transformation, such as deforestation, on continental to global scales (*3*).

Land transformation encompasses a wide variety of activities that vary substantially in their intensity and consequences.

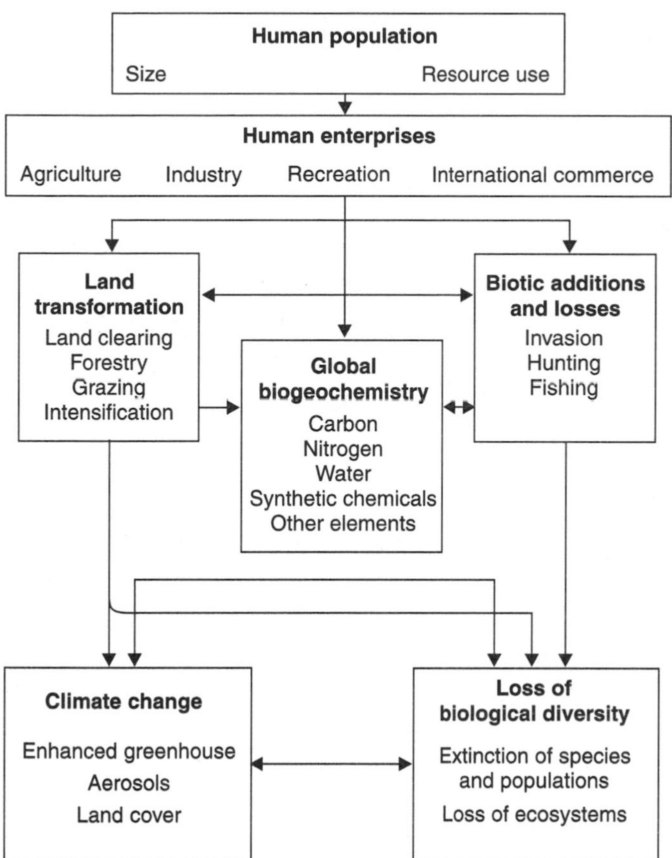

Fig. 1 A conceptual model illustrating humanity's direct and indirect effects on the Earth system [modified from (56)]

At one extreme, 10 to 15% of Earth's land surface is occupied by row-crop agriculture or by urban-industrial areas, and another 6 to 8% has been converted to pastureland (*4*); these systems are wholly changed by human activity. At the other extreme, every terrestrial ecosystem is affected by increased atmospheric carbon dioxide (CO_2), and most ecosystems have a history of hunting and other low-intensity resource extraction. Between these extremes lie grassland and semiarid ecosystems that are grazed (and sometimes degraded) by domestic animals, and forests and woodlands from which wood products have been harvested; together, these represent the majority of Earth's vegetated surface.

The variety of human effects on land makes any attempt to summarize land transformations globally a matter of semantics as well as substantial uncertainty. Estimates of the fraction of land transformed or degraded by humanity (or its corollary, the fraction of the land's biological production that is used or dominated) fall in the range of 39 to 50% (*5*) (Fig. 2). These numbers have large uncertainties, but the fact that they are large is not at all uncertain. Moreover, if anything these estimates understate the global impact of land transformation, in that land that has not been transformed often has been divided into fragments by human alteration of the surrounding areas. This fragmentation affects the species composition and functioning of otherwise little modified ecosystems (*6*).

Overall, land transformation represents the primary driving force in the loss of biological diversity worldwide. Moreover, the effects of land transformation extend far beyond the boundaries of transformed lands. Land transformation can affect climate directly at local and even regional scales. It contributes ~20% to current anthropogenic CO_2 emissions, and more substantially to the increasing concentrations of the greenhouse gases methane and nitrous oxide; fires associated with it alter the reactive chemistry of the troposphere, bringing elevated carbon monoxide concentrations and episodes of urban-like photochemical air pollution to remote tropical areas of Africa and South America; and it causes runoff of sediment and nutrients that drive substantial changes in stream, lake, estuarine, and coral reef ecosystems (*7–10*).

The central importance of land transformation is well recognized within the community of researchers concerned with global environmental change. Several research programs are focused on aspects of it (*9, 11*); recent and substantial progress toward understanding these aspects has been made (*3*), and much more progress can be anticipated. Understanding land transformation is a difficult challenge; it requires integrating the social, economic, and cultural causes of land transformation with evaluations of its biophysical nature and consequences. This interdisciplinary approach is essential to predicting the course, and to any hope of affecting the consequences, of human-caused land transformation.

Oceans

Human alterations of marine ecosystems are more difficult to quantify than those of terrestrial ecosystems, but several kinds of information suggest that they are substantial. The human population is concentrated near coasts—about 60% within 100 km—and the oceans' productive coastal margins have been affected strongly by humanity. Coastal wetlands that mediate interactions between land and sea have been altered over large areas; for example, approximately 50% of mangrove ecosystems globally have been transformed or destroyed by human activity (*12*). Moreover, a recent analysis suggested that although humans use about 8% of the primary production of the oceans, that fraction grows to more than 25% for upwelling areas and to 35% for temperate continental shelf systems (*13*).

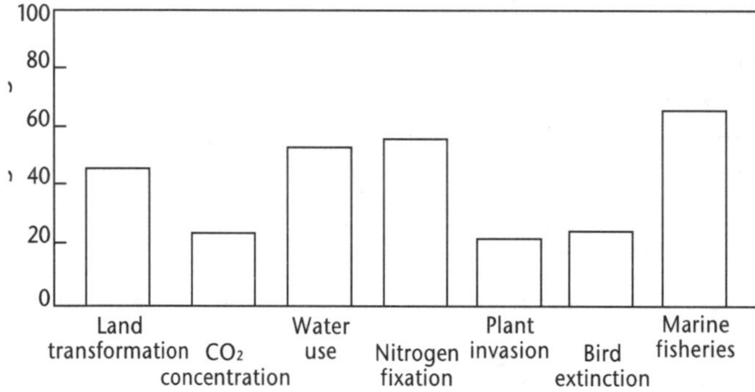

Fig. 2. Human dominance or alteration of several major components of the Earth system, expressed as (from left to right) percentage of the land surface transformed (*5*); percentage of the current atmospheric CO_2 concentration that results from human action (*17*); percentage of accessible surface fresh water used (*20*); percentage of terrestrial N fixation that is human-caused (*28*); percentage of plant species in Canada that humanity has introduced from elsewhere (*48*); percentage of bird species on Earth that have become extinct in the past two millennia, almost all of them as a consequence of human activity (*42*); and percentage of major marine fisheries that are fully exploited, overexploited, or depleted (*14*).

Many of the fisheries that capture marine productivity are focused on top predators, whose removal can alter marine ecosystems out of proportion to their abundance. Moreover, many such fisheries have proved to be unsustainable, at least at our present level of knowledge and control. As of 1995, 22% of recognized marine fisheries were overexploited or already depleted, and 44% more were at their limit of exploitation (*14*) (Figs. 2 and 3). The consequences of fisheries are not restricted to their target organisms; commercial marine fisheries around the world discard 27 million tons of nontarget animals annually, a quantity nearly one-third as large as total landings (*15*). Moreover, the dredges and trawls used in some fisheries damage habitats substantially as they are dragged along the sea floor.

A recent increase in the frequency, extent, and duration of harmful algal blooms in coastal areas (*16*) suggests that human activity has affected the base as well as the top of marine food chains. Harmful algal blooms are sudden increases in the abundance of marine phytoplankton that produce harmful structures or chemicals. Some but not all of these phytoplankton are strongly pigmented (red or brown tides). Algal blooms usually are correlated with changes in temperature, nutrients, or salinity; nutrients in coastal waters, in particular, are much modified by human activity. Algal blooms can cause extensive fish kills through toxins and by causing anoxia; they also lead to paralytic shellfish poisoning and amnesic shellfish poisoning in humans. Although the existence of harmful algal blooms has long been recognized, they have spread widely in the past two decades (*16*).

Alterations of the Biogeochemical Cycles

Carbon. Life on Earth is based on carbon, and the CO_2 in the atmosphere is the primary resource for photosynthesis. Humanity adds CO_2 to the atmosphere by mining and burning fossil fuels, the residue of life from the distant past, and by converting forests and grasslands to agricultural and other low-biomass ecosystems. The net result of both activities is that organic carbon from rocks, organisms, and soils is released into the atmosphere as CO_2.

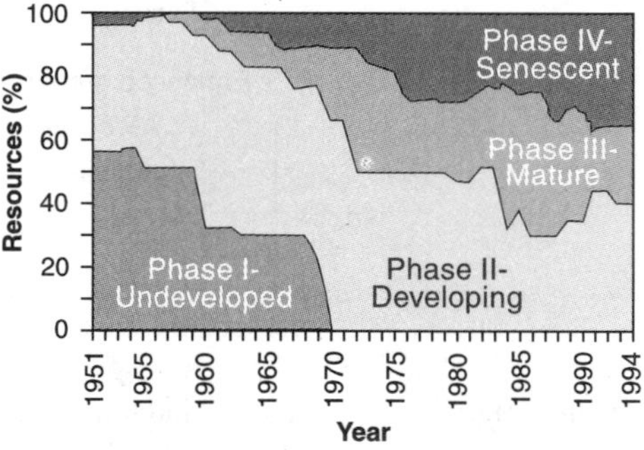

Fig. 3. Percentage of major world marine fish resources in different phases of development, 1951 to 1994 [from (57)]. Undeveloped = a low and relatively constant level of catches; developing = rapidly increasing catches; mature = a high and plateauing level of catches; senescent = catches declining from higher levels.

The modern increase in CO_2 represents the clearest and best documented signal of human alteration of the Earth system. Thanks to the foresight of Roger Revelle, Charles Keeling, and others who initiated careful and systematic measurements of atmospheric CO_2 in 1957 and sustained them through budget crises and changes in scientific fashions, we have observed the concentration of CO_2 as it has increased steadily from 315 ppm to 362 ppm. Analysis of air bubbles extracted from the Antarctic and Greenland ice caps extends the record back much further; the CO_2 concentration was more or less stable near 280 ppm for thousands of years until about 1800, and has increased exponentially since then (*17*).

There is no doubt that this increase has been driven by human activity, today primarily by fossil fuel combustion. The sources of CO_2 can be traced isotopically; before the period of extensive nuclear testing in the atmosphere, carbon depleted in ^{14}C was a specific tracer of CO_2 derived from fossil fuel combustion, whereas carbon depleted in ^{13}C characterized CO_2 from both

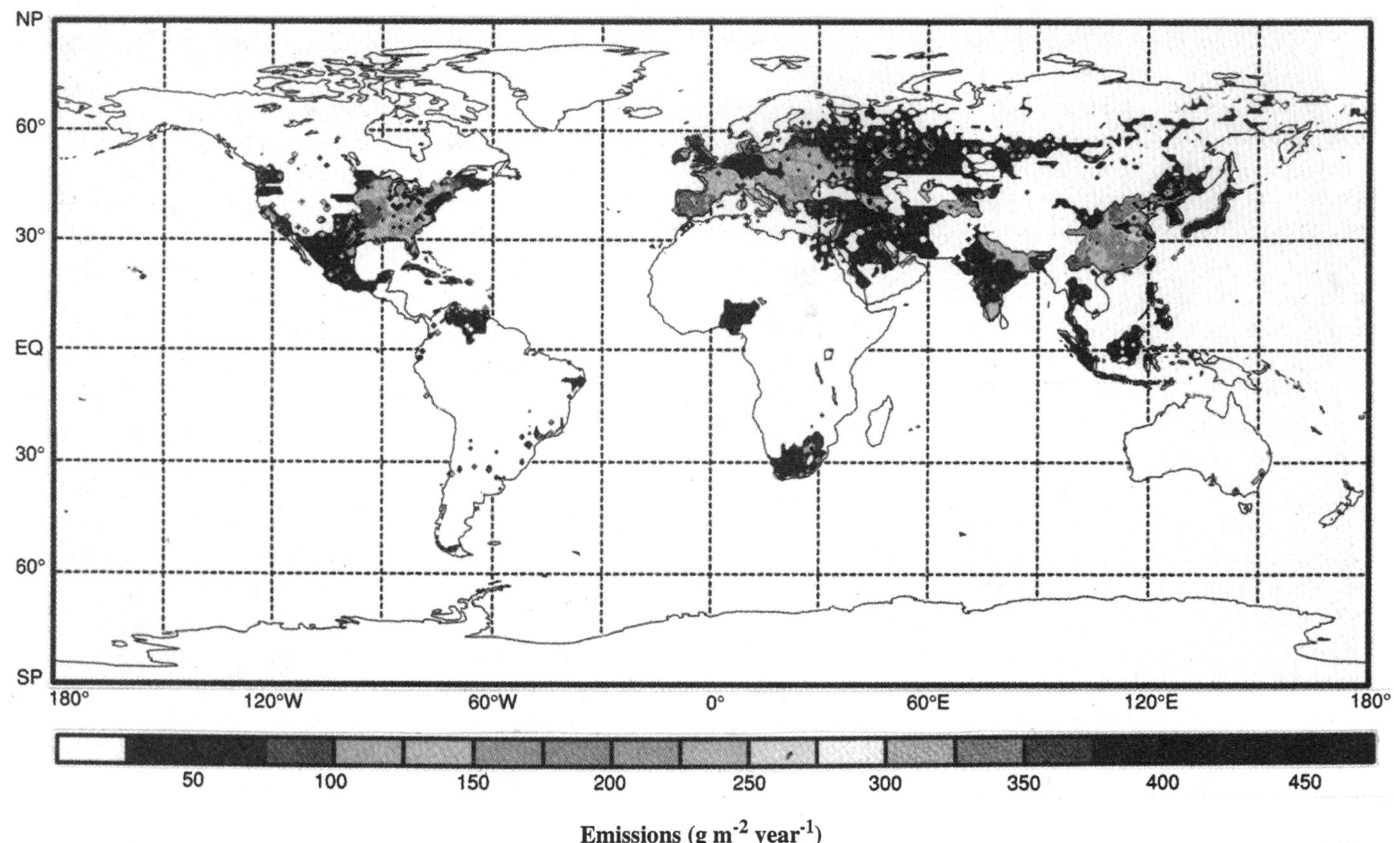

Fig. 4 Geographical distribution of fossil fuel sources of CO_2 as of 1990. The global mean is 12.2 g m^{-2} $year^{-1}$; most emissions occur in economically developed regions of the north temperate zone. EQ, equator; NP, North Pole; SP, South Pole. [Prepared by A.S. Denning, from information in (*18*)]

fossil fuels and land transformation. Direct measurements in the atmosphere, and analyses of carbon isotopes in tree rings, show that both ^{13}C and ^{14}C in CO_2 were diluted in the atmosphere relative to ^{12}C as the CO_2 concentration in the atmosphere increased.

Fossil fuel combustion now adds 5.5 ± 0.5 billion metric tons of CO_2-C to the atmosphere annually, mostly in economically developed regions of the temperate zone (*18*) (Fig. 4). The annual accumulation of CO_2-C has averaged 3.2 [[EQ]] 0.2 billion metric tons recently (*17*). The other major terms in the atmospheric carbon balance are net ocean-atmosphere flux, net release of carbon during land transformation, and net storage in terrestrial biomass and soil organic matter. All of these terms are smaller and less certain than fossil fuel combustion or annual atmospheric accumulation; they represent rich areas of current research, analysis, and sometimes contention.

The human-caused increase in atmospheric CO_2 already represents nearly a 30% change relative to the pre-industrial era (Fig. 2), and CO_2 will continue to increase for the foreseeable future. Increased CO_2 represents the most important human enhancement to the greenhouse effect; the consensus of the climate research community is that it probably already affects climate detectably and will drive substantial climate change in the next century (*1*). The direct effects of increased CO_2 on plants and ecosystems may be even more important. The growth of most plants is enhanced by elevated CO_2, but to very different extents; the tissue chemistry of plants that respond to CO_2 is altered in ways that decrease food quality for animals and microbes; and the water use efficiency of plants and ecosystems generally is increased. The fact that increased CO_2 affects species differentially means that it is likely to drive substantial changes in the species composition and dynamics of all terrestrial ecosystems (*19*).

Water. Water is essential to all life. Its movement by gravity, and through evaporation and condensation, contributes to driving Earth's biogeochemical cycles and to controlling its climate. Very little of the water on Earth is directly usable by humans; most is either saline or frozen. Globally, humanity now uses more than half of the runoff water that is fresh and reasonably accessible, with about 70% of this use in agriculture (*20*) (Fig. 2). To meet increasing demands for the limited supply of fresh water, humanity has extensively altered river systems through diversions and impoundments. In the United States only 2% of the rivers run unimpeded, and by the end of this century the flow of about two-thirds of all of Earth's rivers will be regulated (*21*). At present, as much as 6% of Earth's river runoff is evaporated as a consequence of human manipulations (*22*). Major rivers, including the Colorado, the Nile, and the Ganges, are used so extensively that little water reaches the sea. Massive inland water bodies, including the Aral Sea and Lake Chad, have been greatly reduced in extent by water diversions for agriculture. Reduction in the volume of the Aral Sea resulted in the demise of native fishes and the loss of other biota; the loss of a major fishery; exposure of the salt-laden sea bottom, thereby providing a major source of windblown dust; the production of a drier and more continental local climate and a decrease in water quality in the general region; and an increase in human diseases (*23*).

Impounding and impeding the flow of rivers provides reservoirs of water that can be used for energy generation as well as for agriculture. Waterways also are managed for transport, for flood control, and for the dilution of chemical wastes. Together, these activities have altered Earth's freshwater ecosystems profoundly, to a greater extent than terrestrial ecosystems have been altered. The construction of dams affects biotic habitats indirectly as well; the damming of the Danube River, for example, has altered the silica chemistry of the entire Black Sea. The large number of operational dams (36,000) in the world, in conjunction with the many that are planned, ensure that humanity's effects on aquatic biological systems will continue (*24*). Where surface water is sparse or over-exploited, humans use groundwater—and in many areas the groundwater that is drawn upon is nonrenewable, or fossil, water (*25*). For example, three-quarters of the water supply of Saudi Arabia currently comes from fossil water (*26*).

Alterations to the hydrological cycle can affect regional climate. Irrigation increases atmospheric humidity in semiarid areas, often increasing precipitation and thunderstorm frequency (*27*). In contrast, land transformation from forest to agriculture or pasture increases albedo and decreases surface roughness; simulations suggest that the net effect of this transformation is to increase temperature and decrease precipitation regionally (*7, 26*).

Conflicts arising from the global use of water will be exacerbated in the years ahead, with a growing human population and with the stresses that global changes will impose on water quality and availability. Of all of the environmental security issues facing nations, an adequate supply of clean water will be the most important.

Nitrogen. Nitrogen (N) is unique among the major elements required for life, in that its cycle includes a vast atmospheric reservoir (N_2) that must be fixed (combined with carbon, hydrogen, or oxygen) before it can be used by most organisms. The supply of this fixed N controls (at least in part) the productivity, carbon storage, and species composition of many ecosystems. Before the extensive human alteration of the N cycle, 90 to 130 million metric tons of N (Tg N) were fixed biologically on land each year; rates of biological fixation in marine systems are less certain, but perhaps as much was fixed there (*28*).

Human activity has altered the global cycle of N substantially by fixing N_2—deliberately for fertilizer and inadvertently during fossil fuel combustion. Industrial fixation of N fertilizer increased from <10 Tg/year in 1950 to 80 Tg/year in 1990; after a brief dip caused by economic dislocations in the former Soviet Union, it is expected to increase to 135 Tg/year by 2030 (29). Cultivation of soybeans, alfalfa, and other legume crops that fix N symbiotically enhances fixation by another ~40 Tg/year, and fossil fuel combustion puts >20 Tg/year of reactive N into the atmosphere globally—some by fixing N_2, more from the mobilization of N in the fuel. Overall, human activity adds at least as much fixed N to terrestrial ecosystems as do all natural sources combined (Fig. 2), and it mobilizes >50 Tg/year more during land transformation (*28, 30*).

Alteration of the N cycle has multiple consequences. In the atmosphere, these include (i) an increasing concentration of the greenhouse gas nitrous oxide globally; (ii) substantial increases in fluxes of reactive N gases (two-thirds or more of both nitric oxide and ammonia emissions globally are human-caused); and (iii) a substantial contribution to acid rain and to the photochemical smog that afflicts urban and agricultural areas throughout the world (*31*). Reactive N that is emitted to the atmosphere is deposited downwind, where it can influence the dynamics of recipient ecosystems. In regions where fixed N was in short supply, added N generally increases productivity and C storage within ecosystems, and ultimately increases losses of N and cations from soils, in a set of processes termed "N saturation" (*32*). Where added N increases the productivity of ecosystems, usually it also decreases their biological diversity (*33*).

Human-fixed N also can move from agriculture, from sewage systems, and from N-saturated terrestrial systems to streams, rivers, groundwater, and ultimately the oceans. Fluxes of N through streams and rivers have increased markedly as human alteration of the N cycle has accelerated; river nitrate is highly correlated with the human population of river basins and with the sum of human-caused N inputs to those basins (*8*). Increases in river N drive the eutrophication of most estuaries, causing blooms of nuisance and even toxic algae, and threatening the sustainability of marine fisheries (*16, 34*).

Other cycles. The cycles of carbon, water, and nitrogen are not alone in being altered by human activity. Humanity is also the largest source of oxidized sulfur gases in the atmosphere; these affect regional air quality, biogeochemistry, and climate. Moreover, mining and mobilization of phosphorus and of many metals exceed their natural fluxes; some of the metals that are concentrated and mobilized are highly toxic (including lead, cadmium, and mercury) (*35*). Beyond any doubt, humanity is a major biogeochemical force on Earth.

Synthetic organic chemicals. Synthetic organic chemicals have brought humanity many beneficial services. However, many are toxic to humans and other species, and some are hazardous in concentrations as low as 1 part per billion. Many chemicals persist in the environment for decades; some are both toxic and persistent. Long-lived organochlorine compounds provide the clearest examples of environmental consequences of persistent compounds. Insecticides such as DDT and its relatives, and industrial compounds like polychlorinated biphenyls (PCBs), were used widely in North America in the 1950s and 1960s. They were transported globally, accumulated in organisms, and magnified in concentration through food chains; they devastated populations of some predators (notably falcons and eagles) and entered parts of the human food supply in concentrations higher than was prudent. Domestic use of these compounds was phased out in the 1970s in the United States and Canada, and their concentrations declined thereafter. However, PCBs in particular remain readily detectable in many organisms, sometimes approaching thresholds of public health concern (*36*). They will continue to circulate through organisms for many decades.

Synthetic chemicals need not be toxic to cause environmental problems. The fact that the persistent and volatile chlorofluorocarbons (CFCs) are wholly nontoxic contributed to their widespread use as refrigerants and even aerosol propellants. The subsequent discovery that CFCs drive the breakdown of stratospheric ozone, and especially the later discovery of the Antarctic ozone hole and their role in it, represent great surprises in global environmental science (*37*). Moreover, the response of the international political system to those discoveries is the best extant illustration that global environmental change can be dealt with effectively (*38*).

Particular compounds that pose serious health and environmental threats can be and often have been phased out (although PCB production is growing in Asia). Nonetheless, each year the chemical industry produces more than 100 million tons of organic chemicals representing some 70,000 different compounds, with about 1000 new ones being added annually (*39*). Only a small fraction of the many chemicals produced and released into the environment are tested adequately for health hazards or environmental impact (*40*).

Biotic Changes

Human modification of Earth's biological resources—its species and genetically distinct populations—is substantial and growing. Extinction is a natural process, but the current rate of loss of genetic variability, of populations, and of species is far above background rates; it is ongoing; and it represents a wholly irreversible global change. At the same time, human transport of species around Earth is homogenizing Earth's biota, introducing many species into new areas where they can disrupt both natural and human systems.

Losses. Rates of extinction are difficult to determine globally, in part because the majority of species on Earth have not yet been identified. Nevertheless, recent calculations suggest that rates of species extinction are now on the order of 100 to 1000 times those before humanity's dominance of Earth (*41*). For particular well-known groups, rates of loss are even greater; as many as one-quarter of Earth's bird species have been driven to extinction by human activities over the past two millennia, particularly on oceanic islands (*42*) (Fig. 2). At present, 11% of the remaining birds, 18% of the mammals, 5% of fish, and 8% of plant species on Earth are threatened with extinction (*43*). There has been a disproportionate loss of large mammal species because of hunting; these species played a dominant role in many ecosystems, and their loss has resulted in a fundamental change in the dynamics of those systems (*44*), one that could lead to further extinctions. The largest organisms in marine systems have been affected similarly, by fishing and whaling. Land transformation is the single most important cause of extinction, and current rates of land transformation eventually will drive many more species to extinction, although with a time lag that masks the true dimensions of the crisis (*45*). Moreover, the effects of other components of global environmental change—of altered carbon and nitrogen cycles, and of anthropogenic climate change—are just beginning.

As high as they are, these losses of species understate the magnitude of loss of genetic variation. The loss to land transformation of locally adapted populations within species, and of genetic material within populations, is a human-caused change that reduces the resilience of species and ecosystems while precluding human use of the library of natural products and genetic material that they represent (*46*).

Although conservation efforts focused on individual endangered species have yielded some successes, they are expensive—and the protection or restoration of whole ecosystems often represents the most effective way to sustain genetic, population, and species diversity. Moreover, ecosystems themselves may play important roles in both natural and human-dominated landscapes. For example, mangrove ecosystems protect coastal areas from erosion and provide nurseries for offshore fisheries, but they are threatened by land transformation in many areas.

Invasions. In addition to extinction, humanity has caused a rearrangement of Earth's biotic systems, through the mixing of floras and faunas that had long been isolated geographically. The magnitude of transport of species, termed "biological invasion," is enormous (*47*); invading species are present almost everywhere. On many islands, more than half of the plant species are nonindigenous, and in many continental areas the figure is 20% or more (*48*) (Fig. 2).

As with extinction, biological invasion occurs naturally—and as with extinction, human activity has accelerated its rate by orders of magnitude. Land transformation interacts strongly with biological invasion, in that human-altered ecosystems generally provide the primary foci for invasions, while in some cases land transformation itself is driven by biological invasions (*49*). International commerce is also a primary cause of the breakdown of biogeographic barriers; trade in live organisms is massive and global, and many other organisms are inadvertently taken along for the ride. In freshwater systems, the combination of upstream land transformation, altered hydrology, and numerous deliberate and accidental species introductions has led to particularly widespread invasion, in continental as well as island ecosystems (*50*).

In some regions, invasions are becoming more frequent. For example, in the San Francisco Bay of California, an average of one new species has been established every 36 weeks since 1850, every 24 weeks since 1970, and every 12 weeks for the last decade (*51*). Some introduced species quickly become invasive over large areas (for example, the Asian clam in the San Francisco Bay), whereas others become widespread only after a lag of decades, or even over a century (*52*).

Many biological invasions are effectively irreversible; once replicating biological material is released into the environment and becomes successful there, calling it back is difficult and expensive at best. Moreover, some species introductions have consequences. Some degrade human health and that of other species; after all, most infectious diseases are invaders over most of their range. Others have caused economic losses amounting to billions of dollars; the recent invasion of North

America by the zebra mussel is a well-publicized example. Some disrupt ecosystem processes, altering the structure and functioning of whole ecosystems. Finally, some invasions drive losses in the biological diversity of native species and populations; after land transformation, they are the next most important cause of extinction (*53*).

Conclusions

The global consequences of human activity are not something to face in the future—as Fig. 2 illustrates, they are with us now. All of these changes are ongoing, and in many cases accelerating; many of them were entrained long before their importance was recognized. Moreover, all of these seemingly disparate phenomena trace to a single cause—the growing scale of the human enterprise. The rates, scales, kinds, and combinations of changes occurring now are fundamentally different from those at any other time in history; we are changing Earth more rapidly than we are understanding it. We live on a human-dominated planet—and the momentum of human population growth, together with the imperative for further economic development in most of the world, ensures that our dominance will increase.

The papers in this special section summarize our knowledge of and provide specific policy recommendations concerning major human-dominated ecosystems. In addition, we suggest that the rate and extent of human alteration of Earth should affect how we think about Earth. It is clear that we control much of Earth, and that our activities affect the rest. In a very real sense, the world is in our hands—and how we handle it will determine its composition and dynamics, and our fate.

Recognition of the global consequences of the human enterprise suggests three complementary directions. First, we can work to reduce the rate at which we alter the Earth system. Humans and human-dominated systems may be able to adapt to slower change, and ecosystems and the species they support may cope more effectively with the changes we impose, if those changes are slow. Our footprint on the planet (*54*) might then be stabilized at a point where enough space and resources remain to sustain most of the other species on Earth, for their sake and our own. Reducing the rate of growth in human effects on Earth involves slowing human population growth and using resources as efficiently as is practical. Often it is the waste products and by-products of human activity that drive global environmental change.

Second, we can accelerate our efforts to understand Earth's ecosystems and how they interact with the numerous components of human-caused global change. Ecological research is inherently complex and demanding: It requires measurement and monitoring of populations and ecosystems; experimental studies to elucidate the regulation of ecological processes; the development, testing, and validation of regional and global models; and integration with a broad range of biological, earth, atmospheric, and marine sciences. The challenge of understanding a human-dominated planet further requires that the human dimensions of global change—the social, economic, cultural, and other drivers of human actions—be included within our analyses.

Finally, humanity's dominance of Earth means that we cannot escape responsibility for managing the planet. Our activities are causing rapid, novel, and substantial changes to Earth's ecosystems. Maintaining populations, species, and ecosystems in the face of those changes, and maintaining the flow of goods and services they provide humanity (*55*), will require active management for the foreseeable future. There is no clearer illustration of the extent of human dominance of Earth than the fact that maintaining the diversity of "wild" species and the functioning of "wild" ecosystems will require increasing human involvement.

REFERENCES AND NOTES

1. Intergovernmental Panel on Climate Change, *Climate Change 1995* (Cambridge Univ. Press, Cambridge, 1996), pp. 9–49.
2. United Nations Environment Program, *Global Biodiversity Assessment*, V. H. Heywood, Ed. (Cambridge Univ. Press, Cambridge, 1995).
3. D. Skole and C. J. Tucker, *Science* **260**, 1905 (1993).
4. J. S. Olson, J. A. Watts, L. J. Allison, *Carbon in Live Vegetation of Major World Ecosystems* (Office of Energy Research, U.S. Department of Energy, Washington, DC, 1983).
5. P. M. Vitousek, P. R. Ehrlich, A. H. Ehrlich, P. A. Matson, *Bioscience* **36**, 368 (1986); R. W. Kates, B. L. Turner, W. C. Clark, in (35), pp. 1–17; G. C. Daily, *Science* **269**, 350 (1995).
6. D. A. Saunders, R. J. Hobbs, C. R. Margules, *Conserv. Biol.* **5**, 18 (1991).
7. J. Shukla, C. Nobre, P. Sellers, *Science* **247**, 1322 (1990).
8. R. W. Howarth *et al.*, *Biogeochemistry* **35**, 75 (1996).
9. W. B. Meyer and B. L. Turner II, *Changes in Land Use and Land Cover: A Global Perspective* (Cambridge Univ. Press, Cambridge, 1994).
10. S. R. Carpenter, S. G. Fisher, N. B. Grimm, J. F. Kitchell, *Annu. Rev. Ecol. Syst.* **23**, 119 (1992); S. V. Smith and R. W. Buddemeier, *ibid.*, p. 89; J. M. Melillo, I. C. Prentice, G. D. Farquhar, E.-D. Schulze, O. E. Sala, in (*1*), pp. 449–481.
11. R. Leemans and G. Zuidema, *Trends Ecol. Evol.* **10**, 76 (1995).
12. World Resources Institute, *World Resources 1996–1997* (Oxford Univ. Press, New York, 1996).
13. D. Pauly and V. Christensen, *Nature* **374**, 257 (1995).
14. Food and Agricultural Organization (FAO), *FAO Fisheries Tech. Pap.* **335** (1994).
15. D. L. Alverson, M. H. Freeberg. S. A. Murawski, J. G. Pope, *FAO Fisheries Tech. Pap.* **339** (1994).
16. G. M. Hallegraeff, *Phycologia* **32**, 79 (1993).
17. D. S. Schimel *et al.*, in *Climate Change 1994: Radiative Forcing of Climate Change*, J. T. Houghton *et al.*, Eds. (Cambridge Univ. Press, Cambridge, 1995), pp. 39–71.

18. R. J. Andres, G. Marland, I. Y. Fung, E. Matthews, *Global Biogeochem. Cycles* **10**, 419 (1996).
19. G. W. Koch and H. A. Mooney, *Carbon Dioxide and Terrestrial Ecosystems* (Academic Press, San Diego, CA, 1996); C. Kömer and F. A. Bazzaz, *Carbon Dioxide, Populations, and Communities* (Academic Press, San Diego, CA, 1996).
20. S. L. Postel, G. C. Daily, P. R. Ehrlich, *Science* **271**, 785 (1996).
21. J. N. Abramovitz, *Imperiled Waters, Impoverished Future: The Decline of Freshwater Ecosystems* (Worldwatch Institute, Washington, DC, 1996).
22. M. I. L'vovich and G. F. White, in (*35*), pp. 235–252; M. Dynesius and C. Nilsson, *Science* **266**, 753 (1994).
23. P. Micklin, *Science* **241**, 1170 (1988), V. Kotlyakov, *Environment* **33**, 4 (1991).
24. C. Humborg, V. Ittekkot, A. Cociasu, B. Bodungen, *Nature* **386**, 385 (1997).
25. P. H. Gleick, Ed., *Water in Crisis* (Oxford Univ. Press, New York, 1993).
26. V. Gornitz, C. Rosenzweig, D. Hillel, *Global Planet. Change* **14**, 147 (1997).
27. P. C. Milly and K. A. Dunne, *J. Clim.* **7**, 506 (1994).
28. J. N. Galloway, W. H. Schlesinger, H. Levy II, A. Michaels, J. L. Schnoor, *Global Biogeochem. Cycles* **9**, 235 (1995).
29. J. N. Galloway, H. Levy II, P. S. Kasibhatla, *Ambio* **23**, 120 (1994).
30. V. Smil, in (*35*), pp. 423–436.
31. P. M. Vitousek *et al., Ecol. Appl.*, in press.
32. J. D. Aber, J. M. Melillo, K. J. Nadelhoffer, J. Pastor, R. D. Boone, *ibid.* **1**, 303 (1991).
33. D. Tilman, *Ecol. Monogr.* **57**, 189 (1987).
34. S. W. Nixon et al., *Biogeochemistry* **35**, 141 (1996).
35. B. L. Turner II *et al.*, Eds., *The Earth As Transformed by Human Action* (Cambridgc Univ. Prcss, Cambridgc, 1990).
36. C. A. Stow, S. R. Carpenter, C. P. Madenjian, L. A. Eby, L. J. Jackson, *Bioscience* **45**, 752 (1995).
37. F. S. Rowland, *Am. Sci.* **77**, 36 (1989); S. Solomon, *Nature* **347**, 347 (1990).
38. M. K. Tolba *et al.*, Eds., *The World Environment 1972–1992* (Chapman & Hall, London, 1992).
39. S. Postel, *Defusing the Toxics Threat: Controlling Pesticides and Industrial Waste* (Worldwatch Institute, Washington, DC, 1987).
40. United Nations Environment Program (UNEP). *Saving Our Planet—Challenges and Hopes* (UNEP, Nairobi, 1992).
41. J. H. Lawton and R. M. May, Eds., *Extinction Rates* (Oxford Univ. Press, Oxford, 1995); S. L. Pimm, G. J. Russell, J. L. Gittleman, T. Brooks, *Science* **269**, 347 (1995).
42. S. L. Olson, in *Conservation for the Twenty-First Century*, D. Western and M. C. Pearl, Eds. (Oxford Univ. Press, Oxford, 1989), p. 50; D. W. Steadman, *Science* **267**, 1123 (1995).
43. R. Barbault and S. Sastrapradja. in (*2*), pp. 193–274.
44. R. Dirzo and A. Miranda, in *Plant-Animal Interactions*, P. W. Price, T. M. Lewinsohn, W. Fernandes, W. W. Benson, Eds. (Wiley Interscience, New York, 1991), p. 273.
45. D. Tilman, R. M. May, C. Lehman, M. A. Nowak, *Nature* **371**, 65 (1994).
46. H. A. Mooney, J. Lubchenco, R. Dirzo, O. E. Sala, in (*2*). pp. 279–325.
47. C. Elton, *The Ecology of Invasions by Animals and Plants* (Methuen, London, 1958); J. A. Drake *et al.*, Eds., *Biological Invasions. A Global Perspective* (Wiley, Chichester, UK, 1989).
48. M. Rejmanek and J. Randall, *Madrono* **41**, 161 (1994).
49. C. M. D'Antonio and P. M. Vitousek, *Annu. Rev. Ecol. Syst.* **23**, 63 (1992).
50. D. M. Lodge, *Trends Ecol. Evol.* **8**, 133 (1993).
51. A. N. Cohen and J. T. Carlton, *Biological Study: Nonindigenous Aquatic Species in a United States Estuary. A Case Study of the Biological Invasions of the San Francisco Bay and Delta* (U.S. Fish and Wildlife Service, Washington, DC, 1995).
52. I. Kowarik, in *Plant Invasions—General Aspects and Special Problems*, P. Pysek, K. Prach, M. Rejmánek, M. Wade, Eds. (SPB Academic, Amsterdam, 1995), p. 15.
53. P. M. Vitousek, C. M. D'Antonio, L. L. Loope, R. Westbrooks, *Am. Sci.* **84**, 468 (1996).
54. W. E. Rees and M. Wackernagel, in *Investing in Natural Capital: The Ecological Economics Approach to Sustainability*, A. M. Jansson, M. Hammer, C. Folke, R. Costanza, Eds. (Island, Washington, DC, 1994).
55. G. C. Daily, Ed., *Nature's Services* (Island, Washington, DC, 1997).
56. J. Lubchenco *et al., Ecology*, **72**, 371 (1991), P. M. Vitousek, *ibid.* **75**, 1861 (1994).
57. S. M. Garcia and R. Grainger. *FAO Fisheries Tech. Pap.* 359 (1996).

58. We thank G. C. Daily, C. B. Field, S. Hobbie, D. Gordon, P.A. Matson, and R. L. Naylor for constructive comments on this paper, A. S. Denning and S. M. Garcia for assistance with illustrations, and C. Nakashima and B. Lilley for preparing text and figures for publication.

P. M. Vitousek and H. A. Mooney are in the Department of Biological Sciences, Stanford University, Stanford, CA 94305, USA. J. Lubchenco is in the Department of Zoology, Oregon State University, Corvallis, OR 97331, USA. J. M. Melillo is at the U.S. Office of Science and Technology Policy, Old Executive Office Building, Room 443, Washington, DC 20502, USA.

Sculpting the Earth from Inside Out

Powerful motions deep inside the planet do not merely shove fragments of the rocky shell horizontally around the globe—they also lift and lower entire continents

by Michael Gurnis

Credit for sculpting the earth's surface typically goes to violent collisions between tectonic plates, the mobile fragments of the planet's rocky outer shell. The mighty Himalayas shot up when India rammed into Asia, for instance, and the Andes grew as the Pacific Ocean floor plunged beneath South America. But even the awesome power of plate tectonics cannot fully explain some of the planet's most massive surface features.

Take southern Africa. This region boasts one of the world's most expansive plateaus, more than 1,000 miles across and almost a mile high. Geologic evidence shows that southern Africa, and the surrounding ocean floor, has been rising slowly for the past 100 million years, even though it has not experienced a tectonic collision for nearly 400 million years.

The African superswell, as this uplifted landmass is known, is just one example of dramatic vertical movement by a broad chunk of the earth's surface. In other cases from the distant past, vast stretches of Australia and North America bowed down thousands of feet—and then popped up again.

Scientists who specialize in studying the earth's interior have long suspected that activity deep inside the earth was behind such vertical changes at the surface. These geophysicists began searching for clues in the mantle—the middle layer of the planet. This region of scalding-hot rock lies just below the jigsaw configuration of tectonic plates and extends down more than 1,800 miles to the outer edge of the globe's iron core. Researchers learned that variations in the mantle's intense heat and pressure enable the solid rock to creep molassesslike over thousands of years. But they could not initially decipher how it could give rise to large vertical motions. Now, however, powerful computer models that combine snapshots of the mantle today with clues about how it might have behaved in the past are beginning to explain why parts of the earth's surface have undergone these astonishing ups and downs.

The mystery of the African superswell was among the easiest to decipher. Since the early half of the 20th century, geophysicists have understood that over the unceasing expanse of geologic time, the mantle not only creeps, it churns and roils like pot of thick soup about to boil. The relatively low density of the hottest rock makes that material buoyant, so it ascends slowly; in contrast, colder, denser rock sinks until heat escaping the molten core warms it enough to make it rise again. These three-dimensional motions, called convection, are known to enable the horizontal movement of tectonic plates, but it seemed unlikely that the forces they created could lift and lower the planet's surface. That skepticism about the might of the mantle began to fade away when researchers created the first blurry images of the earth's interior.

About 20 years ago scientists came up with a way to make three-dimensional snapshots of the mantle by measuring vibrations that are set in motion by earthquakes originating in the planet's outer shell. The velocities of these vibrations, or seismic waves, are determined by the chemical composition, temperature and pressure of the rocks they travel through. Waves become sluggish in hot, low-density rock, and they speed up in colder, denser regions. By recording the time it takes for seismic waves to travel from an earthquake's epicenter to a particular recording station at the surface, scientists can infer the temperatures and densities in a given segment of the interior. And by compiling a map of seismic velocities from thousands of earthquakes around the globe they can begin to map temperatures and densities throughout the mantle.

These seismic snapshots, which become increasingly more detailed as researches find more accurate ways to compile their measurements, have recently revealed some unexpectedly immense formations in the deepest parts of the mantle. The largest single structure turns out to lie directly below Africa's southern tip. About two years ago seismologists Jeroen Ritsema and Hendrik-Jan van Heijst of the California Institute of Technology calculated that this mushroom-shaped mass stretches some 900 miles upward from the core and spreads across several thousand miles [*see "Mantle Map".*]

The researchers immediately began to wonder whether this enormous blob could be shoving Africa skyward. Be-

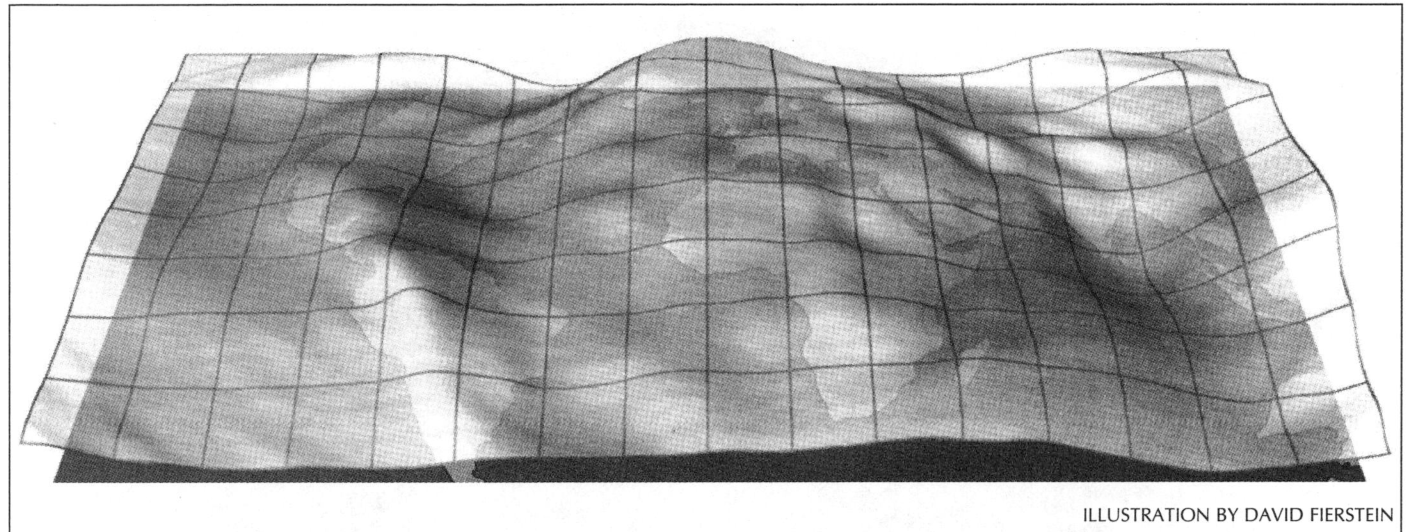

ILLUSTRATION BY DAVID FIERSTEIN

BULGES AND TROUGHS in the transparent surface above the world map represent natural variations in the earth's gravitational field. High points indicate stronger-than-normal gravity caused by a pocket of excess mass within the planet's interior; low areas occur above regions where a deficiency of mass produces a band of low gravity. Such differences in gravity hint at the location of oddities in the structure of the earth' s mantle.

cause the blob is a region where seismic waves are sluggish, they assumed that it was hotter than the surrounding mantle. The basic physics of convection suggested that a hot blob was likely to be rising. But a seismic snapshot records only a single moment in time and thus only one position of a structure. If the blob were of a different composition than the surrounding rock, for instance, it could be hotter and still not rise. So another geophysicist, Jerry X. Mitrovica of the University of Toronto, and I decided to create a time-lapse picture of what might be happening. We plugged the blob's shape and estimated density, along with estimates of when southern Africa began rising, into a computer program that simulates mantle convection. By doing so, we found last year that the blob is indeed buoyant enough to rise slowly within the mantle—and strong enough to push Africa upward as it goes.

Seismic snapshots and computer models—the basic tools of geophysicists—were enough to solve the puzzle of the African superswell, but resolving the up-and-down movements of North America and Australia was more complicated and so was accomplished in a more circuitous way. Geophysicists who think only about what the mantle looks like today cannot fully explain how it sculpts the earth's surface. They must therefore borrow from the historical perspective of traditional geologists who think about the way the surface has changed over time.

Ghosts from the Past

The insights that would help account for the bobbings of Australia and North America began to emerge with investigations of a seemingly unrelated topic: the influence of mantle density on the earth's gravitational field. The basic principles of physics led scientists in the 1960s to expect that gravity would be lowest above pockets of hot rock, which are less dense and thus have less mass. But when geophysicists first mapped the earth's gravitational variations, they found no evidence that gravity correlated with the cold and hot parts of the mantle—at least not in the expected fashion.

Indeed, in the late 1970s and early 1980s Clement G. Chase uncovered the opposite pattern. When Chase, now at the University of Arizona, considered geographic scales of more than 1,000 miles, he found that the pull of gravity is strongest not over cold mantle but over isolated volcanic regions called hot spots. Perhaps even more surprising was what Chase noticed about the position of a long band of low gravity that passes from Hudson Bay in Canada northward over the North Pole, across Siberia and India, and down into Antarctica. Relying on estimates of the ancient configuration of tectonic plates, he showed that this band of low gravity marked the location of a series of subduction zones—that is, the zones where tectonic plates carrying fragments of the seafloor plunge back into the mantle—from 125 million years ago. The ghosts of ancient subduction zones seemed to be diminishing the pull of gravity. But if cold, dense chunks of seafloor were still sinking through the mantle, it seemed that gravity would be high above these spots, not low, as Chase observed.

In the mid-1980s geophysicist Bradford H. Hager, now at the Massachusetts Institute of Technology, resolved this apparent paradox by proposing that factors other than temperature might create pockets of extra or deficient mass within the mantle. Hager developed his theory from the physics that describe moving fluids, whose behavior the mantle imitates over the long term. When a low-density fluid rises upward, as do the hottest parts of the mantle, the force of the flow pushes up the higher-density fluid above it. This gentle rise atop the upwelling itself creates an excess of mass (and hence stronger gravity) near the planet's surface. By the same token, gravity can be lower over cold, dense material: as this heavy matter sinks, it drags down

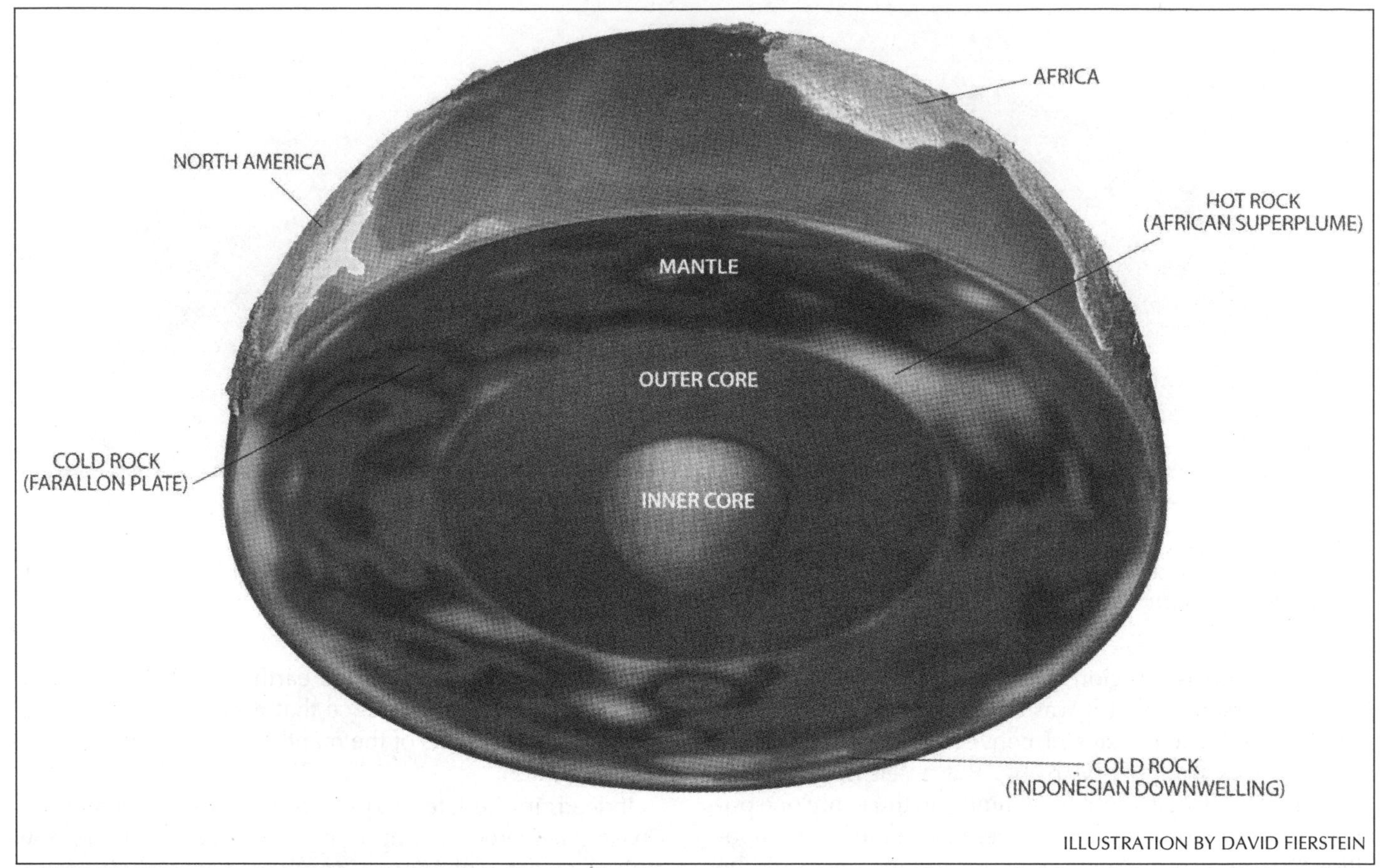

ILLUSTRATION BY DAVID FIERSTEIN

MANTLE MAP integrates measurements of thousands of earthquake vibrations, or seismic waves, that have traveled through the planet. Regions where waves moved quickly usually denote cold, dense rock. Regions where waves slowed down denote hot, less compact rock. Under southern Africa and the South Atlantic lies a pocket of sluggish velocities—a buoyant blob of hot rock called the African superplume. The map also reveals cold, sinking material that is tugging on North America and Indonesia.

mass that was once near the surface. This conception explained why the ghosts of subduction zones could generate a band of low gravity: some of that cold, subducted seafloor must still be sinking within the mantle—and towing the planet's surface downward in the process. If Hager's explanation was correct, it meant that the mantle did not merely creep horizontally near the planet's surface; whole segments of its up-and-down movements also reached the surface. Areas that surged upward would push the land above it skyward, and areas that sank would drag down the overlying continents as they descended.

Bobbing Continents

At the same time that Chase and Hager were discovering a mechanism that could dramatically lift and lower the earth's surface, geologists were beginning to see evidence that continents might actually have experienced such dips and swells in the past. Geologic formations worldwide contain evidence that sea level fluctuates over time. Many geologists suspected that this fluctuation would affect all continents in the same way, but a few of them advanced convincing evidence that the most momentous changes in sea level stemmed from vertical motions of continents. As one continent moved, say, upward relative to other landmasses, the ocean surface around that continent would become lower while sea level around other landmasses would stay the same.

Most geologists, though, doubted the controversial notion that continents could move vertically—even when the first indications of the bizarre bobbing of Australia turned up in the early 1970s. Geologist John J. Veevers of Macquarie University in Sydney examined outcrops of ancient rock in eastern Australia and discovered that sometime in the early Cretaceous period (about 130 million years ago), a shallow sea rapidly covered that half of Australia while other continents flooded at a much more leisurely pace. Sea level climaxed around those landmasses by the late Cretaceous (about 70 million years ago), but by then the oceans were already retreating from Australia's shores. The eastern half of the continent must have sunk several thousand feet relative to other landmasses and then popped back up before global sea level began to fall.

Veevers's view of a bobbing continent turned out to be only part of Australia's enigmatic story. In 1978 geologist Gerard C. Bond, now at Columbia University's Lamont-Doherty Earth Observatory, discovered an even stranger turn of events while he was searching global history for examples of vertical continental motion. After Australia's dip and rise during the Cretaceous, it sank again, this time by 600 feet, between then

How the mantle shapes the Earth's surface

SINKING CONTINENT
RISING SEA LEVEL
SUBDUCTION ZONE
A trench where one tectonic plate plunges beneath another
WHY LAND SINKS
A fragment of a subducted tectonic plate begins to fall through the mantle but remains too cold and dense to mix with the surrounding rock. As the plate sinks, a downward flow of material is created in its wake, pulling the overlying continent down with it
SINKING TECTONIC PLATE
MANTLE
A layer of scalding-hot rock that extends between the base of the tectonic plates and the planet's iron core

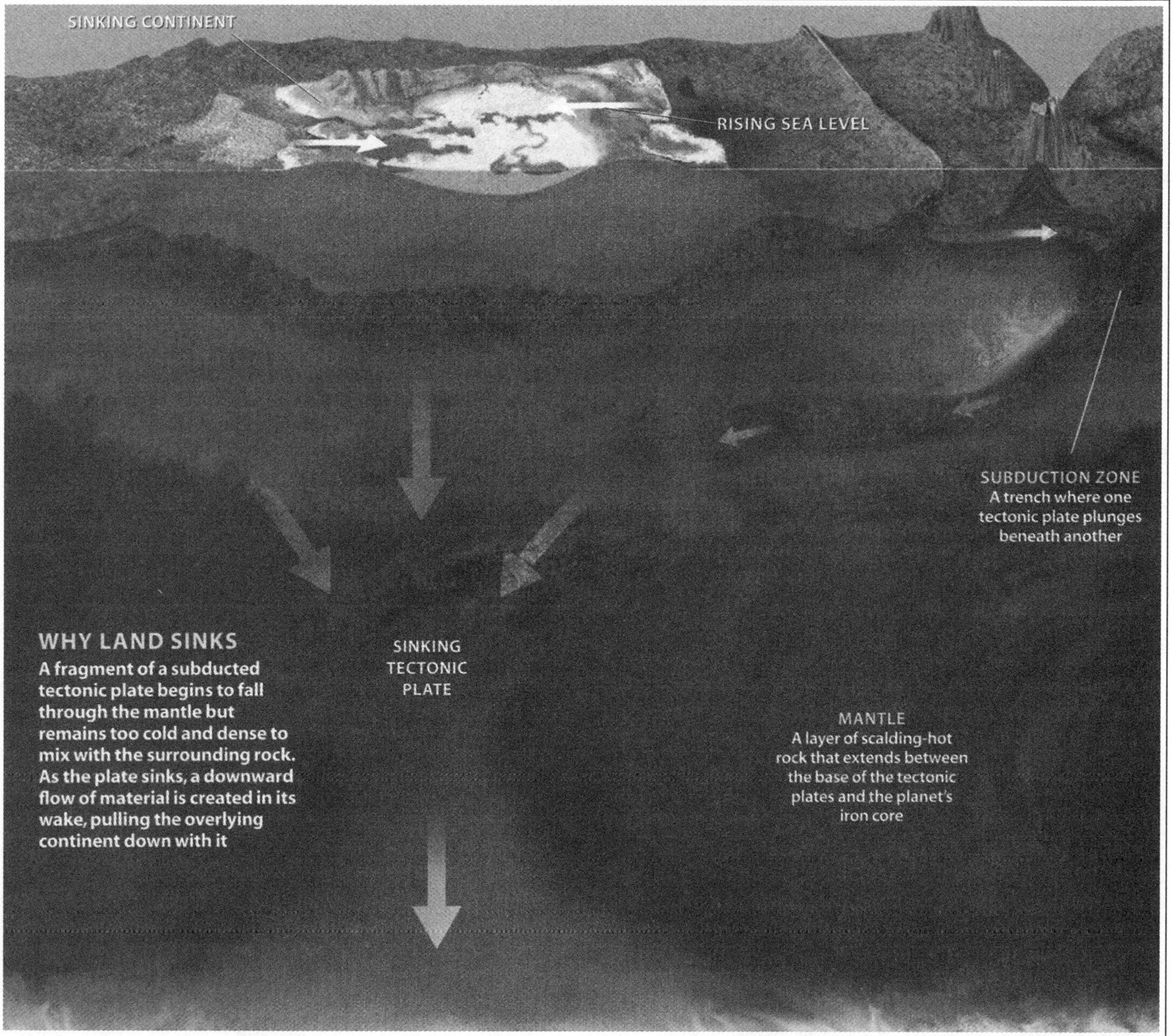

(graphic continued) ILLUSTRATION BY DAVID FIERSTEIN

and the present day. No reasonable interpretation based on plate tectonics alone could explain the widespread vertical motions that Bond and Veevers uncovered. Finding a satisfactory explanation would require scientists to link this information with another important clue: Hager's theory about how the mantle can change the shape of the planet's surface.

The first significant step in bringing these clues together was the close examination of another up-and-down example from Bond's global survey. In the late 1980s this work inspired Christopher Beaumont, a geologist at Dalhousie University in Nova Scotia, to tackle a baffling observation about Denver, Colo. Although the city's elevation is more than a mile above sea level, it sits atop flat, undeformed marine rocks created from sediments deposited on the floor of a shallow sea during the Cretaceous period. Vast seas covered much of the continents during that time, but sea level was no more than about 400 feet higher than it is today. This means that the ocean could never have reached as far inland as Denver's current position—unless this land was first pulled down several thousand feet to allow waters to flood inland.

Based on the position of North America's coastlines during the Cretaceous, Beaumont estimated that this bowing downward and subsequent uplift to today's elevation must have affected an area more than 600 miles across. This geographic scale was problematic for the prevailing view that plate tectonics alone molded the surface. The mechanism

How the mantle shapes the Earth's surface (continued)

FALLING SEA LEVEL
CONTINENTAL CRUST
TECTONIC PLATE
MID-OCEAN RIDGE
A crack in the seafloor that is filled in by material from the mantle as two tectonic plates separate
WHY LAND RISES
A superplume—a blob of hot, buoyant rock originating from the outer surface of the core—expands upward through the mantle because it is less dense than the surrounding material. It pushes the continent up as it goes
SUPERPLUME

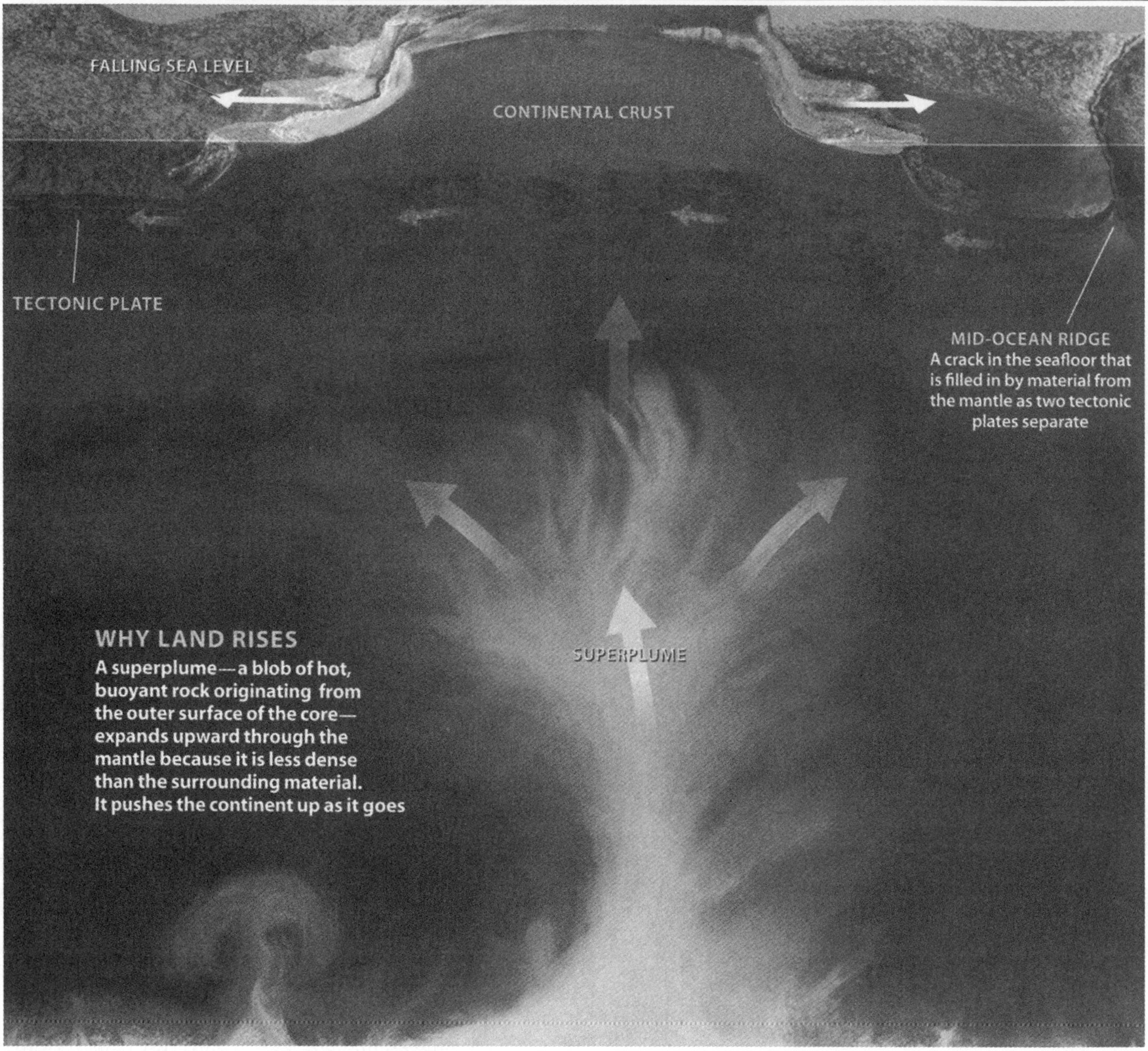

ILLUSTRATION BY DAVID FIERSTEIN

of plate tectonics permits vertical motions within only 100 miles or so of plate edges, which are thin enough to bend like a stiff fishing pole, when forces act on them. But the motion of North America's interior happened several hundred miles inland—far from the influence of plate collisions. As entirely different mechanism had to be at fault.

Beaumont knew that subducted slabs of ancient seafloor might sit in the mantle below North America and that such slabs could theoretically drag down the center of a continent. To determine whether downward flow of the mantle could have caused the dip near Denver, Beaumont teamed up with Jerry Mitrovica, then a graduate student at the University of Toronto, and Gary T. Jarvis of York University in Toronto. They found that the sinking of North America during the Cretaceous could have been caused by a plate called the Farallon as it plunged into the mantle beneath the western coast of North America. Basing their conclusion on a computer model, the research team argued that the ancient plate thrust into the mantle nearly horizontally. As it began sinking, it created a downward flow in its wake that tugged North America low enough to allow the ocean to rush in. As the Farallon plate sank deeper, the power of its trailing wake decreased. The continent's tendency to float eventually won out, and North America resurfaced.

When the Canadian researchers advanced their theory in 1989, the Farallon plate had long since vanished into the

Australia's Ups and Downs

A computer model reveals how the ghost of an ancient subduction zone dragged down a continent

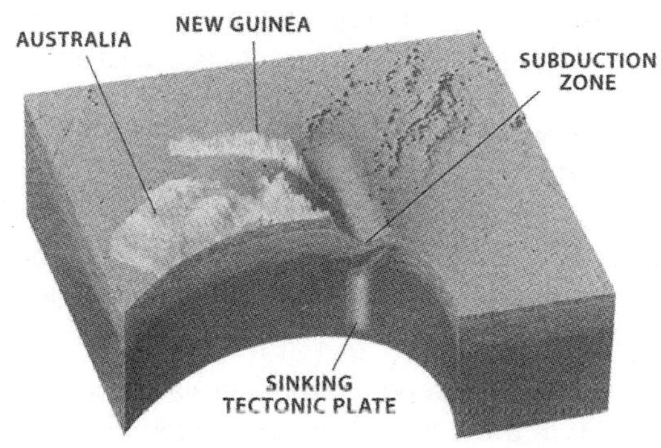

130 Million Years Ago

Australia is bordered by a subduction zone, a deep trench where the tectonic plate to the east plunges into the mantle. The sinking plate pulls the surrounding mantle and the eastern edge of Australia down with it. Later, subduction ceases and the continent begins to drift eastward.

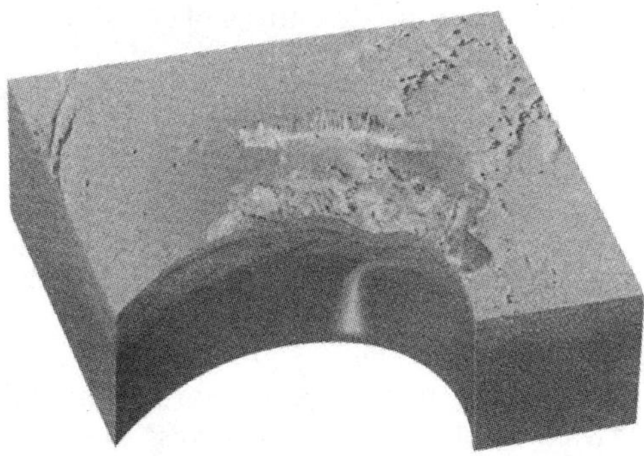

90 Million Years Ago

The entire eastern half of Australia sinks about 1,000 feet below sea level as the continent passes eastward over the sinking tectonic plate. About 20 million years later the plate's downward pull diminishes as it descends into the deeper mantle. As a result, the continent then pops up again.

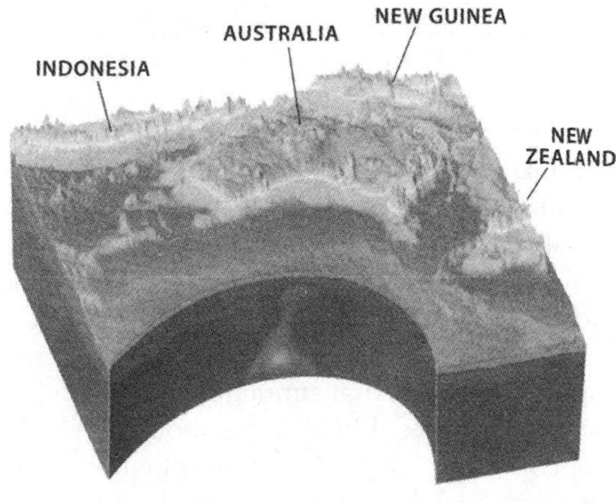

Today

Australia lies north of its former site, having been pushed there by activity in adjacent tectonic plates beginning about 45 million years ago. The entire continent has dropped relative to its greatest elevation as the result of a downward tug in the mantle under Indonesia—a landmass that is also sinking.

mantle, so its existence had only been inferred from geologic indications on the bottom of the Pacific Ocean. At that time, no seismic images were of high enough resolution to delineate a structure as small as a sinking fragment of the seafloor. Then, in 1996, new images of the mantle changed everything. Stephen P. Grand of the University of Texas at Austin and Robert D. van der Hilst of M.I.T., seismologists from separate research groups, presented two images based on entirely different sets of seismic measurements. Both pictures showed virtually identical structures, especially the cold-mantle down-wellings associated with sinking slabs of seafloor. The long-lost Farallon plate was prominent in the images as an arching slab 1,000 miles below the eastern coast of the U.S.

Moving Down Under

Connecting the bobbing motion of North America to the subduction of the seafloor forged a convincing link between ancient sea-level change and goings-on in the mantle. It also became clear that the ancient Farallon slab sits within the band of low gravity that Chase had observed two decades earlier. I suspected that these ideas could also be applied to the most enigmatic of the continental bobbings, that of Australia during and since the Cretaceous. I had been simulating mantle convection with computer models for 15 years, and many of my results showed that the mantle was in fact able to lift the surface by thousands of feet—a difference easily great enough to cause an apparent drop in sea level. Like Chase, Veevers and other researchers before me, I looked at the known history of plate tectonics for clues about whether something in the mantle could have accounted for Australia's bouncing. During the Cretaceous period, Australia, South America, Africa, India, Antarctica and New Zealand were assembled into a vast supercontinent called Gondwana, which had existed for more than 400 million years before it fragmented into today's familiar landmasses. Surrounding Gondwana for most of this time was a huge subduction zone where cold oceanic plates plunged into the mantle.

I thought that somehow the subduction zone that surrounded Gondwana for hundreds of millions of years might have caused Australia's ups and downs. I became more convinced when I sketched the old subduction zones on maps of ancient plate configurations constructed by R. Dietmar Müller, a seagoing geophysicist at Sydney University. The sketches seemed to explain the Australian oddities. Australia would have passed directly over Gondwana's old subduction zone at the time it sank.

To understand how the cold slab would behave in the mantle as Gondwana broke apart over millions of years, Müller and I joined Louis Moresi of the Commonwealth Scientific and Industrial Research Organization in Perth to run a computer simulation depicting the mantle's influence on Australia over time. We knew the original position of the ancient subduction zone, the history of horizontal plate motions in the region and the estimated properties—such as viscosity—of the mantle below. Operating under these constraints, the computer played out a scenario for Australia that fit our hypotheses nearly perfectly [*see "Australia's Ups and Downs"*.]

The computer model started 130 million years ago with ocean floor thrusting beneath eastern Australia. As Australia broke away from Gondwana, it passed over the cold, sinking slab, which sucked the Australian plate downward. The continent rose up again as it continued its eastward migration away from the slab.

Our model resolved the enigma of Australia's motion during the Cretaceous, originally observed by Veevers, but we were still puzzled by the later continentwide sinking of Australia that Bond discovered. With the help of another geophysicist, Carolina Lithgow-Bertelloni, now at the University of Michigan, we confirmed Bond's observation that as Australia moved northward toward Indonesia after the Cretaceous, it subsided by about 6500 feet. Lithgow-Bertelloni's global model of the mantle, which incorporated the history of subduction, suggested that Indonesia is sucked down more than any other region in the world because it lies at the intersection of enormous, present-day subduction systems in the Pacific and Indian oceans. And as Indonesia sinks, it pulls Australia down with it. Today Indonesia is a vast submerged continent—only its highest mountain peaks protrude above sea level.

Which brings us back to Africa. In a sense, Indonesia and Africa are opposites; Indonesia is being pulled down while Africa is being pushed up. These and other changes in the mantle that have unfolded over the past few hundred million years are intimately related to Gondwana. The huge band of low gravity that Chase discovered 30 years ago is created by the still-sinking plates of a giant subduction zone that once encircled the vast southern landmass. At the center of Gondwana was southern Africa, which means that the mantle below this region was isolated from the chilling effects of sinking tectonic plates at that time—and for the millions of years since. This long-term lack of cold, downward motion below southern Africa explains why a hot superplume is now erupting in the deep mantle there.

With all these discoveries, a vivid, dynamic picture of the motions of the mantle has come into focus. Researchers are beginning to see that these motions sculpt the surface in more ways than one. They help to drive the horizontal movement of tectonic plates, but they also lift and lower the continents. Perhaps the most intriguing discovery is that motion in the deep mantle lags behind the horizontal movement of tectonic plates. Positions of ancient plate boundaries can still have an effect on the way the surface is shaped many millions of years later.

Our ability to view the dynamics of mantle convection and plate tectonics will rapidly expand as new ways of observing the mantle and techniques for simulating its motion are introduced. When mantle convection changes, the gravitational field changes. Tracking variations in the earth's gravitational field is part of a joint U.S. and German space mission called GRACE, which is set for launch in June. Two spacecraft, one chasing the other in earth orbit, will map variations in gravity every two weeks and perhaps make it possible to infer the slow, vertical flow associated with convection in the mantle. Higher-resolution seismic images will also play a pivotal role in revealing what the mantle looks like today. Over the five- to 10-year duration of a project called USArray, 400 roving seismometers will provide a 50-mile-resolution view into the upper 800 miles of the mantle below the U.S.

Plans to make unprecedented images and measurements of the mantle in the coming decade, together with the use of ever more powerful supercomputers, foretell an exceptionally bright future for deciphering the dynamics of the earth's interior. Already, by considering the largest region of the planet—the mantle—as a chuck of rock with a geologic history, earth scientists have made extraordinary leaps in understanding the ultimate causes of geologic changes at the surface.

Further Information

DYNAMICS OF CRETACEOUS VERTICAL MOTION OF AUSTRALIA AND THE AUSTRALIAN-ANTARCTIC DISCORDANCE. Michael Gurnis, R. Dietmar Müller and Louis Moresi in *Science,* Vol. 279, pages 1499–1504; March 6, 1998.

DYNAMIC EARTH: PLATES, PLUMES AND MANTLE CONVECTION. Geoffrey F. Davies. Cambridge University Press, 2000.

CONSTRAINING MANTLE DENSITY STRUCTURE USING GEOLOGICAL EVIDENCE OF SURFACE UPLIFT RATES: THE CASE OF THE AFRICAN SUPERPLUME. Michael Gurnis, Jerry X. Mitrovica, Jeroen Ritsema and Hendrik-Jan van Heijst in *Geochemistry, Geophysics, Geosystems,* Vol. 1, Paper No. 1999GC000035; 2000. Available online at http://146.201.254.53/publicationsfinal/articles/1999GC000035/fs1999G000035.html

Gurnis's Computational Geodynamics Research Group Web site: www.gps.caltech.edu/~gurnis/geodynamics.html

---

MICHAEL GURNIS is a geophysicist who is interested in the dynamics of plate tectonics and the earth's interior. These physical processes, which govern the history of the planet, have intrigued him since he began studying geology as an undergraduate 20 years ago. With his research group at the California Institute of Technology, Gurnis now develops computer programs that simulate the evolving motions of the mantle and reveal how those motions have shaped the planet over time. Gurnis's research highlights over the past three years have been deciphering the mysteries of the present-day African superswell and the bobbings of Australia during the Cretaceous period.

Nuclear power

A renaissance that may not come

This week, the Bush administration unveiled an energy policy that strongly supports nuclear power. This may revive a flagging industry, but the doubts remain as strong as ever

THREE MILE ISLAND

THE gently rolling farmlands of central Pennsylvania do not prepare the casual visitor for what lies outside Middletown. Farmers tend cows and corn, diners serve simple food, and the occasional Amish buggy saunters by. But suddenly, there on the horizon, loom the cooling towers of the nuclear plant at Three Mile Island.

The words still send a shiver down the spine. It was here, early in the morning of March 28th 1979, that a reactor started to overheat. A combination of mechanical failure and human error sent the temperature in the reactor core soaring, threatening a blast that would have released huge quantities of lethal radiation. With the lives of perhaps half a million people at stake, politicians and scientists argued over what to do. In the end, disaster was averted; but the world did not forget.

For a while, it seemed that the accident at Three Mile Island (TMI) had killed off nuclear power. No new plants have been built in the United States since then. In Europe, too, people began to have second thoughts. TMI led directly to a referendum in Sweden in 1980 that demanded an end to nuclear power.

In 1986, an even worse accident, at Chernobyl in the Soviet Union, seemed to put the nail in the coffin of nuclear power in Europe. A number of countries, following Sweden's lead, campaigned for a ban. In Germany, the greens succeeded: the government has just agreed to end reprocessing of nuclear fuel by mid-2005. Moreover, Germany and Belgium have decided to ban new nuclear plants, although existing ones may serve out their useful lives. Even pro-nuclear France seemed to lose its enthusiasm for new plants.

For a while, Asia remained a bright spot for the nuclear industry. But the Asian financial crisis of 1998 cooled that enthusiasm. In recent months the new government in Taiwan, once a big fan of nuclear power, has tried to reverse course. In Japan, an accident soured public opinion: shoddy management practices at an experimental fuel-reprocessing plant in Tokaimura led in September 1999 to the deaths of two workers after they were exposed to radiation over 10,000 times the level considered safe. The Japanese government quietly scaled back its plans for 20 new plants.

The industry also hurt itself. In 1999, it emerged that British Nuclear Fuels (BNFL) had falsified records relating to shipments of nuclear fuel to Japan, sparking outrage in both countries. The firm had also understated the cost of nuclear clean-ups in Britain by some $13 billion. Clumsiness with deadly stuff, and now mendacity; in one way or another, nuclear power seemed to spell nothing but trouble.

Votes of confidence

Yet some did not lose faith, and are even looking at nuclear power in a new way. South Africa's Eskom is working with BNFL and Exelon, America's biggest nuclear-energy firm, to build a reactor using new "pebble-bed" technology. In Finland, a power company is now requesting permission to build a €2.5 billion ($2.2 billion) nuclear plant.

Robin Jeffrey, the new chairman-designate of British Energy, Britain's largest nuclear operator, also sees a bright future for his industry. "The mood is buoyant," he says. "Utilities with a nuclear portfolio are seen to be attractive places to put your money." In fact, he has just completed a deal to take over the operation and maintenance of several reactors in Canada. Through AmerGen, a joint venture with Exelon, British Energy already manages a number of plants in the United States.

This week has produced the biggest boost of all for nuclear power: a strong endorsement from the Bush administration. On May 17th, a cabinet-level task-force unveiled a new energy policy that firmly supports the nuclear option. Vice-President Dick Cheney, the head of the task-force, argues forcefully not only for giving existing nuclear plants a new lease of life, but also for building more: "We'd like to see an increase in the percentage of our electricity generated from nuclear power."

To understand why fans of nuclear power have become so optimistic, look back to Three Mile Island itself—now managed, as it happens, by AmerGen. The accident destroyed one of the plant's two reactors, but the surviving reactor has been back in service for some years now. In that time, TMI has become one of the most efficiently run and safest nuclear plants in America, as well as one of the most profitable. Corbin McNeill, Exelon's boss, is certain that financial success and operational safety are closely linked. TMI, he thinks, is a shining symbol of the future for nuclear power.

What explains this burst of enthusiasm? The short answer is the arrival, at long last, of market forces in the electricity business. After decades of being run as monopolies, either by the state or the private sector, the electricity industry is being deregulated the world over. As a result of this, and of the current high price of fossil fuels, existing nuclear plants look attractive, and are beginning to be run as proper businesses by serious managers.

The charm of consolidation

This is best seen in America, which deregulated its wholesale markets for power in 1996. The result of deregulation was a painful squeeze on America's dozens of nuclear plants, many of which were run as one-off investments by local utilities. That is rapidly changing, however, thanks to the flurry of deals that have led to mega-mergers (like the one that created Exelon), joint ventures (like AmerGen), and other sorts of management coalitions. Nearly 30 gigawatts, about a quarter of the country's nuclear capacity, has already been affected by this consolidation. In the near future, today's 50 nuclear utilities will probably be reduced to a dozen.

The advantages of such consolidation are many. Plant managers can benefit from economies of scale and can apply best practices more widely. As a result, plants are running at higher capacity-utilisation rates and making better use of their fuel. Plant operators have also tried to expand capacity by upgrading their steam generators and turbines. Last winter, America's nuclear plants cranked out power at an operating cost of just 1.8 cents per kilowatt (kW)-hour; coal plants produced it for 2.1 cents per kW-hour, while those using natural gas (the price of which soared last winter) did no better than 3.5 cents.

Such improvements, argue nuclear fans, make a clear case for extending the licences of existing nuclear-power plants beyond their original limit of 40 years or so. In America, for example, a number of these permits will start expiring in 2006, and nearly all will have gone by 2030. The story is similar in Europe and elsewhere.

The fans are surely correct. Plants have been able to achieve such low operating costs because they are better managed and more efficient, and that, in turn, is linked to improved operational safety. When plants are safe, people do not mind living near them. Two plants have already received approvals from America's Nuclear Regulatory Commission (NRC) for another 20 years of operation. More will follow.

Cheaper tomorrow...

Tomorrow, the advocates say, nuclear power will be even cheaper. They point to promising new designs (such as pebble-bed technology) and argue that power plants are on the way that are safer and more cost-effective than today's. The industry is also mature now, they say; both companies and regulators know how to avoid the costly bureaucratic quagmire that followed the TMI accident. In future, new plants will be "cheaper than coal".

Maybe; maybe not. The new designs for nuclear plants are undoubtedly improvements. Technical experts agree that they are probably inherently safer, as they use "passive" safety features that make a TMI-style meltdown virtually impossible. The NRC has already given its blessing to three advanced designs. However, critics argue that some new designs "put all the safety eggs in the prevention basket", while short-changing systems that might limit an accident if one occurred.

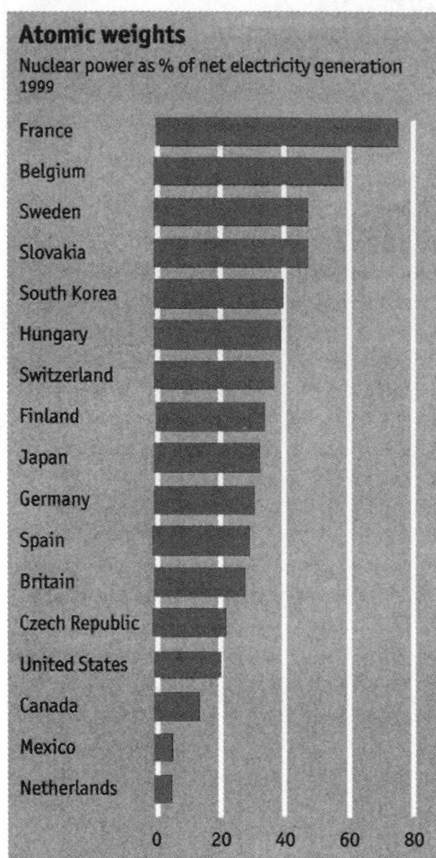

Source: Intrenational Energy Agency

Even if they do prove safer, the new designs may not necessarily be cheaper. By the reckoning of the International Energy Agency (IEA), which has just produced a new analysis of the economics of nuclear power*, the capital cost for today's nuclear designs runs at about $2,000 per kW, against about $1,200 per kW for coal and just $500 per kW for a combined-cycle gas plant. History also suggests that not everything goes as planned when turning clever paper designs into real-life nuclear plants. What is more, the debts of any new plants, unlike the debts of existing plants, will not be written off. In fact, the true cost of power from today's plants is at least double the apparent figure, argues Florentin Krause, an American economist, once debt write-offs, government subsidies and externalities are accounted for. More on that later.

Capital cost clearly remains a big hurdle for nuclear power. When considering the full life-cycle costs of a new project in today's money, some 60–75% of a nuclear plant's costs may be front-loaded; for a gas plant, about a quarter may be. That is before considering interest accrued during construction, which, over the many years it takes to build nuclear plants, can make or break a project. All these dismal sums explain why nuclear projects are exceptionally sensitive to the cost of capital.

...and cheap forever?

Never mind that, the nuclear industry argues; tomorrow's plants will prove cheaper to operate in several ways. For a start, some say, plants will be bigger, to take advantage of economies of scale. Second, there will be a whole series of plants, rather than the uneconomic one-off structures of the past, and these (in imitation of France's *dirigiste* approach) will be standardised replicas of new designs, rather than endless permutations.

Each of these bright ideas has problems. Building bigger plants introduces more complexity, which, experts say, means greater uncertainty and cost. The idea of building many plants is thwarted by the fact that the electricity market in the developed world is not growing fast enough to need them. In fact, the trend since the mid-1970s has been towards smaller plants. It is micropower, not megapower, that the market favours, thanks to the far smaller financial risk involved.

It is true that regulators are becoming lighter-handed. They no longer drag out the completion of plants for ten or 15 years. Even so, careful analysis of the delays after the TMI accident shows that technical hitches were largely to blame, rather than red tape. Many new plants happened to come on line at around that time, and a number had generic technical faults. Even the French programme, touted as a model, suffered from such problems as late as the 1990s: its latest N4 design developed cracks in its heat-removal systems.

A dubious special case

The industry's advocates point to other benefits: security of supply, environmental benefits, and so on. In some countries and in some circumstances, such arguments might have merit. But, taken together, do they make nuclear energy a special case that justifies subsidies or other forms of government intervention?

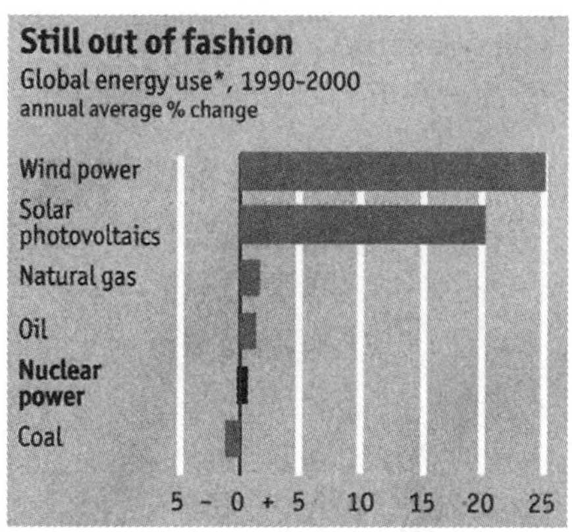

*Based on installed capacity for wind and nuclear power, shipments for solar PV and consumption for natural gas, oil and coal

Source: Worldwatch Institute

The energy-security arguments vary, but mostly involve reduced reliance on fossil fuels, less vulnerability to an OPEC embargo, or a smaller bill for imported fuel. Whatever the political soundness of such arguments, an analysis done in 1998 by several agencies affiliated with the OECD is quite clear about the relative costs and benefits: "For many countries, the additional energy security obtained from investing in non-fossil-fuelled generation options is likely to be worth less than the cost of obtaining that security."

On environmental grounds, too, nuclear power does not emerge a clear winner. It is true that nuclear energy does not produce carbon dioxide, the chief culprit behind man-made global warming. That, say fans like Mr Cheney, means that the world "ought to" build more such plants. But handing out public money to the nuclear-power industry (through production or investment tax credits, for example) is an inefficient way for governments to discourage global warming.

The better way would be through some sort of carbon tax, which would penalise fossil fuels but not any fuel free of carbon emissions, whether nuclear power or renewables. The IEA's boffins have analysed how much of a boost nuclear power could get from a carbon tax, and the answer is quite a lot—possibly enough to compete with coal. Assume that the carbon tax falls between $25 and $85 per tonne of carbon, the level many experts think may be needed if industrialised countries are serious about the emissions targets agreed on in 1997 at Kyoto (some would set it higher still). The IEA thinks that the highest of those taxes would boost the competitiveness of nuclear electricity against coal by two cents per kW-hour, and against natural gas by one cent. At the low end, nuclear gains an advantage of half a cent and a quarter-cent respectively.

But nuclear energy, even if boosted by a carbon tax, also carries grave environmental liabilities. Radiation is a threat to human health at every stage of the process, from uranium mining to plant operation (even in those new ultra-safe plants) to waste disposal. And waste disposal, despite decades of research and politicking, remains a farce. No country has yet built a "permanent" waste-disposal site. The United States hopes to have one finished at Yucca Mountain, in the Nevada desert, in a decade's time; the European countries are a decade behind that. Even if these geological storage sites are completed, they are not the final answer. Nuclear waste may remain deadly for 100,000 years. To bury it in a big hole in the ground, and pray that some future generation may discover how to make it safe, is simply passing the buck.

Lastly, when costing nuclear power, it is essential to remember the scope, scale and subtlety of the subsidies it has received. The IEA analysis of nuclear economics shows that various OECD governments subsidise the industry's fuel-supply services, waste disposal, fuel reprocessing and R&D. They also limit the liability of plants in case of accident, and help them clean up afterwards. Antony Froggatt, an industry expert who has advised Greenpeace, points to export loans and guarantees as another unfair boost.

How much does all this add up to? The IEA's otherwise comprehensive analysis falls strangely silent on this topic, doubtless for political reasons. Reliable, comprehensive and up-to-date global figures from neutral analysts are scarce. Estimates by nuclear opponents typically carry too many zeroes to fit on this page. They are about as rigorous and credible as those put forth by the industry, which usually maintains the outrageous fiction that it no longer receives any subsidies at all.

Coddled to the hilt

Liability insurance is a good example of this. The American industry's official position is that there is no subsidy involved in the Price-Anderson Act, by which Congress limits the civilian nuclear industry's liability for nuclear catastrophes to less than $10 billion (a small fraction of what a Chernobyl-scale disaster would cost in America). Since there is no subsidy involved, why not let the act lapse when it comes up for renewal next year? Mr Cheney's response is revealing: "It needs to be renewed…[if not], nobody's going to invest in nuclear-power plants."

One concrete figure gives an idea of how enormous the overall subsidy pie might be. According to official figures, OECD governments poured $159 billion in today's money into nuclear research between 1974 and 1998. Some of that breathtaking sum is a sunk cost from the early days of the industry, but not all: governments still shell out about half their energy R&D budgets on this mature industry. Even so, says the industry, those have been tapering off over time. But so will all the other subsidies, as the liberalisation of markets advances. The pillar on which the strength of the nuclear industry has rested is crumbling away.

In the end, nuclear energy's future may be skewered by the same sword that is making it fashionable today: the deregulation of electricity markets. This liberalising movement has put a shine on old nuclear plants that are already paid for. TMI, for example, was bought for a pittance and so cranks out power for virtually nothing.

Yet liberalisation is also exposing the true economics of new plants, and is aiming a fierce spotlight at the hefty subsidies that nuclear power has long enjoyed. As these fade, the industry will once again be brought down to earth.

"Nuclear Power in the OECD". International Energy Agency, 2001.

A broken heartland

Nothing manifest about the destiny of small towns on the Great Plains

BY JEFF GLASSER

LARSON, N.D.—The white steeple of St. John's German Lutheran Church lists from the weight of its rusted, half-ton church bell. The 93-year-old church's pews, pulpit, baptismal font, and, most important, congregants have vanished. At the end of a deserted Main Street, tumbleweeds obscure the Great Northern Railroad tracks where trains once routinely carried the world's finest durum wheat to the trade centers of the Midwest.

Across from the tracks stands the Larson Hotel, its paint peeling, its roof about to be patched with discarded aluminum newspaper printing plates. It is now home to a disabled construction worker and his family who moved here from Pennsylvania last fall, saying they could only afford to live in the middle of nowhere. An empty lot away sits the X-treme North Bar and Barely South Restaurant, a last-chance saloon with a rich history of bourbon and burlesque.

Welcome to Larson, population 17, the least populated place in one of the nation's fastest-declining counties. Burke County, N.D., lost 25.3 percent of its population in the past 10 years, falling from 3,002 to 2,242, according to 2000 census figures released this spring. Its neighbor, Divide County, shrank by 21 percent, from 2,899 to 2,283, during the same period. The two counties are littered with dozens of Larsons, Northgates, and Alkabos—virtual ghost towns that grew up as stops for steam trains and died along with the railroads. Larson has withered to the point where none of its residents—including the candidate—bothered to vote in last June's election for alderman. Four miles down state Highway 5 in Columbus, all that remains of the 74-year-old brick high school are 700 commemorative letter openers hand carved by the town elder out of its maple floors and given away as mementos. To the north, dozens of Canadian oil rigs, coal mines, and a SaskPower plant loom in the distance, a mirage of economic activity 25 miles away but a country apart. To the west, past forgotten little houses on the prairie, Crosby's cemeteries have so many fresh mounds that it looks like badgers have dug there all winter. "We're going to have to start importing pallbearers," jokes Crosby farmer Ole Svangstu, 55, noting there were 48 more deaths than births last year.

Ghost towns. Up and down the Great Plains, the country's spine, from the Sandhills of western Nebraska to the sea of prairie grass in eastern Montana, small towns are decaying, and in some cases, literally dying out. The remarkable prosperity of the last decade never reached this far. Nearly 60 percent (250 of 429) of the counties on the Great Plains lost population in the 1990s, according to a *U.S. News* analysis of the new census data.

The emptying out of the nation's rural breadbasket was all the more surprising considering the population resurgence in cities and suburbs. The nation as a whole grew at a robust 13 percent. The 10 states of the Plains, too, expanded by 10 percent overall, a 672,554-person increase fueled by the growth of cities like Billings, Mont., and the tremendous urban sprawl that swallowed the countryside adjacent to Denver, Austin, and San Antonio. Some larger rural areas in the Plains also blossomed from their natural beauty as recreation areas, but the picture was bleak in counties with fewer than 15,000 people, where 228 of 334 (nearly 70 percent) of the counties regressed. "It's like the parting of the Red Sea," says Fannie Mae demographer Robert Lang, a census expert. "There are rivers of people flowing out of the [rural] Plains."

The degeneration of a large swath of this country's midsection—covering a

317,320-square-mile area spread over parts of the 10 states—has not seeped into the conscience of urban America. City dwellers might still perceive small towns as refuges from society's maddening stew of gridlock, smog, and crime. Where else can a visitor leave a car unlocked, not to mention *running*, on a quick trip to the post office? Farmers in small towns are considered the ultimate entrepreneurs, "our national icon of autonomy," as Yale Prof. Kathryn Marie Dudley writes in *Debt and Dispossession: Farm Loss in America's Heartland*. But, as Dudley points out, the contemporary ideal collides with a harsh economic reality.

The problem is seemingly intractable. Once thriving mining and railroad commerce are distant memories. The farm economy has been in a state of contraction for at least 30 years. Forty-two percent of Midwestern farmers, the dominant economic group, earn less than $20,000 annually. A lack of Plains industry limits other opportunities for professionals. Jeff Peterson, 53, Burke County's sole lawyer, sighs wistfully as he explains why he's packing it in after 26 years. "There just aren't so many people for clients now," says Peterson. There aren't even enough people to justify having county judges. Nearly everyone else has already left Burke County, bailing out when their farming and oil and gas jobs dried up in the late 1980s and early 1990s. Peterson says he will have to write off his $120,000 office building. So far, he has found no takers for his $135,000 house. "This wasn't a smart place to invest in," he says.

Manifest destiny. That wasn't always the case. From Thomas Jefferson's stewardship of the Louisiana Purchase, which included present day Burke and Divide counties, sprang forth the concept of America's " Manifest Destiny" to inhabit all the nation's land. In 1862, Congress passed the Homestead Act, giving immigrants free 160-acre parcels called "quarters." Northwestern North Dakota was one of the final places homesteaded. At the turn of the 20th century, the region filled with Norwegians, Swedes, Danes, Belgians, and a few Germans. The territory was so forbidding that it had no trees, so the pioneers built sod homes on a virgin landscape described by novelist Willa Cather as "nothing but land, not a country at all, but the material out of which countries are made."

Postmaster Columbus Larson's settlement on the western tip of Burke County split in two with the coming of the railroads. Half set up in front of the Great Northern tracks at "Larson," half 4 miles to the northeast next to the Soo Line at "Columbus." By 1930, every quarter in Burke and Divide was inhabited, with what would be a peak 19,634 people on the land. Crowds gathered on Saturday nights at the Opera House in Larson to dance the polka and listen to traditional Norwegian yodeling. Colorful vaudeville troops headlined the marquee at Columbus Theater. Lawrence Welk and his dance band played his signature "champagne music" there. Bootleggers peddled liquor during Prohibition, and the Larson Opera House was the place for bawdy pantomime. Occasionally the townspeople gathered on Main Street and fearfully watched local young men test their strength against that of bears for cash prizes (provided they won).

In the "dirty Thirties," pioneer women placed wet bedsheets over windows to keep out dust. The perseverance and courage of the settlers—lionized by Cather in her novel *O Pioneers!*—were tested as the soil crumbled in a series of crop disasters. Most of Larson's 114 residents left the Dust Bowl behind in search of an easier life. Columbus continued to boom in the immediate post-World War II period, though, with coal miners, power-plant workers, farmers, and a few oil roughnecks keeping the place full. The town peaked with nearly 700 people in the early 1950s. Then the coal mines closed, and the local power plant shut down. Advances in technology improved crop yields, so far fewer people were needed to farm the land. A series of government conservation programs prompted hundreds of local farmers to retire to Arizona, exacerbating the exodus.

In 1972, Columbus still had 20 businesses. Larson was hanging on with six shops, including Witty's grocery store and Ole Johnson's gas station. Virtually all are gone today. Columbus, with just 151 residents, has one cafe and a farm tool supplier, both set to close later this year. The only eatery left in Larson is the X-treme North Bar and Barely South Restaurant, which may also close. "The handwriting's on the wall," says Harold Pasche, 80, a retired farmer from Larson who now lives in Columbus. "Every little town in this whole area here is going down." The collapse of the retail trade in Columbus and Larson mirrors a national decline. From 1977 to 1997, the number of American grocery stores fell by 61.2 percent, men's clothing stores dropped by 46.6 percent, and hardware stores slipped by 40.6 percent, according to the Census of Retail Trade. Ken Stone, an Iowa State University economist specializing in rural development, says small-town Main Streets are going the way of the railroads. "There's very little way to bring [them] back," he says.

On the farm, net income is projected to decline 20 percent in the next two years because of a worldwide depression in commodity prices and higher energy costs. Without government intervention, 10 percent of farmers could not survive one year, says former Agriculture Secretary Dan Glickman. He calls federal farm subsidies "rural support" programs and fears "economic devastation in large parts of rural America" if the government nixes them. Yet President Bush's budget package does not allocate any disaster money for farmers, who in the past three years received $25 billion in extra federal relief. Despite Glickman's warnings, there is little room in today's debate for Jeffersonian programs to resettle the Plains. People simply do not want to deal with harsh winters and broiling summers. "It's still a loser in [Plains] politics to say, 'Let them die,'" says Frank Popper, a Rutgers University land-use expert. "You've got an ongoing aversion, a denial of what's going on. But every year there are fewer farmers and ranchers. Every year they are losing their kids." In 1988, Popper and his wife, Deborah, also a professor, dreamed up a radical alternative for the rural Plains: a vast "Buffalo Commons," in which the federal government would return the territory to its pristine state before white settlement, when the buffalo roamed and the prairie grasses grew undisturbed.

Where the buffalo roam? Farmers hated the idea. But in the decade that followed, thousands of miles on the Northern Plains have reverted to "wilderness" areas with buffalo herds and fewer than two people per square mile. "I actually think this is the last American frontier," says Larson's town treasurer, Debra Watterud, 53.

That leaves places like Larson and Columbus with even fewer totems of their town histories. The latter held its final Columbus Day Parade in 1992, when Pasche drove his treasured 1932 Chevrolet Roadster down Main one last time. At the last major civic gathering in 1994, residents scooped up bricks and floor planks from the soon-to-be-demolished high school. Doug Graupe, 56, a Divide County farmer, argues that the remaining residents have an obligation to their ancestors to persevere.

"Economics shouldn't drive every decision," he says. "Do you have to have money to have a good quality of life?... People in small towns are always there to help others, to raise kids. You have a sense of community." Graupe and others in the region are excited about a $2.5 million pasta processing plant that they're planning to build in nearby Crosby, but not everyone's confident it will succeed, given the perilous demographics and the area's previous failed attempts at renewal.

In Larson, Debra Watterud proposed shutting down the town after the no-show election because the level of interest was so low. Her father-in-law, retired farmer Myron Watterud, 76, opposed the idea. If Larson deincorporated, he said, who would pay for the lights (which consumes half the $3,000 town budget)? The town would disappear from maps. No one would ever bring it back, a possibility that's hard to fathom for a man who has spent his life here. His daughter-in-law agreed to table her suggestion, but Myron Watterud says he's "scared" to watch the town in the approaching darkness of its final demise. "If the leaders of this town saw what happened," he says, "they'd turn over in their graves."

UNIT 2

Human-Environment Relationships

Unit Selections

10. **Global Warming: The Contrarian View**, Willliam K. Stevens
11. **The Future of Our Forests**, Ted Kerasote
12. **Restoring Life to the 'Dead Zone': How a Sound Farm Policy Could Save Our Oceans**, *Environmental Defense Newsletter*
13. **Texas and Water: Pay Up or Dry Up**, *The Economist*
14. **Beyond the Valley of the Dammed**, Bruce Barcott
15. **The Himba and the Dam**, Carol Ezzell
16. **Past and Present Land Use and Land Cover in the USA**, William B. Meyer
17. **Operation Desert Sprawl**, William Fulton and Paul Shigley
18. **A Modest Proposal to Stop Global Warming**, Ross Gelbspan
19. **A Greener, or Browner, Mexico?** *The Economist*

Key Points to Consider

- What are the long-range implications of atmospheric pollution? Explain the greenhouse effect.
- How can the problem of regional transfer of pollutants be solved?
- The manufacture of goods needed by humans produces pollutants that degrade the environment. How can this dilemma be solved?
- Where in the world are there serious problems of desertification and drought? Why are these areas increasing in size?
- What will be the major forms of energy in the twenty-first century?
- How are you as an individual related to the land? Does urban sprawl concern you? Explain.
- Can humankind do anything to ensure the protection of the environment? Describe.

Links: www.dushkin.com/online/

These sites are annotated in the World Wide Web pages.

Alliance for Global Sustainability (AGS)
http://www.global-sustainability.org

Environment News Service: Global Warming Could Make Water a Scarce Resource
http://ens.lycos.com/ens/dec2000/2000L-12-15-06.html

Human Geography
http://www.geog.le.ac.uk/cti/hum.html

The North-South Institute
http://www.nsi-ins.ca/ensi/index.html

United Nations Environment Programme (UNEP)
http://www.unep.ch

World Health Organization
http://www.who.int

The home of humankind is Earth's surface and the thin layer of atmosphere enveloping it. Here the human populace has struggled over time to change the physical setting and to create the telltale signs of occupation. Humankind has greatly modified Earth's surface to suit its purposes. At the same time, we have been greatly influenced by the very environment that we have worked to change.

This basic relationship of humans and land is important in geography and, in unit 1, William Pattison identified it as one of the four traditions of geography. Geographers observe, study, and analyze the ways in which human occupants of Earth have interacted with the physical environment. This unit presents a number of articles that illustrate the theme of human-environment relationships. In some cases, the association of humans and the physical world has been mutually beneficial; in others, environmental degradation has been the result.

At the present time, the potential for major modifications of Earth's surface and atmosphere is greater than at any other time in history. It is crucial that the environmental consequences of these modifications be clearly understood before such efforts are undertaken.

The first article in this unit contends that greenhouse gas accumulations in the atmosphere are highly exaggerated. The next two articles deal with familiar and recurring themes: overcutting forests and pollution of water from agricultural chemicals. Next are three articles dealing with dams. In the first, the movement to reduce the number of dams in the United States is discussed. The second reports on a new dam in Africa that may lead to the demise of the Himba culture group. William Meyer then addresses changing land use in the United States. "Operation Desert Sprawl" follows with an analysis of Las Vegas's reliance on transportation systems and the availability of fresh water. The next article provides a reasoned approach to global warming. Finally, the question of NAFTA's impact on economics and the environment is covered.

This unit provides a small sample of the many ways in which humans interact with the environment. The outcomes of these interactions may be positive or negative. They may enhance the position of humankind and protect the environment, or they may do just the opposite. We human beings are the guardians of the physical world. We have it in our power to protect, to neglect, or to destroy.

Global Warming: The Contrarian View

By WILLIAM K. STEVENS

Over the years, skeptics have tried to cast doubt on the idea of global warming by noting that measurements taken by earth satellites since 1979 have found little or no temperature rise in large parts of the upper atmosphere. The satellites' all-encompassing coverage yields more reliable results than temperature samplings showing a century-long warming trend at the earth's surface, they argued.

In January, a special study by the National Research Council, the research arm of the National Academy of Sciences, declared that the "apparent disparity" between the two sets of measurements over the 20-year history of the satellite measurements "in no way invalidates the conclusion that surface temperature has been rising." The surface warming "is undoubtedly real," the study panel said.

But the dissenters are a long way from conceding the debate, and they have seized on other aspects of the panel's report in an effort to bolster their case.

To be sure, according to interviews with some prominent skeptics, there is now wide agreement among them that the average surface temperature of the earth has indeed risen.

"I don't think we're arguing over whether there's any global warming," said Dr. William M. Gray, an atmospheric scientist at Colorado State University, known for his annual predictions of Atlantic hurricane activities as well as his staunch, longtime dissent on global climate change. "The question is, 'What is the cause of it?'"

On that issue, and on the remaining big question of how the climate might change in the future, skeptics continue to differ sharply with the dominant view among climate experts.

The dominant view is that the surface warming is at least partly attributable to emissions of heat-trapping waste industrial gases like carbon dioxide, a product of the burning of fossil fuels like coal, oil and natural gas. A United Nations scientific panel has predicted that unless

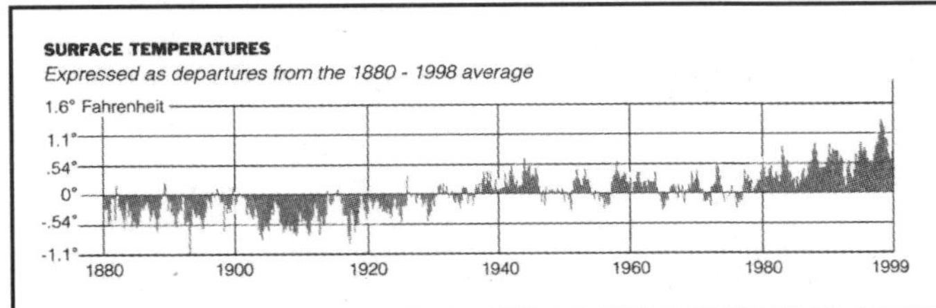

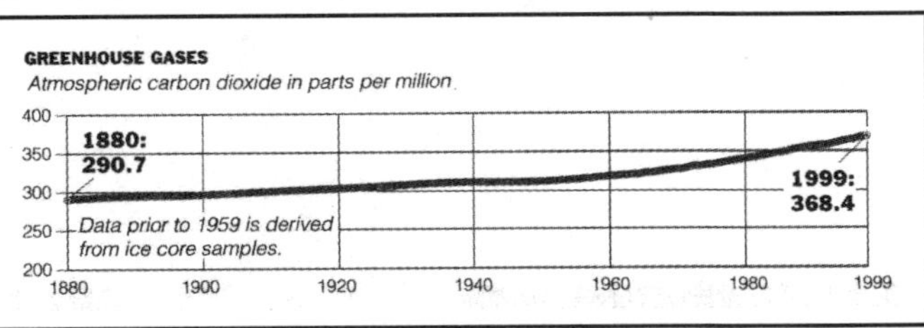

these greenhouse gas emissions are reduced, the earth's average surface temperature will rise by some 2 to 6 degrees Fahrenheit over the next century, with a best estimate of about 3.5 degrees, compared with a rise of 5 to 9 degrees since the depths of the last ice age 18,000 to 20,000 years ago. This warming, the panel said, would touch off widespread disruptions in climate and weather and cause the global sea level to rise and flood many places.

Dr. Gray and others challenge all of this. To them, the observed surface warming of about 1 degree over the last century—with an especially sharp rise in the last quarter century—is mostly or wholly natural, and there is no significant human influence on global climate. They also adhere firmly to their long-held opinion that any future warming will be inconsequential or modest at most, and that its effects will largely be beneficial.

In some ways, though, adversaries in the debate are not so far apart. For instance, some dissenters say that future warming caused by greenhouse gases will be near the low end of the range predicted by the United Nations

Two sides, two data sets

In support of their position, skeptics in the debate over climate change cite an apparent disparity between two sets of temperature data.

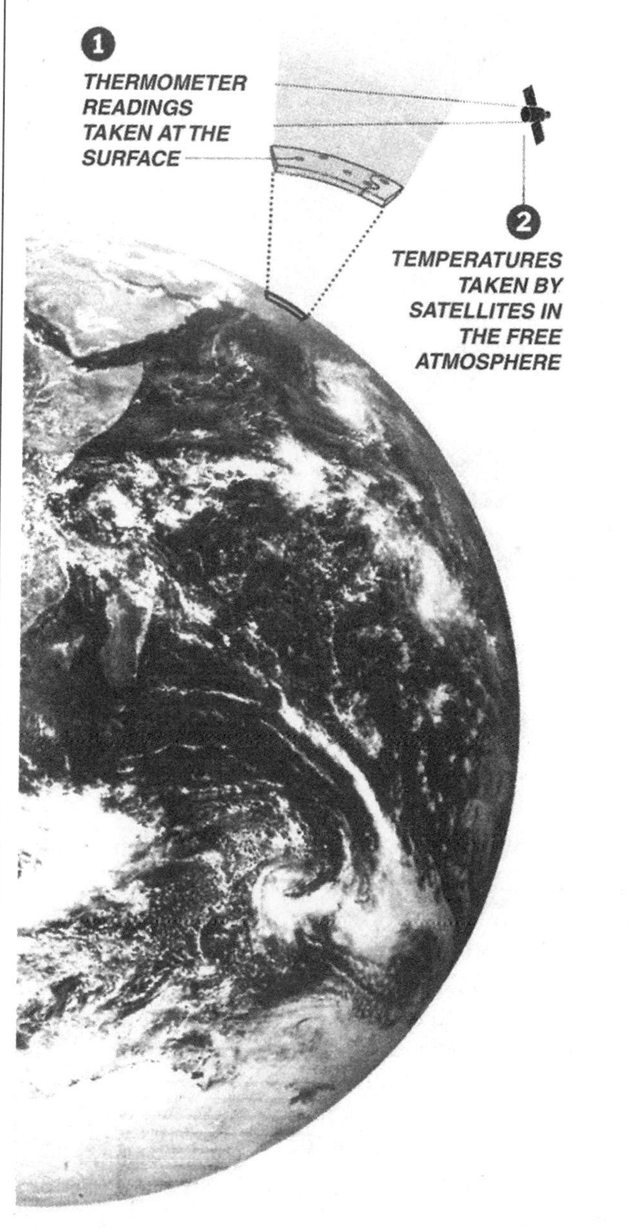

Sources: National Research Council; Carbon Dioxide Information Analysis Center

scientific panel. And most adherents of the dominant view readily acknowledge that the size of the human contribution to global warming is not yet known.

The thrust-and-parry of the climate debate goes on nevertheless.

With the National Research Council panel's conclusion that the surface warming is real, "one of the key arguments of the contrarians has evaporated," said Dr. Michael Oppenheimer, an atmospheric scientist with Environmental Defense, formerly the Environmental Defense Fund.

But those on the other side of the argument see things differently.

To them, the most important finding of the panel is its validation of satellite readings showing less warming, and maybe none, in parts of the upper atmosphere, said Dr. S. Fred Singer, an independent atmospheric scientist who is an outspoken dissenter.

The surface warming is real; humanity's role is at issue.

For him and other climate dissenters, this disparity is key, in that it does not show up in computer models scientists use to predict future trends. The fact that these models apparently missed the difference in warming between the surface and the upper air, the skeptics say, casts doubt on their reliability over all.

Experts on all sides of the debate acknowledge that the climate models are imperfect, and even proponents of their use say their results should be interpreted cautiously.

A further problem is raised by the divergent temperatures at the surface and the upper air, said Dr. Richard S. Lindzen, an atmospheric scientist at the Massachusetts Institute of Technology, who is a foremost skeptic. "Both are right," But, he said, increasing levels of greenhouse gases should warm the entire troposphere (the lower 6 to 10 miles of the atmosphere). That they have not, he said, suggests that "what's happening at the surface is not related to the greenhouse effect."

Skeptics also argue that the lower temperatures measured by the satellites are confirmed by instruments borne aloft by weather balloons. But over a longer period, going back 40 years, there is no discrepancy between surface readings and those obtained by the balloons, said Dr. John Michael Wallace, an atmospheric scientist at the University of Washington in Seattle, who was chairman of the research council study panel.

Although the climate debate has usually been portrayed as a polarized argument between believers and contrarians, there is actually a broad spectrum of views among scientists. And while the views of skeptics display some common themes, there are many degrees of dissent, many permutations and combinations of individual opinion. The views of some have changed materially over the years, while others have expressed essentially the same basic opinions all along.

One whose views have evolved is Dr. Wallace, who describes himself as "more skeptical than most people" but "fairly open to arguments on both sides" of the debate. He says the especially sharp surface warming trend of the

1. TEMPERATURE CHANGES AT OR NEAR THE EARTH'S SURFACE, 1979–1998

CLIMATE DEBATE:

THE DOMINANT VIEW

Surface warming is at least partly attributable to emissions of heat-trapping gases, like carbon dioxide, produced by the burning of fossil fuels.

THE SKEPTICS

Although the surface does appear to be warming, the cause is wholly or mostly natural.

Thermometers at land stations and aboard ships show a general global warming trend. The data are subject to distortion, but a recent study by the National Research Council says, nevertheless, that the surface warming is "undoubtedly real."

The *New York Times;* Images by NASA (Earth); National Academy of Science (Temperature maps)

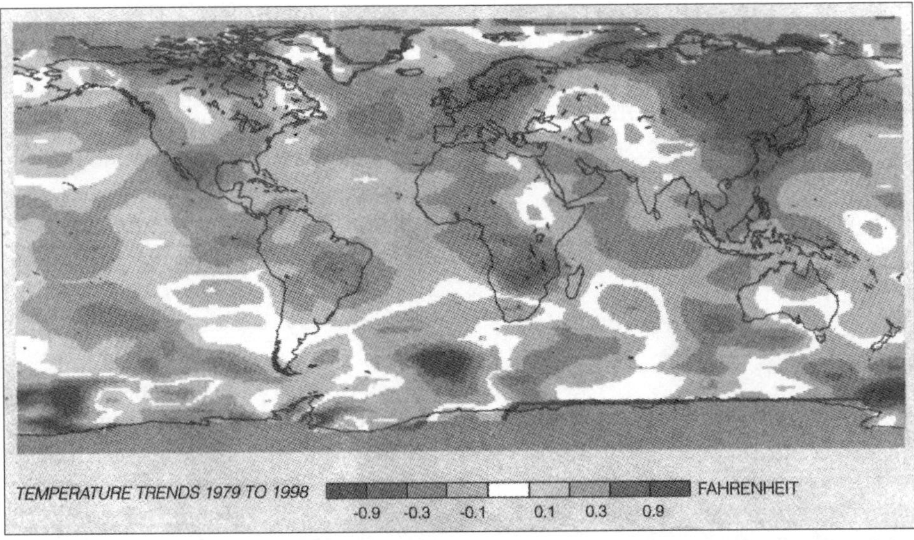

1990's has "pulled me in a mainstream direction." While he once believed the warming observed in recent decades was just natural variation in climate, he said, he is now perhaps 80 percent sure that it has been induced by human activity—"but that's still a long way from being willing to stake my reputation on it."

A decade ago, Dr. Wallace said, many skeptics questioned whether there even was a surface warming trend, in part because what now appears to be a century-long trend had been interrupted in the 1950's, 1960's and early 1970's, and it had not yet resumed all that markedly. But the surge in the 1980's and 1990's changed the picture substantially.

Today, Dr. Wallace said, few appear to doubt that the earth's surface has warmed. One prominent dissenter on the greenhouse question, Dr. Robert Balling, a climatologist at Arizona State University, says, "the surface temperatures appear to be rising, no doubt," and other skeptics agree.

There also appears to be general agreement that atmospheric concentrations of greenhouse gases are rising. At 360 parts per million, up from 315 parts in the late 1950's, the concentration of carbon dioxide is nearly 30 percent higher than before the Industrial Revolution, and the highest in the last 420,000 years.

Mainstream scientists, citing recent studies, suggest that the relatively rapid warming of the last 25 years cannot be explained without the greenhouse effect. Over that period, according to federal scientists, the average surface temperature rose at a rate equivalent to about 3.5 degrees per century—substantially more than the rise for the last century as a whole, and about what is predicted by computer models for the 21st century.

But many skeptics, including Dr. Gray and Dr. Singer, maintain that the warming of the past 25 years can be explained by natural causes, most likely changes in the circulation of heat-bearing ocean waters. In fact, Dr. Gray says he expects that over the next few decades, the warming will end and there will be a resumption of the cooling of the 1950's and 1960's.

At bottom, people on all sides of the debate agree, the question of the warming's cause has not yet been definitively answered. In December, a group of 11 experts on the question looked at the status of the continuing quest to detect the greenhouse signal amid the "noise" of the climate's natural variability.

2. TEMPERATURE CHANGES IN THE FREE ATMOSPHERE, UP TO 5 MILES, 1979–1998

CLIMATE DEBATE:

THE SKEPTICS

Computer models on which projections of future warming are based failed to reflect the surface-satellite disparity, casting doubt on the projections' accuracy. They say future warming will be small to modest, and largely beneficial.

THE DOMINANT VIEW

Scientists adhere to the computer models which say the average global surface temperature will rise by 2 to 6 degrees Fahrenheit over the next century if greenhouse gas emissions are not reduced.

Instruments aboard satellites show little warming, and even some cooling, in the lower to middle part of the free atmosphere, mainly in the tropics. Although scientists cannot fully explain the disparity, some say that over a longer period it might disappear.

The *New York Times*; Images by NASA (Earth); National Academy of Science (Temperature maps)

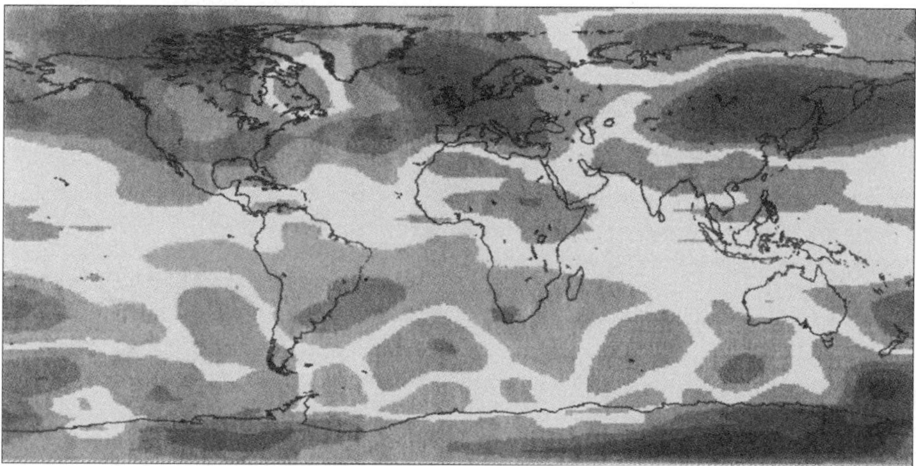

The lead author of the study was Dr. Tim P. Barnett, a climatologist at the Scripps Institution of Oceanography in La Jolla, Calif. Dr. Barnett, who has long worked on detecting the greenhouse signal, describes himself as a "hard-nosed" skeptic on that particular issue, even though he believes that global warming in the long run will be a serious problem.

The study by Dr. Barnett and others, published in The Bulletin of the American Meteorological Society, concluded that the "most probable cause" of the observed warming had been a combination of natural and human-made factors. But they said scientists had not yet been able to separate the greenhouse signal from the natural climate fluctuations. This state of affairs, they wrote, "is not satisfactory."

Two big questions complicate efforts to predict the course of the earth's climate over the next century: how sensitive is the climate system, inherently, to the warming effect of greenhouse gases? And how much will atmospheric levels of the gases rise over coming decades?

The mainstream view, based on computerized simulations of the climate system, is that a doubling of greenhouse gas concentrations would produce a warming of about 3 to 8 degrees. But Dr. Lindzen and Dr. Gray, pointing to what they consider the models' problems with the physics of the atmosphere, say they overestimate possible warming. It "will be extremely little," Dr. Gray said. How little? Dr. Lindzen pegs it at about half a degree to a bit less than 2 degrees, if atmospheric carbon dioxide doubles.

Other factors in the climate system modify the response to heat-trapping gases, and the United Nations panel's analysis included these to arrive at its projection of a 2- to 6-degree rise in the average global surface temperature by 2100. One factor is various possible levels of future carbon dioxide emissions. Dr. Singer, saying that improving energy efficiency will have a big impact on emissions, predicts a warming of less than 1 degree by 2100.

Dr. Balling projects a warming just shy of 1 degree for the next 50 years, not out of line with the United Nations panel's lower boundary. Another skeptic, Dr. Patrick J. Michaels, a climatologist at the University of Virginia, similarly forecasts a greenhouse warming rise of 2.3 degrees over the next century. As is now the case, he says, the warming would be most pronounced in the winter, at night, and in sub-Arctic regions like Siberia and Alaska. A warming of that magnitude, he and others insist, could not be very harmful, and would in fact confer benefits like longer growing seasons and faster plant growth.

"It should be pretty clear," he said, that the warming so far "didn't demonstrably dent health and welfare very much," and he said he saw no reason "to expect a sudden turnaround in the same over the next 50 years." After that, he said, it is impossible to predict the shape of the world's energy system and, therefore, greenhouse gas emissions.

A warming in the low end of the range predicted by the United Nations panel may well materialize, said Dr. Oppenheimer, the environmentalist. But, he said, the high end may also materialize, in which case, mainstream scientists say, there would be serious, even catastrophic, consequences for human society. "There is no compelling evidence to allow us to choose between the low end, or the high end, or the middle," Dr. Oppenheimer said.

If business continues as usual, the world is likely at some point to find out who is right.

THE FUTURE OF OUR FORESTS

TED KERASOTE

"America's vast green treasure house can be made self-perpetuating ... with scientific help," proclaimed a 1967 booklet from Weyerhaeuser, the timber and paper company. In fact, unlike oil or minerals, trees are the ultimate renewable resource. Some species, including aspen, one of the five species highlighted on the following pages, are prolific and prevalent enough to meet today's commercial demands. Such gifts from the forest provide the house you live in and the magazine you are holding.

But as a logger once noted, milk doesn't come from cartons, and pigs don't lay bacon. If you're going to build a deck or a hot tub, a tree has to fall. In this issue, *Audubon* seeks to give consumers the information they need to buy certified wood—the fruit of careful, selective forestry that takes into account preserving wildlife, water quality, and other resources.

Unfortunately, many logging operations take a much heavier toll, as we note in the following profiles of five forests where native trees are at risk. Imagine logging 625-acre swaths of old-growth aspen that are home to dozens of migratory birds just to make paper and strand board. That's what's happening in a virgin boreal forest near Swan River, Manitoba.

Ultimately, these forests and trees share a fate that will be determined by you, the consumer. You may have to go the extra mile to find lumber bearing a certified-wood logo or to call a company to trace the flow of wood back to the place where it grew. But when you do, you can be heartened by the part you are playing in protecting a forest.

Western Red Cedar *Thuja plicata*
THE TREE THAT KEEPS ON GIVING

THE LIVES of the indigenous people, urbanites, mammals, birds, and fish of the Pacific Northwest are all intimately tied to the western red cedar. Without exaggeration, this species can be called one of the planet's most important trees, and the overcutting of the western red cedar in the Elaho Valley near Vancouver represents the destruction of an entire ecosystem.

Here, in coastal British Columbia's temperate rainforest, 1,000-year-old cedars soar to 100 feet, their trunks fluted and their bark reddish-brown and shaggy. Commercially, the trees are valuable for their soft, straight-grained, and aromatic wood, which is easy to work with, takes a satiny finish, and holds paint extremely well. Even untreated, cut cedar is immune to decay for decades. Historically, the region's indigenous people used cedar for homes, bows and arrows, totem poles, and 65-foot voyaging canoes. Today western red cedar is widely used as paneling in homes, and it remains North America's most popular wood for shingles.

The tree also plays a vital role for wildlife. When a red cedar grows big and old, it develops heart rot, thus creating homes for pine martens, black bears, and owls. Woodpeckers feed on carpenter ants that live in the tree, and numerous birds and squirrels eat its seeds. The endangered southern populations of mountain caribou depend on the lichen found in low-elevation old-growth cedar and hemlock forests during early winter. When alive, the moisture-loving cedar shades streams, keeping the water cool for fish and aquatic insects. Dead and fallen cedars provide the woody debris that sustains bacteria and insects, which, in turn, become food for other creatures. Indeed, even after a life that can last a millennium, a red cedar keeps on giving for centuries. Downed trees anchor the soil, and their decaying wood replenishes the earth with incredibly rich nutrients, nursing the growth of new trees.

Six timber companies—Weyerhaeuser, Canadian Forest Products, Fletcher Challenge Canada, International Forest Products, West Fraser Timber, and Western Forest Products—continue to log western red cedar on the coast of British Columbia. In the province's interior,

Slocan Forest Products and Louisiana-Pacific log this cedar. British Columbia's Ministry of Forestry insists that old growth abounds in parks; environmentalists say the parks are primarily rock and ice.

Boycotts in Europe and Canada have forced companies to reconsider their cutting of old-growth cedar. More sustainable logging practices are now being negotiated between conservationists, timber companies, and the province. Still, a recent report by the World Resources Institute called the rate of cutting of Canada's old-growth forests unsustainable.

In the meantime, consumers should buy old-growth western red cedar only in its certified form, which is available in extremely limited supplies. As Wayne McCrory, the well-known Canadian bear biologist, says, "Using 800-year-old wood for cedar shakes to put on your roof is totally irresponsible, especially when there are so many other substitutes." If you need a new roof, try asphalt shingles, which usually last longer and are more fire-resistant.

Sugar Pine *Pinus lambertiana*
THE NOBLEST PINE

JUST south of the Oregon-California border, on Indian Creek, a tributary of the Klamath River, stands a dignified grove of enormous trees. Some of them are skeletons, killed by a blister rust that affects some species of pine. The sugar pine can grow to more than 200 feet, and it litters the ground with 20-inch-long cones. The species derives its name from its sweet and edible resin, which John Muir liked to chew, though wildlife seems to avoid it. Muir called the sugar pine "the noblest pine yet discovered, surpassing all others ... in kingly beauty and majesty." But his rhapsodic line hardly describes the species' ecological and commercial value.

Ranging from central Oregon to northern Baja California, sugar pines are used extensively by cavity-nesting birds such as the northern flicker and the red-breasted nuthatch, and especially by birds that nest in tall snags. Species that forage on its bole include pileated and hairy woodpeckers, red-breasted sapsuckers, red-breasted nuthatches, chestnut-backed chickadees, and brown creepers. White-headed woodpeckers, field mice, and pine squirrels eat the tree's seeds, and fishers, martens, weasels, raccoons, and black bears hunt on or near sugar pines.

"It doesn't matter if the operations are big or small. If they've got sugar pine, they're going to be cutting it."

Ever since the California gold rush, wood from sugar pines has been valued as much as any in the West. Cut extensively throughout the Sierra Nevada and Cascade ranges, the tree has been used to make mine props, railroad ties, and shingles. The produce industry still favors the wood for packing crates because it does not affect the flavor of the fruit and vegetables it holds. Millions of board feet of sugar pine were used to ship oranges and raisins; store coffee, tea, and spices; and make musical instruments. The sugar pine's light weight and resistance to shrinkage make it ideal for many other uses, including doors and windows, fine paneling and furniture, piano keys, and organ pipes.

Part of the sugar pine's range is protected in national parks and wilderness areas and old-growth forests that are spotted owl habitat. But logging continues in national forests and on private holdings. According to Connie Millar of the U.S. Forest Service, "It doesn't matter if the operations are big or small. If they've got sugar pine, they're going to be cutting it."

The question isn't whether sugar pine should be cut, but rather how much and at what age. The issue—which triggered a three-day conference held by the U.S. Forest Service in 1992—is assuming even greater importance given the devastating effects of blister rust. This pathogen, introduced into western North America in 1910, is wiping out stands like the one on Indian Creek. On rare occasions, individual sugar pines appear genetically resistant to blister rust, and the U.S. Forest Service prohibits logging these trees on its land. But Bohun Kinloch, a research geneticist with the agency, believes that as many sugar pines as possible should be spared, since even those that aren't resistant to blister rust can contribute to the genetic diversity of a local population.

Aspen *Populus tremuloides*
SUCKERS FOR WILDLIFE

SPECKLING mountains with flaming gold, pouring over canyon rims, and meandering through dark coniferous forests like sea currents of lighter green, aspen is the most widespread tree in North America. The species ranges from Alaska to Mexico and from British Columbia to Newfoundland. As "pioneer trees," aspens are among the first species to take root after fires and logging. In mountain environments, aspens' lateral roots create "suckers," or vertical shoots. Some of these suckers grow into mature trees, forming an extensive network of interconnected roots that can fan across the landscape for hundreds of miles and can produce new trees for more than 1,000 years. The ability of aspens to regenerate makes them one of the safest choices for buying sustainable commercial wood.

How strange, then, that the aspen might be in danger. Since many of the accessible parts of North America's temperate rainforest have been cut, and much of the remaining old growth is being placed off limits, lumber companies have turned to the little-known Canadian taiga, the subarctic evergreen forest where aspen are prevalent, as the fiber cache of the 21st century. One area that has been especially hard hit is a more than 2 million-acre swath of boreal forest near Swan River, Manitoba, where Louisiana-Pacific is cutting aspens for the wafers that go into oriented strand board (OSB), a strong, plywoodlike building material.

Alberta, Saskatchewan, and Manitoba have leased more than 104 million acres of their woodlands for cutting—an area that's slightly larger than New England, New York, and Pennsylvania combined.

Ironically, industrialists and some environmentalists have touted OSB as "ecofriendly" because it uses, in the parlance of the timber industry, weed species such as aspen—thus sparing old-growth species such as cedar and Douglas fir. However, 75-year-old aspens like those near Swan River are old growth for the species (the tree has a lifespan of about 100 years). They provide nesting sites for many species of warblers, vireos, and other birds that find cover among their foliage, which protects the birds from aerial predators like owls and hawks. Old-growth aspen trunks, which can be as thick as three feet, are home to cavity-nesting ducks such as buffleheads, wood ducks, and goldeneye, and a variety of woodpeckers such as the downy and the hairy. The trees' twigs and foliage are browsed by elk, moose, and caribou. Beavers, rabbits, and other mammals eat the bark, foliage, and buds; those animals are preyed upon by martens, fishers, lynxes, and black bears. Indigenous people, who make up 70 percent of the Canadian taiga's human population, also depend on this wooded landscape, which is now being removed in mind-boggling clearcuts that reach hundreds of acres and are transforming the boreal forest into a fragmented checkerboard. Alberta, Saskatchewan, and Manitoba have leased more than 104 million acres of their woodlands for cutting—an area that's slightly larger than New England, New York, and Pennsylvania combined. "What we have is forestry as strip mining," says Gray Jones, the executive director of the Western Canada Wilderness Committee.

It can be hard to trace the origins of pulp and paper made with aspen. But strand board is sold under company logos, which tells you where to call. Since companies are under considerable market pressure these days to be environmental, they're more responsive to inquiries than in the past. Besides Louisiana-Pacific, another major cutter of this forest is Saskfor Macmillan, which is owned by Weyerhaeuser. Canadian conservationists are pressuring the forest industry and their provincial governments to log more sustainably by leaving older trees and using smaller clearcuts and longer rotations.

Longleaf Pine *Pinus palustris*

A PRAIRIE HOME COMPANION

IN THE 1600s, when European settlers first arrived, the longleaf pine ecosystem, known as a "prairie with trees," covered 93 million acres from Virginia to central Florida and as far west as Texas. Open savannas filled with wire grass, bluestem, and wildflowers lay under widely spaced, 100-foot-high pines, their bark orange-brown, their needles as long as 18 inches and arranged in bunches of three.

Today the longleaf pine ecosystem comprises just 3 million acres. It has been lost to agriculture, industrial forestry, and development, says Jeff Hardesty, director of ecological management for the Nature Conservancy. What remains are scattered stands of trees, some measuring thousands of acres in extent.

Some of the plant species that grow alongside the longleaf pine, such as Apalachicola rosemary, are endangered. In addition, longleaf country is home to an array of reptiles, amphibians, and birds. Some 1,100 species in the Southeast, many associated with longleaf pine, are of "conservation concern," including the federally listed eastern indigo snake, the flatwoods salamander, and the red-cockaded woodpecker. This woodpecker thrives in the open, parklike long-leaf forests, where it carves cavities in the live old-growth pines, using them for both nesting and roosting. The tree's long needles make superior nesting materials, as well as thick duff for browse and cover. White-tailed deer, wild turkeys, fox squirrels, and bobwhite quail also abound in the remaining longleaf pine forests.

Called "southern," "yellow," or "pitch" pines by timbermen, longleaf pines have been a mainstay of the American forest industry because the tree's straight grain and dense wood make it a superior building material. For years it was used for lumber, bridge trestles, posts, and wharves along the Atlantic and Gulf coasts. Turpentine, pine tar, and pitch extracted from longleaf pines thinned paints and caulked wooden ships worldwide. The longleaf is still used in the construction industry and for utility poles. Its extravagant needles, known as pine straw, are coveted as mulch for flower beds and trees.

Depleted by development and by industrial forestry, all that remains of the original longleaf pine ecosystem is scattered stands of trees, some measuring thousands of acres.

Longleaf forests rely on frequent fires to expose mineral soils for the germination of seeds, so modern fire suppression has taken a heavy toll. Above all, the conversion of southeastern forests to vast monoculture plantations of loblolly pine is reducing the biological diversity that sustains a wide variety of the region's wildlife.

These trees are destined for pulp. Longleaf is being replaced by loblolly pine here in Mobile County, Alabama, on a site owned by the University of South Alabama Foundation (a private fund-raising institution affiliated with the university but not actually overseen by it).

To prevent further fragmentation of the longleaf ecosystem, public-private partnerships have sprung up among the U.S. Forest Service, the U.S. Fish and Wildlife Service, state fish and game agencies, the forest industry, and the Nature Conservancy. The Longleaf Alliance, based in Andalusia, Alabama, acts as a clearinghouse for these entities and provides silvicultural and economic consulting, demonstrating how well-managed longleaf stands can be more profitable for landowners than loblolly or slash pine because they produce so many valuable needles and better wood. These stakeholders are key to restoring the longleaf ecosystem, since half the remaining longleaf pines grow on private land. Certified longleaf lumber and pine straw are now entering the marketplace, and consumers can help restore this ecosystem by choosing a product certified by the Forest Stewardship Council or a third-party certifier such as SmartWood.

Northern White Cedar *Thuja occidentalis*
THE TREE OF LIFE

THE northern white cedar isn't well known by the average hiker because it lives in hard-to-reach country. Nonetheless, it has been one of the most important arboreal species in the Northeast and upper Midwest. It's used for shingles, poles, split-rail fences, and boats—particularly canoes—because of its very light weight and its resistance to decay. It remains a mainstay of the log-home and outdoor-furniture industries; L.L. Bean, for instance, uses it in its camp and patio line. An oil distilled from the cedar's needles is used to make perfumes as well as pharmaceuticals like Vicks Vapo Rub, and the tree's leaves and bark are high in vitamin C, a property that inspired the tree's name. While exploring the St. Lawrence River in 1535, Jacques Cartier and his crew drank cedar tea to cure themselves of scurvy, prompting King Francis I to name it arborvitae, or "tree of life."

An often perfectly conical tree that can rise 70 feet and live for almost 1,000 years, northern white cedar grows along tangled stream banks and in swamps all the way from Maine to Tennessee and up the St. Lawrence River valley to the Great Lakes. One such forest is in the Shingleton State Forest near Shingleton, Michigan.

Eighty-four species of birds, mammals, reptiles, and amphibians rely on northern white cedar stands like this one, feeding on its seeds, leaves, and inner bark, and nesting in its snags. Grouse and owls, pileated woodpeckers and winter wrens, white-winged crossbills, and more than a dozen kinds of wood warblers feed on or make their homes in northern white cedar stands, as do shrews, bats, martens, snowshoe hares, wood frogs, and blue-spotted salamanders.

"If we continue to use northern white cedar without dealing with the fundamental challenge of regeneration, we may soon be dealing with an issue of its biological endangerment."

But no animal relies on the tree more than the white-tailed deer, which uses it for forage and for shelter, yarding under its boughs during the winter to conserve energy and avoid predators. Where populations of deer have grown dramatically, the animals eat all the regenerating cedar, mowing down one stand after another. Ray Miller, a research forester at Michigan State University, points out that despite the damage white-tails cause (as is evident in the Shingleton stand), there is tremendous pressure from sportsmen to manage for high deer numbers. What is sacrificed is a healthy forest.

Richard Donovan, the director of SmartWood, a forest-certification program, echoes Miller's concerns about the double whammy of logging cedar while letting deer populations grow. "If we continue to use northern white cedar without dealing with the fundamental challenge of regeneration, we may soon be dealing with an issue of its biological endangerment. We have to improve the forestry side of the equation, and control deer populations, as politically unsavory as that may be in some quarters." The logging of cedar on public lands has been reduced to help stands regenerate. Yet with less cedar in the marketplace, the price of the wood has risen, driving up the cut on private lands.

Longtime *Audubon* contributor Ted Kerasote knows the value of a forest. He often repairs to Bridger-Teton National Forest, near his Wyoming hometown, to hike, birdwatch, hunt, and fish. Kerasote believes that apathy is at the root of unsustainable forestry. "Until consumers take some initiative," he asserts, "and refuse to accept products grown in an environmentally destructive way, forests will continue to be felled in an irresponsible way."

Restoring life to the 'dead zone'

How a sound farm policy could save our oceans

It sounds like something out of a zombie movie, but the spreading "dead zone" in the Gulf of Mexico is real. Extending from the mouth of the Mississippi River, the zone is almost barren of marine life. This void, an area the size of New Jersey, is caused largely by nutrients, primarily nitrogen, washing down from farms in the Midwest.

The greatest threat to our coastal waters today is nutrient pollution from diffuse "non-point" sources such as agricultural and urban runoff and airborne nitrogen pollution that settles on land and water.

Reducing runoff from farms will shrink the dead zone.

In the Gulf of Mexico, nitrogen from the Mississippi causes algae blooms and red and brown tides, which block sunlight and devastate the marine ecosystem. When the algae dies, decomposition uses up available oxygen. Seagrass communities are destroyed. Bottom feeders like red snapper, red and black drum, croaker, sting rays and some sharks can't find food. Worms, clams, starfish and crabs disappear.

"The fish swim out of the area, but the others can't escape," says our Oceans program director Dr. Bob Howarth.

Howarth has been studying nutrient pollution in coastal waters for 15 years and leads an international coalition of 250 scientists researching the problem. This work led to a federal assessment of what causes the dead zone, and a National Academy of Sciences committee chaired by Howarth last summer endorsed the assessment.

An Environmental Defense recommendation for prompt government action helped bring about a multi-state agreement to reduce nutrient pollution of the Mississippi 30% by 2015. This would reduce the dead zone to one-third its present size.

"This goal can be achieved voluntarily by farmers with little or no loss of crop productivity if the federal government comes through with appropriate encouragement and incentives," said Howarth.

DIRECTOR'S MESSAGE

An encounter by the river

Early one recent morning, I was rowing on Connecticut's Norwalk River not far from my home. As I glided past an asphalt factory in the pre-dawn mist, the sight of a great blue heron wading along the shore was an unexpected gift.

Thanks to the Clean Water Act, we've made great progress reducing industrial waste dumped into waterways. Once-moribund rivers are again capable of sustaining life. But many rivers are still far from healthy. More than half our coastal rivers and bays are polluted with nitrogen from farm runoff, municipal effluent and power plant and auto emissions.

Buffer zones can protect our waters.

Nitrogen chokes off oxygen and creates "dead zones" in coastal waters. Because there are so many hard-to-trace sources, the problem has eluded control. Yet simple buffer zones along the water's edge, like the mile of restored stream banks near where I row, can help shield our rivers.

When Congress debates the farm bill this summer, it should expand incentives to create buffers, restore wetlands and reduce pesticide use. As individuals, we can cut back on lawn fertilizers and buy cleaner cars that emit fewer nitrogen oxides. If we help nature, nature—like my riverside heron—will help itself.

—Fred Krupp

WILL WASHINGTON LISTEN?

Environmental Defense sees the upcoming reauthorization of the federal farm bill as a chance to restore the gulf and other degraded coastal waters around the nation. Direct support for farmers increased from $9 billion in the early 1990s to $32 billion in 2000. Yet only about $2 billion went to conservation programs like restoring and protecting wetlands that soak up nitrogen or planting winter cover crops to keep nitrogen in the soil. As debate on the massive farm bill began, we helped orchestrate a letter from 25 senators to the Budget Committee urging more funds for conservation.

Our recent report, *Losing ground: Failing to meet farmer demand for conservation assistance*, found that most farmers who seek federal help to improve water quality, combat sprawl or protect wildlife are rejected for lack of funds. The report found that 2,700 farmers hoping to restore 560,000 acres of lost wetlands were turned down. Much of this acreage would have filtered nitrogen in Indiana, Illinois, Iowa, Minnesota and Ohio—the major sources of the dead zone.

"Many farmers know their practices contribute to the dead zone and want to do something about it," said our attorney Scott Faber. "Yet the government continues to favor methods that make the problem worse. We believe Congress will want to correct this in the new farm bill."

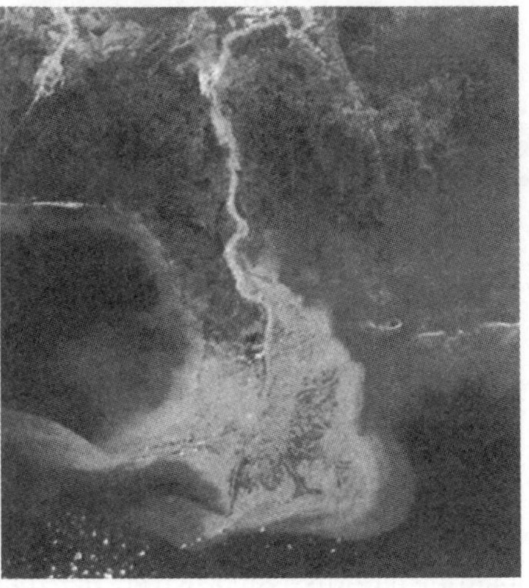

NASA
Nitrogen-saturated sediment clogs the Mississippi delta.

Article 13

Texas and Water

Pay up or dry up

Another state trying not to go thirsty

Austin

OIL built Texas, but water will shape its future. With five droughts in the past four years, water is running out fast. The Rio Grande, one of the state's main sources, has failed to reach the Gulf of Mexico for the first time in about 50 years. And demand is soaring, with the number of Texans expected to double by 2050. If this goes on, El Paso will run out of water in 20 years and other cities not much later.

Can the supply be increased? Texas has been squabbling with its neighbours about the division of the Rio Grande's water. There is talk of new reservoirs, but they may not be ready before El Paso and other cities have gone dry. Since surface water is so scarce, many people want to pump more water from underground aquifers. This would help—55% of the state's population already depends on such water for drinking and agriculture—but reliance on well water, if not handled carefully, could create vast environmental problems and leave the state with no water reserves.

So Texas is again wondering how to cut demand. Nobody can stop the state's population growing. But there are surely ways to limit the amount of water each Texan uses. Americans consume more water per head than most people, yet the price (a third of a cent per gallon) is lower than in most other rich countries. Water takes up less than 0.8% of the average American household budget. In theory, a price increase could achieve two things. It could raise money to help build better pipelines. It could also tame consumption, perhaps by as much as 20% in some areas.

Meanwhile, however, T. Boone Pickens, an erstwhile corporate raider, has been working on the supply side. He has been busy buying water rights in western Texas, setting up a consortium of landowners who have agreed to sell him their water at a given price. Mr Pickens hopes to pipe 150,000-200,000 acre-feet of water from the vast Ogallala aquifer in the Texas Panhandle to the state's parched cities. (An acre-foot, enough water to cover an acre a foot deep, is 326,000 gallons, or some 1.2m litres.)

The cities would pay on a sliding scale, depending on the distance Mr Pickens has to pump the stuff. Far-away El Paso would pay $1,400 per acre-foot, Dallas around $800. Much of the projected revenue of $200m would go into building pipelines to carry the stuff. But these are still stiff prices: the state of California recently paid $260 an acre-foot in a similar deal.

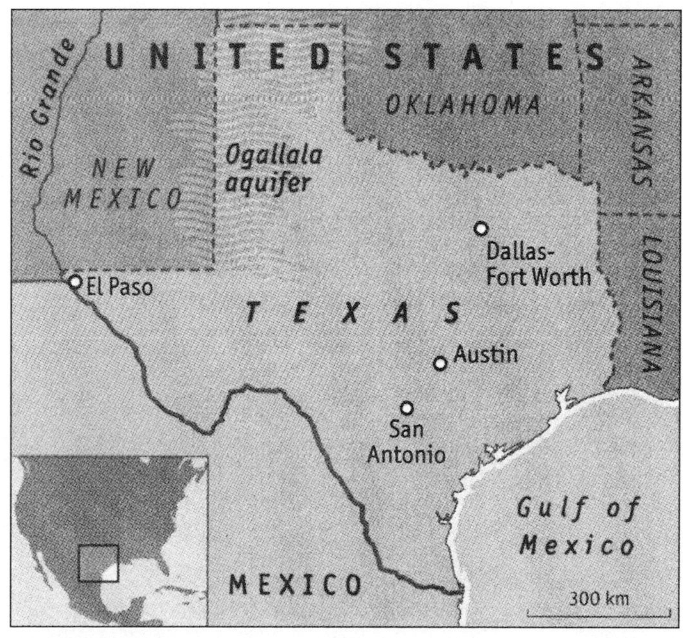

Environmentalists have reason to worry, too. The Ogallala replenishes itself at a rate of less than one acre-foot a year. In these circumstances water extraction is little different from mining. Indeed, Texas law treats water much as it does oil or gold: anybody who has access to the stuff can extract as much as he wants.

In theory, such water is protected by Texas's Groundwater Conservation Districts. But the state's strong tradition of property rights limits the GCDs' ability to control men like Mr Pickens. C.E. Williams, general manager of the Panhandle's Groundwater Conservation District No. 3, which deals with Mr Pickens, thinks the current crisis justifies pumping up to 50% of the Ogallala. But Mr Pickens's methods, he argues, would empty it within 25 years.

Mr Williams is pinning his hopes on a bill that is currently being discussed in the state legislature. This would allow more GCDs to be established, and empower them to levy a fee of at least two-and-a-half cents per 1,000 gallons to study the effects of pumping and set up replenishment projects. The only trouble is, Mr Pickens may have already got himself exempted from the fee.

Beyond the Valley of THE DAMMED

A strange alliance of fish lovers, tree huggers, and bureaucrats say what went up must come down

By God but we built some dams! We backed up the Kennebec in Maine and the Neuse in North Carolina and a hundred creeks and streams that once ran free. We stopped the Colorado with the Hoover, high as 35 houses, and because it pleased us we kept damming and diverting the river until it no longer reached the sea. We dammed our way out of the Great Depression with the Columbia's Grand Coulee; a dam so immense you had to borrow another fellow's mind because yours alone wasn't big enough to wrap around it. Then we cleaved the Missouri with a bigger one still, the Fort Peck Dam, a jaw dropper so outsized they put it on the cover of the first issue of *Life*. We turned the Tennessee, the Columbia, and the Snake from continental arteries into still bathtubs. We dammed the Clearwater, the Boise, the Santiam, the Deschutes, the Skagit, the Willamette, and the McKenzie. We dammed Crystal River and Muddy Creek, the Little River and the Rio-Grande. We dammed the Minnewawa and the Minnesota and we dammed the Kalamazoo. We dammed the Swift and we dammed the Dead.

One day we looked up and saw 75,000 dams impounding more than half a million miles of river. We looked down and saw rivers scrubbed free of salmon and sturgeon and shad. Cold rivers ran warm, warm rivers ran cold, and fertile muddy banks turned barren.

And that's when we stopped talking about dams as instruments of holy progress and started talking about blowing them out of the water.

BY BRUCE BARCOTT

Surrounded by a small crowd, Secretary of the Interior Bruce Babbitt stood atop McPherrin Dam, on Butte Creek, not far from Chico, California, in the hundred-degree heat of the Sacramento Valley. The constituencies represented—farmers, wildlife conservationists, state fish and game officials, irrigation managers—had been wrangling over every drop of water in this naturally arid basin for most of a century. On this day, however, amity reigned.

With CNN cameras rolling, Babbitt hoisted a sledgehammer above his head and—with "evident glee," as one reporter later noted—brought this tool of destruction down upon the dam. Golf claps all around.

The secretary's hammer strike in July 1998 marked the beginning of the end for that ugly concrete plug and three other Butte Creek irrigation dams. All were coming out to encourage the return of spring-run chinook salmon, blocked from their natural spawning grounds for more than 75 years. Babbitt then flew to Medford, Oregon, and took a swing at 30-year-old Jackson Street Dam on Bear Creek. Last year alone, Babbitt cracked the concrete at four dams on Wisconsin's Menominee River and two dams on Elwha River in Washington state; at Quaker Neck Dam on North Carolina's Neuse River; and at 160-year-old Edwards Dam on the Kennebec in Maine.

By any reckoning, this was a weird inversion of that natural order. Interior secretaries are supposed to christen dams, not smash them. Sixty years ago, President Franklin D. Roosevelt and his interior secretary, Harold Ickes, toured the West to dedicate four of the largest dams in the history of civilization. Since 1994, Babbitt, who knows his history, has been following in their footsteps, but this secretary is preaching the gospel of dam-going-away. "America overshot the mark in our dam-building frenzy," he told the Ecological Society of America. "The public is now learning that we have paid a steadily accumulating price for these projects.... We did not build them for religious purposes and they do not consecrate our values. Dams do, in fact, outlive their function. When they do, some should go."

Many dams continue, of course, to be invaluable pollution-free power plants. Hydroelectric dams provide 10 percent of the nation's electricity (and half of our renewable energy). In the Northwest, dams account for 75 percent of the region's power and bestow the lowest electrical rates in the nation. In the past the public was encouraged to believe that hydropower was almost free; but as Babbitt has been pointing out, the real costs can be enormous.

What we know now that we didn't know then is that **a river isn't a water pipe.**

What we know now that we didn't know in 1938 is that a river isn't a water pipe. Dam a river and it will drop most of the sediment it carries into a still reservoir, trapping ecologically valuable debris such as branches, wood particles, and gravel. The sediment may be mixed with more and more pollutants—toxic chemicals leaching from abandoned mines, for example, or naturally occurring but dangerous heavy metals. Once the water passes through the dam it continues to scour, but it can't replace what it removes with material from upstream. A dammed river is sometimes called a "hungry" river, one that eats its bed and banks. Riverbeds and banks may turn into cobblestone streets, large stones cemented in by the ultrafine silt that passes through the dams. Biologists call this "armoring."

Naturally cold rivers may run warm after the sun heats water trapped in the reservoir; naturally warm rivers may run cold if their downstream flow is drawn from the bottom of deep reservoirs. Fish adapted to cold water won't survive in warm water, and vice versa.

As the toll on wild rivers became more glaringly evident in recent decades, opposition to dams started to go mainstream. By the 1990s, conservation groups, fishing organizations, and other river lovers began to call for actions that had once been supported only by environmental extremists and radical groups like Earth First! Driven by changing economics, environmental law, and most of all the specter of vanishing fish, government policy makers began echoing the conservationists. And then Bruce Babbitt, perhaps sensing the inevitable tide of history, began to support decommissioning as well.

So far, only small dams have been removed. Babbitt may chip away at all the little dams he wants, but when it comes to ripping major federal hydropower projects out of Western rivers, that's when the politics get national and nasty. Twenty-two years ago, when President Jimmy Carter suggested pulling the plug on several grand dam projects, Western senators and representatives politically crucified him. Although dam opponents have much stronger scientific and economic arguments on their side in 1999, the coming dam battles are apt to be just as nasty.

Consider the Snake River, where a major confrontation looms over four federal hydropower dams near the Washington-Idaho state line. When I asked Babbitt about the Snake last fall, he almost seemed to be itching for his hammer. "The escalating debate over dams is going to focus in the coming months on the Snake River," he declared. "We're now face to face with this question: Do the people of this country place more value on Snake River salmon or on those four dams? The scientific studies are making it clear that you can't have both."

Brave talk—but only a couple of weeks later, after a bruising budget skirmish with congressional dam proponents who accused him of planning to tear down dams across the Northwest, Babbitt sounded like a man who had just learned a sobering lesson in the treacherous politics of dams. The chastened interior secretary assured the public that "I have never advocated, and do not advocate, the removal of dams on the main stem of the Columbia-Snake river system."

Showdown on the Snake

Lewiston, Idaho, sits at the confluence of the Snake and Clearwater Rivers. It's a quiet place of 33,000 solid citizens, laid out like a lot of towns these days: One main road leads into the dying downtown core, the other to a thriving strip of Wal-Marts, gas stations, and fast-food greaseries. When Lewis (hence the name) and Clark floated through here in 1805, they complained about the river rapids—"Several of them verry bad," the spelling-challenged Clark scrawled in his journal. Further downriver, where the Snake meets the Columbia, the explorers were amazed to see the local Indians catching and drying incredible numbers of coho salmon headed upriver to spawn.

The river still flows, though it's been dammed into a lake for nearly 150 miles. Between 1962 and 1975, four federal hydroelectric projects were built on the river by the Army Corps of Engineers: Ice Harbor Dam, Lower Monumental Dam, Little Goose Dam, and Lower Granite Dam. The dams added to the regional power supply, but more crucially, they turned the Snake from a whitewater roller-coaster into a navigable waterway. The surrounding wheat farmers could now ship their grain on barges to Portland, Oregon, at half the cost of overland transport, and other industries also grew to depend on this cheap highway to the sea.

Like all dams, however, they were hell on the river and its fish—the chinook, coho, sockeye, and steelhead. True, some salmon species still run up the river to spawn, but by the early 1990s the fish count had dwindled from 5 million to less than 20,000. The Snake River coho have completely disappeared, and the sockeye are nearing extinction.

In and around Lewiston, the two conflicting interests—livelihoods that depend on the dams on the one side, the fate of the fish on the other—mean that just about everyone is either a friend of the dams or a breacher. The Snake is the dam-breaching movement's first major test case, but it is also the place where dam defenders plan to make their stand. Most important, depending in part on the results of a study due later this year, the lower Snake could become the place where the government orders the first decommissioning of several big dams.

In the forefront of those who hope this happens is Charlie Ray, an oxymoron of a good ol' boy environmentalist whose booming Tennessee-bred baritone and sandy hair lend him the aspect of Nashville Network host. Ray makes his living as head of salmon and steelhead programs for Idaho Rivers United, a conservationist group that has been raising a fuss about free-flowing rivers since 1991. At heart he's not a tree hugger, but a steelhead junkie: "You hook a steelhead, man, you got 10,000 years of survival instinct on the end of that line."

Despite Ray's bluff good cheer, it's not easy being a breacher in Lewiston. Wheat farming still drives a big part of the local economy, and the pro-dam forces predict that breaching would lead to financial ruin. Lining up behind the dam defenders are Lewiston's twin pillars of industry: the Potlatch Corporation and the Port of Lewiston. Potlatch, one of the country's largest paper producers, operates its flagship pulp and paper mill in Lewiston, employing 2,300 people. Potlatch executives will tell you the company wants the dams mainly to protect the town's economy, but local environmentalists say the mill would find it more difficult to discharge warm effluent into a free-flowing, shallow river.

Potlatch provides Charlie Ray with a worthy foil in company spokesman Frank Carroll, who was hired after spending 17 years working the media for the U.S. Forest Service. Frankie and Charlie have been known to scrap. At an anti-breaching rally in Lewiston last September, Carroll stood off-camera watching Ray being interviewed by a local TV reporter. Fed up with hearing Ray's spin, Carroll started shouting "Bullshit, Charlie, that's bullshit!" while the video rolled. Ray's nothing more than a "paid operative," Carroll says. Ray's reaction: "Yeah, like Frankie's not."

"A lot of people are trying to trivialize the social and economic issues," Carroll says, "trying to tell us the lives people have here don't count, that we'll open up a big bait shop and put everyone to work hooking worms. We resent that. Right now, there's a blanket of prosperity that lies across this whole region, and that prosperity is due to the river in its current state—to its transportation."

Ever since the dams started going up along the Snake River, biologists and engineers have been trying to revive the rapidly declining salmon runs. Their schemes include fish ladders, hatcheries, and a bizarre program in which young smolts are captured and shipped downriver to the sea in barges. By the late 1980s, it was clear that nothing was working; the fish runs continued to plummet. In 1990, the Shoshone-Bannock Indians, who traditionally fished the Snake's sockeye run, successfully petitioned the National Marine Fisheries Service to list the fish as endangered. Every salmon species in the Snake River is now officially threatened or endangered, which means the agencies that control the river must deal with all kinds of costly regulations.

In 1995, under pressure from the federal courts, the National Marine Fisheries Service and the Army Corps of Engineers (which continues to operate the dams) agreed to launch a four-year study of the four lower Snake River dams. In tandem with the Fisheries Service, the Corps made a bombshell announcement. The study would consider three options: maintain the status quo, turbocharge the fish-barging operation, or initiate a "permanent natural river drawdown"—breaching. The study's final report is due in December, but whatever its conclusions, that initial statement marked a dramatic shift. Suddenly, an action that had always seemed unthinkable was an officially sanctioned possibility.

Two separate scientific studies concluded that breaching presented the best hope for saving the river. In 1997 the *Idaho Statesman*, the state's largest newspaper, published a three-part series arguing that breaching the four dams would net local taxpayers and the region's economy $183 million a year. The dams, the paper concluded, "are holding Idaho's economy hostage."

"That series was seismic," says Reed Burkholder, a Boise-based breaching advocate. Charlie Ray agrees. "We've won the scientific argument," he says. "And we've won the economic argument. We're spending more to drive the fish to extinction than it would cost to revive them."

In fact, the economic argument is far from won. The *Statesman*'s numbers are not unimpeachable. The key to their prediction, a projected $248 million annual boost in recreation and fishing, assumes that the salmon runs will return to pre-1960s levels. Fisheries experts say that could take up to 24 years, if it happens at all. The $34 million lost at the Port of Lewiston each year, however, would be certain and immediate.

The Northwest can do without the power of the four lower Snake River dams: They account for only about 4 percent of the region's electricity supply. The dams aren't built for flood control, and contrary to a widely held belief, they provide only a small amount of irrigation water to the region's farmers. What the issue comes down to, then, is the Port of Lewiston. You take the dams out, says port manager Dave Doeringsfeld, "and transportation costs go up 200 to 300 percent."

To breach or to blow?

The pro-dam lobbyists know they possess a powerful, not-so-secret weapon: Senator Slade Gorton, the Washington Republican who holds the commanding post of chairman of the Subcommittee on Interior Appropriations. Gorton has built his political base by advertising himself as the foe of liberal Seattle environmentalists, and with his hands on Interior's purse strings, he can back up the role with real clout. As determined as Bruce Babbitt is to bring down a big dam, Slade Gorton may be more determined to stop him.

During last October's federal budget negotiations, Gorton offered to allocate $22 million for removing two modest dams in the Elwha River on the Olympic Peninsula, a salmon-restoration project dear to the hearts of dam-breaching advocates. But Gorton agreed to fund the Elwha breaching if—and only if—the budget included language forbidding federal officials from unilaterally ordering the dismantling of any dam, including those in the Columbia River Basin. Babbitt and others balked at Gorton's proposal. As a result, the 1999 budget includes zero dollars for removal of the Elwah dams.

Gorton's Elwha maneuver may have been hardball politics for its own sake, but it was also a clear warning: If the Army Corps and the National Marine Fisheries Service recommend breaching on the Snake in their study later this year, there will be hell to pay.

Meanwhile, here's a hypothetical question: If you're going to breach, how do you actually do it? How do you take those behemoths out? It depends on the dam, of course, but the answer on the Snake is shockingly simple.

"You leave the dam there," Charlie Ray says. We're standing downstream from Lower Granite Dam, 35 million pounds of steel encased in concrete. Lower Granite isn't a classic ghastly curtain like Hoover Dam; it resembles nothing so much as an enormous half-sunk harmonica. Ray points to a berm of granite boulders butting up against the concrete structure's northern end. "Take out the earthen portion and let the river flow around the dam. This is not high-tech stuff. This is front-end loaders and dump trucks."

It turns out that Charlie is only a few adjectives short of the truth. All you do need are loaders and dump trucks—really, really big ones, says Steve Tatro of the Army Corps of Engineers. Tatro has the touchy job of devising the best way to breach his agency's own dams. First, he says, you'd draw down the reservoir, using the spillways and the lower turbine passages as drains. Then you'd bypass the concrete and steel entirely and excavate the dam's earthen portion. Depending on the dam, that could mean excavating as much as 8 million cubic yards of material.

Tatro's just-the-facts manner can't disguise the reality that there is something deeply cathartic about the act he's describing. Most environmental restoration happens at the speed of nature. Which is to say, damnably slow. Breaching a dam—or better yet, blowing a dam—offers a rare moment of immediate gratification.

The Glen Canyon story

From the Mesopotamian canals to Hoover Dam, it took the human mind about 10,000 years to figure out how to stop a river. It has taken only 60 years to accomplish the all-too-obvious environmental destruction.

Until the 1930s, most dam projects were matters of trial and (often) error, but beginning with Hoover Dam in 1931, dam builders began erecting titanic riverstoppers that approached an absolute degree of reliability and safety. In *Cadillac Desert*, a 1986 book on Western water issues, author Marc Reisner notes that from 1928 to 1956, "the most fateful transformation that has ever been visited on any landscape, anywhere, was wrought." Thanks to the U.S. Bureau of Reclamation, the Tennessee Valley Authority, and the Army Corps, dams lit a million houses, turned deserts into wheat fields, and later powered the factories that built the planes and ships that beat Hitler and the Japanese. Dams became monuments to democracy and enlightenment during times of bad luck and hunger and war.

Thirty years later, author Edward Abbey became the first dissenting voice to be widely heard. In *Desert Solitaire* and *The Monkey Wrench Gang*, Abbey envisioned a counterforce of wilderness freaks wiring bombs to the Colorado River's Glen Canyon Dam, which he saw as the ultimate symbol of humanity's destruction of the American West. Kaboom! Wildness returns to the Colorado.

Among environmentalists, the Glen Canyon Dam has become an almost mythic symbol of riparian destruction. All the symptoms of dam kill are there. The natural heavy metals that the Colorado River used to disperse into the Gulf of California now collect behind the dam in Lake Powell. And the lake is filling up: Sediment has reduced the volume of the lake from its original 27 million acre-feet to 23 million. One million acre-feet of water are lost to evaporation every year—enough, environmentalists note, to revive the dying upper reaches of the Gulf of California. The natural river ran warm and muddy, and flushed its channel with floods; the dammed version runs cool, clear, and even. Trout thrive in the Colorado. This is like giraffes thriving on tundra.

In 1963, the most beautiful of all the canyons of the Colorado **began disappearing beneath Lake Powell.**

Another reason for the dam's symbolic power can be traced to its history. For decades ago, David Brower, then executive director of the Sierra Club, agreed to a compromise that haunts him to this day: Conservationists would not oppose Glen Canyon and 11 other projects if plans for the proposed Echo Park and Split Mountain dams, in Utah and Colorado, were abandoned. In 1963, the place Wallace Stegner once called "the most serenely beautiful of all the canyons of the Colorado" began disappearing beneath Lake Powell. Brower led the successful fight to block other dams in the Grand Canyon area, but he remained bitter about the compromise. "Glen Canyon died in 1963," he later wrote, "and I was partly responsible for its needless death."

In 1981 Earth First! inaugurated its prankster career by unfurling an enormous black plastic "crack" down the face of Glen Canyon Dam. In 1996 the Sierra Club rekindled the issue by calling for the draining of Lake Powell. With the support of Earth Island Institute (which Brower now chairs) and other environmental groups, the proposal got a hearing before a subcommittee of the House Committee on Resources in September 1997. Congress has taken no further action, but a growing number of responsible voices now echo the monkey-wrenchers' arguments. Even longtime Bureau of Reclamation supporter Barry Goldwater admitted, before his death last year, that he considered Glen Canyon Dam a mistake.

Defenders of the dam ask what we would really gain from a breach. The dam-based ecosystem has attracted peregrine falcons, bald eagles, carp, and catfish. Lake Powell brings in $400 million a year from tourists enjoying houseboats, powerboats, and personal watercraft—a local economy that couldn't be replaced by the thinner wallets of rafters and hikers.

"It would be completely foolhardy and ridiculous to deactivate that dam," says Floyd Dominy during a phone conversation from his home in Boyce, Virginia. Dominy, now 89 years old and retired since 1969, was the legendary Bureau of Reclamation commissioner who oversaw construction of the dam in the early 1960s. "You want to lose all that pollution-free energy? You want to destroy a world-renowned tourist attraction—Lake Powell—that draws more than 3 million people a year?"

It goes against the American grain: the notion that knocking something down and returning it to nature might be progress just as surely as replacing wildness with asphalt and steel. But 30 years of environmental law, punctuated by the crash of the salmon industry, has shifted power from the dam builders to the conservationists.

The most fateful change may be a little-noticed 1986 revision in a federal law. Since the 1930s, the Federal Energy Regulatory Commission has issued 30- to 50-year operating licenses to the nation's 2,600 or so privately owned hydroelectric dams. According to the revised law, however, FERC must consider not only power generation, but also fish and wildlife, energy conservation, and recreational uses before issuing license renewals. In November 1997, for the first time in its history, FERC refused a license against the will of a dam owner, ordering the Edwards Manufacturing Company to rip the 160-year-old Edwards Dam out of Maine's Kennebec River. More than 220 FERC hydropower licenses will expire over the next 10 years.

If there is one moment that captures the turning momentum in the dam wars, it might be the dinner Richard Ingebretsen shared with the builder of Glen Canyon Dam, Floyd Dominy himself. During the last go-go dam years, from 1959 to 1969, this dam-building bureaucrat was more powerful than any Western senator or governor. Ingebretsen is a Salt Lake City physician, a Mormon Republican, and a self-described radical environmentalist. Four years ago, he founded the Glen Canyon Institute to lobby for the restoration of Glen Canyon. Ingebretsen first met Dominy when the former commissioner came to Salt Lake City in 1995 to debate David Brower over the issue of breaching Glen Canyon Dam. To his surprise, Ingebretsen found that he liked the man. "I really respect him for his views," he says.

Their dinner took place in Washington, D.C., in early 1997. At one point Dominy asked Ingebretsen how serious the movement to drain Lake Powell really was. Very serious, Ingebretsen replied. "Of course I'm opposed to putting the dam in mothballs," Dominy said. "But I heard what Brower wants to do." (Brower had suggested that Glen Canyon could be breached by coring out some old water bypass tunnels that had been filled in years ago.) "Look," Dominy continued, "those tunnels are jammed with 300 feet of reinforced concrete. You'll never drill that out."

With that, Dominy pulled out a napkin and started sketching a breach. "You want to drain Lake Powell?" he asked. "What you need to do is drill new bypass tunnels. Go through the soft sandstone around and beneath the dam and line the tunnels with waterproof plates. It would be an expensive, difficult engineering feat. Nothing like this has ever been done before, but I've done a lot of thinking about it, and it will work. You can drain it."

The astonished Ingebretsen asked Dominy to sign and date the napkin. "Nobody will believe this," he said. Dominy signed.

Of course, it will take more than a souvenir napkin to return the nation's great rivers to their full wildness and health. Too much of our economic infrastructure depends on those 75,000 dams for anyone to believe that large numbers of river blockers, no matter how obsolete, will succumb to the blow of Bruce Babbitt's hammer anytime soon. For one thing, Babbitt himself is hardly in a position to be the savior of the rivers. Swept up in the troubles of a lame-duck administration and his own nagging legal problems (last spring Attorney General Janet Reno appointed an independent counsel to look into his role in an alleged Indian casino-campaign finance imbroglio), this interior secretary is not likely to fulfill his dream of bringing down a really big dam. But a like-minded successor just might. It will take a president committed and powerful enough to sway both Congress and the public, but it could come to pass.

Maybe Glen Canyon Dam and the four Snake River dams won't come out in my lifetime, but others will. And as more rivers return to life, we'll take a new census of emancipated streams: We freed the Neuse, the Kennebec, the Allier, the Rogue, the Elwah, and even the Tuolumne. We freed the White Salmon and the Souradabscook, the Ocklawaha and the Genesee. They will be untidy and unpredictable, they will flood and recede, they will do what they were meant to do: run wild to the sea.

Bruce Barcott is the author of The Measure of a Mountain: Beauty and Terror on Mount Rainier (*Sasquatch, 1997*).

From *Utne Reader,* May/June 1999, pp. 50–57. Originally appeared in *Outside,* February 1999.

The Himba and the Dam

A questionable act of progress may drown this African tribe's way of life. Similar dramas are playing out around the world

In our world a dam is a small thing that gives cattle water,
What you are talking about is something else and will finish the Himba.
—Chief Katjira Muniombara

By Carol Ezzell

Not until we stand on a ridge overlooking the Kunene River—which forms part of the border between the southern African nations of Angola and Namibia—does tribal leader Jakatunga Tjiuma comprehend the immensity of the proposed dam. "Look there," I tell him with the help of an interpreter, pointing to a distant notch in the river gorge that a feasibility study says would be the most likely site of the wall of concrete. "That's where the dam would be." Turning, I point to hills in the east. "And the water would back up behind the dam to make a lake that would stretch to there." I can see the shock and incredulity in his eyes as he begins to understand how high the water would rise up the faraway hillsides, flooding more than 140 square miles of Himba settlements, grazing land and grave sites. He clutches a blanket around his shoulders and crouches on a rock, speechless.

The situation surrounding the proposed dam on the Kunene River can be viewed as a microcosm of dam projects around the world that are affecting indigenous peoples.

Tjiuma is a counselor to one of the headmen for the Himba tribe, an essentially self-sufficient band of 16,000 people who eke out an existence from the barren, rocky terrain of northwest Namibia, living off the milk and meat of their cattle and goats, along with the occasional pumpkin or melon. The Himba are sometimes called the Red People because they traditionally cover their bodies, hair and the animal skins they wear with a mixture of butterfat and a powder ground from the iron ore ocher. They say they use the ocher-butter mixture because they like the way it looks, although it undoubtedly also protects their skin against the arid climate.

For decades, the Himba have lived in relative isolation. No other tribes wanted their hardscrabble land, and the Germans who colonized the area in the late 19th century rarely interacted with them. More recently, the Himba's main contact with outsiders has been with soldiers during the fight for Namibia's independence from South Africa (which was won in 1990), with marauding combatants spilling over from Angola's ongoing civil war, and with the occasional caravan of hippie Americans or Europeans. But if the Namibian government has its way, by 2008 more than 1,000 foreign workers will have settled in a temporary village just downstream from Epupa Falls, the site the government favors for the dam. With them will come a cash economy, alcohol, prostitution and AIDS—as well as improved roads, better access to medical care, schools and perhaps even electricity.

The situation surrounding the proposed dam on the Kunene River can be viewed as a microcosm of dam projects around the world that are affecting indigenous peoples. A survey by the World Commission on Dams, which issued its controversial final report last November, found that 68 of the 123 dams worldwide they studied would displace people, many of them in tribes that had little prior contact with the technological world. The largest dam project, the massive Three Gorges Dam on the Yangtze River, will require the resettlement of up to two million Chinese. Nearly all the dams will change local peoples' livelihoods and cultures—for good or ill, or some combination of the two.

How should global society weigh the right of such peoples to be left alone against, in some cases, the very real necessity for developing countries to take advantage of their resources? Should such countries have the autonomy to decide what is in the best interests of all their citizens, even if some of them don't want to change? Perhaps most important, how can traditional peoples decide such issues for themselves when they have only a shaky idea of how more developed societies live and what they might be getting themselves into?

Into the Desert

KAOKOLAND, THE CORNER OF NAMIBIA where the Himba live, is truly the back of beyond. We arrive at Epupa Falls, the modest waterfall on the Kunene River that would be inundated by the dam's reservoir, two days after leaving the last tarred road. Our 4 × 4 truck is packed with everything from jerricans of gasoline (the closest gas pump is a day's drive away) to cases of bottled water, spare tires, emergency medical supplies, camping gear, and small gifts of tobacco, sugar and blankets. Tied to the top of our vehicle is a brand-new bicycle—the payment requested by our Himba translator, Staygon Reiter, in exchange for his services, although how he will use it in this inhospitable landscape I don't know. He has asked specifically that the bicycle come equipped with a carrier basket large enough to hold a goat.

Much of our journey is bumpy, jerky and slow as we attempt to follow the rough track while swerving to avoid washouts and potentially tire-puncturing rocks. More than once we get stuck in sand while trying to cross a dry riverbed, our tires spinning and squealing until we jump out to deflate them a bit or to stuff branches behind them for traction. At one point we stop to look at a particularly large scorpion in our path; I comment that I've seen smaller lobsters.

The settlement at Epupa Falls, where we camp, is a kind of crossroads, a no-man's-land where Namibian Himba mix with their Himba relatives from across the river in Angola and with other tribes such as the Herero—to whom the Himba are closely related—as well as with the Zemba, Thwa and Ngambwe. There is a modest thatched church built by missionaries; a tiny but deluxe safari camp; a corrugated-metal store that sells mostly bags of cheap tobacco, maize meal, and tepid Coke, Sprite and Fanta; and a community-run campsite where visitors like us can pitch a tent under the palmlike *omerungu* trees for 50 Namibian dollars (about US$6) per night. Scarcely any people live at the settlement permanently: the Himba come for a few weeks or months at a time and build temporary huts while they attend funerals, divide inheritances, sell cattle, conduct other business, and visit with friends and relatives.

Our first stop is to meet Chief Hikuminwe Kapika at his compound near Epupa Falls, which is part of the territory he controls. It is immediately clear that Kapika—who is one of roughly a dozen Himba chiefs—is sick of talking about the proposed dam with outsiders but eager for us to appreciate the importance of his rank. From his shock of grayish hair and weathered face, I guess him to be in his 70s, although Himba don't have a calendar system, so they usually don't know the year in which they were born. He keeps us standing beside his white metal camp chair (the only one in his compound) swatting flies from our faces as I try to catch his attention long enough to answer my questions. Several times during our interview he spits through a gap in his front teeth created in his teens when, in keeping with Himba tradition, his lower two central incisors were knocked out and the top two filed to create a V-shaped opening. He makes a point of demonstrating what a busy man he is by continuing to sew a black fabric loincloth and interrupting our translators to correct a group of rowdy children.

Eventually Kapika tells us that he vehemently opposes the proposed dam. He is afraid that the people who will come to build it will steal the Himba's cattle—not an irrational fear, because the Himba were nearly wiped out at the end of the 19th century as a result of cattle raids by the Nama tribe, which lives to the south. And cattle theft continues today. He is also worried that the newcomers will take valuable grazing land, which the Himba are careful not to overuse. Family groups move their households several times a year so that extensively grazed regions can grow back. The area around Kapika's compound illustrates the need for such conservation: the cattle and goats have eaten everything green they can reach, leaving the bushes and trees top-heavy with scraggly growth overhanging trunks like lollipop sticks.

How do you describe a megadam to someone who has never seen electricity? Or a building more than one story high?

Himba leaders also object to the dam because it would flood hundreds of graves, which play a central role in the tribe's religious beliefs and social structure. In times of crisis, family patriarchs consult their forebears through special ceremonies at grave sites, and graves are often used to settle disputes over access to land. Acreage is owned communally, but each permanent settlement is guarded by an "owner of the land," usually the oldest man of the family who has lived at that place for the longest time. When deciding who should be able to graze their cattle in a particular area, Himba compare the number of ancestors they have buried there. They ask, "Whose ancestral graves are older, ours or theirs?"

Kapika says the Himba will resist and fight "with stones and spears" if the Namibian government tries to build a hydroelectric dam at Epupa Falls. "I'm a big man," he tells. "I'm a man who can stand on his own."

Dammed If They Do

HOW DO YOU DESCRIBE a megadam to someone who has never seen electricity? Or a building more than one story high? The dam planned for Epupa Falls would rise 535 feet—only 15 feet shorter than the massive Grand Coulee Dam in Washington State. It would generate 360 megawatts of electricity per day and cost more than US$500 million to build.

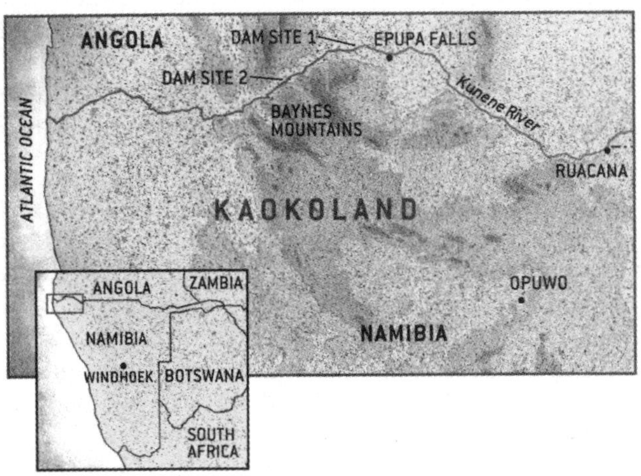

The Kunene River forms the northwest border between Angola and Namibia; the Himba live in the rocky, arid region known as Kaokoland.

A dam was first proposed near Epupa Falls in 1969, when Namibia was South West Africa, a territory of South Africa. The idea went nowhere, but it was revived in 1991, a year after Namibia's independence, when Namibia and Angola commissioned a feasibility study to evaluate such a scheme. The study considered two sites for the dam: Epupa Falls and a spot in the Baynes Mountains farther downstream. It concluded that Epupa Falls made more economic sense, but Angola has favored the Baynes site in part because building a dam there would mean that the country would also get funds to renovate a dam on an Angolan tributary that was damaged during the civil war. That cost is one reason the Baynes site would be more expensive.

When the study's consultants first came to discuss the intended dam with the Himba, the tribal leaders initially had no objections, thinking it was going to be a small earthen dam like the ones they built to help water their cattle. The degree of miscommunication took a while to become apparent. Margaret Jacobsohn of Integrated Rural Development and Nature Conservation, a Namibian journalist turned anthropologist who worked on the social impact part of the feasibility study, recalls a telling incident a few months into the process. She went to visit a Himba family compound near Epupa Falls and began asking their views about the proposed dam. Oddly, they didn't seem to know anything about it, even though the Namibian government had told her that they had been informed. As she finished her questionnaire, a family member asked her to help them with a mysterious piece of paper they had received some time before. When the man brought an ocher-smeared envelope out of his hut, she recognized it as a letter about the dam in English that they had never even opened. After she translated it for them, an old man of the family shook his head and said, "You're talking about the great death of the Himba."

Lifeways of the Himba

THE HIMBA ARE ONE of the last tribes of traditional people who are generally self-supporting and fully or partially isolated from global society. Anthropologists find them particularly interesting because they observe a system of bilateral descent. Every tribe member belongs to two clans, one through the father (a patriclan) and another through the mother (a matriclan). Tribes that practice bilateral descent are rare: besides the Himba, the custom occurs among only a few peoples in West Africa, India, Australia, Melanesia and Polynesia.

Each Himba patriclan is led by the oldest man in the family. Sons live with their fathers; following marriage, daughters leave to join their husband's family's household and become a member of that patrician. But the inheritance of material wealth—in the Himba's case, primarily cattle—is determined by the matriclan. Accordingly, a son does not inherit his father's cattle but his maternal uncle's instead.

Bilateral descent is particularly advantageous for tribes that live in precarious environments, such as the drought-prone region of the Himba, because during a crisis it allows an individual to rely on two sets of relatives spread over different areas. The system could also play a role in alleviating inbreeding among Himba livestock. Various patriclans have taboos prohibiting their members from owning cattle or goats of a certain color or coat pattern. When cattle are born that violate a patriclan's taboos, they must be swapped with nonoffending cattle from another patriclan.

The religion of the Himba is also organized according to bilateral descent and is practiced through an individual's patriclan. Himba believe in a god-creator, but that entity is very remote from human affairs and can be petitioned only by invoking dead paternal ancestors to act as intercessors. The tribe's religious observances center on holy fires that were initially kindled at the graves of ancestors and are maintained by the leader of each respective patriclan in his family compound.

The holy fire is small, often just a smoldering log surrounded by several rocks. It is always located between the opening of the headman's hut and the corral where the cattle are penned at night. That area of the compound is considered sacred: strangers cannot cross between the holy fire and the corral or between the holy fire and the headman's hut without first asking permission. Traditionally, the headman keeps the fire going during the day as he sits by it to commune with his ancestors about any problems facing the family. At night, the headman's wife takes an ember of the fire into the main hut; in the morning, the ember is taken outside to the hearth again.

The Himba are also intriguing to anthropologists as subjects of rapid social change. One way in which this change is manifesting itself is in patterns of dress. Many more Himba men than Himba women have adopted Western clothing and hairstyles. At Epupa Falls, where Himba occasionally have contact with outsiders, a Himba man can be seen one day bare-chested and wearing a Himba apron-skirt and jewelry, and the next day dressed in pants and a shirt. Few young men there wear the "bachelor ponytail" that is traditional for unmarried men, and even fewer married men follow the custom of not cutting their hair and of covering their heads with a cloth. And it is extremely rare to find a Himba man at Epupa Falls who wears ocher: indeed, many wash daily in the Kunene River using soap.

Himba women, however, are much more conservative in their dress. Even at Epupa Falls, most of the women go bare-breasted and wear traditional apron-skirts made of calfskins or goatskins; they smear themselves liberally from head to toe every morning with the ocher-butter mixture and almost never use water to wash. Young girls wear their hair in two thick braids that drape over their foreheads and faces, whereas women have a cascade of long, thin braids, each of which they coat with a mud mixture that dries to a hard shell.

The recent report by the World Commission on Dams declares that tribal peoples such as the Himba often get caught between a dam and a hard place.

According to anthropologists, Himba women are not merely clinging passively to their traditional dress: they are actively rejecting change because it is the only way they can maintain their prestige and value. Himba men occasionally earn money doing menial jobs or selling livestock, but Himba women have not had such opportunities. By preserving their ocher-covered bodies, braids and calfskin skirts, Himba women are engaged in what modern anthropological theory calls "change through continuity" or "active conservatism." "Remaining apparently traditional can be a strategic—and rational—response to modern events," Margaret Jacobsohn says.

The recent report by the World Commission on Dams declares that tribal peoples such as the Himba, whether they are actively conservative or not, often get caught between a dam and a hard place. Such projects have "inadequately addressed the special needs and vulnerabilities of indigenous and tribal peoples," the report concludes, adding that the effects of a dam on local peoples are "often not acknowledged or considered in the planning process." It calls for improving existing water and energy facilities rather than constructing new megadams and stipulates that sponsoring countries and international lenders base their decisions to build new dams on agreements with affected communities.

Namibia's minister of mines and energy says that his country currently imports 60 percent of its power from South Africa. "No one seems to see our need for independent power."

But in February the World Bank said it would use the commission's guidelines only as "reference points" rather than as binding procedures for financing large dam projects. A group of 150 nongovernmental organizations from 39 countries—including Namibia—countered in March with a letter to World Bank president James Wolfensohn to reconsider that stance and to place a moratorium on funding new dams until the bank implements the commission's guidelines. The organizations are requesting that the bank conduct independent reviews of planned and ongoing projects and set up procedures for providing reparations to people harmed by earlier dams. In the letter, they insinuate that the World Bank helped create the World Commission on Dams in 1998 with the World Conservation Union—IUCN only "to deflect opposition or to buy time." Unless the bank amends its position, they write, they "may be less inclined to engage in future... dialogues with the World Bank." According to the commission, the bank has provided an estimated $75 billion for 538 large dams in 92 countries.

So what is the case for a dam at Epupa Falls? Jesaya Nyamu, Namibia's minister of mines and energy, emphasizes that his country currently imports 60 percent of its power from South Africa and needs to pull the plug as a matter of national sovereignty. "No one seems to see our need for independent power," he laments.

Ensconced in the deep upholstery of a sofa in his cabinet minister's office in Windhoek, Namibia's capital, he labels the foreign environmental groups that oppose the dam as meddlers with a double standard: one for their own industrial countries and another for countries they consider untouched and exotic. "The whole of Europe and America is damned," Nyamu says. "These people live in their own countries on hydropower."

Indeed, according to a trade group of dam builders, the International Commission on Large Dams, the U.S. has the second-largest number of large dams (higher than 90 meters) in the world, after China. And the American experience with dams and indigenous peoples is less than laudatory: the Grand Coulee Dam inundated the lands of Native Americans from the Colville and Spokane tribes and ruined their salmon fishery. The tribes sued for reparations in 1951, but the government took 43 years to settle the lawsuit. In 1994 the tribes accepted a $54-million lump sum and $15 million per year as long as the dam produces electricity.

But Katuutire Kaura, president of Namibia's main opposition party, the Democratic Turnhalle Alliance/United Democratic Front Coalition, contends that another dam on the Kunene River is "absolutely not necessary." An existing dam that was built in the 1970s upstream at Ruacana is running at less than 20 percent capacity, he points out. And the recently discovered Kudu gas field off Namibia's southern coast is estimated to contain 20 trillion cubic feet of natural gas—more than enough for Namibia's needs. "The Kudu gas field can last us 25 to 30 years," Kaura asserts. Shell Oil and the Namibian government are currently working to tap those gas fields.

Kaura adds that the Himba will reap few of the dam's benefits while paying high costs. They are not qualified to work on the dam, so it will not bring them jobs. They are also unlikely to get electricity from the project. Electricity did not come to the residents of Opuwo, the town closest to the Ruacana Dam, until 1994, more than 20 years after it was built. In the meantime, a dam at Epupa Falls would destroy the Himba's livelihood. It "will dislocate the Himba to the margins of society where they cannot survive," predicts Phil Ya Nangoloh, executive director of Namibia's National Society for Human Rights.

In a way, the dam will take the river away from the Himba and confer its benefits to people outside Kaokoland. According to the World Commission on Dams report, "Dams take a set of resources… generating food and livelihood for local people and transform them into another set of resources… providing benefits to people living elsewhere. There is a sense, therefore, in which large dams export rivers and lands."

Toward a Struggle?

ONE MORNING when Tjiuma comes to our camp to share a cup of coffee, I ask him what he really thinks will happen if the government goes ahead with its plans for the proposed dam. I know he is no stranger to combat, having been drafted as a tracker to fight on South Africa's side during the war for independence. As we gaze over the Kunene River in the still of the early morning, he admits that the Himba have a plan for resistance. More than 50 of the Himba headmen were in the military during the war, he says, and they still have their old .303 rifles in their compounds.

A week later, when I visit the minister of mines and energy in Windhoek, I tentatively ask him what the Namibian government would do if the Himba resist with violence. His response is chilling: "We know them; they cannot do anything. If they try anything, we will neutralize them, of course. But I don't think it will come to that."

MORE TO EXPLORE

Himba: Nomads of Namibia. Margaret Jacobsohn, Peter Pickford and Beverly Pickford. Struik Publishers, Cape Town, 1990. Published in the U.S. by Appleton Communications, 1992.

Dams and Development: A New Framework for Decision-Making. World Commission on Dams, 2000. Available at **www.dams.org/report/**

For information on dam projects around the world, including the proposed Kunene River dam, visit the International Rivers Network site at **www.irn.org**

Carol Ezzell is a staff editor and writer.

Past and Present Land Use and Land Cover in the USA

WILLIAM B. MEYER

"Land of many uses," runs a motto used to describe the National Forests, and it describes the United States as a whole just as well. "Land of many covers" would be an equally apt, but distinct, description. *Land use* is the way in which, and the purposes for which, human beings employ the land and its resources: for example, farming, mining, or lumbering. *Land cover* describes the physical state of the land surface: as in cropland, mountains, or forests. The term land cover originally referred to the kind and state of vegetation (such as forest or grass cover), but it has broadened in subsequent usage to include human structures such as buildings or pavement and other aspects of the natural environment, such as soil type, biodiversity, and surface and groundwater. A vast array of physical characteristics—climate, physiography, soil, biota—and the varieties of past and present human utilization combine to make every parcel of land on the nation's surface unique in the cover it possesses and the opportunities for use that it offers. For most practical purposes, land units must be aggregated into quite broad categories, but the frequent use of such simplified classes should not be allowed to dull one's sense of the variation that is contained in any one of them.

Land cover is affected by natural events, including climate variation, flooding, vegetation succession, and fire, all of which can sometimes be affected in character and magnitude by human activities. Both globally and in the United States, though, land cover today is altered principally by direct human use: by agriculture and livestock raising, forest harvesting and management, and construction. There are also incidental impacts from other human activities such as forests damaged by acid rain from fossil fuel combustion and crops near cities damaged by tropospheric ozone resulting from automobile exhaust.

Changes in land cover by land use do not necessarily imply a degradation of the land. Indeed, it might be presumed that any change produced by human use is an improvement, until demonstrated otherwise, because someone has gone to the trouble of making it. And indeed, this has been the dominant attitude around the world through time. There are, of course, many reasons why it might be otherwise. Damage may be done with the best of intentions when the harm inflicted is too subtle to be perceived by the land user. It may also be done when losses produced by a change in land use spill over the boundaries of the parcel involved, while the gains accrue largely to the land user. Economists refer to harmful effects of this sort as *negative externalities*, to mean secondary or unexpected consequences that may reduce the net value of production of an activity and displace some of its costs upon other parties. Land use changes can be undertaken because they return a net profit to the land user, while the impacts of negative externalities such as air and water pollution, biodiversity loss, and increased flooding are borne by others. Conversely, activities that result in secondary benefits (or *positive externalities*) may not be undertaken by landowners if direct benefits to them would not reward the costs.

Over the years, concerns regarding land degradation have taken several overlapping (and occasionally conflicting) forms. *Conservationism* emphasized the need for careful and efficient management to guarantee a sustained supply of productive land resources for future generations. *Preservationism* has sought to protect scenery and ecosystems in a state as little human-altered as possible. Modern *environmentalism* subsumes many of these goals and adds new concerns that cover the varied secondary effects of land use both on land cover and on other related aspects of the global environment. By and large, American attitudes in the past century have shifted from a tendency to interpret human use as improving the condition of the land towards a tendency to see human impact as primarily destructive. The term "land reclamation" long denoted the conversion of land from its natural cover; today it is more often used to describe the restoration and repair of land damaged by human use. It would be easy, though, to exaggerate the shift in attitudes. In truth, calculating the balance of costs and benefits from many land use and land cover changes is enormously difficult. The full extent and consequences of proposed changes are often less than certain, as is their possible irreversibility and thus their lasting significance for future generations.

WHERE ARE WE?

The United States, exclusive of Alaska and Hawaii, assumed its present size and shape around the middle of the 19th century. Hawaii is relatively small, ecologically distinctive, and profoundly affected by a long and distinctive history of human use; Alaska is huge and little affected to date by direct land use. In this review assessment we therefore survey land use and land cover change, focusing on the past century and a half, only in the conterminous or lower 48 states. Those states cover an area of almost 1900 million acres, or about 3 million square miles.

The adjustments that are made in land use and land cover in coming years will in some way alter the life of nearly every living thing on Earth.

How land is *used*, and thus how *land cover* is altered, depends on who owns or controls the land and on the pressures and incentives shaping the behavior of the owner. Some 400 million acres in the conterminous 48 states—about 21% of the total—are federally owned. The two largest chunks are the 170 million acres of western rangeland controlled by the Bureau of Land Management and the approximately equal area of the National Forest System. Federal land represents 45% of the area of the twelve western states, but is not a large share of any other regional total. There are also significant land holdings by state governments throughout the country.

Most of the land in the United States is privately owned, but under federal, state, and local restrictions on its use that have increased over time. The difference between public and private land is important in explaining and forecasting land use and land coverage change, but the division is not absolute, and each sector is influenced by the other. Private land use is heavily influenced by public policies, not only by regulation of certain uses but through incentives that encourage others. Public lands are used for many private activities; grazing on federal rangelands and timber extraction from the national forests by private operators are the most important and have become the most controversial. The large government role in land use on both government and private land means that policy, as well as economic forces, must be considered in explaining and projecting changes in the land. Economic forces are of course significant determinants of policy—perhaps the most significant—but policy remains to some degree an independent variable.

There is no standard, universally accepted set of categories for classifying land by either use or cover, and the most commonly used, moreover, are hybrids of land cover and land use. Those employed here, which are by and large those of the U.S. National Resources Inventory conducted every five years by relevant federal agencies, are cropland, forest, grassland (pasture and rangeland), wetlands, and developed land.

- *Cropland* is land in farms that is devoted to crop production; it is not to be confused with total farmland, a broad land use or land ownership category that can incorporate many forms of land cover.
- *Forest land* is characterized by a predominance of tree cover and is further divided by the U.S. Census into timberland and non-timberland. By definition, the former must be capable of producing 20 cubic feet of industrial wood per acre per year and remain legally open to timber production.
- *Grassland* as a category of land cover embraces two contrasting Census categories of use: pasture (enclosed and what is called improved grassland, often closely tied to cropland and used for intensive livestock raising), and range (often unenclosed or unimproved grazing land with sparser grass cover and utilized for more extensive production).
- *Wetlands* are not a separate Census or National Resources Inventory category and are included within other categories: swamp, for example, is wetland forest. They are defined by federal agencies as lands covered all or part of the year with water, but not so deeply or permanently as to be classified as water surface *per se*.
- The U.S. government classifies as *developed* land urban and built-up parcels that exceed certain size thresholds. "Developed" or "urban" land is clearly a use rather than a cover category. Cities and suburbs as they are politically defined have rarely more than half of their area, and often much less, taken up by distinctively "urban" land cover such as buildings and pavement. Trees and grass cover substantial areas of the metropolitan United States; indeed, tree cover is greater in some settlements than in the rural areas surrounding them.

By the 1987 U.S. National Resources Inventory, nonfederal lands were divided by major land use and land cover classes as follows: cropland, about 420 million acres (22% of the entire area of the 48 states); rangeland, about 400 million (21%); forest, 390 million (21%); pasture, 130 million (7%); and developed land, 80 million (4%). Minor covers and uses, including surface water, make up an-

Land Use and Cover
in the Conterminous U.S.

Land Class	Area in Million Acres	Fraction of Total Area
Privately Owned (shown in diagram below)		
Cropland	422	22.4%
Rangeland	401	21.3
Forest	391	20.8
Pasture	129	6.9
Developed	77	4.1
Other Catagories[1]	60	3.2
Federally Owned[2]	404	21.4
TOTAL[3]	1884	100%

[1] Other minor covers and surface water
[2] Federal land is approximately half forest and half rangeland
[3] Included in various catagories is about 100 million acres of wetland, covering about 5% of the national area

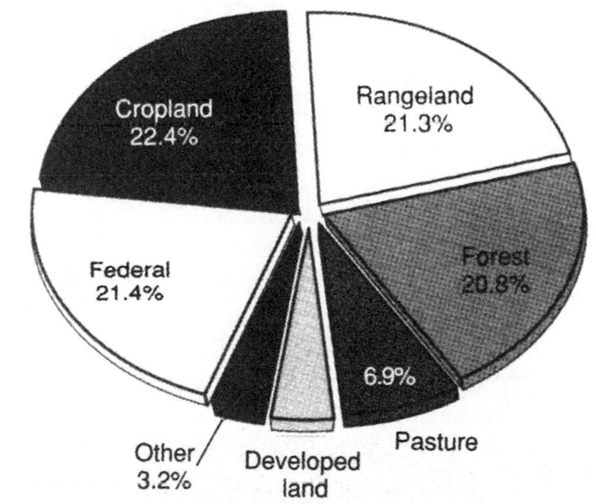

Table 1 Source: U.S. 1987 National Resources Inventory, published in 1989. U.S. Government Printing Office.

other 60 million acres (Table l). The 401 million acres of federal land are about half forest and half range. Wetlands, which fall within these other Census classes, represent approximately 100 million acres or about five percent of the national area; 95 percent of them are freshwater and five percent are coastal.

These figures, for even a single period, represent not a static but a dynamic total, with constant exchanges among uses. Changes in the area and the location of cropland, for example, are the result of the *addition* of new cropland from conversion of grassland, forest, and wetland and its *subtraction* either by abandonment of cropping and reversion to one of these less intensive use/cover forms or by conversion to developed land. The main causes of forest *loss* are clearing for agriculture, logging, and clearing for development; the main cause of forest *gain* is abandonment of cropland followed by either passive or active reforestation. Grassland is converted by the creation of pasture from forest, the interchange of pasture and cropland, and the conversion of rangeland to cropland, often through irrigation.

Change in wetland is predominantly loss through drainage for agriculture and construction. It also includes natural gain and loss, and the growing possibilities for wetland creation and restoration are implicit in the Environmental Protection Agency's "no *net* loss" policy (emphasis added). Change in developed land runs in only one direction: it expands and is not, to any significant extent, converted to any other category.

Comparison of the American figures with those for some other countries sets them in useful perspective. The United States has a greater relative share of forest and a smaller relative share of cropland than does Europe as a whole and the United Kingdom in particular.

Though Japan is comparable in population density and level of development to Western Europe, fully two-thirds of its area is classified as forest and woodland, as opposed to ten percent in the United Kingdom; it preserves its largely mountainous forest area by maintaining a vast surplus of timber imports over exports, largely from the Americas and Southeast Asia.

Regional patterns within the U.S. (using the four standard government regions of Northeast, Midwest, South, and West) display further variety. The Northeast, though the most densely populated region, is the most heavily wooded, with three-fifths of its area in forest cover. It is also the only region of the four in which "developed" land, by the Census definition, amounts to more than a minuscule share of the total; it covers about eight percent of the Northeast and more than a quarter of the state of New Jersey. Cropland, not surprisingly, is by far the dominant use/cover in the Midwest, accounting for just under half of its expanse. The South as a whole presents the most balanced mix of land types: about 40 percent forest, 20 percent each of cropland and rangeland, and a little more than ten percent pasture. Western land is predominantly rangeland, with forest following and cropland a distant third. Wetlands are concentrated along the Atlantic seaboard, in the Southeast, and in the upper Midwest. Within each region, of course, there is further variety at and below the state level.

WHERE HAVE WE BEEN?

The public domain, which in 1850 included almost two-thirds of the area of the present conterminous states, has gone through two overlapping phases of management goals. During the first, dominant in 1850 and long thereafter, the principal goal of management was to transfer public land into private hands, both to raise revenue and to encourage settlement and land improvements. The government often attached conditions (which were sometimes complied with) to fulfill other national goals, such as swamp drainage, timber planting, and railroad construction in support of economic development.

The second phase, that of federal retention and management of land, began with the creation of the world's first national park, Yellowstone, shortly after the Civil War. It did not begin to be a significant force, however, until the 1890s, when 40 million acres in the West were designated as federal forest reserves, the beginning of a system that subsequently expanded into other regions of the country as well. Several statutory vestiges of the first, disposal era remain (as in mining laws, for example), but the federal domain is unlikely to shrink noticeably in coming decades, in spite of repeated challenges to the government retention of public land and its regulation of private land. In recent years, such challenges have included the "Sagebrush Rebellion" in the rangelands of the West in the 1970s and 1980s calling for the withdrawal of federal control, and legal efforts to have many land use regulations classified as "takings," or as exercises of the power of eminent domain. This classification, where it is granted, requires the government to compensate owners for the value of development rights lost as a result of the regulation.

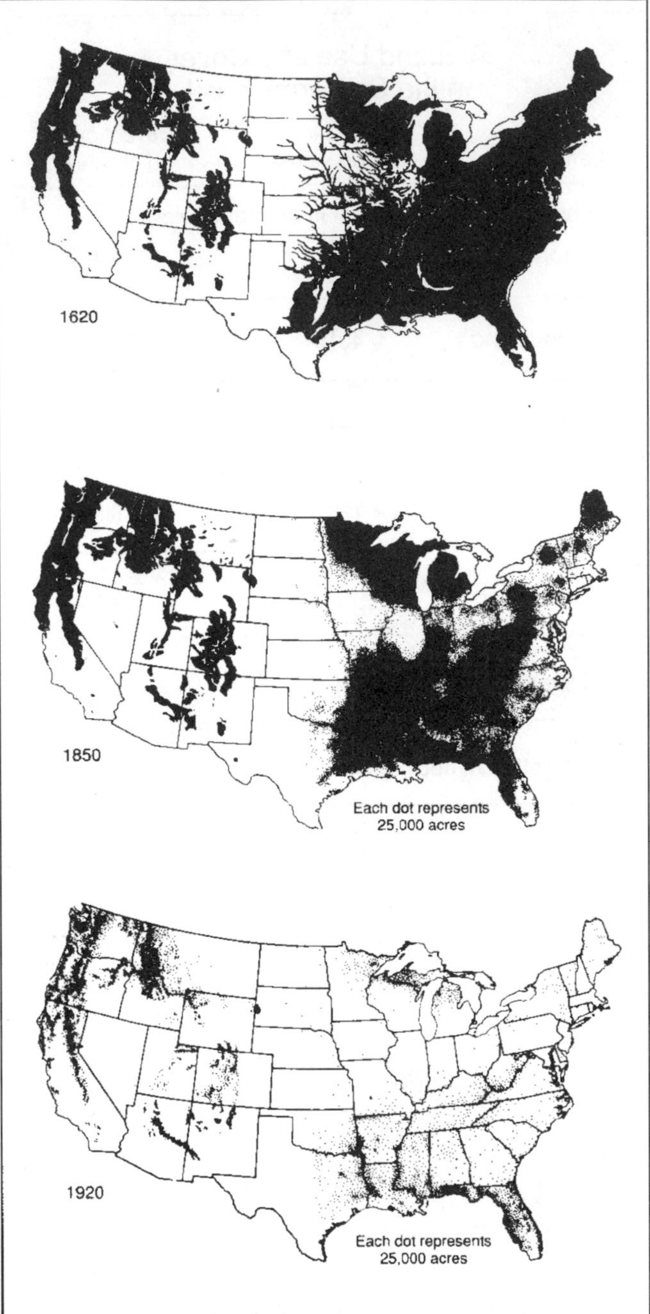

Figure 1 Area of vigin forest: top to bottom 1620, 1850, and 1920 as published by William B. Greeley, "The Relation of Geography to Timber Supply," Economic Geography, vol. 1, pp. 1-11 (1925). The depiction of U. S. forests in the later maps may be misleading in that they show only old-growth forest and not total tree cover.

Cropland

Total cropland rose steadily at the expense of other land covers throughout most of American history. It reached a peak during the 1940s and has subsequently fluctuated in the neighborhood of 400 million acres, though the precise figure depends on the definition of cropland used. Long-term regional patterns have displayed more variety. Cropland abandonment in some areas of New England began to be significant in some areas by the middle of the nineteenth century. Although total farmland peaked in the region as late as 1880 (at 50%) and did not decline sharply until the turn of the century, a steady decline in the subcategory of cropland and an increase in other farmland covers such as woodland and unimproved pasture was already strongly apparent. The Middle Atlantic followed a similar trajectory, as, more recently, has the South. Competition from other, more fertile sections of the country in agricultural production and within the East from other demands on land and labor have been factors; a long-term rise in agricultural productivity caused by technological advances has also exerted a steady downward pressure on total crop acreage even though population, income, and demand have all risen.

Irrigated cropland on a significant scale in the United States extends back only to the 1890s and the early activities in the West of the Bureau of Reclamation. Growing rapidly through about 1920, the amount of irrigated land remained relatively constant between the wars, but rose again rapidly after 1945 with institutional and technological developments such as the use of center-pivot irrigation drawing on the Ogallala Aquifer on the High Plains. It reached 25 million acres by 1950 and doubled to include about an eighth of all cropland by about 1980. Since then the amount of irrigated land has experienced a modest decline, in part through the decline of aquifers such as the Ogallala and through competition from cities for water in dry areas.

Forests

At the time of European settlement, forest covered about half of the present 48 states. The greater part lay in the eastern part of the country, and most of it had already been significantly altered by Native American land use practices that left a mosaic of different covers, including substantial areas of open land.

Forest area began a continuous decline with the onset of European settlement that would not be halted until the early twentieth century. Clearance for farmland and harvesting for fuel, timber, and other wood products represented the principal sources of pressure. From an estimated 900 million acres in 1850, the wooded area of the entire U.S. reached a low point of 600 million acres around 1920 (Fig. 1).

It then rose slowly through the postwar decades, largely through abandonment of cropland and regrowth on cutover areas, but around 1960 began again a modest decline, the result of settlement expansion and of higher rates of timber extraction through mechanization. The agricultural censuses recorded a drop of 17 million acres in U.S. forest cover between 1970 and 1987 (though data uncertainties and the small size of the changes relative to the total forest area make a precise dating of the reversals difficult). At the same time, if the U.S. forests have been shrinking in area they have been growing in density and volume. The trend in forest biomass has been consistently upward; timber stock measured in the agricultural censuses from 1952 to 1987 grew by about 30%.

National totals of forested area again represent the aggregation of varied regional experiences. Farm abandonment in much of the East has translated directly into forest recovery, beginning in the mid- to late-nineteenth century (Fig. 2). Historically, lumbering followed a regular pattern of harvesting one region's resources and moving on to the next; the once extensive old-growth forest of the Great Lakes, the South, and the Pacific Northwest represented successive and overlapping frontiers. After about 1930, frontier-type exploitation gave way to a greater emphasis on permanence and management of stands by timber companies. Wood itself has declined in importance as a natural resource, but forests have been increasingly valued and protected for a range of other services, including wildlife habitat, recreation, and streamflow regulation.

Grassland

The most significant changes in grassland have involved impacts of grazing on the western range. Though data for many periods are scanty or suspect, it is clear that rangelands have often been seriously overgrazed, with deleterious consequences including soil erosion and compaction, increased streamflow variability, and floral and faunal biodiversity loss as well as reduced value for production. The net value of grazing use on the western range is nationally small, though significant locally, and pressures for tighter management have increasingly been guided by ecological and preservationist as well as production concerns.

Wetland

According to the most recent estimates, 53% of American wetlands were lost between the 1780s and the 1980s, principally to drainage for agriculture. Most of the conversion presumably took place during the twentieth century; between the 1950s and the 1970s alone, about 11 million acres were lost. Unassisted private action was long thought to drain too little; since mid-century, it has become apparent that the opposite is true, that unfettered private action tends to drain too much, i.e., at the expense of now-valued wetland. The positive externalities once expected from drainage—improved public health and beautification of an unappealing natural landscape—carry less weight today than the negative ones that it produces. These include the decline of wildlife, greater extremes of streamflow, and loss of a natural landscape that is now seen as more attractive than a human-modified one. The rate of wetland loss has now been cut significantly by regulation and by the removal of incentives for drainage once offered by many government programs.

Developed land

As the American population has grown and become more urbanized, the land devoted to settlement has increased in at least the same degree. Like the rest of the developed world, the United States now has an overwhelmingly non-farm population residing in cities, suburbs, and towns and villages. Surrounding urban areas is a classical frontier of rapid and sometimes chaotic land use and land cover change. Urban impacts go beyond the mere subtraction of land from other land uses and land covers for settlement and infrastructure; they also involve the mining of building materials, the disposal of wastes, the creation of parks and water supply reservoirs, and the introduction of pollutants in air, water, and soil. Long-term data on urban use and cover trends are unfortunately not available. But the trend in American cities has undeniably been one of residential dispersal and lessened settlement densities as transportation technologies have improved; settlement has thus required higher amounts of land per person over time.

WHERE ARE WE GOING?

The most credible projections of changes in land use and land cover in the United States over the next fifty years have come from recent assessments produced under the federal laws that now mandate regular national inventories of resource stocks and prospects. The most recent inquiry into land resources, completed by the Department of Agriculture in 1989 (and cited at the end of this article), sought to project their likely extent and condition a half-century into the future, to the year 2040. The results indicated that only slow changes were expected nationally in the major categories of land use and land cover: a loss in forest area of some 5% (a slower rate of loss than was experienced in the same period before); a similarly modest decline in cropland; and an increase in rangeland of about 5% through 2040. Projections are not certainties, however: they may either incorrectly identify the consequences of the factors they consider or fail to consider important factors that could alter the picture. Because of the significant impacts of policy, its role—notoriously difficult to forecast and assess— demands increased attention, in both its deliberate and its inadvertent effects.

Trends in the United States stand in some contrast to those in other parts of the developed world. While America's forest area continues to decline somewhat, that of many comparable countries has increased in modest degree, while the developing world has seen significant clearance in the postwar era. There has been substantial stability, with slow but fluctuating decline, in cropland area in the United States. In contrast, cropland and pasture have declined modestly in the past several decades in Western Europe and are likely to decline sharply there in the future as longstanding national and European Community agricultural policies subsidizing production are revised; as a result, the European countryside faces the prospect of radical change in land use and cover and considerable dislocation of rural life.

WHY DOES IT MATTER?

Land use and land cover changes, besides affecting the current and future supply of land resources, are important sources of many other forms of environmental change. They are also linked to them through synergistic connections that can amplify their overall effect.

Loss of plant and animal biodiversity is principally traceable to land transformation, primarily through the fragmentation of natural habitat. Worldwide trends in land use and land cover change are an important source of the so-called greenhouse gases, whose accumulation in the atmosphere may bring about global climate change. As much as 35% of the increase in atmospheric CO_2 in the last 100 years can be attributed to land use change, principally through deforestation. The major known sources of increased methane—rice paddies, landfills, biomass burning, and cattle—are all related to land use. Much of the increase in nitrous oxide is now thought due to a collection of sources that also depend upon the use of the land, including biomass burning, livestock raising, fertilizer application and contaminated aquifers.

In most of the world, both fossil fuel combustion and land transformation result in a net release of carbon dioxide to the atmosphere.

Land use practices at the local and regional levels can dramatically affect soil condition as well as water quality and water supply. And finally, vulnerability or sensitivity to existing climate hazards and possible climate change is very much affected by changes in land use and cover. Several of these connections are illustrated below by examples.

Carbon emissions

In most of the world, both fossil fuel combustion and land transformation result in a net release of carbon dioxide to the atmosphere. In the United States, by contrast, present land use and land cover changes are thought to absorb rather than release CO_2 through such processes as the rapid growth of relatively youthful forests. In balance, however, these land-use-related changes reduce U.S. contributions from fossil fuel combustion by only about 10%. The use of carbon-absorbing tree plantations to help diminish global climate forcing has been widely discussed, although many studies have cast doubt on the feasibility of the scheme. Not only is it a temporary fix (the trees sequester carbon only until the wood is consumed, decays, or ceases to accumulate) and requires vast areas to make much of a difference, but strategies for using the land and its products to offset some of the costs of the project might have large and damaging economic impacts on other land use sectors of the economy.

Effects on arable land

The loss of cropland to development aroused considerable concern during the 1970s and early 1980s in connection with the 1981 National Agricultural Lands Study, which estimated high and sharply rising rates of conversion. Lower figures published in the 1982 National Resource Inventory, and a number of associated studies, have led most experts to regard the conversion of cropland to other land use categories as representing something short of a genuine crisis, likely moreover to continue at slower rather than accelerating rates into the future. The land taken from food and fiber production and converted to developed land has been readily made up for by conversion of land from grassland and forest.

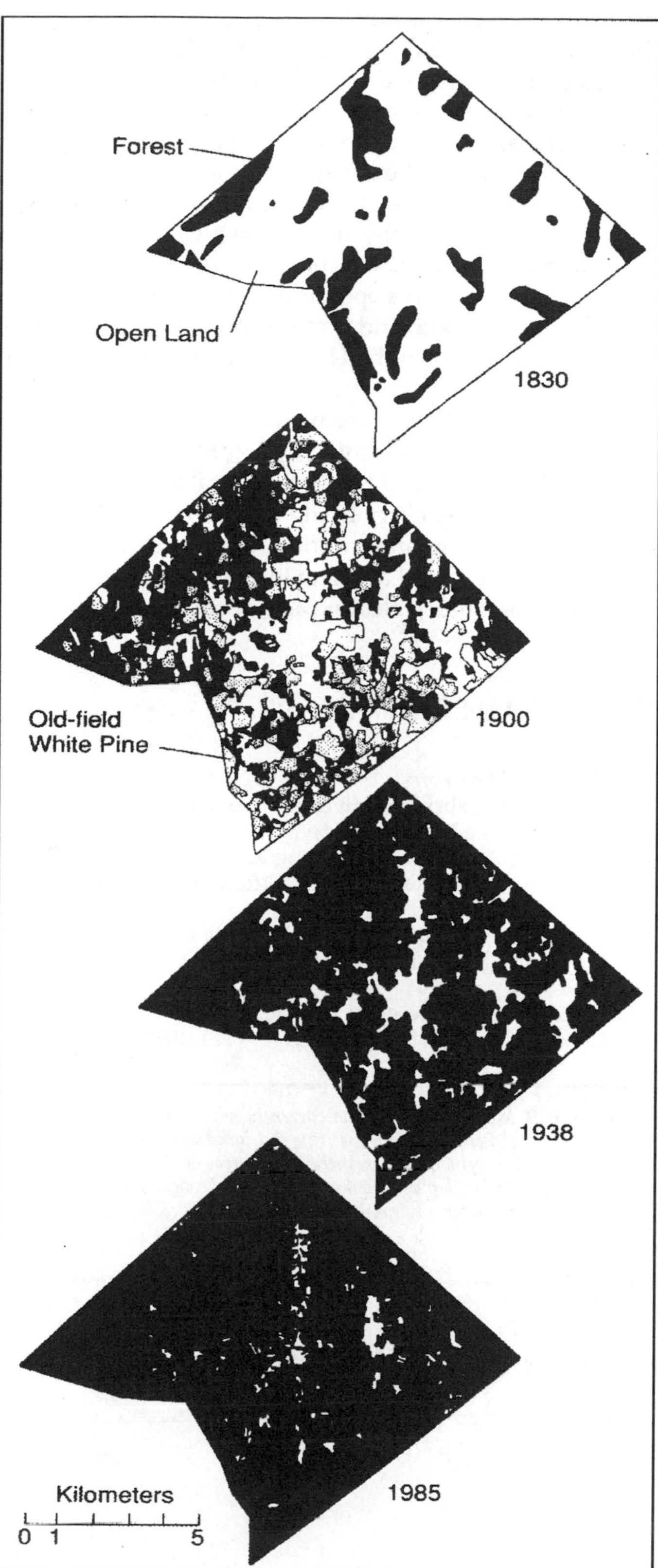

Figure 2 Modern spread of forest (shown in black) in the township of Petersham, Massachusetts, 1830 through 1985. White area is that considered suitable for agriculture; shaded portions in 1900 map indicate agricultural land abandoned between 1870 and 1900 that had developed forest of white pine in this period. From "Land-use History and Forest Transformations," by David R. Foster, in *Humans as Components of Ecosystems*, edited by M. J. McDonnell and S.T.A. Pickett, Springer-Verlag, New York, pp. 91-110, 1993.

The new lands are not necessarily of the same quality as those lost, however, and some measures for the protection of prime farmland are widely considered justified on grounds of economics as well as sociology and amenities preservation.

Vulnerability to climate change

Finally, patterns and trends in land use and land cover significantly affect the degree to which countries and regions are vulnerable to climate change—or to some degree, can profit from it. The sectors of the economy to which land use and land cover are most critical—agriculture, livestock, and forest products—are, along with fisheries, among those most sensitive to climate variation and change. How vulnerable countries and regions are to climate impacts is thus in part a function of the importance of these activities in their economies, although differences in ability to cope and adapt must also be taken into account.

Shifting patterns of land use in the U.S. and throughout the world are a proximate cause of many of today's environmental concerns.

These three climate-sensitive activities have steadily declined in importance in recent times in the U.S. economy. In the decade following the Civil War, agriculture still accounted for more than a third of the U.S. gross domestic product, or GDP. In 1929, the agriculture-forest-fisheries sector represented just under ten percent of national income. By 1950, it had fallen to seven percent of GDP, and it currently represents only about two percent. Wood in 1850 accounted for 90 percent of America's total energy consumption; today it represents but a few percent. These trends suggest a lessened macroeconomic vulnerability in the U.S. to climate change, though they may also represent a lessened ability to profit from it to the extent that change proves beneficial. They say nothing, however, about primary or secondary impacts of climate change on other sectors, about ecological, health, and amenity losses, or about vulnerability in absolute rather than relative terms, and particularly the potentially serious national and global consequences of a decline in U.S. food production.

The same trend of lessening vulnerability to climate changes is apparent even in regions projected to be the most exposed to the more harmful of them, such as reduced rainfall. A recent study examined agro-economic impacts on the Missouri-Iowa-Nebraska-Kansas area of the Great Plains, were the "Dust Bowl" drought and heat of the 1930s to recur today or under projected conditions of the year 2030. It found that although agricultural production would be substantially reduced, the consequences would not be severe for the regional economy overall: partly because of technological and institutional adaptation and partly because of the declining importance of the affected sectors, as noted above. The 1930s drought itself had less severe and dramatic effects on the population and economy of the Plains than did earlier droughts in the 1890s and 1910s because of land use, technological, and institutional changes that had taken place in the intervening period.

Shifting patterns in human settlement are another form of land use and land cover change that can alter a region's vulnerability to changing climate. As is the case in most other countries of the world, a disproportionate number of Americans live within a few miles of the sea. In the postwar period, the coastal states and counties have consistently grown faster than the country as a whole in population and in property development. The consequence is an increased exposure to hazards of hurricanes and other coastal storms, which are expected by some to increase in number and severity with global warming, and to the probable sea-level rise that would also accompany an increase in global surface temperature. It is unclear to what extent the increased exposure to such hazards might be balanced by improvements in the ability to cope, through better forecasts, better construction, and insurance and relief programs. Hurricane fatalities have tended to decline, but property losses per hurricane have steadily increased in the U.S., and the consensus of experts is that they will continue to do so for the foreseeable future.

CONCLUSIONS

How much need we be concerned about changes in land use and land cover in their own right? How much in the context of other anticipated environmental changes?

As noted above, shifting patterns of land use in the U.S. and throughout the world are a proximate cause of many of today's environmental concerns. How land is used is also among the human activities most likely to feel the effects of possible climate change. Thus if we are to understand and respond to the challenges of global environmental change we need to understand the dynamics of land transformation. Yet those dynamics are notoriously difficult to predict, shaped as they are by patterns of individual decisions and collective human behavior, by history and geography, and by tangled economic and political considerations. We should have a more exact science of how these forces operate and how to balance them for the greatest good, and a more detailed and coherent picture of how land in the U.S. and the rest of the world is used.

The adjustments that are made in land use and land cover in coming years, driven by worldwide changes in population, income, and technology, will in some way alter the life of nearly every living thing on Earth. We need to understand them and to do all that we can to ensure that policy decisions that affect the use of land are made in the light of a much clearer picture of their ultimate effects.

FOR FURTHER READING

Americans and Their Forests: A Historical Geography, by Michael Williams. Cambridge University Press, 599 pp, 1989.

An Analysis of the Land Situation in the United States: 1989–2040. USDA Forest Service General Technical Report RM-181. U.S. Government Printing Office, Washington, D.C., 1989.

Changes in Land Use and Land Cover: A Global Perspective. W. B. Meyer and B. L. Turner II, editors. Cambridge University Press, 537 pp, 1994.

"Forests in the Long Sweep of American History," by Marion Clawson. *Science,*vol. 204, pp 1168–1174, 1979.

***Dr. William B. Meyer** is a geographer currently employed on the research faculty of the George Perkins Marsh Institute at Clark University in Worcester, Massachusetts. His principal interests lie in the areas of global environmental change with particular emphasis on land use and land cover change, in land use conflict, and in American environmental history.*

INFRASTRUCTURE

Operation Desert Sprawl

The biggest issue in booming Las Vegas isn't growth. It's finding somebody to pay the staggering costs of growth.

BY WILLIAM FULTON AND PAUL SHIGLEY

On a late spring afternoon, the counters at the Las Vegas Development Services Center are only slightly less crowded than those at the nearby McDonald's. Here, in a nondescript office building some eight blocks from City Hall, a small army of planners occupies counters and cubicles, standing ready to process the daily avalanche of building projects. Several times a minute, people with blueprints tucked under their arms hurry in or out the door.

Upstairs, Tim Chow, the city's planning and development director, shakes his head and smiles. He says he has "the toughest planning job in the country," and he may be right. Two hundred new residents arrive in Las Vegas every day; a house is built every 15 minutes. Last year alone, the city issued 7,700 residential building permits, plus permits for $200 million worth of commercial construction—enough to build a good-sized Midwestern county seat from scratch.

Before he came to Nevada in April, Chow held a similar position in a smaller county in California. There, he points out, the planning process grinds slowly. State law—and local politics—require extensive environmental studies and public hearings before planners approve subdivisions and retail centers.

But this isn't California. It's Las Vegas, the nation's fastest-growing community, and the policy is to build first and ask questions later. "We just don't have time to do the kinds of rigorous analysis done in other places with regard to compatibility, impacts, infrastructure, coordination," Chow says. "Sometimes you make mistakes, and the impacts of those mistakes are felt many years later."

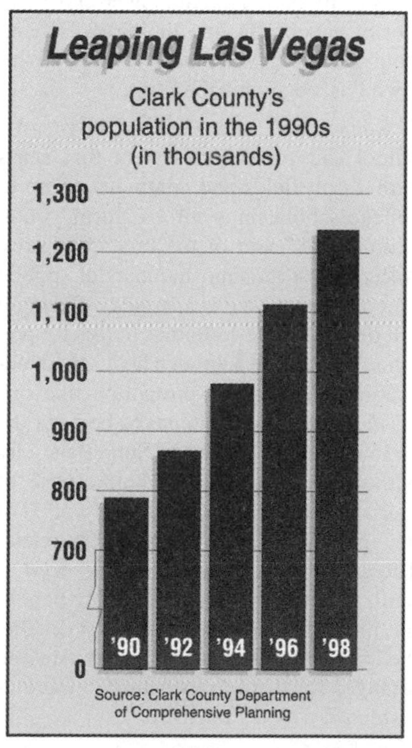

Tim Chow's planning counter isn't the only one in this area that looks like a fast-food restaurant. Fifteen miles to the southeast, his counterpart in Henderson, Mary Kay Peck, is presiding over the rapid creation of the second-largest city in Nevada. Henderson officials claim to have "the highest development standards in the Las Vegas Valley," but that hasn't stopped the city from growing seven-fold in the past two decades, to 170,000 people. The city recently annexed 2,500 acres to accommodate a new Del Webb project, and is lining up a federal land exchange that will allow the addition of 8,000 more acres near McCarran International Airport.

Henderson is in a running argument with well-established Reno over which city is second most populous in the state after Las Vegas. But that argument won't last much longer. "We have room," Peck says, "to grow and grow and grow." Henderson is expected to add another 100,000 people in the next decade—pushing it far past Reno. By 2010, Henderson will be as big as Las Vegas was in 1990.

The new residential subdivisions built all over the Las Vegas Valley in the past few years have created an enormous unsatisfied demand for parks, transportation, and water delivery systems. "Traffic is probably 100 times worse than it was 10 years ago," says Bobby Shelton, spokesman for the Clark County Public Works Department.

Local governments are trying to cope with the onslaught. A rail system connecting downtown, the casino-lined Strip and the airport is on the drawing board. Voters recently approved two tax increases—one for transportation projects, one for water projects—that together will produce some $100 million a year. But even with these projects moving forward Vegas-style—

ready, fire, aim—the problem is getting worse, not better. Even the local building industry acknowledges that growth has gotten far ahead of the infrastructure that is needed to support it.

"Someone back in the '70s and '80s should have said, 'Hey, we are going to need parks and schools and roads,' " says Joanne Jensen, of the Southern Nevada Home Builders, who moved to Las Vegas from Chicago in 1960. "We're playing catch-up." After two months in town, Planning Director Chow uses the same words to describe the situation.

Take the infrastructure needs faced by any fast-growing American community, multiply by a factor of about 20, and you get a rough idea of what is going on in Las Vegas. It is similar to other places in that it has come to realize that residential development does not pay for itself. The difference is in the magnitude of its problem. No other city of comparable size is taking on people at anything remotely close to the Las Vegas rate. No other city is being challenged to build so much so quickly.

The infrastructure will be built. That is not really the issue. Las Vegas and Henderson will continue to grow. The question is who will pay the bill.

As in other American cities, property owners have paid for community infrastructure during most of Las Vegas' history. But they have grown weary of the expense, and the one obvious way to grant them relief is to make developers cover more of the cost. Local homebuilders estimate that "impact fees"—fees paid by developers to cover the cost of community infrastructure—already account for a quarter of the cost of a new house in Las Vegas.

It was no surprise this year that a budding politician decided to make a name for himself by proposing that Las Vegas solve its growth problems by soaking its developers. The surprise was who that politician turned out to be, and how potent his message proved.

Nine months ago, Oscar Goodman was known around town as the classic Vegas mob lawyer—a veteran criminal defense attorney, given to wearing dark, double-breasted suits and a short-cropped silver beard. Today, on the strength of his soak-the-developer campaign rhetoric, Oscar Goodman is mayor of Las Vegas.

Ever since the mid 1980s, civic leaders here have worked hard to bury the Bugsy Siegel image—downplaying the gangster past, building suburban-style homes and office parks at a furious pace, and generally trying to re-position Vegas as an affordable, high-energy Sun Belt city attractive to everyone from retirees to young families. A few years ago, the *New York Times Magazine* heralded this new era in Las Vegas by reporting the city's transformation "from vice to nice."

It's true that the gambling industry remains the local economy's bedrock foundation. Las Vegas boasts 110,000 hotel rooms—one for every 11 residents of the region—and attracts 30 million visitors a year. But a fresh-scrubbed image was necessary to catapult Vegas past its sleazy resort-town reputation and support a new wave of mainstream urban growth. And so even as it tried to remain affordable, Las Vegas began to go upscale as well.

Perhaps the most highly publicized success story is Summerlin, the Howard Hughes Corp.'s 35-square-mile development on the valley's west side. On a tract of land that was nothing but empty desert when Hughes bought it, 35,000 people now live in the earth-tone houses and apartments lining cul-de-sacs. The company predicts the population could reach 180,000 by buildout. And lower-end Summerlin knock-offs line the roads leading from the big development toward downtown Las Vegas and the Strip.

Summerlin's sales literature boasts of a school and recreation system that starts with T-ball fields and continues on up to college scholarships for the local youth. "Summerlin," one of the brochures says, "offers a surprising number of public schools and private academies, offering a full range of close-to-home choices for preschool/kindergarten through high school education." It is clever promotion like this that has enabled Las Vegas to become the nation's fastest-growing Sun Belt city without sacrificing its economic base of tourism and gambling. But the cost of all of that growth has been high nevertheless. There was no way to finesse the need to build public infrastructure at an exponential rate. And for most of the past decade, the local governments swallowed hard and arranged for that infrastructure in the old-fashioned way: by raising taxes.

Three years ago, for example, traffic congestion had become so bad that it was decided to speed up completion of the 53-mile Las Vegas Beltway—by 17 years—so it could open in 2003. In Henderson, giant belly scrapers building the road rumble back and forth just beyond the walled-in backyards of brand-new houses.

Amazingly, the $1.5 billion beltway is being finished without federal funds. A 1 percent motor vehicle privilege tax and a "new home fee" of about $500 per house are generating $50 million a year, which goes toward bonds issued to raise capital for the construction.

Seven years ago, Las Vegas had no bus system at all. Today, the Citizen Area Transit system carries 128,000 passengers a day—the same volume as the busiest part of the beltway. Passengers pay 50 percent of the system's costs at the farebox—a higher percentage than in almost any other American city. The Regional Transportation System hopes to begin construction of a 5.2-mile rail line around downtown in 2001—mostly with federal funds and sales-tax revenues—and tie it to a privately funded monorail along the Strip.

Meanwhile, the Southern Nevada Water Authority, which serves as a wholesaler to cities and water districts in the Las Vegas area, is building a $2 billion water delivery project. The project involves a "second straw" from Lake Mead, which Hoover Dam creates about 30 miles southeast of Las Vegas, and 87 miles of large water mains in the Las Vegas Valley. The water agency's goal is to provide enough water for an additional 2 million people.

There is one catch so far as water supply is concerned: Las Vegas still lacks the legal right to draw additional water from Lake Mead. Changing this arrangement will require a massive political deal to overturn the 75-year-old agreement among seven Western states along the Colorado River. But that didn't stop Clark County voters from approving a quarter-cent sales-tax increase last year—expected to generate close to $50 million a year—to pay for the new straw and the other improvements.

So it can't be said that Las Vegas area residents have been unwilling to open their wallets and spend money for growth—they have spent heavily for it. But they realize all too well how much of the bill remains to be paid. This is the issue that is driving Las Vegas politics, and producing its unexpected results.

Even before this year's mayoral campaign, critics of the growth machine began speaking more loudly in the Las Vegas Valley, and their demand that developers pay impact fees had begun to resonate with the voters.

The ringleaders of this new movement have been Jan Laverty Jones, who was Goodman's predecessor as mayor, and

Dina Titus, a political science professor at the University of Nevada–Las Vegas, who is Democratic leader in the Nevada Senate. Because Las Vegas has a city manager form of government, the mayor's job was never viewed as important. But Jones, a former Vegas businesswoman who used to appear as Little Bo Peep in television car ads, adopted a high profile—especially on growth issues—at exactly the moment when growth was creating massive frustration.

Jones pushed to require developers to bear more of the cost of parks, roads and other community improvements. Meanwhile, Titus took an aggressive approach in the legislature. In 1997, she floated a "Ring Around the Valley" urban growth boundary concept. That bill failed, but last year she managed to push through a bill requiring local governments to conduct an impact analysis for large commercial and residential projects. Although the bill doesn't require mitigation of impacts, Titus hopes it will encourage local officials in the Las Vegas area to impose mitigation requirements more often and more rationally. "Right now, it's very capricious," she says. "Somebody has to put in street lights, another developer doesn't have to put in anything. It all depends on the political situation at hand."

Into this combustible situation stepped two mayoral candidates with exactly the wrong credentials to deal with it. Arnie Adamsen, a three-term city council member, was a title company executive; Mark Fine was one of the creators of Summerlin. Their ties to the real estate industry could not have been more conspicuous. Both Fine and Adamsen acknowledged that growth was a problem, but refused to recommend that developers pay more of its cost. That opened the door for Oscar Goodman, an unlikely political leader even in a town as unusual as Las Vegas.

At age 59, Goodman had lived in Las Vegas far longer than most of the voters—more than 30 years. A native of Philadelphia, he once clerked for Arlen Specter, then a prosecutor, now a U.S. senator. In the early '60s, however, Goodman headed for Las Vegas, looking for a place where he could make a reputation on his own.

Before long, he gained a reputation as a colorful—and effective—defender of accused mobsters. He once persuaded a judge to drop mob financier Meyer Lansky as a defendant in a case, apparently because of Lansky's failing health. In his most celebrated victory, he kept Tony "The Ant" Spilotro out of jail in the face of multiple murder and racketeering charges. Spilotro became the model for the character played by Joe Pesci in the movie "Casino"; Goodman played himself in the same movie.

Of course, Goodman always insisted that he had a wide-ranging criminal law practice, and only 5 percent of his clients were alleged mobsters. Furthermore, Goodman and his wife were regarded around town as good citizens who often contributed to, or even spearheaded, civic causes. Even so, when Goodman first announced his candidacy for mayor, it was surprising that he even wanted the job.

It wasn't ties to organized crime that concerned voters in the Las Vegas mayor's race; it was ties to real estate.

Given the structure of Las Vegas' government, most mayors have been part-timers who served as glorified presiding officers for the city council. On the other hand, the most recent occupant of the seat had shown that it could be more than a ceremonial position. "Jones made it a more important job," says Eugene Moehring, author of *Resort City in the Sunbelt*, a history of Las Vegas. "She showed that you could use it as a platform. I think Oscar saw that and decided to go for it."

Goodman announced that, if elected mayor, he would give up his law practice. Even so, he wasn't taken seriously at first by the Las Vegas political establishment. Then he started talking about sprawl, real estate developers and impact fees. "Growth has to pay for growth," Goodman said in his radio and television commercials, using his fast-talking West Philadelphia accent to get his message across. "Either it has to come from taxpayers or developers.... It's time to make developers pay impact fees when they build new homes."

Goodman argued that even a modest impact fee would bring in more than $15 million a year to help pay for sprawl costs and revitalize Las Vegas' downtown. He recommended a fee of roughly $2,000 for each new home, and said he would use it to revitalize neglected downtown neighborhoods. Such a scheme would require a change in state law—and a big fight with the real estate lobby—but Goodman promised to take on both the legislature and the builders. Polls showed that 80 percent of Las Vegans supported higher development fees.

Goodman was widely perceived in Las Vegas as a "Jesse Ventura candidate"—a celebrity from another field with a populist message and enough personal wealth to assure that he would not be bought by special interests. His opponents essentially played into Goodman's hands. Adamsen, his opponent in the June runoff, insisted that the fees would merely be passed on to homebuyers. "Development fees are very popular with the public because they want someone else to pay for it," he said. Adamsen focused on Goodman's criminal connections, saying they would harm the city's new, family-oriented image. If anybody in town knew about extracting money from a community through nefarious means, he charged, it was Goodman, not the developers.

In the end, though, Goodman's contacts with organized crime were a non-issue. In the Las Vegas of 1999, impact fees are a bigger issue than crime, organized or otherwise. What mattered to most voters was that the candidate didn't have any close ties to the real estate business. Goodman won 64 percent of the vote in his runoff with Adamsen. The Jesse Ventura approach worked so well that even many leading members of the Las Vegas political establishment embraced Goodman during the runoff.

On the last Monday in June, Oscar Goodman took the oath of office before an overflow crowd in the Las Vegas City Council chambers, then stepped outside for his first press conference as mayor. At 10:30 in the morning, it was 95 degrees, with a hot, dry desert wind blowing across the City Hall courtyard. Wearing a trademark double-breasted suit, Goodman was unfazed by what was, for Las Vegas, a typical June morning.

And he also seemed unfazed by his quick introduction to the real world of municipal politics in America's most transient city. In the three short weeks between the election and the inauguration, one of Goodman's campaign aides was accused of attempting to charge $150,000 to arrange an appointment to the City Council. The new mayor was faced with the question of what to do about renewing the contract of the city's waste hauler, who had contributed heavily to his campaign. And, of course, during the Goodman interregnum, 4,000 new residents had arrived in Las Vegas.

Goodman insists he will take his plan for a $2,000-a-house impact fee to the legislature. But the next regular session does not begin until January of 2001, and even with 18 months to build support, his task will not be easy. Current state law prevents any such scheme from being implemented—as it does many other development fees—and the real estate lobby has vowed to oppose it.

Meanwhile, says Goodman with his typical glib charm, "I've sat down with the developers, and I've told them we're going to run an efficient City Hall operation that will meet their day-to-day needs. Those guys are going to *want* impact fees to pay us back for all the good things we're going to do for them in the next two years."

Even Goodman sympathizers agree that Goodman—like that other populist, Jesse Ventura—faces a difficult challenge in learning how to govern on the job. "Growth is a tough issue, and he's going to have to hit the ground running on it," says former Mayor Jan Jones. "It's going to be a big learning curve." In particular, Goodman will have to cultivate regional agencies and suburban governments in Las Vegas—with which Jones often clashed—in order to curb growth on the metropolitan fringe and encourage renewal of older areas in Las Vegas itself.

Increasingly, however, there is agreement among both politicians and developers that the future of Las Vegas—like the future of most American communities—involves developers paying for the impact of growth somehow: There simply is no other way to finance the infrastructure costs. Whatever Goodman does, the Southern Nevada Water Authority is planning to levy a hookup fee of several thousand dollars a unit to help pay for the second straw from Lake Mead. That will only increase the average home price in the metro area, which is already up to $142,000.

Oscar Goodman may or may not succeed as mayor, but it's clear that the political sentiment that he tapped into is here to stay. In wide-open Las Vegas—as in so many of the more conventional cities across the country—the crucial votes no longer lie with the upwardly mobile families desperate for a place to live. They lie with the established middle-class residents who are tired of paying the bill.

A MODEST PROPOSAL TO STOP GLOBAL WARMING

While evidence continues to mount that humans are heating the globe, the world's nations squabble over a complex fix too timid to solve the problem. But we *can* stop global warming—by calling an end to the Carbon Age.

by Ross Gelbspan

The United States is constantly warning against the danger posed by "rogue states" like Iraq or North Korea. But last November we behaved very much like an outlaw nation ourselves by unilaterally scuttling climate talks at The Hague, Netherlands. More than half of the world's industrial nations declared their willingness to cut their consumption of fossil fuels to forestall global warming, but when the United States would commit to nothing more than planting a few trees and buying up cheap pollution allowances from poor countries, the talks collapsed.

The meeting was probably irrelevant anyway. As the three years of frustrating negotiations fell apart, the United Nations–sponsored Intergovernmental Panel on Climate Change (IPCC), which had previously projected an increase in average global temperatures of 3 to 7 degrees Fahrenheit this century, raised its upper estimate to 10.4 degrees. To restabilize the climate, declared the 2,000 eminent climatologists and other scientists, humanity needs to cut its greenhouse-gas emissions ten times more than the 5.2 percent reductions discussed at The Hague.

As heat records continue to be broken and extreme weather events intensify around the world, the reality of global warming is sinking in—everywhere, it seems, except on Capitol Hill. At the 1998 World Economic Forum in Davos, Switzerland, the CEOs of the world's 1,000 biggest corporations surprised organizers by voting climate change the most critical problem facing humanity. European countries are planning drastic reductions in their CO_2 emissions, while growing numbers of corporate leaders are realizing that the necessary transition to highly efficient and renewable energy sources could trigger an unprecedented worldwide economic boom.

This growing international consensus may show us the way to a workable global solution. Instead of The Hague's torturous haggling over the complex minutiae of virtually meaningless goals, the earth's nations could jointly initiate an aggressive worldwide effort to halt and turn back the ominous heating of the globe—and come out stronger, safer, and richer.

The alternative is dismal and frightening. A recent report from the National Climatic Data Center predicts ever harsher droughts, floods, heat waves, and tropical storms as the atmosphere continues to warm. "We found that extreme weather events have had increasing impact on human health, welfare, and finances," said the Center's David Easterling. "This trend is likely to become more intense as the climate continues to change and society becomes more vulnerable to weather and climate extremes."

This vulnerability is underscored by a financial forecast from the world's sixth-largest insurance company. Previous reports from property insurers had emphasized the financial risks to the industry itself, but last November Dr. Andrew Dlugolecki, an executive of the United Kingdom's CGNU, released a study projecting that infrastructure and other property damage, bank and insurance industry losses, crop failures, and other costs of unchecked climate change could bankrupt the global economy by 2065.

And the coming changes will occur 50 percent faster than previously thought, say researchers at the Hadley Center, the UK's leading climate-research agency. Previous estimates of the rate of climate change have been based on projections of the earth's capacity—at current temperatures—to absorb carbon dioxide through its vegetation and, to a lesser extent, its oceans. For the last 10,000 years, these natural "carbon sinks" have maintained atmospheric carbon levels of about 280 parts per million. Since the late 19th century, however, human use of coal and oil has escalated dramatically, leading to our present atmospheric carbon level of about 360 parts per million—a level not experienced in 420,000 years. In a blow to the United States' hope that planting forests in developing countries could absolve it of the need to conserve energy, Hadley's researchers found that photosynthesis slows as the climate warms. Plants' absorption of CO_2 diminishes, and soils begin to release more carbon than they absorb, turning what had been carbon sinks into carbon sources.

Life in a Warmer World

by Paul Rauber

Unless we take drastic action—and soon—global warming threatens to plunge the world into a series of climatic crises. The following are some of the impacts foreseen by the Intergovernmental Panel on Climate Change, from a report published in February:

- Average temperatures will increase by 10.4°F over the next 100 years.
- Heavier flooding, especially in coastal cities, will affect 200 million people.
- Deserts will expand, particularly in Asia and Africa. Crop yields will decline, and droughts will grow more severe.
- The Gulf Stream may slow down, which would result in a dramatically colder northern Europe.
- The Greenland or West Antarctic ice sheets will shrink significantly, raising sea level by almost 3 feet this century and causing the inundation of low-lying islands like Samoa, the Maldives, Mauritius, and the Marshalls. Over the course of the millennium, sea level could rise by 20 feet.
- Endangered species will disappear as habitat dwindles. Coastal ecosystems will flood, freshwater fish will be unable to migrate to cooler regions, and animals already adapted to cold may be left with nowhere to go.
- Incidence of heat-related deaths and infectious diseases like malaria and dengue fever will increase, spreading beyond what are now the tropics.

Similarly, a team led by Sydney Levitus, head of the National Oceanic and Atmospheric Administration's Ocean Climate Laboratory, found that while oceans absorb heat, that effect can be temporary. During the 1950s and '60s, the group found, subsurface temperatures in the Atlantic, Pacific, and Indian Oceans rose substantially while atmospheric temperatures remained fairly constant. But in the 1970s atmospheric temperatures trended upward—driven, in part, by warmth released from deep water. "[O]cean heat content may be an early indicator of the warming of surface, air, and sea surface temperatures more than a decade in advance," said Levitus. Later this century, his researchers predicted, the oceans may release even more heat into an already warming atmosphere.

That grim prediction was echoed by a report from the International Geosphere-Biosphere Programme, which cast doubt on the ability of farmland or forests to soak up the vast amounts of CO_2 that humanity is pumping into the atmosphere. "There is no natural 'savior' waiting to assimilate all the anthropogenically produced CO_2 in the coming century," the report concluded.

The inadequacy of the percentage goals haggled over at The Hague was underscored by a research team led by Tom M. W. Wigley of the National Center for Atmospheric Research, which estimated that the world must generate about half its power from wind, sun, and other noncarbon sources by the year 2018 to avoid a quadrupling of traditional atmospheric carbon levels, which would almost certainly trigger catastrophic consequences. Writing in the journal *Nature*, Wigley's team recommended "researching, developing, and commercializing carbon-free primary power technologies ... with the urgency of the Manhattan Project or the Apollo space program."

Far from recognizing that urgency, the United States' official position seems to be to minimize the severity of global warming. This recalcitrance can be traced to a relentless disinformation campaign by the fossil-fuel lobby to dismiss or downplay the climate crisis. For years, coal and oil interests have funded a handful of scientists known as "greenhouse skeptics" who cast doubt on the implications and even existence of global warming. Enormous amounts of money spent by their corporate sponsors have amplified the skeptics' voices out of all proportion to their standing in the scientific community, giving them undue influence on legislators, policymakers, and the media.

But with the skeptics being marginalized by the increasingly united and alarming findings of mainstream science, industry PR campaigns have taken to exaggerating the economic impacts of cutting back on fossil fuels. On the other side are more than 2,500 economists, including 8 Nobel laureates, who proclaimed in a 1997 statement coordinated by the think-tank Redefining Progress that the U.S. economy can weather the change, and even improve productivity in the long run. Industry is also attacking the diplomatic foundations of the Kyoto Protocol—the international agreement The Hague meeting was meant to implement—claiming that the United States would suffer unfairly because developing countries were exempted from the first round of emissions cuts. Yet the rationale for this exemption—that since the industrial nations created the problem, they should be the first to begin to address it—was ratified by President George H. W. Bush himself when he signed the 1992 Rio Treaty.

The average American is responsible for about 25 times more CO_2 than the average Indian.

The central mechanism of the Kyoto Protocol, as promoted by the United States, is "emissions trading." That system was intended to find the cheapest way to reduce global carbon levels. It allocated a certain number of carbon-emission "credits" to each country, and then permitted nations with greater emissions to buy unused credits from other countries—for example, by financing the planting of trees in Costa Rica.

But international carbon trading turned out to be a shell game. Carbon is burned in far too many places—vehicles, factories, homes, fields—to effectively track even if there were an international monitoring system. Trading also became a huge source of contention between industrial and developing countries. In allocating emission "rights," for instance, all countries were given their 1990 emission levels as a baseline, but the developing nations argue that this would lock in the advantages of the already-industrialized First World. Many developing countries advocate what they claim is a far more democratic, "per capita" basis for allocating emissions, which would grant every American the same quantity of emissions as, say, every resident of India. (Currently, the average American is responsible for about 25 times more CO_2 than the average Indian.)

A second level of inequity embedded in emissions trading is that industrialized countries could buy as many credits from poor countries as they want, banking those big, relatively cheap reductions indefinitely into the future. So when developing countries are eventually obliged to cut their emissions, they will be left with only the most expensive options, such as financing the production of fuel cells or solar installations.

Finally, carbon trading in itself can only go so far; its optimal use would be as a fine-tuning mechanism to help countries achieve the last 10 to 15 percent of their obligations. Measured against what it would take to actually cool the planet, emissions trading is ultimately a form of institutional denial.

Despite U.S. obstructionism, several European countries are now setting more ambitious goals. The United Kingdom last year committed to reductions of 12.5 percent by 2010, and a royal commission is calling for 60 percent cuts by 2050. Germany is also considering 50 percent cuts. Holland—a country at particular risk from rising sea levels—just completed a plan to slash its emissions by 80 percent in the next 40 years. It will meet those goals through an ambitious program of wind-generated electricity, low-emission vehicles, photovoltaic and solar installations, and other noncarbon energy sources. And a number of developing countries are voluntarily installing solar, wind, and small-scale hydro projects, despite their exemption under the Kyoto Protocol from the first round of cuts.

Some major industrial players are also reading the handwriting on the wall. British Petroleum, despite its attempts to drill in the Arctic National Wildlife Refuge, is investing substantial resources in solar power. The company, which now promotes itself as "Beyond Petroleum," anticipates doing $1 billion a year in solar commerce by the end of the decade. Shell has created a $500 million renewable-energy company. In fact, most of the major oil companies—with the notable exception of ExxonMobil—now acknowledge the reality of climate change. In the automotive arena, Ford and DaimlerChrysler have invested $1 billion in a joint venture to put fuel-cell-powered cars on the market in 2004. And William Clay Ford recently declared "an end to the 100-year reign of the internal combustion engine."

While some environmentalists dismiss these initiatives as "greenwashing," they mark an enormous change in industry's public posture. Only a year or two ago, working through such groups as the Western Fuels Association and the Global Climate Coalition, the oil and coal companies sought to dismiss the reality of climate change and cast doubt on the findings of the IPCC. Today, with these arguments largely discredited, the Global Climate Coalition has essentially collapsed. Oil and auto executives are beginning to choose a new approach: to position their firms as prominent players in the coming new-energy economy. (This doesn't preclude backsliding. In March, conservatives' complaints persuaded Bush to break a campaign promise to regulate CO_2 emissions from power plants—thus hanging out to dry EPA chief Christie Todd Whitman, who had widely promoted the idea, and Treasury Secretary Paul O'Neill, who has called for a crash program to deal with climate change.)

U.S. labor unions are also facing up to the future, working with environmentalists on an agenda to increase jobs while reducing emissions—witness the recent call by AFL-CIO president John Sweeney and Sierra Club executive director Carl Pope for a "package of worker-friendly domestic carbon-emission reduction measures." Building and maintaining the necessary new energy facilities will take an army of skilled workers, which organized labor can provide.

How to End—and Reverse—Global Warming

Turning down the earth's thermostat will take a 70 percent reduction in our current global level of carbon emissions. That's a big job—but not impossible. Here's one blueprint to get there:

- Redirect the $300 billion the world currently spends on subsidies for fossil fuels to renewable power: solar systems, wind farms, geothermal, and fuel cells.
- Require every country, whether developed or not, to commit to specific reductions in carbon emissions every year—say, 5 percent—until the goal of 70 percent is met.
- Fund renewable-energy projects in the developing world through a tax on international currency speculation. Such a tax could raise $300 billion a year to help other nations avoid the industrial world's mistakes. Combined with the progressive reduction schedule above, it would provide a monetary incentive for innovation and introduction of renewable technologies.

This isn't the only possible formula, but any approach to reversing the warming of the earth's atmosphere must be at least as ambitious. The transformation will be dramatic, but not necessarily painful—unless we delay too long. —*P.R.*

Despite these encouraging developments, the United States continues to obstruct rather than lead the world in addressing climate change. Former president Clinton blamed the media, saying that until the public knows more about the threat there will not be sufficient popular support to address the issue in a meaningful way. George W. Bush and Dick Cheney, oilmen both, are more inclined to protect the petroleum industry's short-term profitability than to promote its inevitable transformation.

Thus, the public debate is still stuck in the ineffective Kyoto framework. So two years ago, a small group of energy executives, economists, energy-policy specialists, and others (including the author) fashioned a bundle of strategies designed to cut carbon emissions by 70 percent, while at the same time creating a surge of new jobs, especially in developing countries.

At present, the United States spends $20 billion a year to subsidize fossil fuels and another $10 billion to subsidize nuclear power. Globally, subsidies for fossil fuels have been estimated at $300 billion a year. If that money were put behind renewable technologies, oil companies would have the incentive to aggressively develop fuel cells, wind farms, and solar systems. (A portion of those subsidies should be used to retrain coal miners and to construct clean-energy manufacturing plants in poor mining regions.)

The strategy also calls on all nations to replace emissions trading with an equitable fossil-fuel efficiency standard. Every country would commit to improving its energy efficiency by a specified amount—say 5 percent—every year until the global 70 percent reduction is attained. By drawing progressively more energy from noncarbon sources, countries would create the mass markets for renewables that would bring down their prices and make them competitive with coal and oil. This approach would be easy to negotiate and easy to monitor: A nation's progress could be measured simply by calculating the annual change in the ratio of its carbon fuel use to its gross domestic product.

A global energy transition will cost a great deal of money (although not nearly as much as ignoring the problem). Until clean-energy infrastructures take root, providing clean energy to poor countries would cost several hundred billion dollars a year, say researchers at the Tellus Institute, an energy-policy think tank in Boston. A prime source for that funding would be a "Tobin tax" on international currency transactions, named after its developer, Nobel prize-winning economist Dr. James Tobin. Every day, speculators trade $1.5 trillion in the world's currency; a tax of a quarter-penny on the dollar would net about $300 billion a year for projects like wind farms in India, fuel-cell factories in South Africa, solar assemblies in El Salvador, and vast, solar-powered hydrogen farms in the Middle East. Unlike a North-South giveaway, the fund is a transfer of resources from the finance sector—in the form of speculative transactions—to the industrial sector-in the form of productive, wealth-generating investments. Banks would be paid a small percentage fee to administer the fund, partly offsetting their loss of income from the contraction of currency trading. Creation of a fund of this magnitude would follow the kind of thinking that gave rise to the Marshall Plan after World War II. Without that investment, the nations of Europe could be a collection of impoverished, squabbling states instead of the fruitful and prosperous trading partners we have today.

This approach has another precedent, in the Montreal Protocol, the treaty that ended the production of ozone-destroying chemicals. It was successful because the same companies that made the destructive chemicals were able to produce their substitutes. The energy industry can be reconfigured in the same way. Several oil executives have said in private conversations that they can, in an orderly fashion, decarbonize their energy supplies. But they need the governments of the world to regulate the process so that all companies can make the transition simultaneously, without losing market share to competitors.

The very act of addressing the crisis would acknowledge that we are living on a finite planet and foster a new ethic of sustainability.

The plan would be driven by two engines: The progressive-efficiency standard would create the regulatory drive for all nations to transform their energy diets, and the tax generating $300 billion a year for developing countries would create a vast market for clean-energy technologies. It has been endorsed by a number of national delegations—India, Bangladesh, Germany, Mexico, and Britain, among others. While the plan will require refinement, it is of a scale appropriate to the magnitude of the problem.

Ultimately, the climate crisis provides an extraordinary opportunity to help us calibrate competition and cooperation in the global economy, harnessing the world's technical ingenuity and the power of the market within a regulatory framework that reflects a consensus of the world's citizens. The very act of addressing the crisis would acknowledge that we are living on a finite planet and foster a new ethic of sustainability that would permeate our institutions and policies in ways unimaginable today. It could subordinate our current infatuation with commerce and materialism to a restored connection to our natural home, ending the exploitative relationship between our civilization and the planet that supports it.

Angry nature is holding a gun to our heads. Drought-driven wildfires last summer consumed 6 million acres in the western United States. Last fall, the United Kingdom experienced its worst flooding since record-keeping began 273 years ago. In Iceland, Europe's biggest glacier is disintegrating. And the sea ice in the Arctic has thinned by 40 percent in the last 40 years.

We have a very small window of opportunity. The choice is clear. The time is short.

ROSS GELBSPAN *is author of* The Heat Is On: The Climate Crisis, the Cover-up, the Prescription *(Perseus Books, 1998). He maintains the Web site* www.heatisonline.org, *a project of the Green House Network.*

A greener, or browner, Mexico?

NAFTA purports to be the world's first environmentally friendly trade treaty, but its critics claim it has made Mexico dirtier. There is evidence on both sides

CIUDAD JUAREZ

GIVEN the industrial invasion that the North American Free-Trade Agreement has brought to the cities that line Mexico's border with the United States, one might expect the skies of Ciudad Juarez to be brown with pollution, and its watercourses solid with toxic sludge. But no. The centre of Ciudad Juarez looks like a poorer version of El Paso, Texas, its cross-border neighbour: flat, dull and full of shopping malls. Since NAFTA took effect on January 1st 1994, Mexico has passed environmental laws similar to those of the United States and Canada, its NAFTA partners; has set up a fully-fledged environment ministry; and has started to benefit from several two- and three-country schemes designed to fulfil "side accords" on the environment—the first such provisions in a trade agreement.

But the debate over NAFTA's impact on Mexico's environment remains polarised. Certainly NAFTA has had the hoped-for result of encouraging industries to move to Mexico. Since 1994, the number of *maquiladoras* (factories using imported raw materials to make goods for re-export, usually to the United States) has doubled, and half of the new factories are in the 100km-wide (60 mile) northern border region.

But that has put pressure on water supplies. The influx of migrant workers is slowly drying out cities like Juarez, which shares its only water source, an underground aquifer, with El Paso (which has other water supplies). Growth is aggravating old deficiencies: 18% of Mexican border towns have no drinking water, 30% no sewage treatment, and 43% inadequate rubbish disposal, according to Franco Barreno, head of the Border Environment Co-operation Commission (BECC), a bilateral agency set up under NAFTA. Putting that right, which is the BECC's job, will cost $2 billion–3 billion.

The problem of toxic waste is more serious still, and is being ignored. Mexico has just one landfill site for hazardous muck, which can take only 12% of the estimated waste from non-*maquila* industry; the rest is dumped illegally. Mexican law says *maquiladoras* must send their toxic waste back to the country the raw materials came from but, with enforcement weak and repatriation expensive, many are probably ignoring the law, says Victoriano Garza, of the Autonomous University of Ciudad Juarez.

Mexico has long been a dumping-ground for unwanted rubbish from the United States. But in fact less than 1% of the country's toxic gunge is generated in the border region. After 1994, despite the growth in *maquiladoras*, Mexico's exports of toxic waste to the United States dropped sharply—suggesting that tougher rules were making companies adopt greener manufacturing policies. But then, in 1997, waste exports mysteriously shot up again (see chart).

Even greens are split about NAFTA. "In 15 years as an environmentalist, I haven't noticed any change in policy," laments Homero Aridjis, a writer. Quite the contrary, says Tlahoga Ruge, of the North American Centre for Environmental Information and Communication: "NAFTA has brought the environment into the mainstream in Mexico, as something to be taken seriously."

Such is the complexity of the issue, only in June did the Commission for Environmental Co-operation (CEC), a Montreal-based body created in 1994 to implement the environmental side-agreement, publish its methodology for assessing NAFTA's impact. An accompanying case study, on maize farming in Mexico, illustrates the difficulties. Lower protective tariffs are forcing Mexico's subsistence maize farmers to modernise, change their

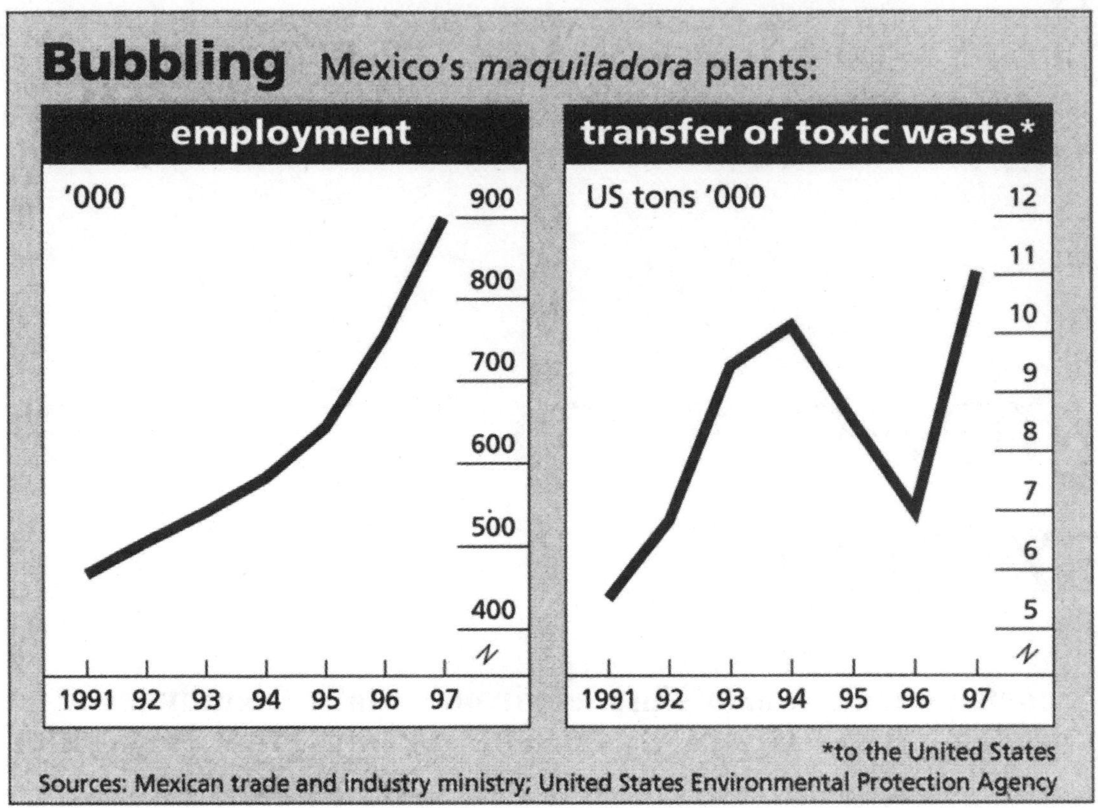

crops or look for other work; each choice has potential impacts, such as soil deterioration, depletion of the maize gene pool, or migration to cities. Social and environmental impacts go hand-in-hand.

Critics say that, as well as being slow, the CEC has too few powers. It can investigate citizens' complaints about breaches of each NAFTA country's national environmental laws, but governments are free to ignore its recommendations. Moreover, the side-agreement's gentle urgings are outgunned by the main accord's firm admonition, in its Chapter 11, to protect foreign investors from uncertainty. A recent report by the International Institute for Sustainable Development, a group based in Winnipeg, Canada, warns that this provision is increasingly being used by business to the detriment of environmental protection. And unlike the CEC, the arbitration bodies that settle Chapter 11 disputes make binding decisions.

Companies have challenged environmental laws in all three NAFTA countries, but Mexico is particularly vulnerable. Its laws are new, its institutions untested and its environmental culture undeveloped. To these handicaps was added the collapse of Mexico's peso in 1995, from which it is still trying to recover. Beefing up environmental institutions has not been its top priority. In Juarez, for example, there are only 15 federal environmental inspectors (and they cover the whole of Chihuahua state). Mexico also lags in data-collection: next week the CEC is due to publish a report on industrial emissions and air pollution, but in the United States and Canada only, because Mexican factories do not have to report their emissions.

These things need to change. NAFTA is supposed to lead to completely free trade after 15 years; its full impact has yet to be felt. In 2001, the *maquiladoras* will lose some of their tax breaks. Increasingly, American firms may opt to set up ordinary factories in Mexico, which would not have to send their waste back home. Mexico badly needs somewhere to put this stuff, but so far attempts to find sites for new toxic-waste landfills have been scuppered by not-in-my-backyard opposition (and, ironically, by the strict stipulations of the new environmental laws).

But not all is murk. Besides better laws and institutions, Mexico has seen a rapid rise in non-governmental organisations, themselves partly an import from the north, which work on the education and awareness-raising that they say the government is neglecting. Ciudad Juarez may be running out of water to drink, but Mexico City's aquifer is so low that the whole place is slowly sinking. And, unlike the capital, Juarez benefits from all kinds of two-country efforts to fix its problem, thanks mainly to NAFTA.

UNIT 3

The Region

Unit Selections

Key Points to Consider

- To what regions do you belong?
- Why are maps and atlases so important in discussing and studying regions?
- What major regions in the world are experiencing change? Which ones seem not to change at all? What are some reasons for the differences?
- What regions in the world are experiencing tensions? What are the reasons behind these tensions? How can the tensions be eased?
- Why are regions in Africa suffering so greatly?
- How will East Asia change as China and Taiwan expand relationships?
- Discuss whether or not the nation-state system is an anachronism.
- Why is regional study important?

Links: www.dushkin.com/online/
These sites are annotated in the World Wide Web pages.

AS at UVA Yellow Pages: Regional Studies
http://xroads.virginia.edu/~YP/regional/regional.html

Can Cities Save the Future?
http://www.huduser.org/publications/econdev/habitat/prep2.html

IISDnet
http://iisd.ca

NewsPage
http://www.individual.com

Telecommuting as an Investment: The Big Picture—John Wolf
http://www.svi.org/telework/forums/messages5/48.html

The Urban Environment
http://www.geocities.com/RainForest/Vines/6723/urb/index.html

Virtual Seminar in Global Political Economy/Global Cities & Social Movements
http://csf.colorado.edu/gpe/gpe95b/resources.html

World Regions & Nation States
http://www.worldcapitalforum.com/worregstat.html

The region is one of the most important concepts in geography. The term has special significance for the geographer, and it has been used as a kind of area classification system in the discipline.

Two of the regional types most used in geography are "uniform" and "nodal." A uniform region is one in which a distinct set of features is present. The distinctiveness of the combination of features marks the region as being different from others. These features include climate type, soil type, prominent languages, resource deposits, and virtually any other identifiable phenomenon having a spatial dimension.

The nodal region reflects the zone of influence of a city or other nodal place. Imagine a rural town in which a farm-implement service center is located. Now imagine lines drawn on a map linking this service center with every farm within the area that uses it. Finally, imagine a single line enclosing the entire area in which the individual farms are located. The enclosed area is defined as a nodal region. The nodal region implies interaction. Regions of this type are defined on the basis of banking linkages, newspaper circulation, and telephone traffic, among other things.

This unit presents examples of a number of regional themes. These selections can provide only a hint of the scope and diversity of the region in geography. There is no limit to the number of regions; there are as many as the researcher sets out to define.

"The Rise of the Region State" suggests that the nation-state is an unnatural and even dysfunctional unit for organizing human activity. "Continental Divide" deals with changing geopolitical situations. The next two articles consider regional changes in Russia and the Balkans. A *Time* map of AIDS in Africa and an article on AIDS in India and China follow. The devastation of this disease is a global problem. The continuing rise of Greenville, South Carolina, is documented in the next article. Janet Raloff summarizes concerns about overfishing in marine sanctuaries and the need for environmental controls. The hard-pressed Rio Grande River is discussed next. Then, "Does It Matter Where You Are?" considers aspects of geographical location principles in the context of the new global economic systems.

THE RISE OF THE REGION STATE

Kenichi Ohmae

The Nation State Is Dysfunctional

THE NATION STATE has become an unnatural, even dysfunctional, unit for organizing human activity and managing economic endeavor in a borderless world. It represents no genuine, shared community of economic interests; it defines no meaningful flows of economic activity. In fact, it overlooks the true linkages and synergies that exist among often disparate populations by combining important measures of human activity at the wrong level of analysis.

For example, to think of Italy as a single economic entity ignores the reality of an industrial north and a rural south, each vastly different in its ability to contribute and in its need to receive. Treating Italy as a single economic unit forces one—as a private sector manager or a public sector official—to operate on the basis of false, implausible and nonexistent averages. Italy is a country with great disparities in industry and income across regions.

On the global economic map the lines that now matter are those defining what may be called "region states." The boundaries of the region state are not imposed by political fiat. They are drawn by the deft but invisible hand of the global market for goods and services. They follow, rather than precede, real flows of human activity, creating nothing new but ratifying existing patterns manifest in countless individual decisions. They represent no threat to the political borders of any nation, and they have no call on any taxpayer's money to finance military forces to defend such borders.

Region states are natural economic zones. They may or may not fall within the geographic limits of a particular nation—whether they do is an accident of history. Sometimes these distinct economic units are formed by parts of states, such as those in northern Italy, Wales, Catalonia, Alsace-Lorraine or Baden-Württemberg. At other times they may be formed by economic patterns that overlap existing national boundaries, such as those between San Diego and Tijuana, Hong Kong and southern China, or the "growth triangle" of Singapore and its neighboring Indonesian islands. In today's borderless world these are natural economic zones and what matters is that each possesses, in one or another combination, the key ingredients for successful participation in the global economy.

Look, for example, at what is happening in Southeast Asia. The Hong Kong economy has gradually extended its influence throughout the Pearl River Delta. The radiating effect of these linkages has made Hong Kong, where GNP per capita is $12,000, the driving force of economic life in Shenzhen, boosting the per capital GNP of that city's residents to $5,695, as compared to $317 for China as a whole. These links extend to Zhuhai, Amoy and Guangzhou as well. By the year 2000 this cross-border region state will have raised the living standard of more than 11 million people over the $5,000 level. Meanwhile, Guangdong province, with a population of more than 65 million and its capital at Hong Kong, will emerge as a newly industrialized economy in its own right, even though China's per capita GNP may still hover at about $1,000. Unlike in Eastern Europe, where nations try to convert entire socialist economies over to the market, the Asian model is first to convert limited economic zones—the region states—into free enterprise havens. So far the results have been reassuring.

These developments and others like them are coming just in time for Asia. As Europe perfects its single market and as the United States, Canada and Mexico begin to explore the benefits of the North American Free Trade Agreement (NAFTA), the combined economies of Asia and Japan lag behind those of the other parts of the globe's economic triad by about $2 trillion—roughly the aggregate size of some 20 additional region states. In other words, for Asia to keep pace existing regions must continue to grow at current rates throughout the next decade, giving birth to 20 additional Singapores.

Many of these new region states are already beginning to emerge. China has expanded to 14 other areas—many of them inland—the special economic zones that have worked so well for Shenzhen and Shanghai. One such project at Yunnan will become a cross-border economic zone encompassing parts of Laos and Vietnam. In Vietnam itself Ho Chi Minh City (Saigon) has launched a similar "sepzone" to attract foreign capital. Inspired in part by Singapore's "growth triangle," the governments of Indonesia, Malaysia and Thailand in 1992 unveiled a larger triangle across the Strait of Malacca to link Medan, Penang and Phuket. These developments are not, of course, limited to the developing economies in Asia. In economic terms the United States has never been a single nation. It is a collection of region states: northern and southern California, the "power corridor" along the East Coast between Boston and Washington, the Northeast, the Midwest, the Sun Belt, and so on.

What Makes a Region State

THE PRIMARY linkages of region states tend to be with the global economy and not with their host nations. Region states make such effective points of entry into the global economy because the very characteristics that define them are shaped by the demands of that economy. Region states tend to have between five million and 20 million people. The range is broad, but the extremes are clear: not half a million, not 50 or 100 million. A region state must be small enough for its citizens to share certain economic and consumer interests but of adequate size to justify the infrastructure—communication and transportation links and quality professional services—necessary to participate economically on a global scale.

It must, for example, have at least one international airport and, more than likely, one good harbor with international-class freight-handling facilities. A region state must also be large enough to provide an attractive market for the brand development of leading consumer products. In other words, region states are not defined by their economies of scale in production (which, after all, can be leveraged from a base of any size through exports to the rest of the world) but rather by their having reached efficient economies of scale in their consumption, infrastructure and professional services.

For example, as the reach of television networks expands, advertising becomes more efficient. Although trying to introduce a consumer brand throughout all of Japan or Indonesia may still prove prohibitively expensive, establishing it firmly in the Osaka or Jakarta region is far more affordable—and far more likely to generate handsome returns. Much the same is true with sales and service networks, customer satisfaction programs, market surveys and management information systems: efficient scale is at the regional, not national, level. This fact matters because, on balance, modern marketing techniques and technologies shape the economies of region states.

Where true economies of service exist, religious, ethnic and racial distinctions are not important—or, at least, only as important as human nature requires. Singapore is 70 percent ethnic Chinese, but its 30 percent minority is not much of a problem because commercial prosperity creates sufficient affluence for all. Nor are ethnic differences a source of concern for potential investors looking for consumers.

Indonesia—an archipelago with 500 or so different tribal groups, 18,000 islands and 170 million people—would logically seem to defy effective organization within a single mode of political government. Yet Jakarta has traditionally attempted to impose just such a central control by applying fictional averages to the entire nation. They do not work. If, however, economies of service allowed two or three Singapore-sized region states to be created within Indonesia, they could be managed. And they would ameliorate, rather than exacerbate, the country's internal social divisions. This holds as well for India and Brazil.

The New Multinational Corporation

WHEN VIEWING the globe through the lens of the region state, senior corporate managers think differently about the geographical expansion of their businesses. In the past the primary aspiration of multinational corporations was to create, in effect, clones of the parent organization in each of the dozens of countries in which they operated. The goal of this system was to stick yet another pin in the global map to mark an increasing number of subsidiaries around the world.

More recently, however, when Nestlé and Procter & Gamble wanted to expand their business in Japan from an already strong position, they did not view the effort as just another pin-sticking exercise. Nor did they treat the country as a single coherent market to be gained at once, or try as most Western companies do to establish a foothold first in the Tokyo area, Japan's most tumultuous and overcrowded market. Instead, they wisely focused on the Kansai region around Osaka and Kobe, whose 22 million residents are nearly as affluent as those in Tokyo but where competition is far less intense. Once they had on-the-ground experience on how best to reach the Japanese consumer, they branched out into other regions of the country.

Much of the difficulty Western companies face in trying to enter Japan stems directly from trying to shoulder their way in through Tokyo. This instinct often proves difficult and costly. Even if it works, it may also prove a trap; it is hard to "see" Japan once one is bottled up in the particular dynamics of the Tokyo marketplace. Moreover, entering the country through a different regional doorway has great economic appeal. Measured by aggregate GNP the Kansai region is the seventh-largest economy in the world, just behind the United Kingdom.

Given the variations among local markets and the value of learning through real-world experimentation, an incremental region-based approach to market entry makes excellent sense. And not just in Japan. Building an effective presence across a landmass the size of China is of course a daunting prospect. Serving the people in and around Nagoya City, however, is not.

If one wants a presence in Thailand, why start by building a network over the entire extended landmass? Instead focus, at least initially, on the region around Bangkok, which represents the lion's share of the total potential market. The same strategy applies to the United States. To introduce a new top-of-the-line car into the U.S. market, why replicate up front an exhaustive coast-to-coast dealership network? Of the country's 3,000 statistical metropolitan areas, 80 percent of luxury car buyers can be reached by establishing a presence in only 125 of these.

The Challenges for Government

TRADITIONAL ISSUES of foreign policy, security and defense remain the province of nation states. So, too, are macroeconomic and monetary policies—the taxation and public investment needed to provide the necessary infrastructure and incentives for region-based activities. The government will also remain responsible for the broad requirements of educating and training citizens so that they can participate fully in the global economy.

Governments are likely to resist giving up the power to intervene in the economic realm or to relinquish their impulses for protectionism. The illusion of control is soothing. Yet hard evidence proves the contrary. No manipulation of exchange rates by central bankers or political appointees has ever "corrected" the trade imbalances between the United States and Japan. Nor has any trade talk between the two governments. Whatever cosmetic actions these negotiations may have prompted, they rescued no industry and revived no economic sector. Textiles, semiconductors, autos, consumer electronics—the competitive situation in these industries did not develop according to the whims of policymakers but only in response to the deeper logic of the competitive marketplace. If U.S. market share has dwindled, it is not because government policy failed but because individual consumers decided to buy elsewhere. If U.S. capacity has migrated to Mexico or Asia, it is only because individual managers made decisions about cost and efficiency.

The implications of region states are not welcome news to established seats of political power, be they politicians or lobbyists. Nation states by definition require a domestic political focus, while region states are ensconced in the global economy. Region states that sit within the frontiers of a particular nation share its political goals and aspirations. However, region states welcome foreign investment and ownership—whatever allows them to employ people productively or to improve the quality of life. They want their people to have access to the best and cheapest products. And they want whatever surplus accrues from these activities to ratchet up the local quality of life still further and not to support distant regions or to prop up distressed industries elsewhere in the name of national interest or sovereignty.

When a region prospers, that prosperity spills over into the adjacent regions within the same political confederation. Industry in the area immediately in and around Bangkok has prompted investors to explore options elsewhere in Thailand. Much the same is true of Kuala Lumpur in Malaysia, Jakarta in Indonesia, or Singapore, which is rapidly becoming the unofficial capital of the Association of Southeast Asian Nations. São Paulo, too, could well emerge as a genuine region state, someday entering the ranks of the Organization of Economic Cooperation and Development. Yet if Brazil's central government does not allow the São Paulo region state finally to enter the global economy, the country as a whole may soon fall off the roster of the newly industrialized economies.

Unlike those at the political center, the leaders of region states—interested chief executive officers, heads of local unions, politicians at city and state levels—often welcome and encourage foreign capital investment. They do not go abroad to attract new plants and factories only to appear back home on television vowing to protect local companies at any cost. These leaders tend to possess an international outlook that can help defuse many of the usual kinds of social tensions arising over issues of "foreign" versus "domestic" inputs to production.

In the United States, for example, the Japanese have already established about 120 "transplant" auto factories throughout the Mississippi Valley. More are on the way. As their share of the U.S. auto industry's production grows, people in that region who look to these plants for their livelihoods and for the tax revenues needed to support local communities will stop caring whether the plants belong to U.S.- or Japanese-based companies. All they will care about are the regional economic benefits of having them there. In effect, as members of the Mississippi Valley region state, they will have leveraged the contribution of these plants to help their region become an active participant in the global economy.

Region states need not be the enemies of central governments. Handled gently, region states can provide the opportunity for eventual prosperity for all areas within a nation's traditional political control. When political and industrial leaders accept and act on these realities, they help build prosperity. When they do not—falling back under the spell of the nationalist economic illusion—they may actually destroy it.

Consider the fate of Silicon Valley, that great early engine of much of America's microelectronics industry. In the beginning it was an extremely open and entrepreneurial environment. Of late, however, it has become notably protectionist—creating industry associations, establishing a polished lobbying presence in Washington and turning to "competitiveness" studies as a way to get more federal funding for research and development. It has also begun to discourage, and even to bar, foreign investment, let alone foreign takeovers. The result is that Boise and Denver now prosper in electronics; Japan is developing a Silicon Island on Kyushu; Taiwan is trying to create a Silicon Island of its own; and Korea is nurturing a Silicon Peninsula. This is the worst of all possible worlds: no new money in California and a host of newly energized and well-funded competitors.

Elsewhere in California, not far from Silicon Valley, the story is quite different. When Hollywood recognized that it faced a severe capital shortage, it did not throw up protectionist barriers against foreign money. Instead, it invited Rupert Murdoch into 20th Century Fox, C. Itoh and Toshiba into Time-Warner, Sony into Columbia, and Matsushita into MCA. The result: a $10 billion infusion of new capital and, equally important, $10 billion less for Japan or anyone else to set up a new Hollywood of their own.

Political leaders, however reluctantly, must adjust to the reality of economic regional entities if they are to nurture real economic flows. Resistant governments will be left to reign over traditional political territories as all meaningful participation in the global economy migrates beyond their well-preserved frontiers.

Canada, as an example, is wrongly focusing on Quebec and national language tensions as its core economic and even political issue. It does so to the point of still wrestling with the teaching of French and English in British Columbia, when that province's economic future is tied to Asia. Furthermore, as NAFTA takes shape the "vertical" relationships between Canadian and U.S. regions—Vancouver and Seattle (the Pacific Northwest region state); Toronto, Detroit and Cleveland (the Great Lakes region state)—will become increasingly important. How Canadian leaders deal with these new entities will be critical to the continuance of Canada as a political nation.

In developing economies, history suggests that when GNP per capita reaches about $5,000, discretionary income crosses an invisible threshold. Above that level people begin wondering whether they have reasonable access to the best and cheapest available products and whether they have an adequate quality of life. More troubling for those in political control, citizens also begin to consider whether their government is doing as well by them as it might.

Such a performance review is likely to be unpleasant. When governments control information—and in large measure because they do—it is all too easy for them to believe that they "own" their people. Governments begin restricting access to certain kinds of goods or services or pricing them far higher than pure economic logic would dictate. If market-driven levels of consumption conflict with a government's pet policy or general desire for control, the obvious response is to restrict consumption. So what if the people would choose otherwise if given the opportunity? Not only does the government withhold that opportunity but it also does not even let the people know that it is being withheld.

Regimes that exercise strong central control either fall on hard times or begin to decompose. In a borderless world the deck is stacked against them. The irony, of course, is that in the name of safeguarding the integrity and identity of the center, they often prove unwilling or unable to give up the illusion of power in order to seek a better quality of life for their people. There is at the center an understandable fear of letting go and losing control. As a result, the center often ends up protecting weak and unproductive industries and then passing along the high costs to its people—precisely the opposite of what a government should do.

The Goal is to Raise Living Standards

THE CLINTON administration faces a stark choice as it organizes itself to address the country's economic issues. It can develop policy within the framework of the badly dated assumption that success in the global economy means pitting one nation's industries against another's. Or it can define policy with the awareness that the economic dynamics of a borderless world do not flow from such contrived head-to-head confrontations, but rather from the participation of specific regions in a global nexus of information, skill, trade and investment.

If the goal is to raise living standards by promoting regional participation in the borderless economy, then the less Washington constrains these regions, the better off they will be. By contrast, the more Washington intervenes, the more citizens will pay for automobiles, steel, semiconductors, white wine, textiles or consumer electronics—all in the name of "protecting" America. Aggregating economic policy at the national level—or worse, at the continent-wide level as in Europe—inevitably results in special interest groups and vote-conscious governments putting their own interests first.

The less Washington interacts with specific regions, however, the less it perceives itself as "representing" them. It does not feel right. When learning to ski, one of the toughest and most counterintuitive principles to accept is that one gains better control by leaning down toward the valley, not back against the hill. Letting go is difficult. For governments region-based participation in the borderless economy is fine, except where it threatens current jobs, industries or interests. In Japan, a nation with plenty of farmers, food is far more expensive than in Hong Kong or Singapore, where there are no farmers. That is because Hong Kong and Singapore are open to what Australia and China can produce far more cheaply than they could themselves. They have opened themselves to the global economy, thrown their weight forward, as it were, and their people have reaped the benefits.

For the Clinton administration, the irony is that Washington today finds itself in the same relation to those region states that lie entirely or partially within its borders as was London with its North American colonies centuries ago. Neither central power could genuinely understand the shape or magnitude of the new flows of information, people and economic activity in the regions nominally under its control. Nor could it understand how counterproductive it would be to try to arrest or distort these flows in the service of nation-defined interests. Now as then, only relaxed central control can allow the flexibility needed to maintain the links to regions gripped by an inexorable drive for prosperity.

Kenichi Ohmae is Chairman of the offices of McKinsey & Company in Japan.

Continental Divide

With 13 countries on the applicant list, the European Union confronts the dilemma of expansion in 2000. But are the advantages worth the price of admission? Even as leaders of Bulgaria, Cyprus, the Czech Republic, Estonia, Hungary, Latvia, Lithuania, Malta, Poland, Romania, the Slovak Republic, Slovenia, and Turkey maneuver to bring their policies in line with EU law, there is dissension within member countries over EU standards and the uniformity of their enforcement. And judging from the recent electoral successes of far-right political parties in Western Europe, nationalist sentiment and distaste for open borders will lend controversy to upcoming EU decisions on such hot-button issues as asylum and immigration policy.

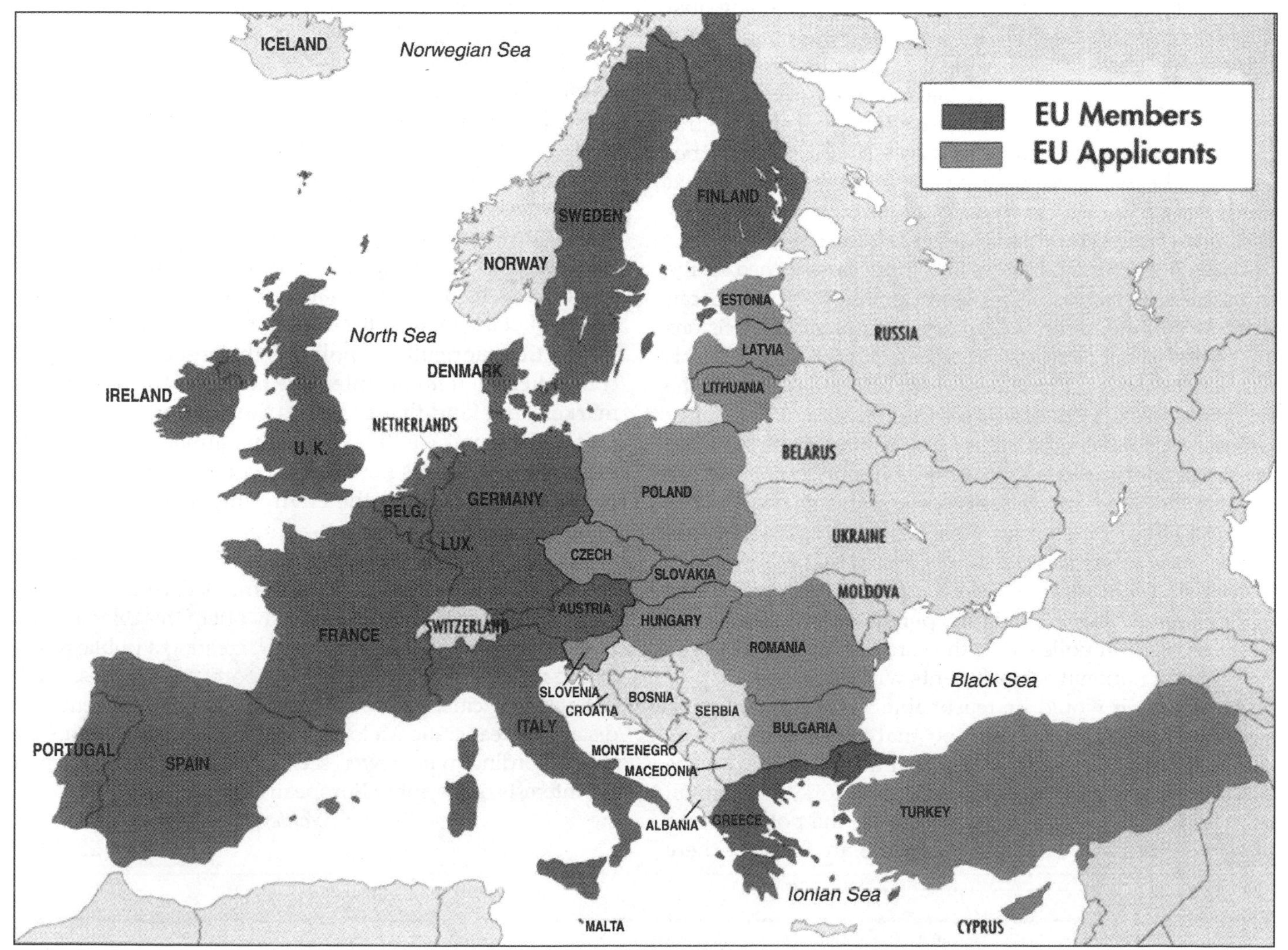

DESPERATELY SEEKING ADMISSION

Limitless Growth?

Eighteen months ago the European Union opened admission negotiations with Estonia, Poland, Slovenia, the Czech Republic, Hungary, and Cyprus. In December this group should expand by six additional nations. If Bulgaria, Latvia, Lithuania, Malta, Romania, and Slovakia are included, the 15-member EU will be dealing with 12 candidates. In addition, Turkey, Albania, and the successor states to Yugoslavia have sought admission.

The candidates are pressing for a quick response, but there is no way to say when the EU will act, since it is not clear when the candidates will meet the performance prerequisites. The only exception is Cyprus. The divided island republic faces political hurdles. Economically, Cyprus has long since met all the criteria. For another reason, it is not at all clear that the EU is ready for any expansion.

Even in its present makeup, it finds it very difficult to function. An EU of 20 or even more members would be practically ungovernable. By 2002 the EU wants, therefore, to finish its internal reforms.

But where the European giant ought to be going, just how large the EU ought to be, and what the political and geographic borders of Europe ought to be are unclear. And not by chance. It is only because the future political shape of the Union has been left vague that the integration process has gone as far as it has. Had it, from the beginning, been based on one of the many suggested models—a federative state, a confederation, a union—the European train would have never left the station.

Now, however, with more and more cars hitched on the train, there is increasing pressure for reform. The EU can scarcely continue with the luxury of unanimous decisions and lengthy negotiations preceding any changes. This is true for the first and until now most important pillar of the EU, the internal market, with a common agricultural policy and the economic and currency union. And it will be all the more true for the second pillar, the common foreign and security policy, and the third, domestic and legal policies.

The EU special summit meeting in Tampere, Finland, [in October] made this dilemma clear. It makes sense, in a Europe that is increasingly closely knit, to have a single set of rules governing legal rights, penal codes, border security, and asylum policies. At the same time, this raises the danger that national achievements will be destroyed.

Therefore, it would be reasonable to begin by moving toward a European constitution that would define basic rights and obligations before tackling agreements on the detailed questions. But how should this work, when up till now both the geographical borders and the political form of this entity have been left vague? So, in Tampere there was an agreement to work out a Charter of Basic Rights for Europe by 2000. Long sought by the European left, the charter would in fact represent remarkable progress.

The Council of Sages created by European Commission President Romano Prodi is also aimed at a quasi-constitution for Europe. Belgium's former Prime Minister Jean-Luc Dehaene; Lord Simon, the former British minister to Europe; and former German President Richard von Weizsäcker advise the EU to restructure its legal framework. The Sages' goal is unmistakable: An expanded EU should, and must, abandon the right to veto and replace it with democratic decisions based on majority votes. That would increase the power of the European Parliament. It would also mean that individual nation-states would have to give up even more of their national sovereignty.

But even this proposed reform is a compromise that would consciously leave the future of European integration open. The candidates for membership are of course profiting from this open character—for otherwise the EU would have long since become a closed club.

At the same time, it means living with an undecided and unfinished integration. Deputies to the European Parliament are elected nationally, EU officials are chosen by national governments, and the first concerns of the European Union's heads of government are always the next election back home, and only then European politics. Common interests always take second priority, and when action is taken, fear of what national interests might be affected often leads to stasis or even retreat at the European level.

Europe has put itself under pressure to integrate in order to preserve peace and its own prosperity. That drives the EU onward, but also feeds the tendency of members to keep what they've got. The result is great pressure for conformity. It turns candidates into petitioners who cannot predict the real results of their negotiations or wishes.

The EU's agricultural policy is the best example of this contradiction. It favors intensive farming, aimed at world markets, the kind that damages the environment. To demand of the new Central European nations that they conform to this recipe is hopeless. It would not serve the EU, or Eastern farmers, or the environment, let alone Third World farmers.

The way out lies in the reform of the EU agriculture policy. But that flies in the face of narrow-minded yet understandable national interests. The only way out of this dilemma lies in forced democratization of the EU, creating a public receptive to new ideas, and winning supportive majorities. Without stronger citizen participation, the Union will remain a distant, bureaucratic Moloch, or a cash cow that each state will, according to its power, seek to milk without regard for the interests of the entire European Community.

—*Torsten Wohlert*, Freitag *(leftist weekly), Berlin, Oct. 22, 1999.*

Russia's regions: Beyond the Kremlin's walls

President Vladimir Putin is trying to bring Russia's regions back into line

UFA, BASHKORTOSTAN

BUSINESS is what matters; democracy is for later, perhaps. There are elections of a sort, but the president's candidates always win. The media do what they are told. Foreigners are welcome so long as they keep their wallets open and their mouths shut. The place stays afloat thanks to oil and the weak rouble.

A gloomy snapshot of President Vladimir Putin's Russia? The description certainly fits Bashkortostan, a family-run republic in mid-Russia that has become the first target of Mr Putin's attempt to tidy up his country's shambolic internal structure.

The immediate argument is about the republic's constitution, which puts Bashkortostan's laws on an equal footing with Russia's. That has allowed the leadership to ignore federal privatisation programmes and keep the press cowed and elections rigged. Last week, Mr Putin fired off a stiff letter to the speaker of the local parliament, saying that the republic must bring its constitution into line with Russia's.

Mr Putin has launched a wider plan too. He is calling for more power to sack regional bosses and wants to end their automatic right to seats in Russia's upper house of parliament. He also wants to parcel out Russia's 89 component republics and regions into seven new districts, each overseen by a presidential appointee. These governors-general, as the Russian media call them, are to manage the local operations of the "power ministries"—those for defence, the interior, security and justice. All this would severely cramp the style of Bashkortostan and other independent-minded bits of the federation, which have largely taken over the central government's outposts of power.

At stake is the future of Russia as a centrally governed country. Over the past ten years, the centre's hold has weakened sharply, and the differences between regions have grown (see map). The local governments are not an advertisement for federalism: most are by turns thuggish, crony-ridden and plain incompetent, though a handful are now dimly aware of the benefits of foreign trade and investment.

The leadership in Bashkortostan is puzzled rather than panicky. The republic is far from being the worst-run place in Russia, and it loyally supported Mr Putin in the presidential election. Next-door Tatarstan is much more outspoken about political and economic sovereignty. Crime in Bashkortostan is not conspicuous. President Murtaza Rakhimov is an autocrat, but his rule is heavy-handed rather than bloody.

The argument, his friends insist, is really about money, and his government is quite ready to talk about it. Bashkortostan is prosperous by Russian standards, with one of the biggest oil companies in the country (coincidentally run by the president's son, Ural) and one of the strongest banks. "Our republic's status will not be a subject of negotiation," says the republic's speaker. And if Mr Putin differs? "A threat would be counter-productive," he frowns intimidatingly.

The noncommittal welcome given by most regional leaders so far to Mr Putin's plans has worked well in the past. Previous attempts to bring order to the provinces have quickly become bogged down. Under pressure, regional leaders pay lip service to the federal leadership and wait until its attention wanders. The 80-plus presidential representatives in the regions appointed by Boris Yeltsin in an attempt to re-establish his authority have usually become little more than figureheads. Mr Putin's planned new governors-general may well meet the same fate.

"This happens when new people are only just starting work," says the head of another republic in central Russia, in a revealingly patronising tone. "The decree just creates one more bureaucracy with thousands more employees."

All the same, Mr Putin could prove a more serious centraliser than Mr Yeltsin. He worries publicly about separatism, and has strongly backed the war against it in Chechnya. He may be able to muster some serious allies in Moscow. He may, for example, be co-ordinating his plan with the barons of the national oil and gas industries,

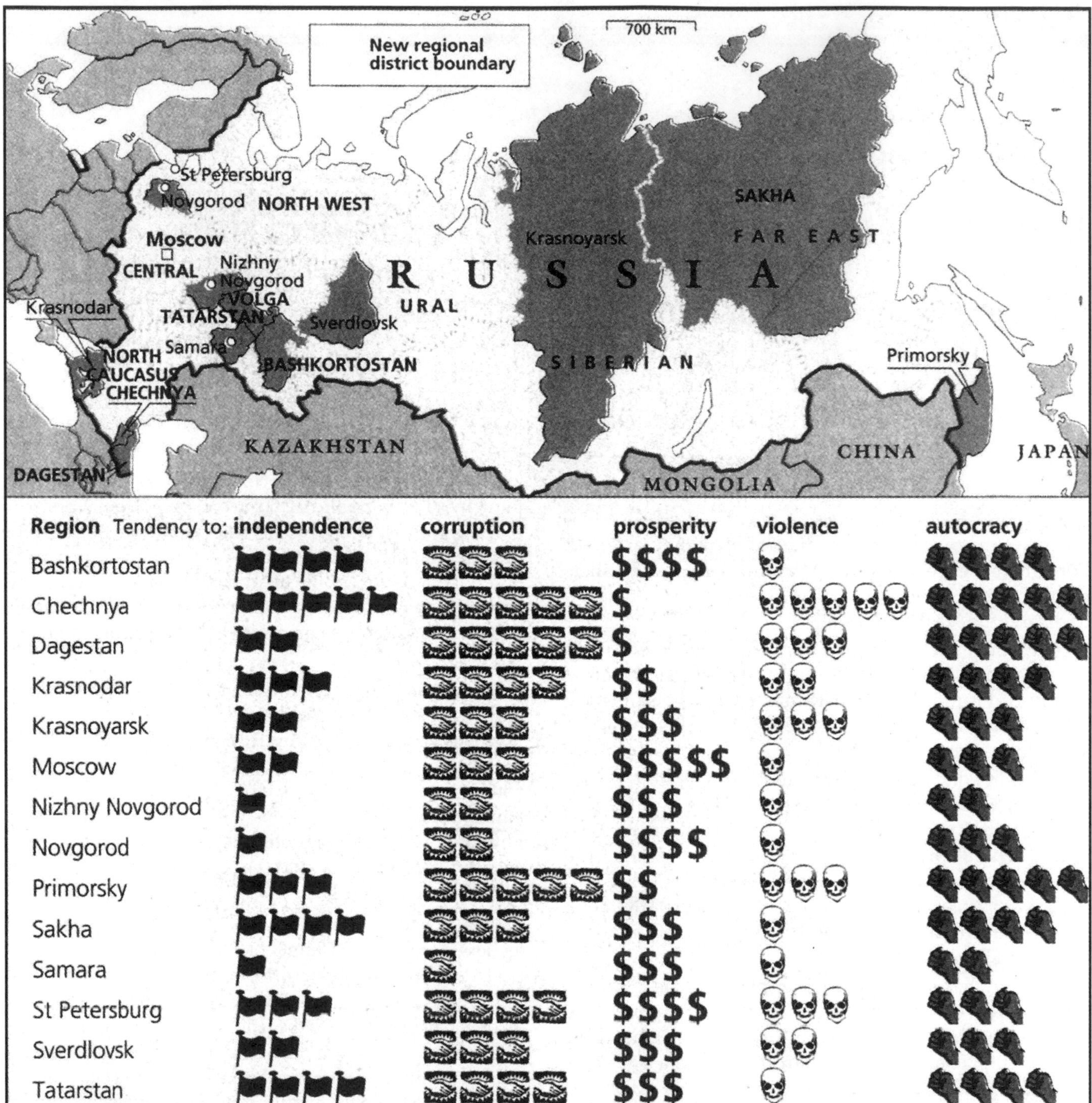

who would also like to cut down self-important regional leaders—with an eye for the spoils.

Even so, any serious attempt to recentralise Russia risks changing the regions' current apathy towards Moscow into hostility. And although democrats in places like Bashkortostan rest their hopes, lightly, on Mr Putin, getting rid of bad local leaders will improve things only if the central government for its part starts working properly.

That could yet happen, but the opening weeks of Mr Putin's presidency give little reason for hope. Journalists are panicking about state harassment of the company that owns NTV, the main independent television channel. And there is no sign yet of government support for the increasingly dog-eared economic-reform plans that have been floating around Moscow. Bashkortostan is a useful target for Mr Putin; pessimists fear it could be a useful model too.

EUROPE

The delicate Balkan balance

This autumn sees the biggest round of elections in the Balkans since ex-Yugoslavia broke up eight years ago. This time, voting could genuinely reshape the region. How, in particular, do Bosnia and Kosovo stand?

BANJA LUKA, PRISTINA AND SARAJEVO

THE rosiest Balkan scenario goes something like this. Slobodan Milosevic, the Yugoslav president who has exploited ethnic loyalties so brutally and successfully to stay in power over the past decade, is voted out of office at the presidential poll on September 24th. He is replaced by a doubtless prickly, but nonetheless more decent, Serb who realises that his country can be rebuilt only if he makes terms with the outside world, and accepts the need for a new constitutional settlement for much of the region—within, and perhaps beyond, the rump of Yugoslavia, which still includes the nominally Serbian province of Kosovo.

Thanks to other elections at various levels, most importantly in Bosnia and Kosovo, there is a swing, however small, towards moderates who believe in co-operation rather than confrontation. This matches other moderate successes at local polls in September in Macedonia. There, reasonable people currently run a frail coalition government, which has to fend off a lot of complaints from the country's Slav majority that the ethnic-Albanian minority (at least a quarter of the population) is being allowed to cause too much trouble. In this bright setting, Albania's local elections in October pass off quietly, easing fears of a return to the chaos of the mid-1990s.

The consequent advent of brave new moderate Balkan politics calms tension across the region, enabling economic help to be delivered more effectively and lightening the outside world's task of peacekeeping and protecting minorities.

All too rosy? Very probably, yes. The biggest imponderable is the Yugoslav elections. The government of Montenegro, Serbia's junior partner in the Yugoslav federation, is refusing to co-operate with the poll—and fears are growing that Mr Milosevic will exploit the smaller republic's internal divisions to stir up a new round of killing.

Nor has a convincing candidate emerged to take him on. With two opposition candidates now standing, the anti-Milosevic vote may well anyway be split. Kosovo remains violent, with ruthless ethnic-Albanian nationalists in the ascendant. Meanwhile, in Bosnia, only some of the Muslims—their leaders style themselves Bosniaks—seem truly to believe in a multi-ethnic state.

Still, of late there have been some hopeful advances, especially in Bosnia. Killings in that former charnel-house have been minimal this year. Thanks to greater calm, the NATO-led peacekeeping force (known as SFOR) has been shrunk by a third, to 20,000. The election of a more sensible, westward-looking coalition government in Croatia, under Ivica Racan, has knocked quite a lot of stuffing out of the more bloody-minded of Bosnia's Croats. In April, the harsh nationalists who ruled their respective roosts during the civil war did worse than usual in local elections across Bosnia. From a wretched base, the economy too has begun to improve, with more trade across the "inter-entity boundary" that demarcates Bosnia's constituent bits. Even the three "entity armed forces"—the Croats, Muslims and Serbs—are each on track to trim their numbers by 15% by the end of the year.

Perhaps the most hopeful feature is that more people are returning to their old homes, even in places where a rival ethnic group holds sway. In the first half of this year, there were 20,000 such "minority returns", a threefold increase over the same period of 1999. At that rate, it will still take a long time to reverse the effects of ethnic cleansing. Some 2m Bosnians, about half the pre-war population, were forced to abandon their homes during the early

1990s. Only 300,000 have gone back, and over 1m do not have secure access to their pre-war homes.

But the accelerating rate of minority returns shows that the vicious circle of violently imposed segregation is not unbreakable. In several towns, such as Drvar, in the Muslim-Croat Federation, where many Serbs have returned, the ethnic balance has tipped against the Croats without, yet, provoking the ructions that many feared.

Another notable success, to date, has been the peace prevailing in the strategically sensitive town of Brcko, a once evenly balanced tri-ethnic town at the northern choke-point that links the western and eastern parts of Bosnia's Serb Republic. A decision by outsiders in March to neutralise and demilitarise the town and its surrounding corridor indefinitely did not provoke the violent outrage that Serb militants had promised.

The particular hope of Bosnia's overseers is that, in the forthcoming elections, the Serbs' assorted moderates, led by Milorad Dodik, the prime minister of their "entity" based at Banja Luka, can team up to beat the old Serb Democratic Party, previously led by Radovan Karadzic. It could be: the arch-nationalists did fairly badly in April's local elections. But, as elsewhere in the Balkans, the forging of coalitions and alliances is always fraught with backbiting.

Alija Izetbegovic, the Muslim member of Bosnia's three-person collective presidency, is poised to resign; his stridently Muslim Party of Democratic Action (SDA) has lost ground. One possible successor is Haris Silajdzic, whose moderate group, the Party of Bosnia and Hercegovina, is on the rise.

Yet most Bosnians still see politics in ethnic terms. Leading Bosnian Croats want to dissolve the Muslim-Croat Federation, and give more powers to the ten cantons that make up their hunk of Bosnia; in practice, to each locally dominant ethnic group. Mr Izetbegovic is sympathetic to the idea. The UN's high representative in Bosnia, Wolfgang Petritsch, is said to be pondering it. Similarly, talk of creating a single Bosnian army wins a hearing from some Muslims, but from few Croats or Serbs. "Only the Bosniaks think of themselves as Bosnian," says an SFOR man.

For now, the informal economy seems to be holding the country together as much as anything else. Some two-fifths of people in the Muslim-Croat Federation have no formal job; in the Serb Republic, about half. Most of the old political parties are intricately tied up with organised crime. Many of those who have returned struggle valiantly to rebuild homes and lives, though many depend on hand-outs. There is a sort of stagnant stability but—despite flickering hopes of an economic revival—no real sign of a state emerging. If SFOR were to clear out, Bosnia would almost certainly relapse into chaos.

And so to Kosovo

If Bosnia is complicated, but with a hint of hope, Kosovo these days has a harsher feel to it. The choices are certainly blunter. Most Albanian Kosovars want all the Serbs to leave—and most have done so. Some 200,000–300,000 Serbs used to live in Kosovo a decade ago. Maybe 100,000 still do, about half of them north of the Ibar river, which cuts through the northern town of Mitrovica. Another 27,000 live in a "Serb crescent" of villages and small towns that curls round the western and southern flanks of Pristina, the province's capital. No more than 700 Serbs remain in the capital itself, out of perhaps 20,000 who were there before NATO's bombing campaign last year.

To the polls

Upcoming elections in the Balkans

	Date	Type of election
Macedonia	September 10th	Local
Serbia	September 24th	Local, and Federal Yugoslav parliamentary and presidential
Montenegro	September 24th	Federal Yugoslav parliamentary and presidential*
Albania	October 1st	Local
Slovenia	October 15th	Parliamentary
Kosovo	October 28th	Local
Bosnia	November 11th	Parliamentary elections in Muslim-Croat Federation and Serb Republic

*Montenegrin government pledged to boycott election

Apart from the land north of Mitrovica and the Serb crescent, Serbs are few and far between. Kosovo's western valleys, where the ethnic-Albanian insurgency of the Kosovo Liberation Army (KLA) was fiercest before the bombing, are virtually empty of Serbs, except for scattered and dwindling groups huddled under the protection of KFOR, the NATO-led force that is trying to prevent the ethnic Albanians from hounding the Serbs out altogether. British troops around Slivovo, east of Pristina, are trying to consolidate and protect a string of villages where Serbs still survive.

Even within the crescent, few Serbs dare to travel without a KFOR escort. If Serbs cross from Serbia proper, as 100-plus do a day, to visit their relations or test the ethnic climate, they queue up at the border and then set off in convoys, protected by KFOR. In Pristina, Serbs are cooped up in a ghetto of tenement blocks, with KFOR guards on watch 24 hours a day. The Albanians refuse to accept them in Pristina's hospital, so the Serb sick have to be taken, often under KFOR supervision, to a Russian field hospital at Kosovo Polje.

Fewer Serbs are now being killed in Kosovo than during the months immediately after NATO ground troops rolled into the province in mid-1999. Then, by UN estimates, more than 60 people a month were killed, most of them Serbs. In the past three months, some 20-odd have been. But a constant undercurrent of violence and intimidation runs through the province. Life for any Serbs south of Mitrovica—and for non-Serbs north of that city—is wretched.

Yet the Serbs are not without help altogether. Serb paramilitaries are moving around, though mostly lying low, in the crescent near Pristina. North of the Ibar, between Mitrovica and Serbia proper, they hold sway. UN and other agencies barely operate there any more. But, this week, Kosovo's protectors made one of their boldest moves. Under a hail of rocks and abuse from furious Serbs, KFOR seized control of the Zvecan lead-smelter, on the northern side of the divide, citing worries about the appalling level of pollution it was giving rise to. The smelter is part of the huge Trepca complex of mines and factories which communist Yugoslavia regarded as one of its prize economic assets. The UN wants a consortium of French, American and Swedish interests to put the plant in order and reopen it, presumably with a more multi-ethnic workforce.

Farther south, the biggest recent source of unrest has consisted of Albanians attacking Albanians, as politicians and criminals—often one and the same—joust for supremacy in the run-up to elections for Kosovo's 30 municipalities.

After NATO's arrival, the 20,000-plus guerrillas of the KLA were disbanded, and were supposed to hand in their arms. Their force was reinvented, under the UN's aegis, as the much smaller Kosovo Protection Corps (KPC). The KPC is meant to do civilian neighbourly good works—putting out fires, building bridges and so on. But in practice the force sees itself as the core of an armed elite that will one day be the vanguard of the army of an independent Kosovo.

Its commander, Agim Ceku, was the KLA commander. It answers, unofficially, to Hashim Thaci, leader of the Democratic Party of Kosovo (PDK), which emerged from the KLA. A lot of the intra-Albanian violence is perpetrated by the PDK against the other main Kosovar factions, especially Ibrahim Rugova's more moderate Democratic League of Kosovo (LDK).

Last month, one of Mr Rugova's advisers was kidnapped and killed. Recently, his party leader in Podujevo just escaped being assassinated. KFOR simply does not fully control these ex-KLA men. The Americans, a central part of KFOR, are loth to take them on, for fear that the perception of NATO troops will turn from that of liberators to oppressors—and that the force will start taking casualties at the hands of the Kosovars. Another ethnic-Albanian guerrilla force, known as UCPMB, operates almost at will in an Albanian-inhabited strip of Serbia proper, with the declared aim of seizing control of three Serbian towns just to the east of Kosovo. The guerrillas, most of them former KLA men, claim they number 500; KFOR guesses 150. They want this bit of Serbia to belong to their would-be Albanian state. The idea of swapping it for the chunk above Mitrovica is in the air—though discounted by western mediators, fearful where this might lead with tricky borders elsewhere.

By all informed accounts, Mr Rugova's lot is far more popular than the young thugs who look to Mr Thaci. But the more militant PDK has more of the local media behind it, more cash, and more criminal and business links. Somewhere between the two stands a new player, Ramush Haradinaj.

Several of Kosovo's most prominent businessmen, such as Mustafa Remi in Podujevo and Saved Geci, are leading lights in Kosovar politics. Of the 50-odd Albanian parties which have registered for the municipal elections, many call for a Greater Albania, embracing a big slice of Macedonia and Albania proper. One even demands the Greek island of Corfu.

Just as KFOR cannot decide how robustly to handle the former KLA people, politicians in the West have little idea how to resolve Kosovo's eventual constitutional status. The judicial system is still weak; the UN's police force, which was meant to number more than 4,700, has yet to reach full strength: not surprisingly, given that it has 42 nationalities, it cannot cope. Besides, a proper criminal investigation unit is badly needed. There is no proper prison. Bernard Kouchner, the French doctor who administers the province in the name of the UN, is struggling to bring in foreign judges to help oversee law and order.

The main immediate hope of Dr Kouchner and the KFOR commanders in charge of some 20,000 overstretched troops is that Mr Rugova, and perhaps Mr Haradinaj, will do well at the elections. Dr Kouchner could then appoint additional people, including Serbs, who are boycotting the polls, to local councils. KFOR might then have more authority to enable it to bring KPD miscreants to book.

In the longer run, however, it may be that the only way to settle the problem of Kosovo would be to hold a new Balkan conference, where the entire gamut of territorial and constitutional issues across the region could be discussed in the round. Might, for instance, Montenegro, Kosovo and Serbia proper be reshaped as three republics linked in one federation? Might Bosnia's constitution be rewritten? Might there be referendums to decide under whose flag the inhabitants of contested areas want to live?

The trouble is that no such bold ideas are worth discussing until Mr Milosevic is out of the way. A defeat for him in the September election would hugely boost the prospects for Balkan peace. Jacques Chirac, president of France, which holds the current six-month presidency of the European Union, has contemplated holding such a grand Balkan summit in the autumn.

But Mr Milosevic could well stay in power for quite some time yet. If he does, the West will simply have to grit its teeth, in Kosovo perhaps more doggedly even than in Bosnia, and prepare itself for a long haul as an unloved policeman in a wretched part of the world. For if SFOR and KFOR were to leave, or to draw down their forces too fast, a Balkan bonfire, in Kosovo, Bosnia and elsewhere, could easily reignite.

A CONTINENT IN PERIL

17 million Africans have died since the AIDS epidemic began in the late 1970s, more than 3.7 million of them children. An additional 12 million children have been orphaned by AIDS. An estimated 8.8% of adults in Africa are infected with HIV/AIDS, and in the following seven countries, at least 1 adult in 5 is living with HIV

HOT SPOT

Of the 36 million adults and children in the world living with HIV/AIDS in 2000, more than 70% were in sub-Saharan Africa. 3.8 million Africans were newly infected last year

1. Botswana

Though it has the highest per capita GDP, it also has the highest estimated adult infection rate—**36%**. 24,000 die each year. 66,000 children have lost their mother or both parents to the disease

2. Swaziland

Swaziland More than **25%** of adults have HIV/AIDS in this small country. 12,000 children have been orphaned, and 7,100 adults and children die each year

3. Zimbabwe

One-quarter of the adult population is infected here. 160,000 adults and children died in 1999, and 900,000 children have been orphaned. Because of AIDS, life expectancy is 43

4. Lesotho

24% of adults are infected with HIV/AIDS. 35,000 children have been orphaned, and 16,000 adults and children die each year

5. Zambia

20% of the adult population is infected, 1 in 4 adults in the cities. 650,00 children have been orphaned, and 99,000 Zambians died in 1999

6. South Africa

This country has the largest number of people living with HIV/AIDS, about **20%** of its adult population, up from 13% in 1997. 420,000 children have been orphaned, and 250,000 people die each year from the disease.

7. Namibia

19.5% of the adult population is living with HIV. 57% of the infected are women. 67,000 children are AIDS orphans, and 18,000 adults and children die each year

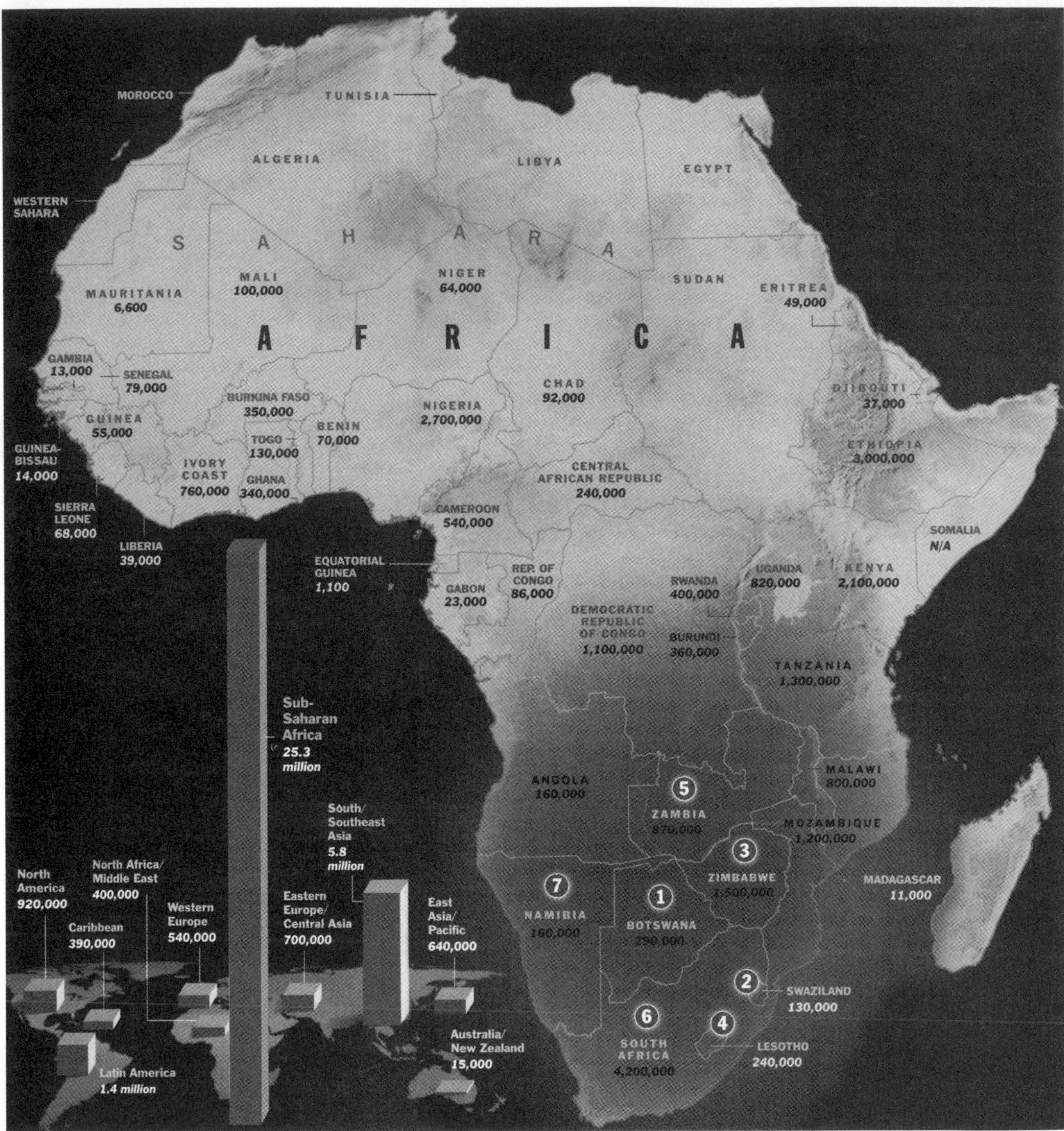

TIME Graphic by Lon Tweeten

Source: UNAIDS

AIDS Has Arrived in India and China

How will the world's two most populous countries cope with the pandemic?

by Ann Hwang

In 1348, the Black Death arrived in Europe from its probable home in Central Asia, and over the next couple of years it is believed to have killed 25 million people. Sometime soon, mortality from AIDS will exceed the death toll of that worst outbreak of bubonic plague. Since the start of the AIDS pandemic roughly 20 years ago, 20 million people have died and over 50 million have been infected. Every 11 seconds, someone dies from AIDS. According to statistics compiled by the World Health Organization, AIDS is now killing more people each year than any other infectious disease. AIDS has become one of the greatest epidemics in the history of our species.

The AIDS epidemic took much longer to build momentum than did the Black Death, but AIDS has far more staying power. For all their intensity, the bubonic plague epidemics were relatively short: *Yersinia pestis*, the plague bacterium, tends to burn itself out quickly. And in any case, *Y. pestis* and *Homo sapiens* are no longer caught up in an intense epidemic cycle. Plague still kills people in various parts of the world, but it does not spark epidemics on a continental scale. Even if it did, antibiotics have made it far less deadly than it was 650 years ago. But HIV, the virus that causes AIDS, shows no sign of releasing us from its grip. Indeed, it has evolved into several new forms, even as it continues to burn through humanity. And although there are now drugs that can prolong the lives of its victims—or at least, those who can afford treatment—there is no cure for the disease and no vaccine for it. (See box, "An AIDS Vaccine?")

Within the AIDS pandemic, sub-Saharan Africa has become the equivalent of mid-14th century Europe. Ignorance of the disease, poverty, war, and frequently, a rather relaxed attitude toward sexual activity (especially when it comes to men)—such factors have allowed HIV to explode through some African societies. In 1996, the Joint United Nations Programme on HIV/AIDS (UNAIDS) predicted that by 2000, over 9 million Africans would be infected with HIV. The actual number turned out to be 25 million. Though Africa is home to less than 9 percent of the world's adults, it has more than two-thirds of adult HIV infections. In Botswana, the county with the world's highest infection rate, one in three adults is now infected. And as the infected continue to die, places like Botswana may become increasingly unstable for lack of farmers, teachers, community leaders, even parents.

But in large measure, the course of the pandemic will depend on what happens not in Africa but in Asia, the continent that is home to nearly 60 percent of the world's people. AIDS is already well established in Asia, although no one knows precisely when or where it first arrived. By the mid-1980s, however, infections were beginning to appear in several Asian counties, including Thailand and India. A few years later, it was obvious that HIV infection was increasing dramatically among two of the best known "high risk populations"—prostitutes and users of injection drugs. As its incidence increased, the disease began to travel the highways of Asia's drug trade, radiating outward from the opium-producing "Golden Triangle," where Myanmar (Burma), Laos, and Thailand converge. The infecting of the world's most populous continent had begun.

That process may now be reaching a kind of critical mass. AIDS has arrived in the two most heavily populated countries in the world: India and China. With populations of 1 billion and 1.3 billion respectively, these countries are home to over a third of the world's population and nearly 70 percent of Asians people. Thus far, neither has suffered the kind of explosive epidemic that has ravaged sub-Saharan Africa. Each still has important opportunities to stem the epidemic. What will the giant societies of Asia make of those opportunities? This is one of the greatest social and ethical issues of our era.

Mapping the Epidemic

Reported Risk of HIV infection in India and China, 1999

Caveat lector: the data in this map, which derive from official country sources, do not give a complete picture of the epidemic. In particular, information on high risk groups is incomplete. The high risk data do not include homosexuals in either India or China, or blood sellers in China. Because the latter group is omitted, the map does not accurately portray the epidemic in central China.

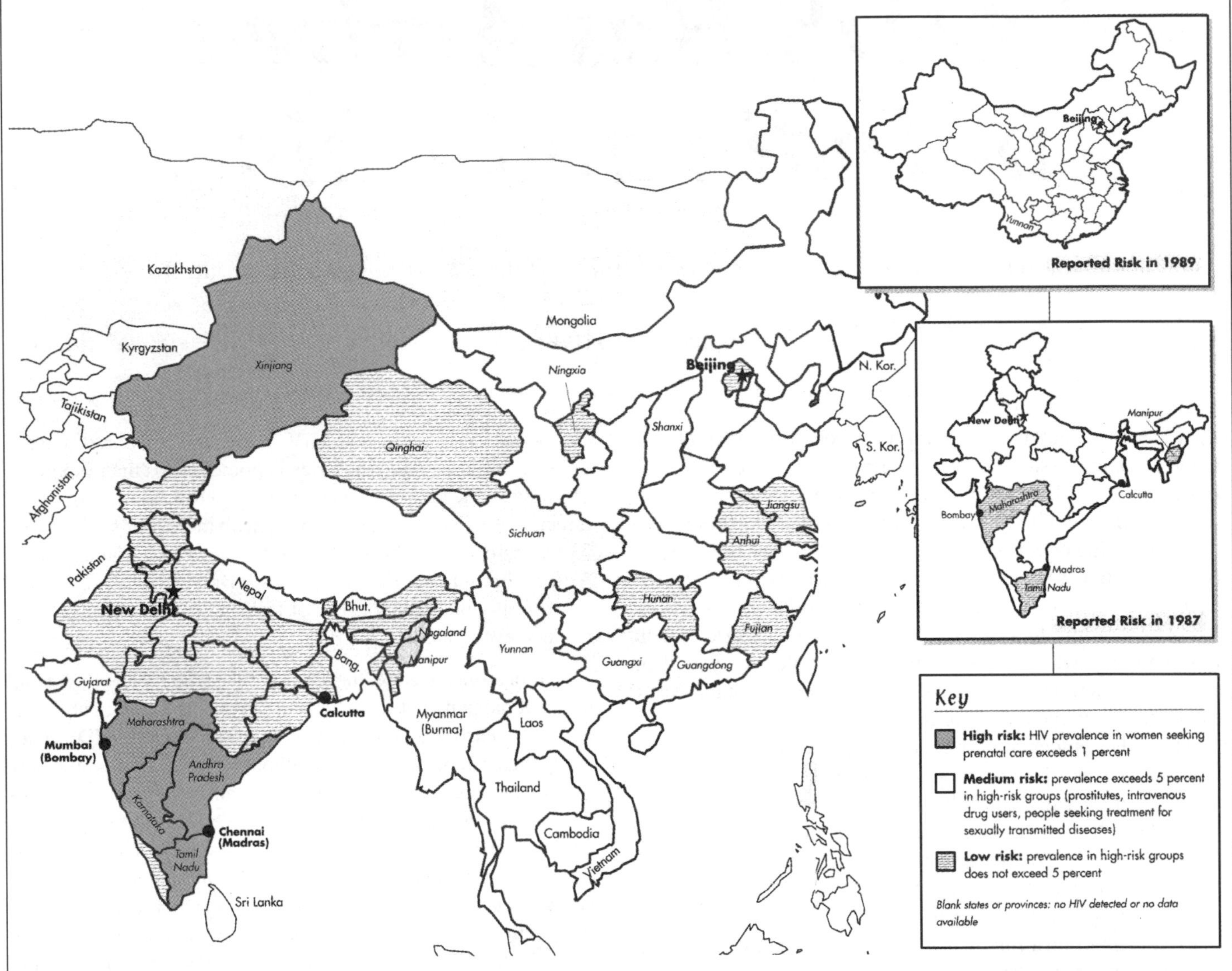

Sources: Indian Ministry of Health and Family Welfare, National AIDS Control Organization; UNAIDS/WHO Epidemiological Fact Sheet: China, 2000 update; UNAIDS Country Profile: China

Four Million Infected in India

India is home to an estimated 4 million people with HIV—more than any other country in the world. Because of India's huge population, the level of infection as a national average is very low—just 0.4 percent, close to the U.S. national level of 0.3 percent. But this apparently comfortable average masks huge regional disparities: in some of India's states, particularly in the extreme northeast, near the Myanmar border, and in much of the south, the rate of infection among adults has reached 2 percent or more—five times the national rate and more than enough to kindle a widespread epidemic.

Among these more heavily infected regions, there is another kind of disparity as well, in the way the virus is spreading. In southern India, AIDS fits the standard profile of a sexually transmitted disease (STD), with particularly high infection rates among prostitutes. Sex is big business in India, generating revenues of $8.7 billion each year, according to the Centre of Concern for Child Labour, a Delhi-based non-profit. Mumbai (Bombay), the country's largest west coast city, has twice the population of New York yet almost 20 times the number of prostitutes. By 1997, over 70 percent of those prostitutes were HIV positive. The prostitutes' clients, in addition to risking infection themselves, put their wives or other sex partners in jeopardy, thereby creating a bridge that allows the virus to spread from a high-risk enclave to the general population.

In some segments of Indian society, that bridge is now very broad. Long-distance truck drivers, for example, are usually away from home for long periods and many visit prostitutes en route. For one study, published in the *British Medical Journal* in 1999, nearly 6,000 long-distance truckers were interviewed and nine out of ten married drivers described themselves as "sexually promiscuous," defined as having frequent and indiscriminate change of sexual partners. Not surprisingly, HIV incidence is now rising among married Indian women. A study from 1993 to 1996 found that over 10 percent of female patients at STD clinics in Pune, near Mumbai, were HIV positive; over 90 percent of these women were married and had had sexual contact only with their husbands. (See box, "Increasingly, A Women's Disease.")

In India's northeast, the epidemic has a very different character. This region has an extensive drug culture—which is hardly surprising, given its proximity to the Golden Triangle. Here, the epidemic has been driven by intravenous drug use, particularly among young unemployed men and students. By sharing contaminated needles, addicts are injecting the virus into their bloodstreams. Data are scarce, but according to government estimates, there are 1 million heroin users in India, and roughly 100,000 of them reside in the comparatively small states that make up the northeast.

In the northeastern state of Manipur, on the Myanmar border, HIV among intravenous drug users and their sexual partners increased from virtually nothing in 1988 to over 70 percent four years later. By 1999, 2.2 percent of pregnant women attending prenatal care clinics in Manipur tested positive for HIV. Because the infection risk in women seeking prenatal care should be roughly representative of the general population, epidemiologists often use this group to estimate trends in the general population. In the northeast, as in the south, HIV is apparently moving into mainstream society.

Perhaps One Million Infected in China

In China, the shadow of AIDS is at present just barely discernable. Current estimates put the number of HIV infections at 500,000 to 1 million. In a country of 1.3 billion, that works out to an infinitesimal national level of infection: eight one-hundredths of a percent at most. But even though the virus is very thinly spread, it seems to be present nearly everywhere: all of the country's 31 provinces have reported AIDS cases.

As with India, the character of this incipient epidemic differs greatly from one region to the next. China's original HIV hotspot is in the south: Yunnan province, which borders Laos and Myanmar, had almost 90 percent of the country's HIV cases in 1990. Yunnan lies on the periphery of the Golden Triangle and is home to a large (but not readily definable) proportion of China's intravenous drug users. Today, however, the virus has moved well beyond Yunnan, in part because of a surge in the popularity of injection drugs. By the middle of the 1990s, half of new infections in intravenous drug users were occurring outside Yunnan, mostly in other southern provinces. Guangxi province, which borders Yunnan to the east, saw infection levels in surveyed drug users climb from zero in 1993 to 40 percent by 1997.

An AIDS Vaccine? No Magic Bullet

"People expect a magic bullet," says Chris Collins, president of the board of the AIDS Vaccine Advocacy Coalition, a network of U.S. activists that seeks to increase funding for HIV vaccine research. But he cautions, "the AIDS vaccine probably isn't going to be that."

It is true that vaccine researchers have made substantial progress over the past few years. A California-based company known as VaxGen is now conducting the first ever large-scale tests in humans of a possible vaccine. An interim analysis of the tests, which involve 8,000 volunteers on three continents, is scheduled for November 2001. Many experts believe that such efforts will eventually pay off, but the results are not likely to compare with the smallpox vaccine, which eventually eliminated that earlier global pandemic.

One big obstacle is the virus's mutation rate. Mutations appear to occur in at least one of the virus's genes each time it replicates, once every 8 hours. In HIV, as in any other organism, most mutations prove to be evolutionary dead ends. But not all of them: the virus has already spawned more than a dozen different subtypes around the globe, and it is unclear whether a single vaccine would be effective against every subtype. China in particular has a very heterogeneous epidemic, with nearly all known subtypes represented. This global mosaic of subtypes may exacerbate the medical North-South divide. How much industrialized-country R&D will be invested in developing vaccines for strains that predominate in developing countries?

Even when a viable vaccine is discovered, researchers are likely to face formidable challenges in determining its use. Suppose, for example, that a vaccine is only 50 percent effective: should it be licensed, given the possibility that people receiving it may be less inclined to have safe sex or use clean needles? Assuming that a strong general case could be made for the use of such a vaccine, who is going to pay for the inoculation of the developing world's high-risk populations? Vaccine researchers may find the sociology of the epidemic as difficult to deal with as the biology of the virus itself. No doubt, an effective vaccine will be a valuable tool against the pandemic, but it is not likely to replace any of the other tools already in use.

Last year, China's official count of registered intravenous drug users reached 600,000—more than double the number in 1992. And as the number of users has grown, so has the custom

Increasingly, A Women's Disease

In the developing world, women now account for more than half of HIV infections, and there is growing evidence that the position of women in developing societies will be a critical factor in shaping the course of the AIDS pandemic. In general, greater gender inequality tends to correlate with higher levels of HIV infection, according to the World Bank researchers who track literacy rates and other general indicators of social well-being.

As in the AIDS-ravaged countries of sub-Saharan Africa, India and China offer women far fewer social opportunities than men. Both countries score in the lower half of the "Gender-Related Development Index," a measure of gender equity developed by the United Nations Development Programme.

Double sexual standards that demand female virginity while condoning male promiscuity put many women at risk. Studies in India and Thailand, by the Washington D.C.-based International Center for Research on Women (ICRW), have found that young, single women are expected not only to be virgins but also to be ignorant of sexual matters. As a result, young women lack basic knowledge about their bodies and are poorly prepared to insist on the use of condoms to protect themselves from HIV or other sexually transmitted diseases (STDs).

Even within marriage, women may have little influence over sex. "A woman does not have much say in the house," said one Indian woman participating in an ICRW focus group. "He is the husband. How long can we go against his wish?" Without adequate legal protection or opportunities for economic independence, such women may have little choice but to remain in abusive marriages and follow their husbands' dictates, Of 600 women living in a slum in Chennai (Madras), a major city on India's east coast, 90 percent said they had no bargaining power with their spouses about sex and couldn't convince them to use condoms. And 95 percent of these women were financially dependent on their husbands.

Women's risk is compounded by biological factors. During vaginal intercourse without a condom, transmission of HIV from an infected man to a woman is two to four times more likely than transmission in the opposite direction. The two key factors appear to be the surface area of exposed tissue and the viral load. Women lose on both counts: the virus concentrates in semen, and the surface area of the vagina is relatively large and subject to injury during sex. Tears in the lining of the vagina or cervix may admit the virus more readily. Women suffer another biological disadvantage as well. In general, STDs are harder to detect in women because the symptoms are more likely to be internal. Lesions from unrecognized STDs can increase a woman's susceptibility to HIV.

Once infected, women are less likely to be treated. In couples where both partners are infected with HIV but where treatment can be afforded only for one, it is the husband who almost invariably gets the drugs. Subhash Hira, director of Bombay's AIDS Research and Control Center, explained it this way to an AP reporter: "It is the woman who is stepping back. She thinks of herself as expendable." A 1991–93 study in Kagera, Tanzania found that in AIDS-afflicted households, more than twice as much, on average, was spent caring for the male victims than for the female victims: $80 versus only $38.

The stigma of infection also seems to fall more heavily upon women. Unease over female sexuality appears to translate readily into a tendency to see infection in women as punishment for sexual promiscuity. Women are sometimes even blamed for being the source of the disease. Suneeta Krishnan, an expert on AIDS in southern India, notes that the local languages contain few words for STDs, but the most commonly used formula is "diseases that come from women." One man explained the term to her: "The man may be the transmitter of the disease, but the source is the woman. She is the one who is blamed. For example, if a well is poisoned, and a man drinks from it and falls ill, people do not blame him. They blame the well. In the same way, people blame women for sexually transmitted diseases."

—*Ann Hwang*

of sharing needles. Information on this habit is hard to come by, but based on the most recent data the government has provided, UNAIDS estimated that 60 percent of users shared needles in 1998, up from 25 percent the year before.

In many parts of China, and particularly in the countryside of the central provinces, the virus is spreading through a very different form of injection. Selling one's own blood is a common way for poor people to make a little extra money, but it puts them at high risk for HIV infection. The government banned blood sales in 1998 (the blood supply in China is supposed to come from voluntary donations). But growing demand for blood virtually ensures the continuation of the practice. In some illegal collection centers, blood of the same blood type may be pooled, the plasma extracted to make valuable clotting and immune factors, and the remaining cells re-injected into the sellers. (Re-injection shortens the recovery period, allowing people to sell their blood more frequently.) The needles and other collection equipment are often reused as well. A January 2000 raid on one such center in Shanxi province, southwest of Beijing, turned up 64 bags of plasma, all of which tested positive for HIV and hepatitis B.

The extent of the black market in blood is unknown. China's news media are banned from reporting on the topic, outside researchers have been prevented from studying it, and government officials won't discuss it. But it's a good bet that the system is not about to be weaned off black market blood anytime soon; official donations are apparently inadequate even though their "voluntary" character is already badly strained. Inland from Hong Kong, for instance, in the city of Guangzhou, work groups are fined if they do not meet their blood donation quotas. Workers sometimes avoid the fines without donating by hiring "professional donors" to take their place. One could argue that such quotas still work, albeit in a somewhat indirect and callous way. But the system is riddled with flaws. The general cultural reluctance to give blood in China has been exacerbated by a widespread perception that donation is dangerous. And unfortunately, that perception is probably justified, since even official blood collection centers may reuse needles and tubing. (Such reuse is not necessarily intentional; sometimes unscrupulous dealers collect used equipment, repackage it, and sell it as new.) Another unfortunate consequence follows when the blood is actually used: apart from the larger urban hospitals, the Chinese blood supply is probably not adequately screened for HIV or other diseases, and "professional donors" have much higher levels of infection than the general public.

In the major cities and especially along China's highly developed southeastern coast, AIDS is primarily an STD. At least in the cities, sexual mores appear to have loosened considerably over the past couple of decades. Not surprisingly, prostitution is becoming more common. For the country as a whole, prostitution arrests now number about 500,000 annually; China's Public Security Department estimates the number of prostitutes to be between 3 and 4 million, a figure that has been increasing since the 1980s. STDs, such as syphilis and gonorrhea, were virtually eradicated in the 1960s under an aggressive public health campaign, but have returned with a vengeance. Infection rates are increasing by 30 to 40 percent each year, according to the Ministry of Health. That portends an increase in AIDS, not only because of what it suggests about the growing sexual permissiveness, but also because the genital sores caused by other STDs make people more vulnerable to HIV.

Sexual contact, intravenous drug use, blood selling—in many parts of the country, these and perhaps other modes of transmission are increasingly likely to "overlap" as the virus spreads. The results may be difficult to anticipate, or to counter. For example, in 1998, the most recent year for which statistics were available, the province reporting the largest number of new HIV infections was not Yunnan or Guangxi, but the remote Xinjiang, in China's arid and lightly populated northwest. Why? In part, the answer appears to be drugs. Despite its apparent isolation, Xinjiang is enmeshed in the opium trade. Some studies have found infection levels of about 80 percent among the province's intravenous drug users. Local prostitutes seem to be heavily infected as well. And HIV has begun to appear in women coming to clinics for prenatal care—a strong indication that the virus is starting to leak into the province's general population. But despite the fact that it has become an HIV hotspot, Xinjiang has attracted little official attention, and that suggests another reason for the province's plight. Most of Xinjiang's inhabitants are Uigur, a people of Turkish descent. (The area is sometimes called "Chinese Turkestan.") Like some of China's other ethnic minorities, the Uigur suffer disproportionately from HIV. The country's AIDS prevention and education programs, very small to begin with, may be even less effective among ethnic minorities. Lack of official interest in minorities may be a factor Xinjiang's epidemic; perhaps also there is some sort of cultural "communications gap."

In early 2000, a group of concerned Chinese scientists—including some members of the Chinese Academy of Sciences—submitted a report to the government that warned, "The spread of AIDS is accelerating rapidly and we face the prospect of remaining inert against the threat." Without decisive action, according to China's National Center for AIDS Prevention and Control (NCAIDS), 10 million people in China could be infected with HIV by 2010.

Death on the Margins

In China and most of India, AIDS is still concentrated among socially marginal high-risk groups—groups engaged in activities that attract mainstream disapproval and that are often illegal. One of the most obscure of these groups is male homosexuals. Despite the prominence of homosexuality in the AIDS controversies of the industrialized countries, very little is known about gay life in China or India. But studies in Chennai (Madras), the largest city on the southeast coast, reveal one ominous characteristic of the Indian homosexual underground: most participants do not appear to be exclusively homosexual. Most are married.

Gay men who are married, heterosexual men who patronize prostitutes, intravenous drug users and their sexual partners: AIDS may still be a disease of the social margins, but in both India and China there are several major bridges between the margins and mainstream society. It's possible that the virus will tend to cross those bridges relatively slowly. If it remains largely in the fringe populations, it should be easier to control. But even this scenario entails serious risk, since it could encourage callousness towards the victims and complacency towards the disease.

Take the complacency potential first: if AIDS is portrayed as a disease of marginalized groups, people who are not in those groups may be reluctant to acknowledge their own vulnerability. Suneeta Krishnan, a researcher at the University of California at Berkeley, has studied HIV for the past three years in southern India and seen this reluctance first hand. "The perception is that AIDS is only a problem of female commercial prostitutes sitting in Bombay," she said. "It's only a problem for us if we have sex with them." Such attitudes could easily heighten the risk of contagion.

The "us-them" mentality can also greatly increase the suffering of those who are already infected. One effect of stigmatizing AIDS-prone minorities is that *all* AIDS sufferers tend to end up stigmatized. Rajesh Vedanthan, one of the founders of Swasthya, a nonprofit that provides HIV counseling to women in the southern Indian state of Karnataka, recalls the story of a pregnant woman who sought care at a hospital for profuse vaginal bleeding. Without her consent or knowledge, she was tested for HIV and found to be infected. The hospital doctor—without informing her of her HIV status—placed gauze to soak up the blood, discharged her from the hospital without treatment, and told her never to return. By the time she came to Swasthya, she had a raging infection. Such inhumanity can greatly compound the contagion of the disease itself.

"Avoiding Unnecessary Agony"

In Beijing, the streets are swept clean by women wielding brooms made from twigs. Licensed taxis queue at the airport waiting for uniformed guards to assign them passengers. But you needn't go far from China's capital before all the taxis have inexplicably broken meters, and beggars crowd the trash-covered streets. A similar duality is apparent in the country's efforts to deal with AIDS. As a totalitarian state with a strong tradition of public health and social services, China would appear to be in good shape to control the AIDS epidemic. But China spends only about seven tenths of 1 percent of its GDP on health care. (The United States is at the other end of the spectrum, with public health care expenditures amounting to 6 percent of its GDP.) China's anti-AIDS efforts thus far have amounted to little more than crackdowns on prostitution, drug use, and blood sales—strong-arm tactics that have had negligible effect.

Public education about the epidemic has been stalled by censorship. The language of official AIDS announcements reflects a deep awkwardness in discussing sexual issues. "The government calls to the attention of its citizens whether their words and deeds conform to the standards of the Chinese nation," explained one official declaration dating from the beginning of the epidemic. The announcement added, with muffled urgency, that citizens should "know what to do and what not to do when making sexual decisions and avoiding unnecessary agony." Though times are changing, China's first nationally televised advertisement promoting condom use to prevent AIDS was taken off the air in December 1999, after just two days of broadcast, because it violated a ban on ads for sex products.

Technical infrastructure for treating and tracking the epidemic is also in short supply. In its most recent report, released in 1997, NCAIDS noted that China had only 400 labs capable of testing for HIV, or roughly one for every 3 million people. There is also a shortage of medical personnel trained to treat people infected with HIV or other STDs. When workers at STD clinics in the southern city of Shenzen were tested on their medical knowledge, only 23 percent passed, according to Xinhua, the official Chinese news agency. According to Zeng Yi, an AIDS researcher and member of the Chinese Academy of Sciences, local officials in various parts of the country are reluctant to collect data on HIV, for fear that their province will be blackballed as a highly infected area. Even more alarming is the apparent drop in resources committed to fighting the epidemic. Following budget cuts of 40 percent, the number of HIV screening tests in disease surveillance programs fell from 3.4 million in 1997 to 1.3 million in 1998.

India, the world's largest democracy, has little reason for complacency either. Early in the epidemic, some Indian politicians were calling for banning sex with foreigners, isolating HIV-positive people, and urging a return to traditional values—cries that were being heard in other countries as well. The proposal to ban sex with foreigners was put forth in 1988 by A.S. Paintal, the government's chief medical researcher, but was scuttled immediately under a barrage of domestic and international criticism. In Goa state, on India's west coast, a law permitting the resting and isolation of anyone suspected of being HIV-positive was overturned only after repeated protests. On the federal level, an unsuccessful 1989 "AIDS Prevention Bill" called for the forcible testing and detention of any HIV-positive person or anyone suspected of being HIV-positive.

In 1992, India's Ministry of Health and Family Welfare established the National AIDS Control Organisation (NACO) to carry out AIDS prevention and education. NACO has put into place a surveillance system to monitor disease trends, but limited resources have hampered prevention and made treatment impossible. Anti-retroviral therapy, the "drug cocktail" that can slow the progression of AIDS, costs $270 to $450 per month. The country's average per capita income is only $444 per year. Even among India's rapidly expanding middle class, the average per capita income is only about $4,800 per year—roughly the same as a year's worth of the cocktail. Nor is there preventive care for the many opportunistic infections that ultimately kill people whose immune systems are ravaged by AIDS, even though in industrialized countries, these infections can usually be held at bay for years with relatively inexpensive medications. Like China, India spends only about 1 percent of its GDP on health care—a number that Jeffrey Sachs, a professor of international trade at Harvard University, calls "shockingly low."

The Sonagachi Prostitutes and the Future of AIDS

In 1989, when surveys of Thai brothels turned up rising levels of HIV infection among prostitutes, the Thai government collaborated with several non-governmental organizations to launch a massive public information campaign urging condom use. The "100% Condom Program" distributed condoms to brothels and massage parlors, and enforced use by tracking the contacts of men who sought care for STDs. Over the course of the next three years, condom use in brothels increased from 14 to 90 percent. By 1995, the number of men treated at government clinics for new sexually transmitted infections had dropped tenfold. A year later, HIV prevalence among conscripts to the army had dropped below 2 percent—less than half of what it had been in mid-1993.

The lesson from the early stages of the epidemic in Thailand is clear: it's worth dispensing with moral scruples to give people a clear sense of the medical issues. Public education works, at least when it's backed by some degree of enforcement. There's no reason to think this approach would be any less effective in China or India. Consider the prostitutes of Calcutta's Sonagachi district. Against considerable odds, these women have managed, not just to inform themselves about AIDS, but to organize themselves. The over 30,000 dues-paying members in their informal union have improved working conditions, educated other prostitutes about AIDS, started reading classes, and reduced the number of child prostitutes. They understand the need for condoms and have even threatened collective action against brothel owners reluctant to require condom use. As a result, their HIV infection levels remain at 5 percent—very low compared to the 60 or 70 percent levels typical of prostitutes in other Indian cities.

Frank talk about condoms and safe sex is of course just a start. An effective AIDS program must also have a reliable, confidential, and voluntary HIV testing program. It must protect the rights of infected people and secure treatment for them. But perhaps the greatest challenge of all is the need to build some form of long-term support for those marginalized, high-risk groups—support that invites the kind of initiative shown by the Sonagachi prostitutes. As Suneeta Krishnan puts it, "HIV is intimately linked to social and economic inequality and deprivations. As long as these problems persist, HIV is going to persist."

That is perhaps one of the lessons from the latter stages of the Thai epidemic. The Asian financial crisis dried up funding for Thailand's AIDS programs. Spending fell from $90 million in 1997 to $30 million in 1998 before rebounding somewhat, to $40 million in 1999 and 2000. The drop in funds has made the weak points in the Thai approach more apparent. Among populations other than brothel workers and their clients, the epidemic has proceeded largely unchecked. Male homosexuals have not generally been included in the program. Neither have intravenous drug users—a group whose infection level has passed 40 percent. And the worst news of all is that the infection level among women receiving prenatal care is now climbing.

In India and China as in many other places, prostitutes, homosexuals, and drug addicts are frequently the objects of contempt and legal sanction. But these are the people who should be top priorities for any serious AIDS program, for both practical and humanitarian reasons. How much of an investment are we really willing to make in the egalitarian principles upon which every public health program is built? AIDS is an acid test of our humanity. Over and over again, the virus teaches its terrifying lesson. There is no such thing as an expendable person.

Ann Hwang is a medical student at the University of California, San Francisco and a former intern at the Worldwatch Institute.

GREENVILLE: FROM BACK COUNTRY to FOREFRONT

Eugene A. Kennedy

What factors are crucial in determining the success or failure of an area? This article explores the past and present and glimpses what may be the future of one area which is experiencing great success. The success story of Greenville County, S.C. is no longer a secret. This article seeks to find the factors which led to its success and whether they will provide a type of yardstick to measure the future.

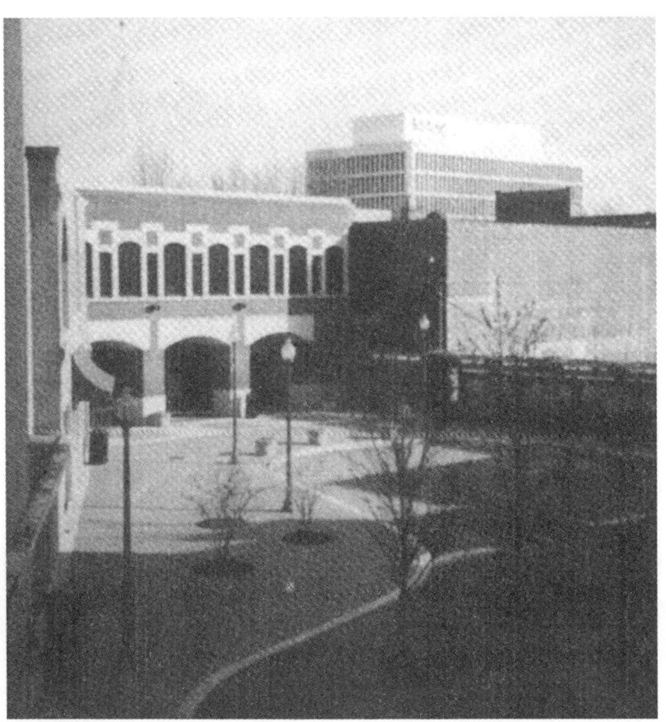

PHOTO: E. KENNEDY

An open courtyard off Main Street, downtown Greenville, S.C.

The physical geography of this area is explored, as well as the economic factors, history, transportation, energy costs, labor costs and new incentive packages designed to lure new industries and company headquarters to the area.

Physical geography: advantageous

Greenville County is situated in the northwest corner of South Carolina on the upper edge of the Piedmont region. The land consists of a rolling landscape butted against the foothills of the Appalachian Mountains. Monadnocks, extremely hard rock structures which have resisted millions of years of erosion, rise above the surface in many places indicating that the surface level was once much higher than today. Rivers run across the Piedmont carving valleys between the plateaus. The cities, farms, highways and rail lines are located on the broad, flat tops of the rolling hills.

Climatologically, the area is in a transition zone between the humid coastal plains and the cooler temperatures of the mountains, resulting in a relatively mild climate with a long agricultural growing season. The average annual precipitation for Greenville County is 50.53 inches at an altitude of 1040 feet above sea level. The soil is classified as being a Utisoil. This type of soil has a high clay base and is usually found to be a reddish color due to the thousands of years of erosion which has leached many of the minerals out of the soil, leaving a reddish residue of iron oxide. This soil will produce good crops if lime and fertilizer containing the eroded minerals are added. Without fertilizers, these soils could sustain crops on freshly cleared areas for only two to three years before the nutrients were exhausted and new fields were needed. This kept large plantations from being created in the Greenville area. The climate and land are such that nearly anything could be cultivated with the proper soil modification. Physical potential, although a limiting factor, is not the only determining factor in the success of an area. As Preston James, one of the fathers of modern geography pointed out, the culture of the population which comes to inhabit the area greatly determines the response to that particular physical environment.

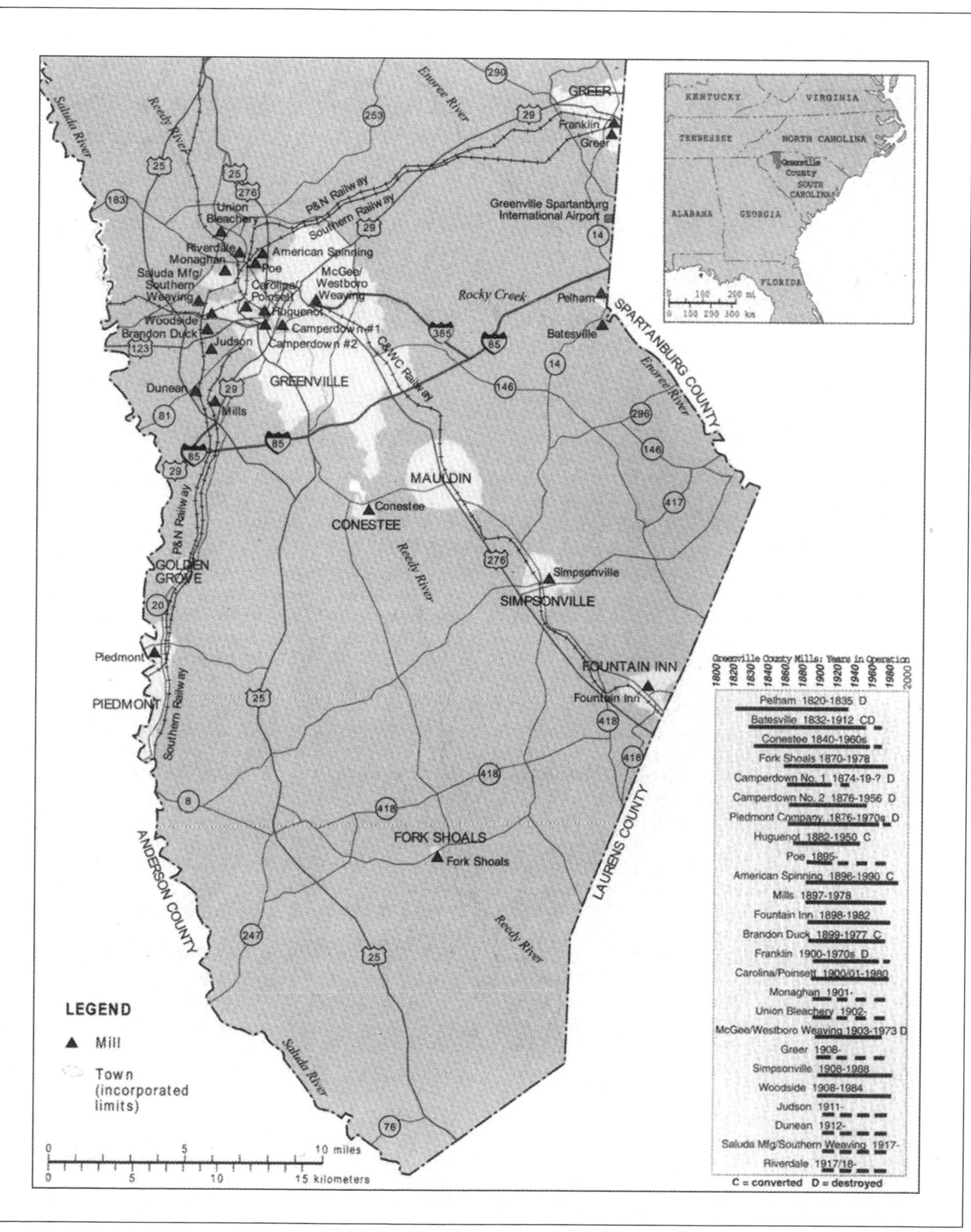
KENTUCKY
VIRGINIA
TENNESSEE
NORTH CAROLINA
Greenville County
SOUTH CAROLINA
ALABAMA
GEORGIA
FLORIDA
0 100 200 mi
0 100 200 300 km
GREER
Franklin
Greer
Greenville Spartanburg International Airport
Enoree River
Saluda River
Reedy River
P&N Railway
Southern Railway
Union Bleachery
Riverdale
Monaghan
American Spinning
Poe
Saluda Mfg/Southern Weaving
Carolina/Poinsett
McGee/Westboro Weaving
Rocky Creek
Pelham
Woodside
Huguenot
Brandon Duck
Camperdown #1
Camperdown #2
Judson
Batesville
C&WC Railway
SPARTANBURG COUNTY
GREENVILLE
Dunean
Mills
MAULDIN
Conestee
CONESTEE
GOLDEN GROVE
Simpsonville
SIMPSONVILLE
Piedmont
PIEDMONT
FOUNTAIN INN
Fountain Inn
LAURENS COUNTY
FORK SHOALS
Fork Shoals
ANDERSON COUNTY
LEGEND
Mill
Town (incorporated limits)
0 5 10 miles
0 5 10 15 kilometers
Greenville County Mills: Years in Operation
1800 1820 1830 1840 1860 1880 1900 1920 1940 1960 1980 2000
Pelham 1820-1835 D
Batesville 1832-1912 CD
Conestee 1840-1960s
Fork Shoals 1870-1978
Camperdown No. 1 1874-19-? D
Camperdown No. 2 1876-1956 D
Piedmont Company 1876-1970s D
Huguenot 1882-1950 C
Poe 1895-
American Spinning 1896-1990 C
Mills 1897-1978
Fountain Inn 1898-1982
Brandon Duck 1899-1977 C
Franklin 1900-1970s D
Carolina/Poinsett 1900/01-1980
Monaghan 1901-
Union Bleachery 1902-
McGee/Westboro Weaving 1903-1973 D
Greer 1908-
Simpsonville 1908-1988
Woodside 1908-1984
Judson 1911-
Dunean 1912-
Saluda Mfg/Southern Weaving 1917-
Riverdale 1917/18-
C = converted D = destroyed

KAREN SEVERUD COOK, UNIVERSITY OF KANSAS MAP ASSOCIATES

From European settlement through the textile era

An Englishman named Richard Pearis was the first to begin to recognize the potential of what was then known as the "Back Country." The area was off limits to white settlers through a treaty between the British and the Indians. In order to get around the law, Pearis married a native American and opened a trading post in 1768 at the falls of the Reedy River. He soon built a grist mill and used the waterfalls for power. Pearis prospered until the end of the Revolutionary War. He had remained loyal to the British, lost all his property when the new nation was established and left the country.

Others soon realized the potential of what was to become Greenville County. Isaac Green built a grist mill and became the area's most prominent citizen. In 1786, the area became a county in South Carolina and was named for Isaac Green. The Saluda, Reedy and Enoree Rivers along with several smaller streams had many waterfalls, making them excellent locations for mills during the era of water power. During the Antebellum period, Greenville County's 789 square miles was inhabited by immigrants with small farms and also served as a resort area for Low Country planters who sought to escape the intense summer heat and the disease carrying mosquitoes which flourished in the flooded rice fields and swampy low country of the coastal plains. Most of the permanent residents farmed and a few mills were built to process the grains grown in the area.

Although very little cotton was ever actually grown in Greenville County, cotton became the driving force behind its early industrialization. Beginning with William Bates in 1820, entrepreneurs saw this area's plentiful rivers and waterfalls as a potential source of energy to harness. William Bates built the first textile mill in the county sometime between 1830 and 1832 on Rocky Creek near the Enoree River. This was known as the Batesville Mill. Water power dictated the location of the early southern textile mills, patterned after the mills built in New England. Mill owners purchased the cotton from farms and hauled it to their mills, but lack of easy transportation severely limited their efforts until 1852. That year, the Columbia and Greenville Railroad finally reached Greenville County. Only the interruption of the Civil War kept the local textile industry from becoming a national force during the 1850s and 1860s.

The area missed most of the fighting of the Civil War and escaped relatively unscathed. This provided the area with an advantage over those whose mills and facilities had been destroyed during the war. The 1870 census reported a total $351,875 in textiles produced in the county. This success encouraged others to locate in Greenville. Ten years later, with numerous mills being added each year, the total reached $1,413,556.11. William Bates' son-in-law, Colonel H. P. Hammett, was owner of the Piedmont Company which was the county's largest producer. Shortly after the construction of the water powered Huguenot Mill in the downtown area of the City of Greenville County in 1882, the manufacture of cotton yarn would no longer be controlled by the geography of water power.

PHOTO: E. KENNEDY

F.W. Poe Manufacturing Co., Old Buncombe Road, Greenville, S.C. Built in 1895, purchased by Burlington Industries and closed in 1997. Palmetto State Dyeing and Finishing Co. opened in 1987. The company employs approximately 110 people.

The development of the steam engine created a revolution in the textile industry. No longer was the location of the mill tied to a fast moving stream, to turn a wheel that moved machinery. Large amounts of water were still needed but the dependence upon the waterfalls was severed. Between 1890 and 1920, four textile plants were built in the county outside the current city limits of the City of Greenville. At least thirteen large mills were built near the city to take advantage of the rail system, as shown on the map, "Greenville County Mills." Thus, with cheaper and more efficient steam power, transportation costs became a deciding factor. These mills built large boiler rooms adjacent to their plants and dug holding ponds for water.

Another drastic change took place in the textile industry around 1900. This change would provide even greater flexibility for the mill owners. A hydroelectric dam was constructed on the Saluda River, five miles west of the city of Greenville. It was completed in 1902 and would provide cheap electricity for the county. John Woodside, a local mill owner who foresaw electricity as the next step in the evolution of the industry, built what was then the largest textile mill in the world in the city of Greenville that same year. He located it further from a water source than previously thought acceptable. However, John had done some primitive locational analysis and chose the new site well. It was located just beyond the city boundary to limit his tax liability and directly between the lines of two competing rail companies—the Piedmont Railroad and the Norfolk and Western (now known as Norfolk and Southern). John Woodside's mill proved to be a

PHOTO: E. KENNEDY

Panorama of downtown Greenville, S.C.

tremendous success. With water no longer a key factor of location, the owners identified transportation as the key factor of location. Others began to build near rail lines.

The textile industry made Greenville County very prosperous. The mills needed workers and shortly outstripped the area's available labor supply. Also, many did not want to work in the hot, poorly ventilated, dangerous conditions found in the mills. When most of the mills were still built of wood, the cotton fibers floating in the air made fire a very real danger. Many businesses sprang up to service the needs of the workers and the textile mill owners. Farmers, sharecroppers, former slaves and children of former slaves were recruited to work in the mills. Housing soon became scarce and the infrastructure wasn't equipped to handle the influx of new workers. To alleviate the problem, the mill owners built housing for their workers. These were very similar to the coal camps of Appalachia and other factory owned housing in the north. They were very simple dwellings built close to the mill so the workers could easily walk to and from work. They also provided company-owned stores, doctors and organized recreational activities for their employees, creating mill communities. Many people who worked for the mills would have told you they lived at Poe Mill or Woodside, the names of their mill communities, rather than Greenville.

In the 1960s, rail transportation of textiles was a cost the owners wished to lower. They found a cheaper, more versatile form of transportation in the trucking industry. The interstate highway system was now well developed and provided a means of keeping costs down for the operators. In the 1970s, owners began to identify wages and benefits as a major factor in their cost of operation and many firms relocated in foreign countries, which offered workers at a fraction of the wages paid in the United States and requiring few if any benefits.

Meeting the challenge of economic diversification

Greenville County used its natural physical advantage to become the "Textile Capital of the World." Many of the other businesses were tied directly or indirectly to the textile industry. These ranged from engineering companies who designed and built textile machinery to companies which cleaned or repaired textile machines. Employment in the textile industry in Greenville County peaked in 1954 with 18,964 workers directly employed in the mills. As the industry began to decline, the leaders of the industry along with local and state leaders showed great foresight by combining their efforts into an aggressive move to transform Greenville County into a production and headquarters oriented economy. A state sponsored system of technical schools greatly facilitated this effort. Workers could get the training they needed to pursue almost any vocation at these centers. This system still is a factor in Greenville County's success.

The group emphasized the ability to make a profit in Greenville County. The focus of their efforts was turned to creating a sound technical education network along with the flexibility to negotiate packages of incentives to lure large employers. Incentives included negotiable tax and utility rates, plus a strong record of worker reliability due to South Carolina's nonunion tradition, with very few work stoppages. The foresight of this group has paid off handsomely. The majority of the textile mills which provided the backbone of the economy of Greenville County are no longer in business. Many of the old buildings still stand. Ten of the mills built before 1920 now are used in other capacities. American Spinning was built in 1896 and now is used as a warehouse, office space and light manufacturing all under one roof. Most of the mills are used for warehouse space or light manufacturing such as the Brandon Duck Mills, which operated between 1899 and 1977 as a cotton mill. It now houses two small factories which assemble golf clubs and part of the mill is used as a distribution center. The low lease cost (from $1 to $15 per square foot) is an enticement for other businesses to locate in these old buildings.

The old Huguenot Mill, the last water powered mill built in the county, was recently gutted and has been rebuilt as offices for the new 35 million dollar Peace Center entertainment complex in downtown Greenville. The Batesville Mill, the first in the county, was built of wood. It burned and was rebuilt in brick in 1881. It closed its doors in 1912 because the water-powered mill was not competitive. The mill was purchased by a husband and wife in 1983, converted into a restaurant, and was the cornerstone and headquarters of a chain of FATZ Restaurants until it burned again in 1997. So, in considering diversification, one of the first steps was to look for other uses for the facilities which already existed.

Other efforts also met with great success. As businesses began to look south during the 1970s for relocation sites, Greenville began to use its natural advantages to gather some impressive companies into its list of residents. By 1992, the combination of these efforts made Greenville County the wealthiest county in the state of South Carolina. Twenty-five companies have their corporate headquarters in the county, as shown in Table 1.

Forty-nine others have divisional headquarters in the county, as shown in Table 2. This constitutes a sizable investment for the area, yet even this list does not include a 150 million dollar investment by G. E. Gas Turbines in 1992 for expansion of their facility. This was the largest recent investment until 1993.

Table 1
CORPORATE HEADQUARTERS IN GREENVILLE COUNTY

1. American Leprosy Mission International
2. American Federal Bank
3. Baby Superstores, Inc.
4. Bowater Inc.
5. Builder Marts of America Inc.
6. Carolina First Bank
7. Delta Woodside Industries Inc.
8. Ellcon National Inc.
9. First Savings Bank
10. Heckler Manufacturing and Investment Group
11. Henderson Advertising
12. Herbert-Yeargin, Inc.
13. JPS Textile Group Inc.
14. Kemet Electronics Corp.
15. Leslie Advertising
16. Liberty Corp.
17. Mount Vernon Mills Inc.
18. Multimedia Inc.
19. Ryan's Family Steakhouses
20. Span America
21. Steel Heddle Manufacturing Co.
22. Stone Manufacturing Co.
23. Stone International.
24. TNS Mills Inc.
25. Woven Electronics Corp.

What ultimately swayed the automaker to choose Greenville? One of the main reasons was physical location.

Along with American companies, foreign investment was sought as well. Companies such as Lucas, Bosch, Michelin, Mita and Hitachi have made major investments in the county. Great effort has been put into reshaping the face of Main Street in Greenville as well. The city is trying to make a place where people want to live and shop. Many specialty stores have opened replacing empty buildings left by such long time mainstays as Woolworths. The Plaza Bergamo was created to encourage people to spend time downtown. The Peace Center Complex provides an array of entertainment choices not usually found in a city the size of Greenville. The Memorial Auditorium, which provided everything from basketball games, to rodeo, concerts, high school graduations and truck pulls has closed its doors and was demolished in 1997 to make way for a new 15,000 seat complex which will be named for its corporate sponsor. It will be called the Bi-Lo Center. Bi-Lo is a grocery store chain and a division of the Dutch Company, Ahold. A new parking garage is being built for this center and two other garages have recently been added to improve the infrastructure of the city. City leaders have traveled to cities such as Portland, Oregon, to study how they have handled and managed growth and yet kept the city friendly to its inhabitants.

The largest gamble for Greenville County came in early 1989. The automaker BMW announced that it was considering building a factory in the United States. Greenville County and the state of South Carolina competed against several other sites in the midwest and southeast for nearly two years. On June 23, 1992, the German automaker chose to locate in the Greenville-Spartanburg area. Although the plant is located in Spartanburg County, the headquarters are in Greenville and both counties will profit greatly. When the announcement was made, the question was: what ultimately swayed the automaker to choose Greenville? One of the main reasons was physical location. The site is only a four hour drive from the deepwater harbor of Charleston, SC. Interstates 26 and 85 are close by for easy transportation of parts to the assembly plant. The Greenville-Spartanburg Airport is being upgraded so that BMW can send fully loaded Boeing 747 cargo planes and have them land within five miles of the factory. Plus, the airport is already designated as a U.S. Customs Port of Entry and the flights from Germany can fly directly to Greenville without having to stop at Customs when entering the country. Other incentives in the form of tax breaks, negotiated utility rates, worker training and state purchased land helped BMW choose the 900 acre site where it will build automobiles.

Table 2
DIVISIONAL HEADQUARTERS IN GREENVILLE COUNTY

1. Ahold, Bi-Lo.
2. BB&T, BB&T of South Carolina.
3. Bell Atlantic Mobile
4. Canal Insurance Company
5. Coats and Clark, Consumer Sewing Products Division.
6. Cryovac—Div. of W. R. Grace & Co.
7. Dana Corp., Mobile Fluid Products Division
8. DataStream Systems, Inc.
9. Dodge Reliance Electric
10. Dunlop Slazenger International, Dunlop Slazenger Corp.
11. EuroKera North America, Inc.
12. Fluor Daniel Inc.
13. Fulfillment of America
14. Frank Nott Co.
15. Gates/Arrow Inc.
16. General Nutrition Inc., General Nutrition Products Corp.
17. Gerber Products Co., Gerber Childrenswear, Inc.
18. GMAC
19. Goddard Technology Corp.
20. Greenville Glass
21. Hitachi, Hitachi Electronic Devices (USA)
22. Holzstoff Holding, Fiberweb North America Inc.
23. IBANK Systems, Inc.
24. Insignia Financial Group, Inc.
25. Jacobs-Sirrine Engineering
26. Kaepa, Inc.
27. Kvaerner, John Brown Engineering Corp.
28. Lawrence and Allen
29. LCI Communications
30. Lockheed Martin Aircraft Logistics Center Inc.
31. Manhattan Bagel Co.
32. Mariplast North America, Inc.
33. Michelin Group, Michelin North America
34. Mita South Carolina, Inc.
35. Moovies, Inc.
36. Munaco Packing and Rubber Company
37. National Electrical Carbon Corp.
38. O'Neal Engineering
39. Personal Communication Services Dev.
40. Phillips and Goot
41. Pierburg
42. Rust Environment and Infrastructure
43. SC Teleco Federal Credit Union
44. Sodotel
45. South Trust Bank
46. Sterling Diagnostic Imaging, Inc.
47. Umbro, Inc.
48. United Parcel Service
49. Walter Alfmeier GmbH & Co.

The large incentive packages might appear self-defeating but BMW's initial investment was scheduled to be between 350 and 400 million dollars. The majority of the companies supplying parts for BMW also looked for sites close enough to satisfy BMW's just-in-time manufacturing needs. The fact that Michelin already made tires for their cars here, Bosch could supply brake and electrical parts from factories already here and J.P. Stevens and others could supply fabrics for automobile carpets and other needs readily from a few miles away also was a factor.

A combination of physical, environmental and cultural factors greatly influence the location of businesses.

One major BMW supplier, Magna International, which makes body parts for the BMW Roadster and parts for other car manufacturers, located its stamping plant in Greenville County. Magna invested $50 million and will invest $35 million more as BMW expands. Magna needed 100 acres of flat land without any wetlands and large rock formations. This land needed to be close enough to provide delivery to BMW. After studying several sites, Magna chose South Donaldson Industrial Park, formerly an Air Force base, just south of the city of Greenville. The county and state will help prepare the location for their newest employer.

PHOTO: E. KENNEDY

Huguenot Mill (lower left). Built in 1882, on Broad Street, Greenville, S.C., it is the last waterpowered mill in Greenville County. It is being refurbished to become part of the Peace Center Complex at right.

Road improvements, the addition of a rail spur and an updating of water and sewer facilities will all be provided to Magna in this agreement. Also, Magna will receive a reduced 20 year fixed tax rate along with other incentives for each worker hired. These incentive packages may seem unreasonable but they have proven to be necessary in the 1990s when large organizations are deciding where to locate.

The future: location, location, and location

From the time of the earliest European settlers, the natural advantages of Greenville County helped bring it to prosperity. The cultural background of the settlers was one of industry and a propensity for changing the physical environment to maximize its industrial potential. Nature provided the swift running rivers and beautiful waterfalls. The cultural background of the settlers caused them to look at these natural resources and see economic potential.

The people worked together to create an environment which led Greenville County to be given the title of "Textile Center of the World" in the 1920s. Then, again taking advantage of transportation opportunities and economic advantages, the area retained its textile center longer than the majority of textile centers.

Today, after 30 years of diversification, economic factors now are normally the deciding factor in the location of a new business or industry. Greenville County with its availability of land, reasonable housing costs, low taxes, willingness to negotiate incentive packages, and positive history of labor relations helped make it a desirable location for business. Proximity to interstate transportation, rail and air transport availability help keep costs low. The county's physical location about half way between the mega-growth centers of Charlotte, North Carolina, and Atlanta, Georgia, places it in what many experts call the mega-growth center of the next two decades. Now, with BMW as a cornerstone industry for the 1990s and beyond, Greenville County looks to be one of the areas with tremendous growth potential.

Thus, a combination of physical, environmental and cultural factors greatly influence the location of businesses. Transportation costs, wage and benefit packages and technical education availability are all interconnected.

The newest variable involves incentive packages of tax, utility reduction, worker training, site leasing and state and local investment into improving the infrastructure for attracting employers. The equation grows more and more complex with no one factor outweighing another; however, economic costs of plant or office facilities, wages and benefits and transportation seem to be paramount. Greenville County is blessed with everything it needs for success. It will definitely be one the places "to be" in the coming years.

References and further readings

DuPlessis, Jim. 1991. Many Mills Standing 60 Years After Textile Heydays. *Greenville News-Piedmont* July 8. pp. 1c–2c.

Greater Greenville Chamber of Commerce, 1990. *1990 Guide to Greenville.*

Greenville News-Piedmont. 1991–1993. *Fact Book 1991; 1992; 1993.*

Patterson, J. H. 1989. *North America*. Oxford University Press: N.Y. Eighth edition.

Scott, Robert. 1993. Upstate Business. *Greenville News-Piedmont*. 15 August. pp. 2–3.

Shaw, Martha Angelette. 1964. *The Textile Industry in Greenville County*. University of Tennessee Master's Thesis.

Strahler, Arthur. 1989. *Elements of Physical Geography*. John Wiley and Sons: N.Y. Fourth edition.

Eugene A. Kennedy is a native of West Virginia who attended Bluefield State College, Bluefield, West Virginia, and received an M.A. in geography from Marshall University in Huntington. He is currently a public educator in the Greenville County School system, Greenville S.C. He was awarded a "Golden Apple" by Greenville television station WYFF in 1997, has been a presenter at the South Carolina Science Conference, and a consultant to the South Carolina State Department of Education. He can be reached at GEOGEAK@aol.com.

Underwater refuge

Efforts are under way to greatly expand coastal no-fishing zones

By JANET RALOFF

Sanctuary. One definition, according to *Merriam Webster's Collegiate Dictionary*, is "a refuge for wildlife where predators are controlled and hunting is illegal."

You'd think, therefore, that the United States' 13 national marine sanctuaries—more than 18,000 square nautical miles of underwater real estate along U.S. coasts—should be safe havens for their denizens. In fact, most are anything but.

All the sanctuaries allow fishing. Most also permit recreational boating, mining of some resources, and a host of other potentially disruptive activities.

That's why calling these regions sanctuaries "is a crock," argues John C. Ogden, director of the Florida Institute of Oceanography in St. Petersburg. The misnomer confuses the public about how well sensitive ecosystems and beleaguered fish are being protected, he contends.

Ogden's assertions are borne out by a national survey commissioned by SeaWeb, a marine-environment advocacy group in Washington, D.C. Of 1,000 U.S. adults polled in February, 31 percent guessed that more than one-fifth of U.S. coastal waters are fully protected from fishing and other activities, notes Vikki Spruill, the group's executive director.

In fact, Ogden notes, only in pockets of some sanctuaries does the federal government prohibit fishing and certain other exploitative activities, such as ship salvaging. He estimates that perhaps only 125 square nautical miles of U.S. marine waters are such "no-take" refuges. The newest and biggest is the month-old 74-square-nautical-mile Tortugas refuge within the Florida Keys National Marine Sanctuary.

Jane Lubchenco of Oregon State University in Corvallis notes that the U.S. tally leaves out many additional no-take areas protected by state or local authorities. Even including these, however, the total would still come to less than 0.01 percent of U.S. coastal waters, she says.

The nation's territorial waters extend 200 nautical miles out from all coasts, encompassing a whopping 3.36 million square nautical miles. This so-called Exclusive Economic Zone (EEZ) is an area considerably larger than the nation's land mass, notes Elliott A. Norse, president of the Marine Conservation Biology Institute in Redmond, Wash.

At a minimum, Norse argues, 20 percent of waters within the EEZ—or some 660,000 square nautical miles—should be set aside within the next 15 years as no-take refuges. Such action is necessary to allow recovery of heavily overfished stocks (SN: 2/7/96, p. 367) and to preserve seafloor communities or rebuild ones that have been wiped out by trawling (SN: 12/19&26/98, p. 388).

Some sensitive old-growth habitats may need a century to mature, Lubchenco says. She would like to see 35 to 50 percent of the EEZ set aside.

Yet U.S. industries that exploit the ocean's resources, especially its fish, have fought virtually every effort to create new refuges. These actions may have been shortsighted, new analyses indicate, because safe havens appear to boost populations of fish outside their borders.

At an American Association for the Advancement of Science symposium in San Francisco in February, Lubchenco and others reported huge benefits to areas in and around no-take refuges. Marine biologists refer to such refuges as marine reserves.

"This was really the first time that the scientific community assessed in depth what the science is telling us about marine reserves," says Roger Griffis of the National Oceanic and Atmospheric Administration in Washington, D.C. The-new findings "show [reserves] have powerful impacts," he says.

The new analyses appear so compelling, both he and Lubchenco note, that the need for more refuges is at last starting to win grudging support—even among some fishing-boat captains.

The United States created its marine-sanctuaries program in 1972, when oil spills and treasure plundering seemed to pose the greatest threat to sea resources. Sanctuaries therefore prohibited oil drilling and salvaging but little else.

Since then, overfishing has emerged as a far bigger threat than oil pollution. Commercial ships have compensated for dwindling fish stocks by spending more time at work. As prized stocks such as cod and haddock crashed in coastal areas, some to the brink of extinction, fleets began targeting species previously discarded as junk, such as dogfish and angler fish.

Biologists have petitioned governments to put the critical spawning grounds and nurseries of valued species off limits. The fishing industry has countered that this could bankrupt many of its members.

In hopes of averting stalemate, Lubchenco and several colleagues in 1998 recruited a group of experts to launch a new program at the National Center for Ecological Analysis and Synthesis (NCEAS) in Santa Barbara, Calif. During the past 30 months, the group has pored over almost 100 studies of marine reserves, looking for specifics on how well their no-take policies protect ecosystems or let fish stocks rebuild.

By pooling data from many small studies around the world, the scientists were able to tease out some strong generalizations. They found, for instance, that reserves generate benefits quickly.

Densities of surveyed species were, on average, twice as high inside reserves as outside, Robert Warner of the University of California, Santa Barbara, reported at the San Francisco meeting. The biomass, or weight of organisms within a reserve, was typically three times that found in an equal-size fished area outside the reserve. Moreover, animals were on average 30 percent bigger inside reserves and the overall species diversity about 20 percent higher, compared with populations outside reserve boundaries.

Some reserves date back to the mid-1970s. Warner's team discovered that substantial benefits typically show up within just 3 years of a reserve being established and endure for decades. "All reserves, large and small, showed this response," he noted.

These data also suggest that a system of small reserves may achieve benefits equal to or greater than a single, large one, Warner says.

The necessary size for a reserve to flourish and to replenish the area around it depends on the flora and fauna present. Until recently, biologists assumed that reserves have to be fairly large to protect the many animal species that flow in and out with the currents and tides.

However, the NCEAS analyses, which are all due to be published this fall as a special issue of ECOLOGICAL APPLICATIONS, uncovered another surprise: Many species tend to be home bodies.

The young of most marine animals spend some of their development time as minute larvae—plankton that drift with ocean currents. Depending on the species, this planktonic stage can last anywhere from a few hours to months. The distance larvae float during this time can also vary dramatically—from 3 feet to 550 nautical miles, notes Louis W Botsford of the University of California, Davis.

In animals with a long planktonic period, larvae hatched in a reserve risk floating beyond their protected home. To ensure that enough of any species with a long larval stage remains in its refuge—creating a self-sustaining population reserve's diameter should be at least as great as the distance that larvae float.

However, where a reserve's primary goal is to breed abundant fish populations that will migrate beyond the reserve's boundaries, that diameter shouldn't be much bigger than this critical size. A series of small reserves would provide a greater total border zone to fishers than one large no-take zone.

Though initial data on planktonic periods suggested that most reserves might need to be hundreds or thousands of kilometers in diameter, the NCEAS analyses may now explain why even many tiny no-take zones seem to build large fish stocks: Their plankton don't wander far.

For instance, Indonesia's manta shrimp should be able to travel thousands of kilometers per generation, given that the animal's larvae drift for about 4 weeks in currents flowing at up to 1 meter per second. At the San Francisco meeting, Stephen R. Palumbi of Harvard University reported, however, that most of the shrimp move only 10 to 30 nautical miles in a single generation. He and his colleagues tracked the movement of eight major populations of the animals by measuring the spread of genes among them.

"And this is not an isolated example," Palumbi says. He notes that various other marine species in Australia and along the northeast U.S. coast have been spreading at rates representing only a small fraction of what their planktonic periods suggest should be likely.

Indeed, Palumbi and others now advocate the development of national networks of no-take zones—in effect, archipelagos of underwater safe havens. The NCEAS scientists' computer modeling suggests that networks of irregularly sized and spaced reserves could sustain a wide variety of species, including animals that begin life as long-distance drifters.

However, cautions Steven D. Gaines, director of the Marine Science Institute at the University of California, Santa Barbara, redundancy will be needed within such networks to offset the effects of occasional catastrophes, such as hurricanes, oil spills, and algal blooms. His analysis suggests that planners should increase the area to be preserved by 10 to 100 percent to account for catastrophes, depending on their historical frequency in a region.

To date, wherever environmental activists and researchers have proposed reserves, fishers have resisted them—and "almost always vigorously," says Callum M. Roberts of York University in England. However, he adds, evidence "from around the world indicates that fishers have nothing to fear."

By way of example, he points to data that he collected at the Soufriere Marine Management Area, a coral-reef park off the Caribbean island of St. Lucia.

Daily patrols by park staff have enforced a fishing prohibition in four no-take zones since 1995. Within 3 years, he reports, the density of commercially important fish stocks inside the protected areas swelled and spilled over to areas just outside the park.

The commercial stocks doubled within the area outside the reserves. "Fishers now agree they are better off with the [reserves] than without," he says.

To probe the long-term impacts of no-take refuges, biologists have been monitoring one of the world's first: New Zealand's 1.5-square-nautical-mile Cape Rodney-Okakari Point Reserve off Auckland. Established in 1975, its density of prized fish like snapper (*Pagrus auratus*) is now 40 times higher inside the reserve than in similar fished areas, Roberts notes. The biomass of spiny lobsters in the reserve has also increased phenomenally—by 5 to 11 percent annually.

Roberts says people quickly learned the advantage of fishing just outside the border of this reserve, and boats line up there daily.

This reserve's impressive benefits have "paved the way for a national network of marine reserves that is now being built in New Zealand," Roberts observes. Heather Leslie at Oregon State, who has been studying this network, says that as of last September, New Zealand already had 16 fully protected reserves. Together, they encompass some 2,900 square nautical miles, or nearly 0.2 percent of that country's territorial waters. Most protected marine areas include some land and adjacent coastal waters, as here at California's San Miguel Island.

U.S. planners are now investigating how best to begin building such networks of reserves here.

For instance, Leslie has adapted an experimental computer program to combine topographic maps of a region with plots of such features as spawning grounds, fish habitat, fisheries, coral reefs, and fragile seafloor biota. The program can generate a host of possible reserve-network configurations for analysis by local stakeholders—from biologists and oceanographers to scuba divers and squid-fishing fleets.

Leslie recently used the program to suggest hundreds of possible networks of reserves that the government might establish within the 1,252-square-nautical-mile Channel Islands National Marine Sanctuary off California. Currently, only one 0.03-square-nautical-mile reserve exists there.

A local stakeholders group commissioned Leslie and other scientific and economic advisors to suggest how much new territory should be designated no-take. The scientists recently recommended that from 30 to 50 percent of the sanctuary should be in reserves. Now, the stakeholders are studying maps of possible set-asides totaling between 8 and 50 percent of the sanctuary.

Some fishers have begun saying that the maps of proposed reserves have allayed some of their initial fears of a Channel Islands refuge network, observes Lubchenco. The experimental computer program, she argues, "is proving a powerful tool."

Under an executive order issued last May—which remains in force under President Bush—President Clinton authorized federal agencies "to strengthen the management, protection, and conservation of existing marine protected areas (MPAs) and establish new or expanded MPAs." These sites include marine sanctuaries and all other fully or partially protected parcels of underwater real estate.

MPAs can range from tidal beaches that are off-limits to visitors during sea turtle nesting periods to areas that ban fishing that disturbs the seafloor. Some MPAs prohibit disturbance of coral or forbid the anchoring of ships; others bar the extraction of sand. One, in Hawaii, outlaws any activities that might disturb young humpback whales.

No existing catalog identifies all U.S. MPAs, let alone the subset that has been granted reserve status, Griffis notes. His office is developing such a registry and will post it on a Web site for use by individuals and government agencies seeking to nominate new MPAs.

Griffis' goal is to have by year's end a list of all MPAs, cross-indexed by location, ecosystem, and level of protection. Knowing what's already out there is an essential first step to building coordinated networks of marine reserves, he says.

However, Lubchenco points out, even reserves can't prevent toxic or nutrient pollution, alien-species invasions, or climate change. Overfishing of top predators in areas outside reserves also can affect populations within no-take areas. That's why, she warns, although "networks of marine reserves may be the single most useful tool at our disposal," they will never, by themselves, be sufficient to protect the increasingly imperiled seas.

From *Science News,* April 28, 2001, pp. 264-266 by Janel Raloff.

The Río Grande

Beloved river faces rough waters ahead

By Steve Larese

Corrales farmer Gus Wagner allows himself just a minute to admire a peach and honey sunrise pouring over the Sandía Mountains, its patchy light filtering through cottonwoods and bobbing on the Río Grande. Turning back to his work, his callused hands turn the wheel of his *compuerta* (floodgate), and the river's paced water soon sluices through the *acequia* to flood his blossoming apple orchard.

"The river's beautiful, *que no?*" he asks, stealing another moment from his busy day. "I thank God everyday for the Río Grande and how it allows my family to live here. The river is our lifeblood."

It's safe to say there's not a Land of Enchanter around who would disagree with Wagner. Three states and two countries lay claim to the Río Grande, but only New Mexico claims it as our soul. To New Mexicans past and present, the Río Grande has been a gentle miracle in a harsh land.

But our beloved river was recently named the seventh most endangered in the nation by the respected American Rivers, a national conservation organization (www.Amrivers.org). "The Río Grande is really on its deathbed," says Betsy Otto, American Rivers' director of river restoration finance. "Increased population, outdated irrigation techniques and misguided engineering are drying the river up. But that being said, the situation isn't hopeless. Rivers are resilient if you let them be rivers. But too many people think of the Río Grande only as an irrigation ditch, drinking fountain or a sewer."

Beginning life as a twist of alpine streams 12,500 feet above sea level in the San Juan Mountains of Colorado, the Río Grande courses through Colorado, New Mexico and forms the 1,000-mile border between Texas and Mexico. Its life ends 1,887 miles later when it merges with salt water in the Gulf of Mexico. Today, the river appears fairly linear through New Mexico, lined by the nation's largest continuous cottonwood forest called the *bosque*, or woods. But this hasn't always been the case, says Dr. Cliff Crawford, a University of New Mexico research professor emeritus who has extensively studied the Río Grande and its ecosystem.

"The river and *bosque* as we see them today look quite different from how they appeared just a few decades ago," he says.

Crawford explains that until about the mid-'50s, the Río Grande was a braided river, meaning several sizable rivulets would snake over one another with cottonwood islands between them. Instead of perfectly lining the river, cottonwoods, coyote willows and other native flora created a mosaic pattern, their seeds deposited on the whim of the river. Depending on the year's runoff, the rivulets would swell to make one river worthy of the name Río Grande.

This seasonal flooding would establish new groves of trees, clean away debris and keep in check non-native species such as salt cedar and Russian olive. During heavy runoff years, the river would occasionally spread past its average bounds and devastate villages and pueblos built within the flood plain. The force of such flooding could reroute the very course of the river, cutting new channels through former farm fields and irrigation ditches.

Ciénegas (marshes) and oxbow lakes remained after the flood subsided. For the most part, New Mexicans ac-

STEVE LARESE

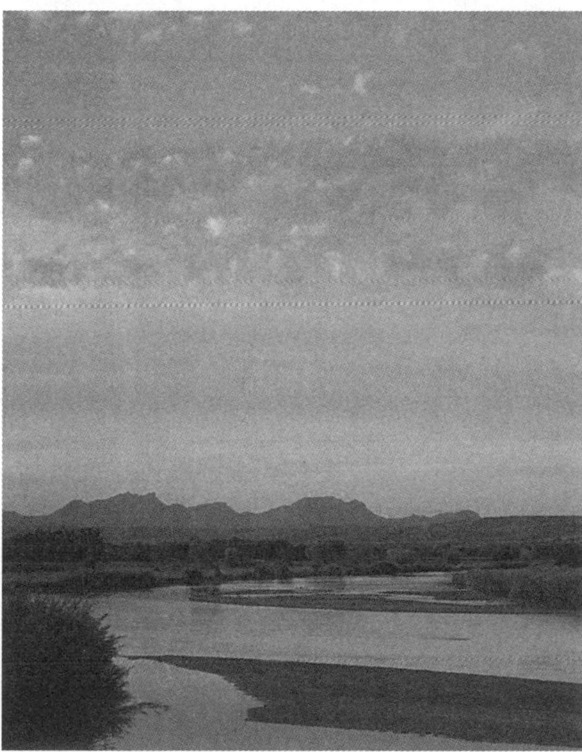

LAURENCE PARENT

Top—*The river courses through the Río Grande Gorge, an impressive feature it carved over millions of years through the volcanic basalt of the Taos Plateau. The canyon starts as a ditch in Colorado's San Juan Hills and eventually plummets to depths of 1,000 feet. Bottom—The Río Grande as it leaves New Mexico and forms the Texas/Mexico border. .*

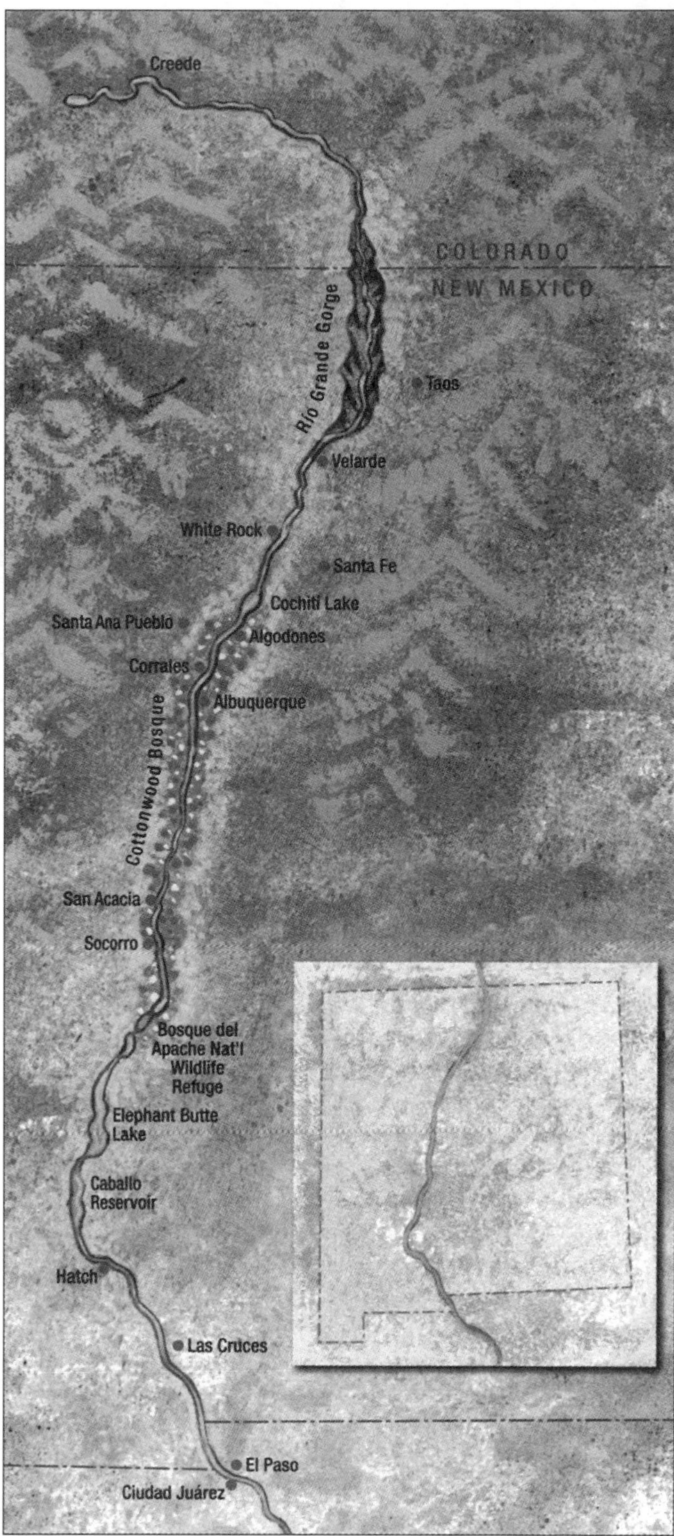

Above—*Map of New Mexico's portion of the Great River*

cepted this fact of life, and many understood it was necessary. Like Egypt's Nile, with the floods came rich silt that was deposited on farmland. The infrequent inconvenience of rebuilding waterlogged adobes was worth the annual gifts provided by the river.

STEVE LARESE

The Middle Río Grande supports the largest continuous cottonwood forest left in the United States, seen here north of Albuquerque. Scientists, citizens and environmentalists worry the forest (bosque) is dying out, partly because the river hasn't been able to flood in the past half century. Flooding is crucial in the establishment of new cottonwoods. Also, deadwood has been allowed to build up, which creates a severe fire hazard. The Catch 22 is that if flooding is allowed, there may not be enough water to meet water commitments to Texas, Chihuahua, Coahuila, Nuevo Leon and Tamaulipas, Mexico. As New Mexico enters an expected period of even drier weather, the growing cities of Albuquerque, El Paso and Ciudad Juárez are also becoming more dependent on the river.

But New Mexico's dynamics were changing. As more people moved to the state and communities—especially Albuquerque—grew, the price of flooding increased. Finally, after Albuquerque in part had to be evacuated because of the floods of 1941 and '42, state and federal governments decided the Great River needed to be controlled.

In the 1950s, the Southwest suffered through a devastating drought. The Río Grande dried up, and New Mexico was unable to meet its water obligations to Texas under the Río Grande Compact, a water-rights agreement signed by Colorado, New Mexico and Texas and approved by Congress in 1939. New Mexico avoided a lawsuit by aggressively pursuing channelization of the river to maximize flow downstream. Levees were built along the river's banks to contain flooding. "Jetty Jacks," the same type of crossed metal structures used to deter amphibious assaults during World War II, made the Río Grande look like Normandy Beach. Jetty Jacks lined the desired channels with other structures directing the water flow into the channels. The result was to trap silt, sand and debris, building up the banks and further confining the river. By narrowing the channel, more water was being delivered downstream, which also greatly reduced flooding.

The efforts worked perfectly. But altering the natural tendencies of the river on such a grand scale couldn't happen without affecting its very nature. Today, Crawford says, we are seeing those effects.

"The changes made to the river were very justified in people's minds at the time," he says. "But the hydrology of the system has completely changed. Unless we allow the system to come back to some level of how its ecosystem used to work, Albuquerque's *bosque* at least will be lost."

"You can't blame people for not wanting their houses washed away or their crops destroyed," says Rob Yaksich, an interpretive ranger at the Río Grande Nature Center State Park in Albuquerque. "But a relatively short time later, we're seeing the cottonwoods are certainly losing ground. Without flooding, they aren't regenerating. Most of the youngest trees we have were established in the floods of the '40s. Without some type of flooding, when they're gone in 40 or so years, that'll be it for the *bosque* as we know it."

Early last century, salt cedar and Russian olive trees were introduced to New Mexico as ornamental vegetation. Some were planted along the river to further stabilize its banks. These newcomers have done extremely

CLAY MARTIN

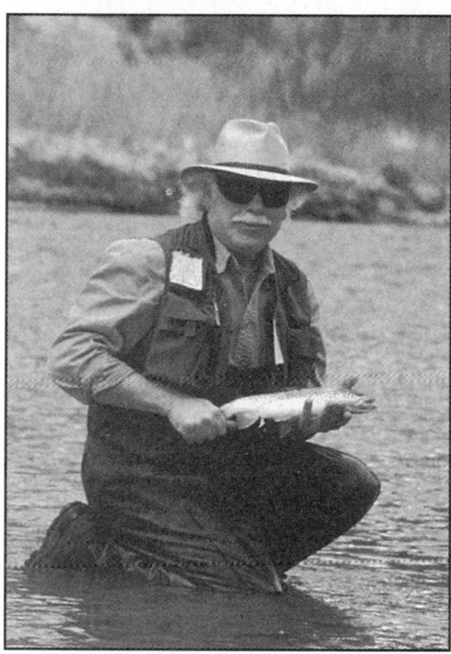

STEVE LARESE

Top—Elephant Butte Dam near Truth or Consequences created the largest reservoir in the world upon the dam's completion in 1916. A major recreation destination, the reservoir impounds 2-million-acre-feet of water for irrigation in southern New Mexico. Cochití Dam, completed in 1975 north of Cochití Pueblo, is one of the largest earth-filled dams in the world at 5.5 miles long and 251 feet high. Constructed and managed by the U.S. Army Corps of Engineers, the no-wake lake is a favorite playground for windsurfers. ***Bottom****—The Upper Río Grande near Pilar is an angler's paradise.*

well, and have choked out native trees such as cottonwoods in areas. Salt cedars have increased the salinity of the soil, and they have also blocked the sun that young cottonwoods need, says Crawford. "New cottonwoods need to be established in the open with lots of sun and silt," he says. "But it's a matter of who wins the shade race."

Realizing the threat, several governments and organizations have begun to take action to maintain and restore New Mexico's *bosque*.

Todd Caplan, department of natural resources director at Santa Ana Pueblo, watches as his crew plants new cottonwoods along part of the six miles of river that crosses the 74,000-acre pueblo. "What we're doing is restoring 7,000 acres of floodplain here," Caplan says. "The river through here used to average 1,200 feet wide. Now it's 300 feet. Cochití Dam has certainly reduced flooding, but now the *bosque* needs help."

Using a combination of state, federal and tribal funds, the Pueblo has painstakingly ripped out hundreds of acres of salt cedar and Russian olive that overran traditional cottonwood and willow habitat. The felled trees are cut and delivered to tribal elders for firewood. Towering piles of disassembled Jetty Jacks await new lives as fence posts. Below what will be the tribe's new Hyatt Regency Tamaya golf resort, 115 acres of native salt grass will be planted, and miles of nature trails will wind through the restored *bosque*, Caplan says. Already, the change is apparent.

STEVE LARESE

The river provides a relaxing respite for New Mexicans and many species of birds that depend upon it during migrations. For more information about the river and its natural history, tour the Río Grande Nature Center State Park in Albuquerque, 2901 Candelaria NW (505) 344–7240 or visit www.unm.edu/~natrcent.

"The best feeling I can have is when the elders come down and take a look at what we've done so far and say, 'This is what it looked like when we were growing up and playing down here.' What we're doing is for the health, recreation and enjoyment of the pueblo, but it will also positively impact the river downstream. The river is a living creature, and what is good for a part is good for the whole."

STEVE LARESE

Having escaped the drought and hardships that befell northwestern New Mexico, many groups of ancestral Pueblo people eventually settled along the Río Grande, creating the oldest communities in the United States. Here, a pet helps out during San Juan Pueblo's deer dance.

Bosque del Apache National Wildlife Refuge is also aggressively maintaining and restoring its 57,191 acres by tearing out salt cedar, planting cottonwoods and conducting controlled flooding this month, says ecologist Gina Dello Russo. "We have one of the nicest examples of what the river used to look like," she says. "We've had great success in bringing back native habitat."

STEVE LARESE

Union and Confederate troops clashed along the Río Grande during the Civil War battle of Valverde near Socorro, which is re-enacted every February. Victorious Confederate troops rebuffed Union attacks from Fort Craig, captured six cannons and continued north to take Albuquerque and Santa Fe. For more information, log on to www2.cr.nps.gov/abpp/battles/nm001.htm.

STEVE LARESE

Glowing red in the late afternoon sun, salt cedar lines much of the river through New Mexico. The non-native, thirsty shrub was introduced from Eurasia as an ornamental plant early last century. Also called tamarisk, it is considered a problem along the Río Grande because it uses much water and chokes out native trees like cottonwoods and coyote willows.

But conditions look like they're going to get harder before they get easier. A major drought is being predicted for New Mexico in the near future. The El Niño weather pattern gets much of the blame, but as old-timers, historians and scientists say, periods of unusually dry conditions aren't so unusual.

"The issues we're seeing with the Río Grande have always, always, always been true," says Steve Hansen, a Bureau of Reclamation hydrologist. "The Río Grande has always been in danger of drying up. It has a long history of water poverty."

True, historic accounts are filled with tales of drought and deluge. Coronado's conquistadores gave the river its impressive name after seeing what was described as a body of water many leagues wide. After seeing a trickle of water pick its way through a dusty riverbed, Will Rogers declared the Río Grande was the only river he'd ever seen in need of irrigation. Both accounts summarize the Great River, which has always been a paradox. It's the country's third-longest river next to the Mississippi and Missouri, yet some years you can step across it.

"We're coming out of a 20-year wet period," Hansen says. "It's going to get drier, which is normal. What has changed is that there's a lot more people depending on the Río Grande now, and we care about the environment a lot more. Fact is, we need more water but there's going to be less to go around. Everybody is going to have a compromise and be neighbors and partners in this."

Above—*This section of river north of Cochití Dam demonstrates the braided nature and oxbows once common for much of New Mexico's Río Grande. By damming and bank reinforcement, the river below Cochití Dam is now fairly straight. This has eliminated flooding and improved water availability downstream, but it has also destroyed much of the habitat needed by endangered species such as the silvery minnow and Southwest willow flycatcher.*
Top left—*Ron J. Sarracino places a beaver cage around a newly planted cottonwood as part of Santa Ana Pueblo's Río Grande Bosque Rehabilitation Project.* ***Top right***—*Todd Caplan, Santa Ana's director of natural resources, explains how his employees have cleared out non-native salt cedar and Russian olive trees from the Pueblo's bosque, leaving cottonwoods and returning the area to how it appeared before the introduction of non-native species.* ***Bottom top right***—*Rafters take advantage of the annual spring snow runoff that turns the Upper Río Grande into a national destination for thrill seekers.*

Article 29

Does it matter where you are?

The cliché of the information age is that instantaneous global telecommunications, television and computer networks will soon overthrow the ancient tyrannies of time and space. Companies will need no headquarters, workers will toil as effectively from home, car or beach as they could in the offices that need no longer exist, and events half a world away will be seen, heard and felt with the same immediacy as events across the street—if indeed streets still have any point.

There is something in this. Software for American companies is already written by Indians in Bangalore and transmitted to Silicon Valley by satellite. Foreign-exchange markets have long been running 24 hours a day. At least one California company literally has no headquarters: its officers live where they like, its salesmen are always on the road, and everybody keeps in touch via modems and e-mail.

Yet such developments have made hardly a dent in the way people think and feel about things. Look, for example, at newspapers or news broadcasts anywhere on earth, and you find them overwhelmingly dominated by stories about what is going on in the vicinity of their place of publication. Much has been made of the impact on western public opinion of televised scenes of suffering in such places as Ethiopia, Bosnia and Somalia. Impact, maybe, but a featherweight's worth.

World television graphically displayed first the slaughter of hundreds of thousands of people in Rwanda and then the flight of more than a million Rwandans to Zaire. Not until France belatedly, and for mixed motives, sent in a couple of thousand soldiers did anyone in the West lift so much as a finger to stop the killing; nor, once the refugees had suddenly poured out, did western governments do more than sluggishly bestir themselves to try to contain a catastrophe.

Rwanda, of course, is small (population maybe 8m before the killings began). More important, it is far away. Had it been Flemings killing Walloons in Belgium (population 10m) instead of Hutus slaying Tutsi in Rwanda, European news companies would have vastly increased their coverage, and European governments would have intervened in force. Likewise, the only reason the Clinton administration is even thinking about invading Haiti is that it lies a few hundred miles from American shores. What your neighbours (or your kith and kin) do affects you. The rest is voyeurism.

The conceit that advanced technology can erase the contingencies of place and time ranges widely. Many armchair strategists predicted during the Gulf war that ballistic missiles and smart weapons would make the task of capturing and holding territory irrelevant. They were as wrong as the earlier seers who predicted America could win the Vietnam war from the air.

In business, too, the efforts to break free of space and time have had qualified success at best. American multinationals going global have discovered that—for all their world products, world advertising, and world communications and control—an office in, say, New York cannot except in the most general sense manage the company's Asian operations. Global strengths must be matched by a local feel—and a jet-lagged visit of a few days every so often does not provide one.

Most telling of all, even the newest industries are obeying an old rule of geographical concentration. From the start of the industrial age, the companies in a fast-growing new field have tended to cluster in a small region. Thus, in examples given by Paul Krugman, an American economist, all but one of the top 20 American carpet-makers are located in or near the town of Dalton, Georgia; and, before 1930, the American tire industry consisted almost entirely of the 100 or so firms carrying on that business in Akron, Ohio. Modern technology has not changed the pattern. This is why the world got Silicon Valley in California in the 1960s. It is also why tradable services stay surprisingly concentrated—futures trading (in Chicago), insurance (Hartford, Connecticut), movies (Los Angeles) and currency trading (London).

History's Heavy Hand

This offends not just techno-enthusiasts but also neo-classical economics: for both, the world should tend towards a smooth dispersion of people, skills and economic competence, not towards their concentration. Save for transport costs, it should not matter where a tradable good or service is produced.

The reality is otherwise. Some economists have explained this by pointing to increasing returns to scale (in labour as well as capital markets), geographically uneven patterns of demand and transport costs. The main reason is that history counts: where you are depends very much on where you started from.

The new technologies will overturn some of this, but not much. The most advanced use so far of the Internet, the greatest of the world's computer networks, has not been to found a global village but to strengthen the local business and social ties among people and companies in the heart of Silicon Valley. As computer and communications power grows and its cost falls, people will create different sorts of space and communities from those that exist in nature. But these modern creations will supplement, not displace, the original creation; and they may even reinforce it. Companies that have gone furthest towards linking their global operations electronically report an increase, not a decline in the face-to-face contact needed to keep the firms running well: with old methods of command in ruins, the social glue of personal relations matters more than ever.

The reason lies in the same fact of life that makes it impossible really to understand from statistics alone how exciting, say, China's economic growth is unless you have physically been there to feel it. People are not thinking machines (they absorb at least as much information from sight, smell and emotion as they do from abstract symbols), and the world is not immaterial: "virtual" reality is no reality at all; cyberspace is a pretence at circumventing true space, not a genuine replacement for it. The weight on mankind of time and space, of physical surroundings and history—in short, of geography—is bigger than any earthbound technology is ever likely to lift.

UNIT 4

Spatial Interaction and Mapping

Unit Selections

Key Points to Consider

- Describe the spatial form of the place in which you live. Do you live in a rural area, a town, or a city, and why was that particular location chosen?
- How does your hometown interact with its surrounding region? With other places in the state? With other states? With other places in the world?
- How are places "brought closer together" when transportation systems are improved?
- What problems occur when transportation systems are overloaded?
- How will public transportation be different in the future? Will there be more or fewer private autos in the next 25 years? Defend your answer.
- How good a map reader are you? Why are maps useful in studying a place?

Links: www.dushkin.com/online/
These sites are annotated in the World Wide Web pages.

Edinburgh Geographical Information Systems
http://www.geo.ed.ac.uk/home/gishome.html

Geography for GIS
http://www.ncgia.ucsb.edu/cctp/units/geog_for_GIS/GC_index.html

GIS Frequently Asked Questions and General Information
http://www.census.gov/ftp/pub/geo/www/faq-index.html

International Map Trade Association
http://www.maptrade.org

PSC Publications
http://www.psc.lsa.umich.edu/pubs/abs/abs94-319.html

U.S. Geological Survey
http://www.usgs.gov/research/gis/title.html

Geography is the study not only of places in their own right but also of the ways in which places interact. Places are connected by highways, airline routes, telecommunication systems, and even thoughts. These forms of spatial interaction are an important part of the work of geographers.

In "Transportation and Urban Growth: The Shaping of the American Metropolis," Peter Muller considers transportation systems, analyzing their impact on the growth of American cities. The next article explores GIS as the technology used to solve a 160-year-old boundary controversy involving Ellis Island. Next, "Mapping the Outcrop" relates the use of digitized topographic maps and GIS in geology. An extensive analysis of satellite imagery and its applications follows. The next two articles illustrate the power of the choropleth map to tell its story. "Do We Still Need Skyscrapers?" questions the need for high-density structures in the new era of extensive communications. "China Journal I" discusses the Three Gorges project in China, including the spatial interaction aspects.

It is essential that geographers be able to describe the detailed spatial patterns of the world. Neither photographs nor words could do the job adequately, because they literally capture too much of the detail of a place. Therefore, maps seem to be the best way to present many of the topics analyzed in geography. Maps and geography go hand in hand. Although maps are used in other disciplines, their association with geography is the most highly developed.

A map is a graphic that presents a generalized and scaled-down view of particular occurrences or themes in an area. If a picture is worth a thousand words, then a map is worth a thousand (or more!) pictures. There is simply no better way to "view" a portion of Earth's surface or an associated pattern than with a map.

Transportation and Urban Growth

The shaping of the American metropolis

Peter O. Muller

In his monumental new work on the historical geography of transportation, James Vance states that geographic mobility is crucial to the successful functioning of any population cluster, and that "shifts in the availability of mobility provide, in all likelihood, the most powerful single process at work in transforming and evolving the human half of geography." Any adult urbanite who has watched the American metropolis turn inside-out over the past quarter-century can readily appreciate the significance of that maxim. In truth, the nation's largest single urban concentration today is not represented by the seven-plus million who agglomerate in New York City but rather by the 14 million who have settled in Gotham's vast, curvilinear outer city—a 50-mile-wide suburban band that stretches across Long Island, southwestern Connecticut, the Hudson Valley as far north as West Point, and most of New Jersey north of a line drawn from Trenton to Asbury Park. This latest episode of intrametropolitan deconcentration was fueled by the modern automobile and the interstate expressway. It is, however, merely the most recent of a series of evolutionary stages dating back to colonial times, wherein breakthroughs in transport technology unleashed forces that produced significant restructuring of the urban spatial form.

The emerging form and structure of the American metropolis has been traced within a framework of four transportation-related eras. Each successive growth stage is dominated by a particular movement technology and transport-network expansion process that shaped a distinctive pattern of intraurban spatial organization. The stages are the Walking/Horsecar Era (pre-1800–1890), the Electric Streetcar Era (1890–1920), the Recreational Automobile Era (1920–1945), and the Freeway Era (1945–present). As with all generalized models of this kind, there is a risk of oversimplification because the building processes of several simultaneously developing cities do not always fall into neat time-space compartments. Chicago's growth over the past 150 years, for example, reveals numerous irregularities, suggesting that the overall metropolitan growth pattern is more complex than a simple, continuous outward thrust. Yet even after developmental ebb and flow, leapfrogging, backfilling, and other departures from the idealized scheme are considered, there still remains an acceptable correspondence between the model and reality.

Before 1850 the American city was a highly compact settlement in which the dominant means of getting about was on foot, requiring people and activities to tightly agglomerate in close proximity to one another. This usually meant less than a 30-minute walk from the center of town to any given urban point—an accessibility radius later extended to 45 minutes when the pressures of industrial growth intensified after 1830. Within this pedestrian city, recognizable activity concentrations materialized as well as the beginnings of income-based residential congregations. The latter was particularly characteristic of the wealthy, who not only walled themselves off in their large homes near the city center but also took to the privacy of horse-drawn carriages for moving about town. Those of means

(LIBRARY OF THE BOSTON ATHENEUM)

Horse-drawn trolleys in downtown Boston, circa 1885.

also sought to escape the city's noise and frequent epidemics resulting from the lack of sanitary conditions. Horse-and-carriage transportation enabled the wealthy to reside in the nearby countryside for the disease-prone summer months. The arrival of the railroad in the 1830s provided the opportunity for year-round daily commuting, and by 1840 hundreds of affluent businessmen in Boston, New York, and Philadelphia were making round trips from exclusive new trackside suburbs every weekday.

As industrialization and its teeming concentrations of working-class housing increasingly engulfed the mid-nineteenth century city, the deteriorating physical and social environment reinforced the desires of middle-income residents to suburbanize as well. They were unable, however, to afford the cost and time of commuting by steam train, and with the walking city now stretched to its morphological limit, their aspirations intensified the pressures to improve intraurban transport technology. Early attempts involving stagecoach-like omnibuses, cablecar systems, and steam railroads proved impractical, but by 1852 the first meaningful transit breakthrough was finally introduced in Manhattan in the form of the horse-drawn trolley. Light street rails were easy to install, overcame the problems of muddy, unpaved roadways, and en-

(LIBRARY OF THE BOSTON ATHENEUM)

Electric streetcar lines radiated outward from central cities, giving rise to star-shaped metropolises. Boston, circa 1915.

abled horsecars to be hauled along them at speeds slightly (about five mph) faster than those of pedestrians. This modest improvement in mobility permitted the opening of a narrow belt of land at the city's edge for new home construction. Middle-income urbanites flocked to these "horsecar suburbs," which multiplied rapidly after the Civil War. Radial routes were the first to spawn such peripheral development, but the relentless demand for housing necessitated the building of cross-town horsecar lines, thereby filling in the interstices and preserving the generally circular shape of the city.

The less affluent majority of the urban population, however, was confined to the old pedestrian city and its bleak, high-density industrial appendages. With the massive immigration of unskilled laborers, (mostly of European origin after 1870) huge blue-collar communities sprang up around the factories. Because these newcomers to the city settled in the order in which they arrived—thereby denying them the small luxury of living in the immediate company of their fellow ethnics—social stress and conflict were repeatedly generated. With the immigrant tide continuing to pour into the nearly bursting industrial city throughout the late nineteenth century, pressures redoubled to further improve intraurban transit and open up more of the adjacent countryside. By the late 1880s that urgently needed mobility revolution was at last in the making, and when it came it swiftly transformed the compact city and its suburban periphery into the modern metropolis.

The key to this urban transport revolution was the invention by Frank Sprague of the electric traction motor, an often overlooked innovation that surely ranks among the most important in American history. The first electrified trolley line opened in Richmond in 1888, was adopted by two dozen other big cities within a year, and by the early 1890s swept across the nation to become the dominant mode of intraurban transit. The rapidity of this innovation's diffusion was enhanced by the immediate recognition of its ability to resolve the urban transportation problem of the day: motors could be attached to existing horsecars, converting them into self-propelled vehicles powered by easily constructed overhead wires. The tripling of average speeds (to over 15 mph) that resulted from this invention brought a large band of open land beyond the city's perimeter into trolley-commuting range.

> Before 1850 the American city was a highly compact settlement in which the dominant means of getting around was on foot, requiring people and activities to tightly agglomerate in close proximity to one another.

The most dramatic geographic change of the Electric Streetcar Era was the swift residential development of those urban fringes, which transformed the emerging metropolis into a decidedly star-shaped spatial entity. This pattern was produced by radial streetcar corridors extending several miles beyond the compact city's limits. With so much new space available for home-building within walking distance of the trolley lines, there was no need to extend trackage laterally, and so the interstices remained undeveloped. The typical streetcar suburb of the turn of this century was a continuous axial corridor whose backbone was the road carrying the trolley line (usually lined with stores and other local commercial facilities), from which gridded residential streets fanned out for several blocks on both sides of the tracks. In general, the quality of housing and prosperity of streetcar subdivisions increased with distance from the edge of the central city. These suburban corridors were populated by the emerging, highly mobile middle class, which was already stratifying itself according to a plethora of minor income and status differences. With frequent upward (and local geographic) mobility the norm, community formation became an elusive goal, a process further retarded by the grid-settlement morphology and the reliance on the distant downtown for employment and most shopping.

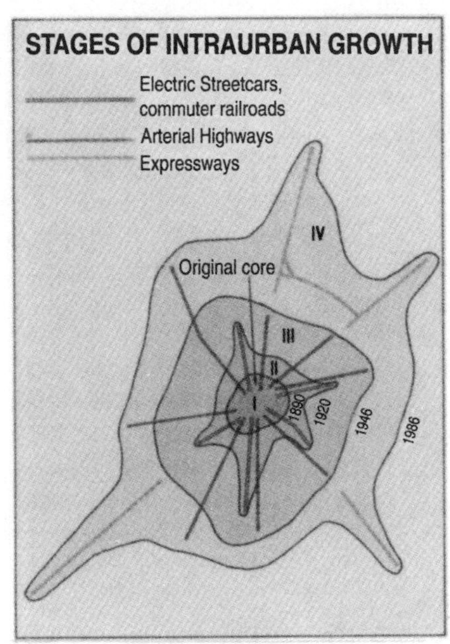

CARTOGRAPHY LAB. DEPT. OF GEOGRAPHY, UNIV. OF MINNESOTA

Within the city, too, the streetcar sparked a spatial transformation. The ready availability and low fare of the electric trolley now provided every resident with access to the intracity circulatory system, thereby introducing truly "mass" transit to urban America in the final years of the nineteenth century. For nonresidential activities this new ease of movement among the city's various parts quickly triggered the emergence of specialized land-use districts for commerce, manufacturing, and transportation, as well as the continued growth of the multipurpose central business district (CBD) that had formed after mid-century. But the greatest impact of the streetcar was on the central city's social geography, because it made possible the congregation of ethnic groups in their own neighborhoods. No longer were these moderate-income masses forced to reside in the heterogeneous jumble of row-houses and tenements that ringed the factories. The trolley brought them the opportunity to "live with their own kind," allowing the sorting of discrete groups into their own inner-city social territories within convenient and inexpensive traveling distance of the workplace.

By World War I, the electric trolleys had transformed the tracked city into a full-fledged metropolis whose streetcar suburbs, in the larger cases, spread out more than 20 miles from the metropolitan center. It was at this point in time that intrametropolitan transportation achieved its greatest level of efficiency—that the bustling industrial city really "worked." How much closer the American metropolis might have approached optimal workability for all its residents, however, will never be known because the next urban transport revolution was already beginning to assert itself through the increasingly popular automobile. Americans took to cars as wholeheartedly as anything in the nation's long cultural history. Although Lewis Mumford and other scholars vilified the car as the destroyer of the city, more balanced assessments of the role of the automobile recognize its overwhelming acceptance for what it was—the long-awaited attainment of private mass transportation that offered users the freedom to travel whenever and wherever they chose. As cars came to the metropolis in ever greater numbers throughout the interwar decades, their major influence was twofold: to accelerate the deconcentration of population through the development of interstices bypassed during the streetcar era, and to push the suburban frontier farther into the countryside, again producing a compact, regular-shaped urban entity.

While it certainly produced a dramatic impact on the urban fabric by the eve of World War II, the introduction of the automobile into the American metropolis during the 1920s and 1930s came at a leisurely pace. The earliest flurry of auto

(BOSTON PUBLIC LIBRARY)

Afternoon commuters converge at the tunnel leading out of central Boston, 1948.

adoptions had been in rural areas, where farmers badly needed better access to local service centers. In the cities, cars were initially used for weekend outings—hence the term "*Recreational* Auto Era"—and some of the earliest paved roadways were landscaped parkways along scenic water routes, such as New York's pioneering Bronx River Parkway and Chicago's Lake Shore Drive. But it was into the suburbs, where growth rates were now for the first time overtaking those of the central cities, that cars made a decisive penetration throughout the prosperous 1920s. In fact, the rapid expansion of automobile suburbia by 1930 so adversely affected the metropolitan public transportation system that, through significant diversions of streetcar and commuter-rail passengers, the large cities began to feel the negative effects of the car years before the auto's actual arrival in the urban center. By facilitating the opening of unbuilt areas lying between suburban rail axes, the automobile effectively lured residential developers away from densely populated traction-line corridors into the suddenly accessible interstices. Thus, the suburban homebuilding industry no longer found it necessary to subsidize privately-owned streetcar companies to provide low-fare access to trolley-line housing tracts. Without this financial underpinning, the modern urban transit crisis quickly began to surface.

The new recreational motorways also helped to intensify the decentralization of the population. Most were radial highways that penetrated deeply into the suburban ring and provided weekend motorists with easy access to this urban countryside. There they obviously were impressed by what they saw, and they soon responded in massive numbers to the sales pitches of suburban subdivision developers. The residential development of automobile suburbia followed a simple formula that was devised in the prewar years and greatly magnified in scale after 1945. The leading motivation was developer profit from the quick turnover of land, which was acquired in large parcels, subdivided, and auctioned off. Understandably, developers much preferred open areas at the metropolitan fringe, where

Central City-Focused Rail Transit

The widely dispersed distribution of people and activities in today's metropolis makes rail transit that focuses in the central business district (CBD) an obsolete solution to the urban transportation problem. To be successful, any rail line must link places where travel origins and destinations are highly clustered. Even more important is the need to connect places where people really want to go, which in the metropolitan America of the late twentieth century means suburban shopping centers, freeway-oriented office complexes, and the airport. Yet a brief look at the rail systems that have been built in the last 20 years shows that transit planners cannot—or will not—recognize those travel demands, and insist on designing CBD-oriented systems as if we all still lived in the 1920s.

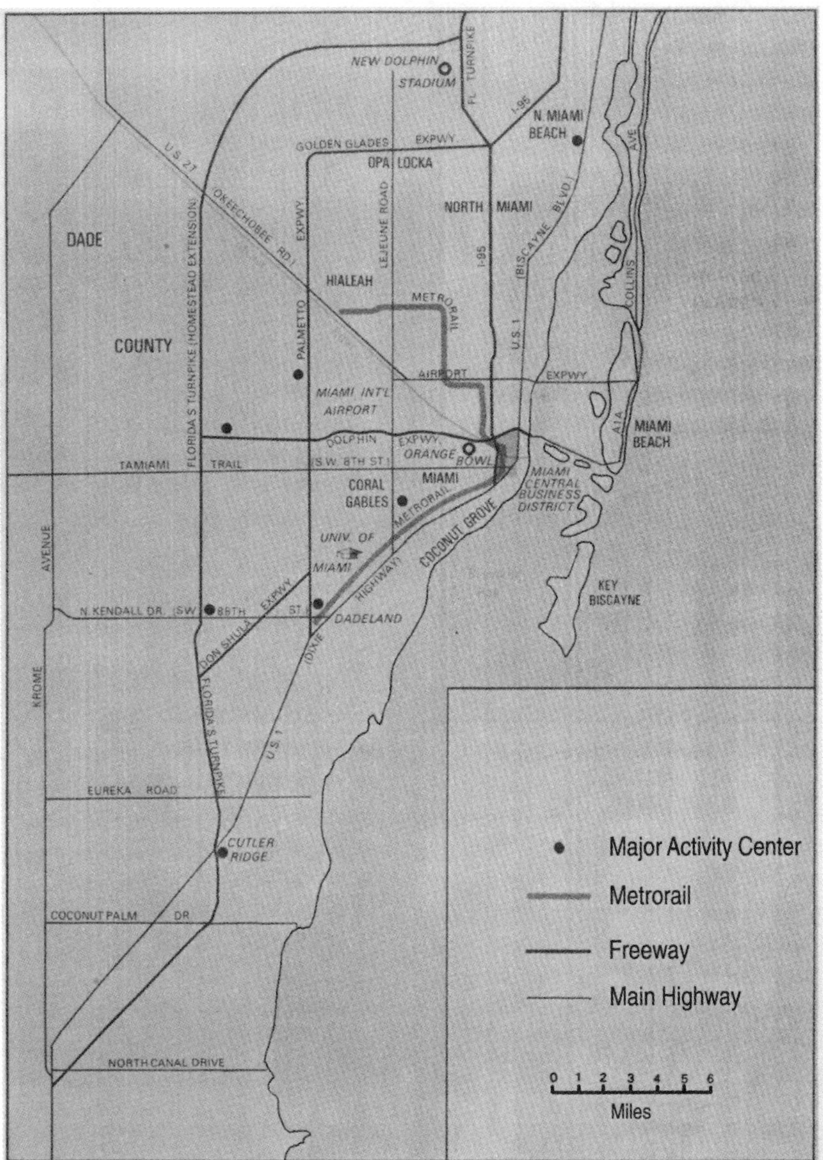

CARTOGRAPHY LAB. DEPT. OF GEOGRAPHY, UNI V OF MINNESOTA

One of the newest urban transit systems is Metrorail in Miami and surrounding Dade County, Florida. It has been a resounding failure since its opening in 1984. The northern leg of this line connects downtown Miami to a number of low- and moderate-income black and Hispanic neighborhoods, yet it carries only about the same number of passengers that used to ride on parallel bus lines. The reason is that the high-skill, service economy of Miami's CBD is about as mismatched as it could possibly be to the modest employment skills and training levels possessed by residents of that Metrorail corridor. To the south, the prospects seemed far brighter because of the possibility of connecting the system to Coral Gables and Dadeland, two leading suburban activity centers. However, both central Coral Gables and the nearby International Airport complex were bypassed in favor of a cheaply available, abandoned railroad corridor alongside U.S. 1. Station locations were poorly planned, particularly at the University of Miami and at Dadeland—where terminal location necessitates a dangerous walk across a six-lane highway from the region's largest shopping mall. Not surprisingly, ridership levels have been shockingly below projections, averaging only about 21,000 trips per day in early 1986. While Dade County's worried officials will soon be called upon to decide the future of the system, the federal government is using the Miami experience as an excuse to withdraw from financially supporting all construction of new urban heavy-rail systems. Unfortunately, we will not be able to discover if a well-planned, high-speed rail system that is congruent with the travel demands of today's polycentric metropolis is capable of solving traffic congestion problems. Hopefully, transportation policy-makers across the nation will heed the lessons of Miami's textbook example of how not to plan a hub-and-spoke public transportation network in an urban era dominated by the multicentered city.

large packages of cheap land could readily be assembled. Silently approving and underwriting this uncontrolled spread of residential suburbia were public policies at all levels of government: financing road construction, obligating lending institutions to invest in new homebuilding, insuring individual mortgages, and providing low-interest loans to FHA and VA clients.

The ready availability and low fare of the electric trolley now provided every resident with access to the intracity circulatory system, thereby introducing truly "mass" transit to urban America.

Because automobility removed most of the pre-existing movement constraints, suburban social geography now became dominated by locally homogeneous income-group clusters that isolated themselves from dissimilar neighbors. Gone was the highly localized stratification of streetcar suburbia. In its place arose a far more dispersed, increasingly fragmented residential mosaic to which builders were only too eager to cater, helping shape a kaleidoscopic settlement pattern by shrewdly constructing the most expensive houses that could be sold in each locality. The continued partitioning of suburban society was further legitimized by the widespread adoption of zoning (legalized in 1916), which gave municipalities control over lot and building standards that, in turn, assured dwelling prices that would only attract newcomers whose incomes at least equaled those of the existing local population. Among the middle class, particularly, these exclusionary economic practices were enthusiastically supported, because such devices extended to them the ability of upper-income groups to maintain their social distance from people of lower socioeconomic status.

Nonresidential activities were also suburbanizing at an increasing rate during the Recreational Auto Era. Indeed, many large-scale manufacturers had decentralized during the streetcar era, choosing locations in suburban freight-rail corridors. These corridors rapidly spawned surrounding working-class towns that became important satellites of the central city in the emerging metropolitan constellation. During the interwar period, industrial employers accelerated their intraurban deconcentration, as more efficient horizontal fabrication methods replaced older techniques requiring multistoried plants-thereby generating greater space needs that were too expensive to satisfy in the high-density central city. Newly suburbanizing manufacturers, however, continued their affiliation with intercity freight-rail corridors, because motor trucks were not yet able to operate with their present-day efficiencies and because the highway network of the outer ring remained inadequate until the 1950s.

Americans took to cars as wholeheartedly as anything in the nation's long cultural history.

The other major nonresidential activity of interwar suburbia was retailing. Clusters of automobile-oriented stores had first appeared in the urban fringes before World War I. By the early 1920s the roadside commercial strip had become a common sight in many southern California suburbs. Retail activities were also featured in dozens of planned automobile suburbs that sprang up after World War I—most notably in Kansas City's Country Club District, where the nation's first complete shopping center was opened in 1922. But these diversified retail centers spread slowly before the suburban highway improvements of the 1950s.

Unlike the two preceding eras, the postwar Freeway Era was not sparked by a revolution in urban transportation. Rather, it represented the coming of age of the now pervasive automobile culture, which coincided with the emergence of the U.S. from 15 years of economic depression and war. Suddenly the automobile was no longer a luxury or a recreational diversion: overnight it had become a necessity for commuting, shopping, and socializing, essential to the successful realization of personal opportunities for a rapidly expanding majority of the metropolitan population. People snapped up cars as fast as the reviving peacetime automobile industry could roll them off the assembly lines, and a prodigious highway-building effort was launched, spearheaded by high-speed, limited-access expressways. Given impetus by the 1956 Interstate Highway Act, these new freeways would soon reshape every corner of urban America, as the more distant suburbs they engendered represented nothing less than the turning inside-out of the historic metropolitan city.

The snowballing effect of these changes is expressed geographically in the sprawling metropolis of the postwar era. Most striking is the enormous band of growth that was added between 1945 and the 1980s, with freeway sectors pushing the metropolitan frontier deeply into the urban-rural fringe. By the late 1960s, the maturing expressway system began to underwrite a new suburban co-equality with the central city, because it was eliminating the metropolitanwide centrality advantage of the CBD. Now any location on the freeway network could easily be reached by motor vehicle, and intraurban accessibility had become a ubiquitous spatial good. Ironically, large cities had encouraged the construction of radial expressways in the 1950s and 1960s because they appeared to enable the downtown to remain accessible to the swiftly dispersing suburban population. However, as one economic activity

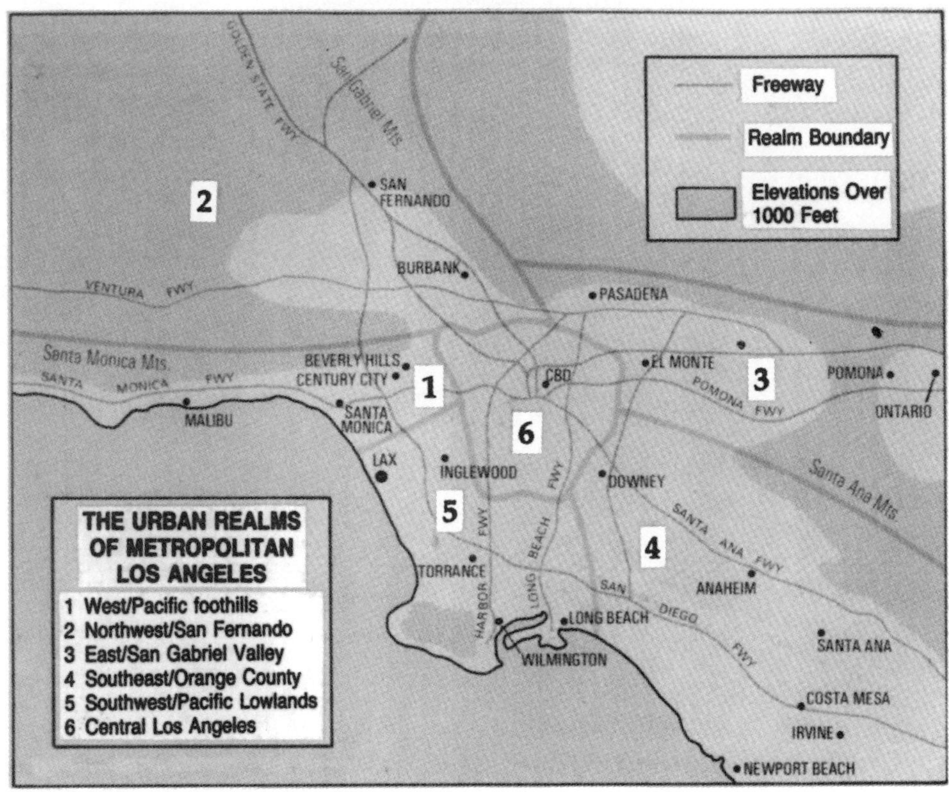

CARTOGRAPHY LAB. DEPT.OF GEOGRAPHY, UNIVERSITY OF MINNESOTA

after another discovered its new locational flexibility within the freeway metropolis, nonresidential deconcentration sharply accelerated in the 1970s and 1980s. Moreover, as expressways expanded the radius of commuting to encompass the entire dispersed metropolis, residential location constraints relaxed as well. No longer were most urbanites required to live within a short distance of their job: the workplace had now become a locus of opportunity offering access to the best possible residence that an individual could afford anywhere in the urbanized area. Thus, the overall pattern of locally uniform, income-based clusters that had emerged in prewar automobile suburbia was greatly magnified in the Freeway Era, and such new social variables as age and lifestyle produced an ever more balkanized population mosaic.

Retail activities were featured in dozens of planned automobile suburbs that sprang up after World War I—most notably Kansas City's Country Club District, where the nation's first complete shopping center was opened in 1922.

The revolutionary changes in movement and accessibility introduced during the four decades of the Freeway Era have resulted in nothing less than the complete geographic restructuring of the metropolis. The single-center urban structure of the past has been transformed into a polycentric metropolitan form in which several outlying activity concentrations rival the CBD. These new "suburban downtowns," consisting of vast orchestrations of retailing, office-based business, and light industry, have become common features near the highway interchanges that now encircle every large central city. As these emerging metropolitan-level cores achieve economic and geographic parity with each other, as well as with the CBD of the nearby central city, they provide the totality of urban goods and services to their surrounding populations. Thus each metropolitan sector becomes a self-sufficient functional entity, or *realm*. The application of this model to the Los Angeles region reveals six broad realms. Competition among several new suburban downtowns for dominance in the five outer realms is still occurring. In wealthy Orange County, for example, this rivalry is especially fierce, but Costa Mesa's burgeoning South Coast Metro is winning out as of early 1986.

The new freeways would soon reshape every corner of urban America, as the more distant suburbs they engendered represented nothing less than the turning inside-out of the historic metropolitan city.

The legacy of more than two centuries of intraurban transportation innovations, and the development patterns they helped stamp on the landscape of metropolitan America, is suburbanization—the growth of the edges of the urbanized area at a rate faster than in the already-developed interior. Since the geographic extent of the built-up urban areas has, throughout history, exhibited a remarkably constant radius of about 45 minutes of travel from the center, each breakthrough in higher-speed transport technology extended that radius into a new outer zone of suburban residential opportunity. In the nineteenth century, commuter railroads, horse-drawn trolleys, and electric streetcars each created their own suburbs—and thereby also created the large industrial city, which could not have been formed without incorporating these new suburbs into the pre-existing compact urban center. But the suburbs that materialized in the early twentieth century began to assert their independence from the central cities, which were ever more perceived as undesirable. As the automobile greatly reinforced the dispersal trend of the metropolitan population, the distinction between central city and suburban ring grew as well. And as freeways eventually eliminated the friction effects of intrametropolitan distance for most urban functions, nonresidential activities deconcentrated to such an extent that by 1980 the emerging outer suburban city had become coequal with the central city that spawned it.

As the transition to an information-dominated, postindustrial economy is completed, today's intraurban movement problems may be mitigated by the increasing substitution of communication for the physical movement of people. Thus, the city of the future is likely to be the "wired metropolis." Such a development would portend further deconcentration because activity centers would potentially be able to locate at any site offering access to global computer and satellite networks.

Further Reading

Jackson, Kenneth T. 1985. *Crabgrass Frontier: The Suburbanization of the United States.* New York: Oxford University Press.

Muller, Peter O. 1981. *Contemporary Suburban America.* Englewood Cliffs, N.J.: Prentice-Hall.

Schaeffer, K. H. and Sclar, Elliot. 1975. *Access for All: Transportation and Urban Growth.* Baltimore: Penguin Books.

GIS Technology Reigns Supreme in Ellis Island Case

Richard G. Castagna, Lawrence L. Thornton and John M. Tyrawski

In 1998, the U.S. Supreme Court ruled on a territorial squabble between the states of New Jersey and New York over Ellis Island that had been brewing for more than 160 years. GIS technology as implemented by the New Jersey Department of Environmental Protection (NJDEP) was instrumental in effecting the outcome. Here's how.

Early agreements between New York and New Jersey set the state boundary line as the middle of the Hudson river down through New York Bay, but the actual boundary around historic Ellis Island was never officially determined. Although the boundary dispute predates the Revolution, the story officially begins with an 1834 compact between the states, which was approved by the U.S. Congress. This compact set the boundary for Ellis Island as follows: *all non-submerged lands of the island belong to New York, and all submerged lands surrounding the island belong to New Jersey*. At that time, the non-submerged area of the island occupied approximately three acres.

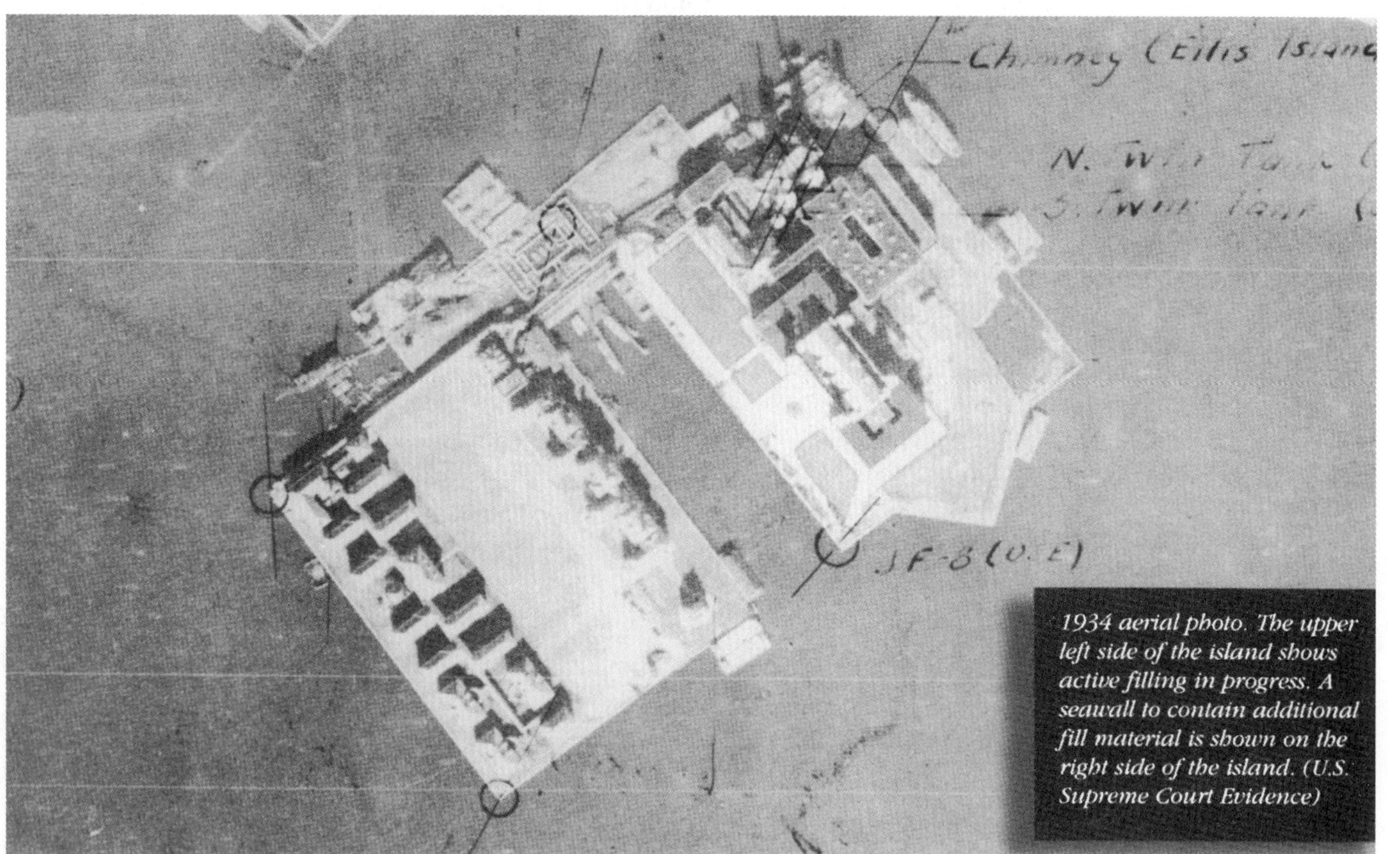

1934 aerial photo. The upper left side of the island shows active filling in progress. A seawall to contain additional fill material is shown on the right side of the island. (U.S. Supreme Court Evidence)

Source: New Jersey Department of Environmental Protection, Aerial Photo Library.

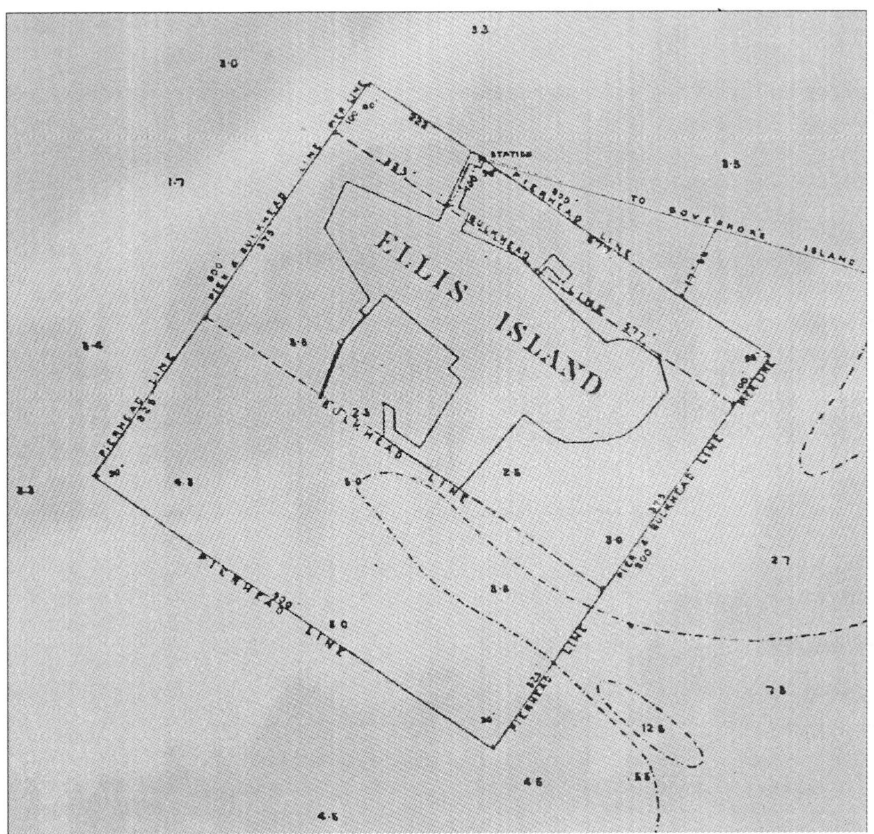

Source: National Archives, June 1890.

This map is titled "Pierhead & Bulkhead Lines for Ellis Island, New Jersey, New York Harbor as recommended by the New York Harbor Line Board." Special Master Paul Verkuil noted, "The significance of this map is that it was approved by the Secretary of War, Elihu Root, and produced over his signature. His signature... with the designation Ellis Island, New Jersey, makes this weighty evidence." (U.S. Supreme Court Evidence)

Enlargement of Non-submerged Area

In the intervening years, the boundary question became more muddled. The United States, which owned the island since 1808, used the island as a fort in the early 19th century and as a powder magazine in the mid-19th century. In 1890, the federal government decided to use Ellis Island as an immigration station. Requiring more space, the federal government began filling the submerged lands around the island. By 1934, the island was enlarged tenfold by successive landfills, from its original 2.75 acres to 27.5 acres. Since 1890, New Jersey has contended that the filling to enlarge and develop the island was done on New Jersey territory.

The NJDEP mapped the natural island as part of the riparian mapping program undertaken by the Bureau of Tidelands in 1980. Using the riparian map as a preliminary claim, New Jersey officially asked the U.S. Supreme Court in 1993 to adjudicate the boundary dispute. Although both states and several congressional mandates had reviewed the boundary question over the years, the U.S. Supreme Court has sole jurisdiction to resolve boundary issues between states.

State Boundary Case Procedures

The process by which a state boundary case is presented to the Supreme Court is an involved one. The Court first names a Special Master, who reviews all pertinent information submitted by the states to support their claims. The Special Master then submits a report to the full Supreme Court summarizing the evidence and making a recommendation on the settlement. The high court then makes its determination on the final boundary settlement.

In preparation for the trial, the NJDEP Bureau of Tidelands, assisted by the NJDEP GIS Unit, the NJDEP Land Use Regulation Program and the Geodetic section of the New Jersey Department of Transportation, prepared several maps on the DEP's GIS showing the proposed boundary line based on the 1857 U.S. Coast Survey map. Also mapped were the perimeter of the existing island as determined using GPS, as well as the locations of a portion of the historic fort built on Ellis Island before 1812. The location of the original wall (which has been excavated in part) was helpful in supporting the alignment of the historical maps used to define New Jersey's claim.

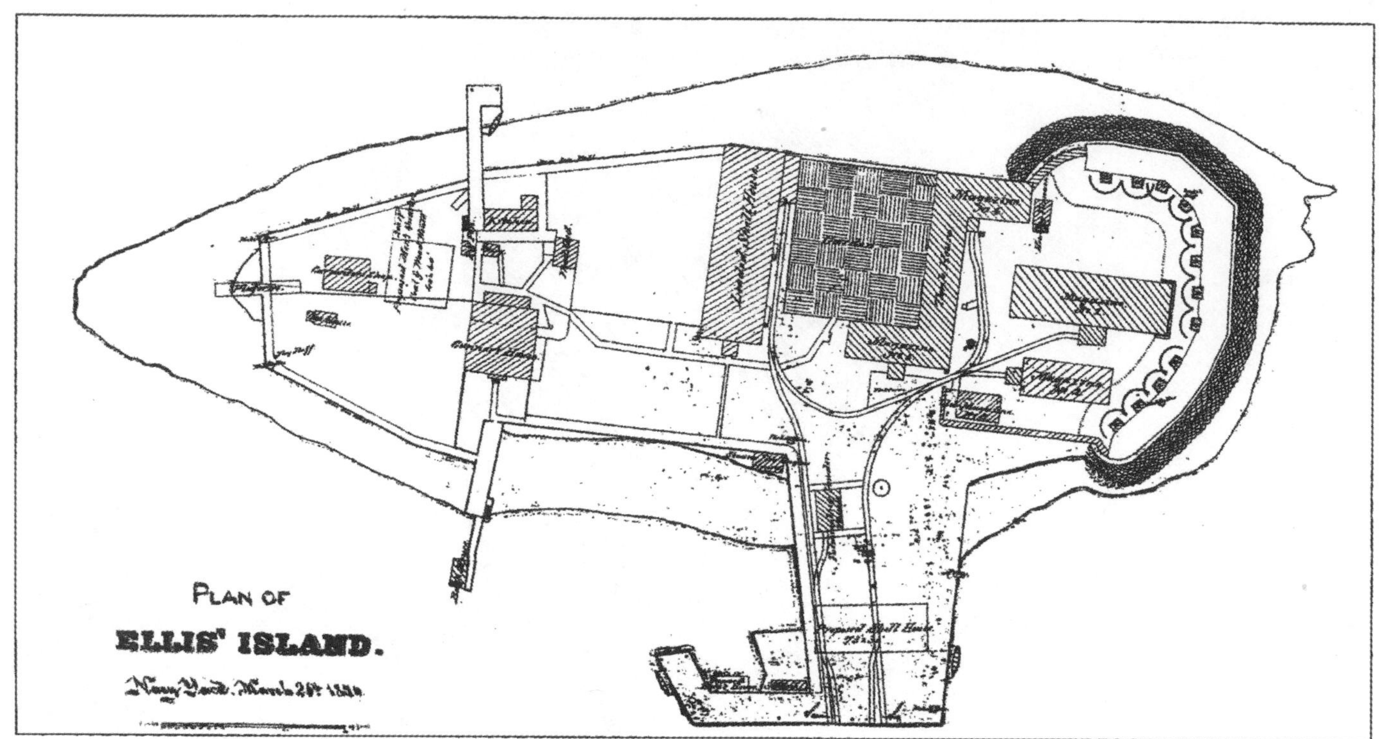

Source: National Archives

"Plan of Ellis' Island 1870," prepared by the Bureau of Ordinance, Navy Department. This map clearly shows the two angles in the Fort Gibson wall used in the 1995 GPS survey. (U.S. Supreme Court Evidence)

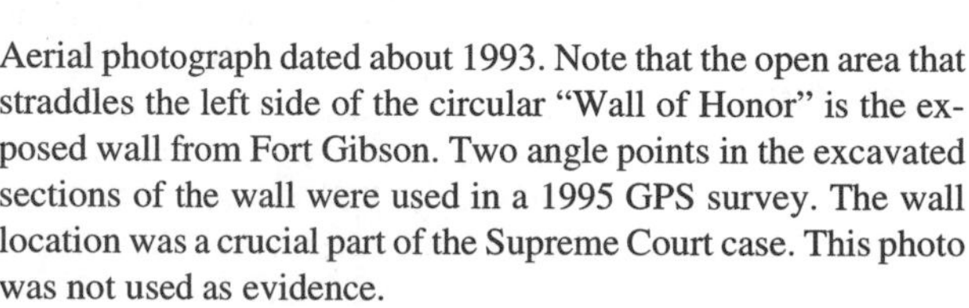
Aerial photograph dated about 1993. Note that the open area that straddles the left side of the circular "Wall of Honor" is the exposed wall from Fort Gibson. Two angle points in the excavated sections of the wall were used in a 1995 GPS survey. The wall location was a crucial part of the Supreme Court case. This photo was not used as evidence.

Ellis Island in 1995 and in 1857 Showing the Low Water Line

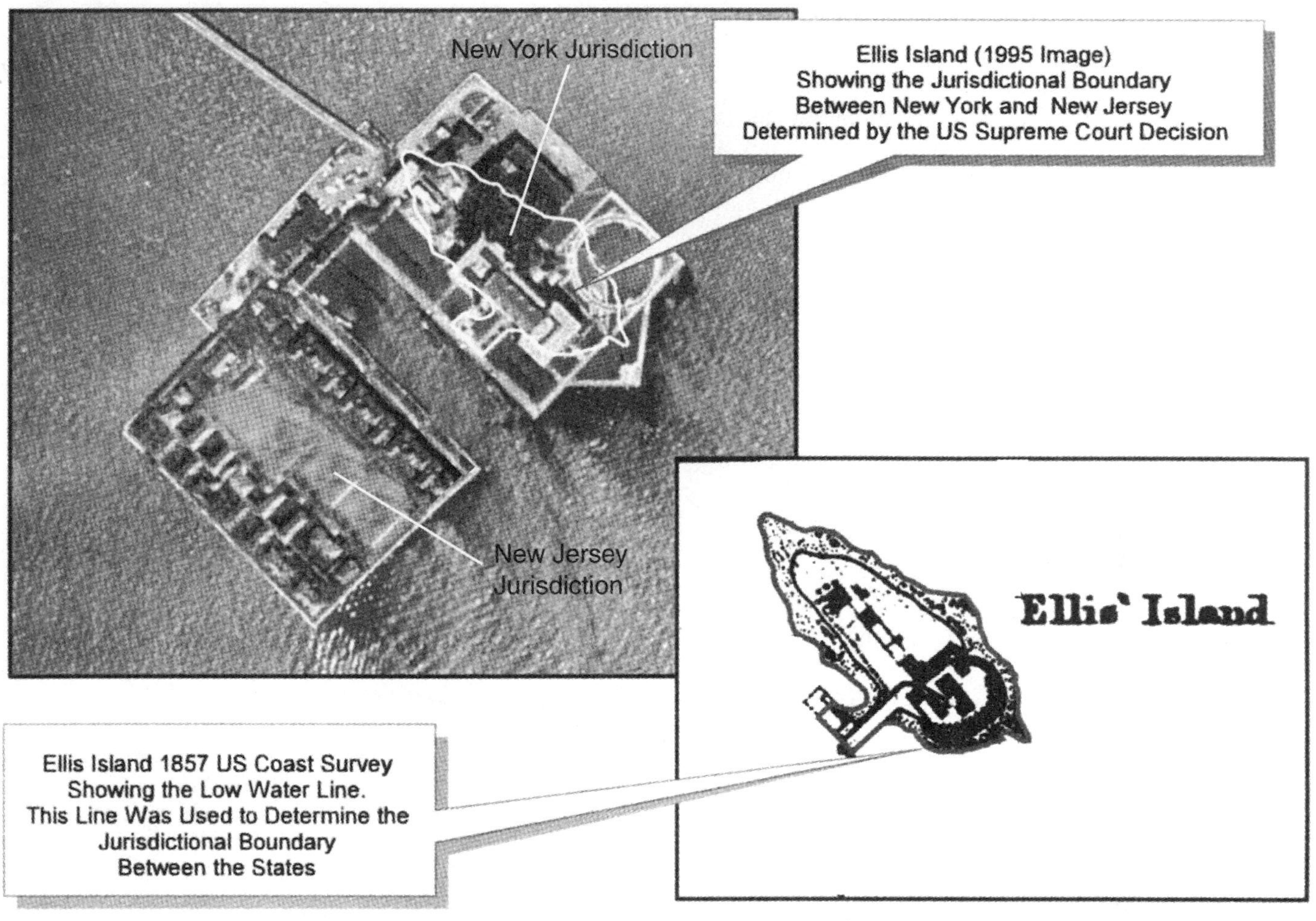

Prepared by Lawrence L. Thornton, New Jersey Department of Environmental Protection. Map Composition: Lawrence L. Thornton

1857 U.S. Coast Survey map and the jurisdictional boundary line from the 1857 map superimposed on a 1995 aerial photograph. This exhibit was prepared after the trial and was not used as evidence.

1857 Map Chosen to Define Boundary

When the Special Master reviewed all of the evidence, he determined that the 1857 U.S. Coast Survey map should define the boundary between the two states. However, the Special Master disagreed with New Jersey's use of the mean high water line on the island as the boundary and directed the state to use the low water line. In May of 1998, after oral arguments were presented by the states, the Supreme Court determined that the 1857 low water line of the natural island should be used to delineate the jurisdictional boundary.

The NJDEP was directed to prepare the Ellis Island boundary based on the Special Master's recommendation. The mapping was completed using GIS. The 1857 U.S. Coast Survey map was scanned and captured as a TIFF image file by the New Jersey Geological Survey. The image file was then brought into ArcView, and the low water line was captured as an edit function. The line depicting low water was represented on the 1857 map by a series of dots. The center of each dot was used to enter each point used to define the low water boundary. Once completed, the points and the line they describe were given geographic referencing by first converting the shape files to coverages—creating tic files for each—and then transforming and projecting the coverages to New Jersey State Plane Feet, NAD83. With this referencing, the line could be plotted on NJDEP's 1995 digital imagery and be integrated into the outer boundary survey, which was completed with the GPS done by NJDOT. The line was then un-generated and sent to NJDOT to prepare a final hard copy map.

New York Officials Approve Map

The map was then presented to New York state officials, who subsequently approved the delineation after several minor changes. The final step in the process is the Special Master's approval of the delineation.

While possibly not the first use of GIS to solve a boundary dispute, this may be a first use of GIS to present and solve a boundary dispute before the U.S. Supreme

Court. The success and power of GIS in the Ellis Island case suggests that it will not be the last. After more than 160 years, the jurisdictional fight over Ellis Island is finally over. The high court issued its final decree and approved the boundary line on May 17, 1999. New Jersey was granted sovereign authority over 22.80 acres, and New York was granted authority over the remaining 4.68 acres.

RICHARD G. CASTAGNA is a regional supervisor with the Bureau of Tidelands, NJDEP. He testified as an expert witness before the U.S. Supreme Court in the Ellis Island case on behalf of the State of New Jersey, describing physical changes to the island from the 18th century to the present.

LAWRENCE L. THORNTON is manager of the GIS Unit for NJDEP in Trenton, New Jersey. He delineated a claims line around Ellis Island for the state's riparian claim in 1980 and assisted in the delineation of the low water line, implementing the Supreme Court's decision in 1998.

JOHN M. TYRAWSKI is currently a research scientist with the GIS Unit of NJDEP. For the Ellis Island case, he assisted in the digital creation of the historic 1857 shoreline and in the development of the exhibits used to present the case for the State of New Jersey.

Mapping the Outcrop

Teaching field geology with laptop computers and geographic information systems brings digital mapping to the outcrop.

By J. Douglas Walker and Ross A. Black

Over the last 20 years, geologists have evolved from die-hard computer-phobes to people using computers in virtually every aspect of their work. Now computers are making inroads into that last bastion of the "old-school" geologist: basic field mapping on the outcrop.

A field mapper can still pull on a pair of boots and grab a backpack, hammer and base map and conduct field work without a computer. Even with the advent of the personal computer, most outcrop mappers remain independent, self-reliant and proud of the low level of technology necessary to make original geological contributions to the scientific community.

With the advent of the Internet, we expect new scientific information to be digital.

But computers have become ubiquitous within our society. This is especially true in higher education. Today's student has been exposed to computers since an early age, and many students now actually see computers as a primary learning tool. Who better, then, to test digital mapping technologies than students? Over the last two years, we have been teaching our geology students to use laptop computers and geographic information system (GIS) software in the field.

Mapping itself is becoming a digital process (*Geotimes*, June 2000). With the advent of the Internet, we expect new scientific information to be digital. Large corporations, government agencies and, to some extent, universities began major efforts to put new information into a digital form many years ago. They also had to come to grips with the fact that it is tedious and expensive to convert older data into a usable digital form.

Making mapping information digital from the earliest point of the mapping process—in the field—could save the mapper many time-consuming steps.

Entering historic data into a system where it can be integrated with other information is a chore. Entering mapping data into the computer is one of the geologist's more onerous tasks. The endearing term "digi-slave" is common in laboratories and offices converting maps into digital data sets. Making mapping information digital from the earliest point of the mapping process—in the field—could save the mapper many time-consuming steps.

Geological data are location dependent: the elevation and location at which an observation is made is just as important as the observation itself. This is why most geological data are recorded in a map-based format. Geological outcrop observations are thus well suited to being recorded and manipulated with existing GIS software packages.

We and our students use GIS software to compile, compose and view geologic maps. We also use such software to merge maps with satellite imagery, aerial photography and other data sets, and for visualizing data in 3-D for modeling geological processes.

Our GIS lab has been integrating large geological and geophysical databases for the last six years. We have put a tremendous amount of time and effort into converting paper-based geological data into a digital form.

Existing geological maps are by far the hardest sources of information to enter into a database. The information on the map consists of on-the-fly interpretations of observations the field geologist made on the outcrop. The person digitizing the map must also interpret the map symbols on-the-fly.

Why not enter the data into the GIS package on the outcrop, eliminating the need for another step in the lab that is technical, time consuming, costly and prone to error?

After asking ourselves this same question, we started putting together a computer-based field-mapping program. Several private companies, government agencies and academic groups were pursuing the same goal, and we met them at meetings of the Geological Society of America, American Association of Petroleum Geologists, American Geophysical Union and the Environmental Research Institute Users Group. Some groups, most notably the Canadian Geological Survey, Bowling Green State University and the University of California at Berkeley, had digital mapping programs in place. But almost everyone was at about the same stage we were.

We investigated the technologies we could pursue and then sought funding for the project. We received funding from the University of Kansas (KU) Technology Fund, the Geothermal Program Office of the U.S. Navy and the KU Department of Geology.

Students in the field

We first used the computers and software in a graduate level mapping course offered in January 1999. Four graduate students signed up. These students had previous mapping experience, and three of the four had used ArcView software.

The students first had to figure out how to carry their laptops into the field. They dug into a box of straps, buckles, clips and tape we had purchased from a camping store, and, after an hour of fiddling, were ready to go into the field. Most of the first day was spent getting used to the computers and trying to enter geologic data on the outcrop.

In a word, the students were very unhappy with the whole operation at the end of the day (mutiny might be a more accurate term). Carrying the nine-pound computers was not fun, digitizing was a pain, the screens were hard to read and the batteries were weak and heavy. We were not very encouraged.

To avoid a total loss of field time, the students printed maps and took them into the field to map on the next day. This went fine until it came time to enter the data into the computer. Predictably, this was a tedious operation. Sensing that the computers could actually save some time and effort, we went out with computers and paper maps the third day. By the end of the day the students were mapping pretty well on the computers and were in better spirits.

We spent another seven days in the field mapping and working out problems with the computers and software. By the end of two weeks, three of the four students were happy with the mapping setup. The fourth remained unconvinced that we had come up with anything useful.

After this session, it was with great uneasiness that we introduced computer mapping into our undergraduate field camp in June of 1999. We taught eight undergraduate students in the last week of a six-week field course. None of them had ever used a GIS program, let alone ArcView. We gave them the same short, three-hour introductory session we'd given the graduate students and then sent them into the field.

The undergraduate experience could not have been more different from the graduate one. The students were very excited about mapping with computers and welcomed the change from paper maps, photos and mylar overlays. Most students were comfortable with the computers by the end of the first day; by mid-morning of the second day they were asking questions about the geology and not about how to use the programs.

We attribute these different reactions to two factors. First, the undergraduates are not set in their ways about mapping. They did not have the background baggage the graduate students carried. Second, the undergraduates were more used to computers. The age difference of a couple of years is just enough that the younger students expect to use computers in all aspects of their education and most aspects of their lives.

The future

We will continue using computers in University of Kansas field courses. We plan to expand the undergraduate component to about half of the six-week course. We still consider conventional mapping skills important. Introducing the computer adds a level of excitement for the students.

Many of our students are now taking GIS courses. This change is a grassroots effort among the undergraduates and not an idea the faculty pushed onto them. They will know more about the basic software components than will some of the field-camp faculty members.

The widespread availability of inexpensive (or free) 7.5-minute topographic maps in various digital formats has been one of the important factors in making digital mapping systems easier.

Some of the problems with field computers are being remedied. Laptops are getting lighter—four pounds instead of nine pounds. Battery life is steadily increasing. We can map all day on a single lithium-ion battery. Touchscreens are now readable in sunlight. Personal digital assistants should soon be powerful enough to run the software and handle the large image files needed to perform efficient mapping.

The widespread availability of inexpensive (or free) 7.5-minute topographic maps in various digital formats has been one of the important factors in making digital mapping systems easier to use. Now we need inexpensive, large scale, aerial photos at digital resolutions useable for geological field studies.

The final component for digital mapping is GPS receivers. Using the Global Positioning System (GPS) promises to give the field geologist real-time, accurate location information. Although we have a method for connecting the GPS unit directly to the laptop and downloading the location, the GIS packages do not automatically update the map with the proper map symbols. Thus it is easier to read the location from the GPS unit and then manually move the laptop cursor to that point on the map and record the field observation. We hope that GPS receivers soon become standard options for ruggedized laptops and that GIS packages include easy-to-use interfaces with standard GPS data.The demise of selective availability in GPS signals (Geotimes, June 2000) has made GPS coordinates almost 10 times more accurate.

Improved, publicly available GPS signals may be what pushes GPS/GIS-driven geological field mapping onto every student's field belt in a one-piece unit that will fit in a Gfeller field case.

Additional Reading

"Bedrock geologic mapping using ArcInfo" by T.E. Waht, J.D. Miller and E.J. Bauer. *Proceedings* of ESRI Users Conference, 1995. p. 167.

"The Bedrock of Geologic Mapping" by P. Chirico. *Geo Info Systems*, 1997. v. 7, n. 10, p. 26–31.

"Development of Geographic Information Systems Oriented Databases for Integrated Geological and Geophysical Applications" by J.D. Walker, R.A. Black, J.K. Linn, A.J. Thomas, R. Wiseman and M.G. D'Attillio. *GSA Today*, 1996 v. 6, n. 3, p.1–7.

Getting to know ArcView GIS by ESRI Press. 1998.

Walker and Black teach in the Department of Geology at the University of Kansas in Lawrence, Kan.

GAINING PERSPECTIVE

The proliferation of satellite technology, from spy-quality photos to low-resolution radar images, is giving us new, more meaningful ways to envision complex information about the Earth. But whether we will act on the picture of ecological destruction this technology is cobbling together—from global climate change to wholesale clearing of forests—remains to be seen.

by Molly O'Meara Sheehan

During the last few decades of the 20th century it became evident that tropical rainforests were endangered not only by road-building, timber-cutting, and other incursions of the bulldozer and saw, but by thousands of wildfires. Historically, relatively small fires have been set by slash-and-burn farmers trying to clear patches of jungle for farm land. But starting in 1997, fires in the world's tropical forests from Brazil to Papua New Guinea raged on a scale never recorded before. The causes of these huge conflagrations raised questions, because tropical rainforests rarely burn naturally.

In the wake of several haze-induced accidents and public health warnings in smoke-covered Indonesia, the need for a clear answer to these questions was given legal significance when President Suharto, under pressure from neighboring countries, passed a decree making it illegal to set forest fires. The politically connected timber industry had managed to direct most of the blame for forest fires on the small-scale, slash-and-burn farmers, but Indonesia's rogue environment minister Sarwono Kusumaatmadja employed a relatively new intelligence-gathering technology to get a clear picture of the situation: he downloaded satellite images of burning Indonesian rainforests from a U.S. government website and compared them to timber concession maps. The satellite images confirmed that many of the blazes were being set in areas the timber companies wanted to clear for plantations. With the satellite evidence in hand, Kusnmaatmadja got his government to revoke the licenses of 29 timber companies.

HIGH SPEED INTELLIGENCE

The environment minister's quick work on the rainforest issue is just one of many recent cases involving environmental questions in which satellite surveillance has been used to provide answers that might otherwise not have been known for years, if ever. The images captured by cameras circling high above the planet are proving effective not only because they scan far more extensively than ground observers can, but because they can be far faster than traditional information-gathering methods.

Pre-satellite studies of the oceans, for example, had to be done from boats, which can only reach a tiny fraction of the oceanic surface in any given month or year. And even after centuries of nautical exploration, most of the information scientists have gathered about winds, currents, and temperatures comes from the commercial trade routes of the North Atlantic between the United States and Europe. Satellites don't replace on-the-water research, as they can't collect water samples, but for some kinds of data collection they can do in minutes what might take boats centuries to do. Satellites can, in principle, watch the whole of the world's oceans, providing almost immediate assessments of environmental conditions everywhere.

Similarly quick surveillance is available for many parts of the biosphere that are otherwise difficult to reach—the polar ice, dense forest interiors, and atmosphere. As a result, says Claire Parkinson of the U.S. National Aeronautics and Space Administration (NASA), "theory and explanations no longer have a database restricted to areas and times where humans have physically [gone] and made observations or left instruments to record the measurements." The speed of environmental research has taken a quantum leap.

Speed isn't only a matter of technical capability, however. In practice, it's also a matter of access. Spy satellites began circling the globe soon after Russia's Sputnik went into orbit in 1957. But the information they relayed to Soviet and U.S. intelligence agencies was kept sequestered.

The difference now is that satellites are increasingly being used for purposes other than espionage or military intelligence. The great majority are for telecommunications. However, more than 45—many owned by governments, but a growing number of them privately owned—are being used for monitoring various phenomena on the ground, on the water, or in the atmosphere. In addition, more than 70 launches are planned during the next 15 years by civil space agencies and private companies. How these instruments are used, and by whom, will have enormous consequences for the world.

THE RACE AGAINST TIME

If incidents like the Indonesian forest fire intervention are any indication, environmental monitoring by orbiting cameras could play a critical role in reversing the global trends of deforestation and ecological collapse that now threaten the long-term viability of civilization. Denis Hayes, the former Worldwatch Institute researcher who is the chairman of Earth Day 2000 asked a few years ago, in a speech, "How can we have won so many environmental battles, yet be so close to losing the war?" Since then, we have edged still closer. Clearly, the number of battles being won is too small, and the time it takes to win them is too long.

FLOODING IN BANGLADESH

10 October 1988

A

B

N

SPOT SATELLITE IMAGERY: © CNES 2000. COURTESY SPOT IMAGE CORPORATION, WWW.SPOT.COM.

This medium resolution SPOT image of the confluence of the Meghna and Ganges Rivers and nearby Dhaka, the capital of Bangladesh, depicts a kind of collision between population growth and the ebbs and flows of the powerful rivers that feed the Ganges Delta. The land here is some of the most fertile--and heavily cultivated--in the world, replenished with rich silt washed down from the Himalayas by annual floods. The sprawling city of Dhaka and a couple of roads are perceptible in the northwest. And a closer view shows considerable development and cultivation throughout the image. (Even though the area is densely populated, this is difficult to see as most of the people live in small towns or villages.)

Another way of posing Hayes's now famous question might be to ask whether the processes of information-gathering and dissemination essential to changing human behavior can be speeded up enough to accelerate the environmental movement. Telecommunications satellites began providing part of the answer several decades ago by facilitating the formation of an active international environmental community that can mobilize quickly—whether to protest a dam on the Narmada River of India or to stop the use of genetically modified organisms in food production in Europe.

But while activism gained momentum, field work remained ominously slow—biologists slogging about in boots and rowboats, while the forces they were trying to understand raced over the Earth on the wings of global commerce, or ripped into it with the blades of industrial agriculture and resource extraction. However, satellite monitoring has begun to help researchers to more quickly assemble the data needed to bring decisive change. Remotely sensed images are contributing to critical areas of environmental research and management, including:

- **Weather**: The first meteorological satellites were launched in the early 1960s, and quickly became a key part of the U.N. World Meteorological Organization's World Weather Watch. In addition to the satellite data, virtually all nations contribute surface measurements of temperature, precipitation, and wind to this program to aid weather prediction, which has enormous social and economic benefits. In recent years, optical sensors that collect data on sea surface temperature and radar sensors that estimate ocean height have proven useful in understanding and predicting El Niño events, which can damage fisheries and agriculture by bringing warmth and wetness to much of the west coasts of South and North America, and drought to Southeast Asia, Australia, and parts of Africa.
- **Climate**: In the 1990s, researchers began to delve into satellite archives to study longer-term climate patterns. For instance, satellite images have helped reveal a decrease in snow in the Northern Hemisphere, a lengthening growing season in northern latitudes, and the breakup of major ice sheets. Radar sensors have been used to construct topographical maps of the ocean bottom, which in turn provide better understanding of the ocean currents, tides, and temperatures that affect climate. However, it was not until recently that space agencies began to design satellite systems dedicated specifically to climate research. In 1999, the United States launched Terra, which carries five different sensors for recording climatic variables such as radiative energy fluxes, clouds, water vapor, snow cover, land use, and the biological productivity of oceans. It is to be the first in a series of satellites that will create a consistent data set for at least 18 years.
- **Coastal boundary changes**: Whether as a result of warmer temperatures contributing to sea-level rise or irrigation projects shrinking lakes, coastal configurations

change over time—sometimes dramatically. Scientists have compared declassified images from covert U.S. military satellites pointed at Antarctica in 1963 to recent images of the same regions, for example, to reveal changes in the continent's ice cover. Other comparisons show the extent to which central Asia's Aral Sea and Africa's Lake Chad have diminished in size.

• **Habitat Protection**: The destruction of habitats as a result of human expansion has been identified as the largest single cause of biodiversity loss. Satellite images have proved quite effective in revealing large-scale forest destruction, whether by fire or clearcutting, not only in Indonesia but in the Amazon and other biological hotspots. New, more detailed imagery may reveal small-scale habitat niches. In Australia, for example, the Australia Koala Foundation plans to use detailed satellite images to identify individual eucalyptus trees. Researchers will compare these images to field data to determine what this species of tree looks like from above, then use the information to more quickly map individual trees or groves than would be possible from the ground. In the oceans, the same satellite-generated maps of undersea topography and sea surface temperature used to study weather and climate can be used to track the upwellings of nutrient-rich water that help to sustain fisheries.

• **Environmental law enforcement**: International organizations and national governments can use remote imaging to put more teeth in environmental laws and treaties. One of the leading fishing nations, Peru, is monitoring its coastal waters to prevent the kind of heavy overfishing that has so often caused fisheries to collapse. In Italy, the city of Ancona plans to buy satellite images to detect illegal waste dumps. Within the next decade, large-scale use of this technology could give urgently needed new effectiveness to such agreements as the Kyoto Protocol to the Climate Convention, the Biodiversity Convention, the Convention on Illegal Trade in Endangered Species (CITES), or the Law of the Sea.

MAKING SENSE OF NONSENSE

Look closely at a small detail of a newspaper or magazine photo—put it under a magnifying glass—and it may make no sense. The dots don't form any recognizable image. But stand back and see the photo as a whole, and it snaps into focus. Satellite images do the same thing, only on a vastly larger scale. Bits of information that might make no meaningful pattern when seen from the ground may, when seen from many kilometers above, resolve themselves into startling pictures.

The first pictures from space were photographs made from film, by astronauts aboard the first manned flights to the moon in the 1960s. These photos, of a fragile blue planet suspended in the vast blackness of space, helped to inspire the nascent environmental movement—one of them becoming the emblem of the first Earth Day in 1970.

In later surveillance from satellites, the imaging was digitized so that the data could be sent down in continuous streams and in much larger quantities than would be possible with film. Although one Russian satellite still uses regular camera film that is dropped to Earth in a canister and retrieved from the North Sea, most remote sensing satellites now use digital electronic sensors. The binary data they send down can be reconstructed into visual images by ground-based computers.

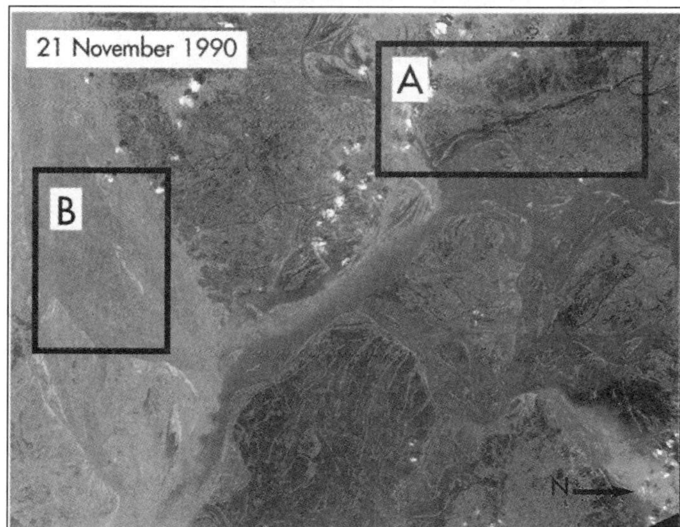

Bangladesh is one of the most densely populated countries in the world, and one of the most low-lying--the majority of the country is barely above sea level--so even the smallest of the annual floods can cause considerable damage. This image, in which darker areas are water-covered, was recorded during a devastating period of flooding, which took thousands of lives. Dhaka (A) is waterlogged and the once-cultivated islands in the Ganges, in the south of the image (B), are completely inundated.

The amount of detail varies with the type of sensor (see table, "Selected Satellite Systems"). For instance, an image of a 1,000 square kilometer tract of land obtained by a fairly low-resolution satellite such as AVHRR, which is used in continental and global studies of land and ocean, might contain 1,000 picture elements—or "pixels" (one piece of data per square kilometer). In contrast, an image of the same tract from the new, high-resolution Ikonos satellite would have 1 *billion* pixels (one per square meter). Between the broad perspective of satellites like AVHRR and the telescopic imaging of those like the new spy-quality satellite Ikonos, are medium-resolution sensors, such as those aboard the Landsat and SPOT satellites, in which one pixel represents a piece of land that is between 30 and 10 meters across. However, the level of detail is also limited by the size of the medium on which an image is displayed. For instance, if an Ikonos image with 1 billion pixels were reproduced in a magazine image one-quarter the size of this page, it would be reduced to 350,000 pixels.

Different tasks require different levels of detail. The value of high resolution lies in its enabling the viewer to hone in on a much smaller piece of the ground and see it in a kind of detail that the lower resolution camera could not capture. For a larger area, a lower resolution would suffice to give the human eye and brain as clear a pattern as it can recognize. Whereas the wide coverage provided by lower-resolution satellites has proved useful in understanding large-scale natural features such as geologic formations and ocean circulation, very detailed imagery may be best able to reveal niche habitats—such as the individual treetops that are home to the koala—and man-made structures, such as buildings, tanks, weapons, and refugee camps.

But satellite surveillance can do much more than provide huge volumes of sharp visual detail of the kind recorded by conventional optical cameras. The orbital industry also deploys a range of sensors that pick up information outside the range of the human eye, which can then be translated into visual form:

- Near-infrared emissions from the ground can be used to assess the health of plant growth, either in agriculture or in natural ecosystems, because healthy green vegetation reflects most of the near-infrared radiation it receives;
- Thermal radiation can reveal fires that would otherwise be obscured by smoke;
- Microwave emissions can provide information about soil moisture, wind speed, and rainfall over the oceans;
- Radar—short bursts of microwaves transmitted from the satellite—can penetrate the atmosphere in all conditions, and thus can "see" in the dark and through haze, clouds, or smoke. Radar sensors launched by European, Japanese, and Canadian agencies in the 1990s have been used mainly to detect changes in the freezing of sea ice in dark, northern latitudes, helping ships to navigate ice fields and steer clear of icebergs. Radar is what enabled satellites to map the ocean bottom, which would otherwise be obscured.

While satellites have the technical capability to monitor the Earth's entire surface—day or night, cloud-covered or clear, on the ground or underwater—this doesn't mean we now have updated global maps of whatever we want. Aside from the World Weather Watch, there is no process for coordinating a worldwide, long-term time series of comparable data from Earth observations. Rather, individual scientists collect data to answer specific questions for their own projects. In recent years, national space administrations have teamed up with research funding agencies and two international research programs to support an Integrated Global Observing Strategy that would create a framework for uniting environmental observations. Researchers are now trying to demonstrate the viability of this approach with a suite of projects, including one on forests and another on oceans.

In addition, to make sense of remotely sensed data requires comparison with field observations. An important element of the weather program's success, for instance, is the multitude of observations from both sky and land. And satellite estimations of sea-surface temperature can't generate El Niño forecasts automatically, but must be combined with other data sources, including readings from a network of ocean buoys that monitor wind speed and a satellite altimeter that measures water height. Similarly, the radar scans used to make maps of the ocean floor are calibrated and augmented by sounding surveys conducted by ships. Even a task as straightforward as the location of eucalyptus trees for the Australia koala project requires initial field observations to confirm that the typical visual pattern being searched out from above is indeed that of the eucalyptus, and not of some other kind of tree.

THE NILE DELTA, EGYPT

SPOT SATELLITE IMAGERY: © CNES 2000. COURTESY SPOT IMAGE CORPORATION, WWW.SPOT.COM.

This medium-resolution SPOT image of the Nile Delta shows the steady march of irrigation (indicated by the dark shades and crop circles) out into the desert near Cairo. While the Nile Delta and its floodplain have been farmed for thousands of years, only within the past 30 years have crops been planted intensively out in the desert. And with good reason: Cairo's population has grown from 5 million in 1970 to more than 11 million today.

Satellite imagery has become even more useful with the advent of geographic information systems (GIS), which allow users to combine satellite images with other data in a computer to create maps and model changes over time. In much the same way that old medical encyclopedias depict human anatomy, with transparencies of the skeleton, circulatory system, nervous system, and organs that can be laid over a picture of the body, a GIS stores multiple layers of geographically referenced information. The data layers might include satellite images, topography, political boundaries, rivers, highways, utility lines, sources of pollution, and wildlife habitat.

Maps that are stored in a GIS allow people to exploit the data storage capacity and calculating power of com-

SELECTED SATELLITE SYSTEMS PRODUCING COMMERCIALLY AVAILABLE IMAGERY

Satellite	Launch Date	Owner	Spatial Resolution	Spectral Range	Price per Square Mile
Landsat series Landsat-7	1972 1999	NASA, (U.S. space agency)	30-120m, 15-60m	visible light (red, green blue); near-short-wave, and thermal infrared	$.02-.03
Terra	1999	NASA	15m-22km	visible, near-, short-wave, mid-, and thermal infrared	N/A
SPOT series SPOT-4	1986 1997	CNES (French space agency)	10-30m	visible, near-and short-wave infrared	$1-3
AVHRR	1979	NOAA (U.S. agency)	1.1km	visible, thermal infrared	$.08-80 per 10,000 square miles
IRS-1D	1997	Indian remote sensing agency	6m	visible, near- and short-wave infrared	$1.30-6.20
Ikonos	1999	Space Imaging Corp.	1-4m	visible; near-infrared	$75-250
Orb View		Orbimage Corp.			
OrbView-1	1995		10 km	visible; near-infrared	
OrbView-2	1997		1 km	visible; near-infrared	$.0003
OrbView-3	2000		1-8m	visible; near-infrared	N/A
OrbView-4	2000-01		1-8m	visible; near-infrared	N/A
QuickBird	2000	Earthwatch Corp.	1-4m	visible; near-infrared	N/A
ERS SAR					
ERS-1 ERS-2	1991 1995	European space agencies	25m	radar; C-band	
IERS-1	1992	Japanese space agency	18m	radar; L-band	
Radarsat					
Radarsat-1	1995	Canadian space agency	8-100m	radar; C-band	$.04-5.40

puters. Thus when geographically referenced data are entered into a GIS, the computer can be harnessed to look at changes over time, to identify relationships between different data layers, to change variables in order to ask "what if" questions, and to explore various alternatives for future action.

Because human perception can often identify patterns more easily on maps than in written text or numbers, maps can help people understand and analyze problems in ways that other types of information cannot. The Washington, D.C.-based World Resources Institute (WRI), for example, has used GIS to analyze threats to natural resources on a global scale. Researchers have combined ground and satellite data on forests with information about wilderness areas and roads to map the world's remaining large, intact "frontier" forests and identify hot-spots of deforestation. A similar WRI study, investigating threats to coral reefs, assembled information from 14 global data sets, local studies of 800 sites, and scientific expertise to conclude that 58 percent of the world's reefs are at risk from development.

With advances in computing power, some GIS software packages can now be run on desktop computers, allowing more people to take advantage of them. In fact, the number of people using GIS is swelling by roughly 20 percent each year, and the leading software company,

ESRI, grew from fewer than 50,000 clients in 1990 to more than 220,000 in 1999.

A related technology spurring the market for geographic information is the Global Positioning System—a network of 24 navigation satellites operated by the U.S. Department of Defense. A GPS receiver on the ground uses signals from different satellites to triangulate position. (For security reasons, the Defense Department purposefully introduces a distortion into the signal so that the location is correct only to within 100 meters.) As GPS receivers have become miniaturized, their cost has come down. The technology is now built into some farm machines, cars, and laptop computers. Researchers can take air or water samples and feed the data directly into a GIS, with latitude and longitude coordinates supplied by the GPS receiver in their computers.

The relatively new field of "precision agriculture" demonstrates how satellite imagery, GIS, and GPS systems can all be used to show farmers precisely how their crops are growing. Conditions in every crop row can be monitored when a farmer walks into the field—or when a satellite flies over—and recorded for analysis in a GIS. During the growing season, satellite monitoring can track crop conditions, such as the amount of pest damage or water stress, and allow farmers to attend to affected areas. The central component of a precision agriculture operation is a yield monitor, which is a sensor in a harvesting combine that receives GPS coordinates. As the combine harvests a crop such as corn, the sensor records the quality and quantity of the harvest from each section of the field. This detailed information provides indicators about the soil quality and irrigation needs of different parts of the field, and allows the farmer to apply water, fertilizer, and pesticides more accurately the following season.

Meanwhile, the growth of the Internet is allowing satellite images and GIS data to be more easily distributed. In late 1997, Microsoft Corporation teamed up with the Russian space agency Sovinformsputnik and image providers such as Aerial Images, Inc. and the U.S. Geological Survey to create TerraServer, the first website to allow people to view, download, and purchase satellite images. Some satellite operators have begun to offer catalogs of their images on the Internet.

Whose Picture Is It?

Throughout history, people have fought for possession of pieces of the Earth's land and water. It was not until the advent of Earth observation satellites that ownership of the images of those places was seriously debated. To legitimize its satellite program, the United States argued strongly that the light reflected off the oceans or mountains, like the air, should be in the public domain—a claim now accepted by many other countries. But for the last two decades, the United States has also promoted the involvement of private U.S. companies in earth observation. Until the end of the Cold War, companies were reluctant to enter the satellite remote sensing business for fear of restrictions related to national security concerns. But in September 1999, a U.S.-based firm called Space Imaging launched the first high-resolution commercial satellite; this year, two other U.S. enterprises, Orbimage and EarthWatch, plan to launch similar instruments.

This trend raises questions about the tension between public and private interests in exploiting space. On the one hand, the widespread availability of detailed images means greater openness in human conduct. With satellite imagery, it is impossible to hide (or not find out about) such harmful or threatening activities as Chernobyl-scale nuclear accidents, or widespread forest clearing, or major troop movements. On the other hand, whether the information will be used to its full potential is up to governments and citizens.

There are obvious benefits to commercially available high-resolution images. Governments wary of revealing secrets have traditionally restricted the circulation of detailed satellite information. Now, images of the Earth that were once available to a select few intelligence agencies are accessible to anyone with a credit card. The information may be valuable to many non-military enterprises—public utilities, transportation planners, telecommunications firms, foresters, and others who already rely on up-to-date maps for routine operations.

In the world of NGOs, the impact of high-resolution imagery may be most dramatic for groups that keep an eye on arms control agreements and government military activities. "When one-meter black-and-white pictures hit the market, a well-endowed non-governmental organization will be able to have pictures better than [those] the U.S. spy satellites took in 1972 at the time of the first strategic arms accord," writes Peter Zimmerman, a remote-sensing and arms control expert, in a 1999 *Scientific American* article.

Indeed, when Ikonos released imagery of a top-secret North Korean missile base last January, the Federation of American Scientists (FAS), a U.S.-based nonprofit group, published a controversial analysis of the images contradicting U.S. military claims that the site is one of the most serious missile threats facing the United States. (The potential threat from this base is a key argument for proponents of a multi-billion dollar missile shield, the construction of which would violate the anti-ballistic missile treaty.) Noting the absence of transportation links, paved roads, propellant storage, and staff housing, the FAS report found the facility "incapable of supporting the extensive test program that would be needed to fully develop a reliable missile system."

In addition, the private entrants in the satellite remote sensing business may spur the whole industry to become more accessible. Already, the new companies are beginning to seek partnerships with government imagery providers, so that customers are able to go to one place to buy a number of different types of images. For instance,

Orbimage, which is scheduled to launch its first high resolution satellite this year, has made agreements to sell medium resolution images from the French SPOT series and radar images from the Canadian Radarsat. Such arrangements may make it easier for people to find and use imagery.

FISHBONE FORESTS

LANDSAT IMAGES COURTESY OF THE TROPICAL RAINFOREST INFORMATION CENTER OF THE BASIC SCIENCE AND REMOTE SENSING INITIATIVE AT MICHIGAN STATE UNIVERSITY, A NASA EARTH SCIENCE INFORMATION PARTNER. WWW.BSRSI.MSU.EDU

These medium-resolution Landsat images show the legacy of the Brazilian government's Polonoreste project, which held out the offer of cheap land to bring farmers to this remote area of the Amazon. The centerpiece of this project, the Trans-Amazon Highway, can be seen following the Jiparaná River, running from the southeast to the northwest through the booming rural cities of Pimenta Bueno (center) and then Cacoal (top left). A tiny outpost in the early 1970s, Cacoal is now home to more than 50,000 people.

LANDSAT IMAGES COURTESY OF THE TROPICAL RAINFOREST INFORMATION CENTER OF THE BASIC SCIENCE AND REMOTE SENSING INITIATIVE AT MICHIGAN STATE UNIVERSITY, A NASA EARTH SCIENCE INFORMATION PARTNER. WWW.BSRSI.MSU.EDU

Highway BR 364, as it is called, has unzipped this part of Amazon, opening the vast forests to the tell-tale "fishbone pattern" of forest clearing. The roads that radiate out from the highway are flanked with once-forested land cleared for agriculture. Heavy rainfall leaches the soil of nutrients within a few seasons and crop yields quickly decline. The cycle of clearing starts anew when the degraded land is sold to cattle ranchers for pasture lands, which can be seen here as large rectangular clearings. The untouched tract of forest to the northwest is an indigenous preserve.

But private ownership of satellite data—making it available only at a price that not all beneficiaries can pay, or protecting it with copyright agreements—could also cause serious impediments to reversing ecological decline:

• One of the most important potential applications of remote sensing could be its use by non-governmental public interest groups, which provide a critical counterweight to the government and corporate sectors. NGOs that monitor arms control or humanitarian emergencies, for example, can use satellite data to pressure governments to live up to international nonproliferation agreements and foreign aid commitments. But a group that buys images from a private satellite company in order to publicize a humanitarian disaster or environmental threat could—depending on copyright laws and restrictions—find itself prohibited from posting the images on its website or distributing them to the media. While low-resolution imagery from government sources is easily shared, citizen groups and governments should quickly set a precedent for sharing information from high-resolution imagery.

• Only a few, very large agricultural operations can afford the high-tech equipment required to practice precision agriculture. Because farmers with small plots of land can simply walk into their fields for an assessment, the technology will remain most useful to larger operations. So although this tool could improve the way large-scale agriculture is practiced in the short term, it could also delay the long-term transition to more sustainable agricultural practices, which tend to require smaller-scale farms.

• Large companies looking for places to extract oil, minerals, or biological resources could purchase detailed satellite data and gain unfair advantage over cash-strapped developing nations in which the resources are located, whose governments cannot afford satellite imagery, GIS software, and technical support staff and systems needed to make and maintain such maps.

Finally, along with the question of who will own the technology, there is the related question of whether there is significant risk of its being badly misused. A few decades ago, the advent of commercially available high-resolution images would likely have been met with great alarm, as a manifestation of the "Big-Brother-is-watching-you" fear that pervaded the Cold War years. That fear may have receded, but what remains is a conundrum that has haunted every powerful new technology, from steel blades to genetic engineering. Could access to detailed images of their enemies cause belligerent nations to become more dangerous than they already are?

In any case, there's no turning back now. Many of the remote sensing satellites now scanning the Earth and scheduled for launch this year will be in orbit until long after the basic decisions affecting the planet's long-term environmental future—and perhaps the future of civilization—have been made. Ultimately, an educated global citizenry will be needed to make use of the flood of data being unleashed from both publicly and privately owned satellites. Policy analyst Ann Florini of the Carnegie Endowment writes: "With states, international organizations, and corporations all prodding one another to release ever more information, civil society can take that information, analyze and compile it, and disseminate it to networks of citizen groups and consumer organizations."

If the Internet has given the world's technological infrastructure a new nervous system, the Earth-observation satellites are giving it a new set of eyes. In precarious times, that could be useful. U.S. Vice President Al Gore, who understands the potential of remote sensing, has called for the completion of a "Digital Earth," a 1-meter resolution map of the world that would be widely accessible. According to Brian Soliday of Space Imaging, the Ikonos instrument alone might be able to assemble a cloud-free map of the world at 1-meter resolution within four to five years. That's about as long as it has taken to do the vaunted Human Genome map, and this map would be much bigger. Arguably, because it covers not only us humans but also the biological and climatic systems in which our genome evolved and must forever continue to depend, it could also be at least as valuable.

Molly O'Meara Sheehan is a research associate at the Worldwatch Institute.

From *World Watch*, March/April 2000, pp. 14–24.

census 2000

Micro Melting Pots

THE COUNTRY IS BECOMING MORE DIVERSE, BUT GROWTH OF ETHNIC POPULATIONS IS ONLY CONCENTRATED IN CERTAIN REGIONS.

BY WILLIAM H. FREY

In the wake of Census 2000, newspaper headlines have bombarded us with messages about the growing and pervasive racial and ethnic diversity across the United States. And nationwide, statistics not only confirm that minorities grew at 12 times the rate of whites, but that fewer than 7 in 10 Americans consider themselves to be white—or "non-Hispanic white only" in census terminology.*

Still, a careful examination of the torrent of statistics flowing from the U.S. Census Bureau reveals that the nation's minority groups, especially Hispanics and Asians, are heavily clustered in selected regions and markets. Rather than witnessing the formation of a homogeneous national melting pot, we are seeing the creation of numerous mini-melting pots—in contrast to the rest of America, which is much less diverse. Through intermarriage and the blending of cultures, each of these melting-pot metros will develop its own politics, tastes for consumer items, and demographic personalities. Commentators, markets, and political analysts should understand and take into account these multiple melting pots and the new ethnic frontiers presaged by their spillover as predictors of America's changing racial/ethnic landscape.

Regional Differences

In a broad swath of the country the minority presence is still quite limited.... America's racial and ethnic patterns have taken on distinctly regional dimensions. Hispanics dominate large portions of counties in a span of states stretching from California to Texas. Blacks are strongly represented in counties of the South as well as selected urban areas in the Northeast and Midwest. The Asian presence is relatively small and highly concentrated in a few scattered counties, largely in the West. And Native Americans are concentrated in select pockets in Oklahoma, the Southeast, upper Midwest, and the West. Multiethnic counties are most prominent in California and the Southwestern U.S., with mixes of Asians and Hispanics, or Hispanics and Native Americans.

The most notable aspect... is the broad stretch of counties from the upper West and Rocky Mountains to the Midwest and Northeast that are mostly white, and where none of the minority groups come close to approximating their national averages. Of the 3,141 counties in the U.S., over three-quarters (2,419) of them have white shares greater than the nation as a whole, and well over half of all counties (1,822) are at least 85 percent white.

In contrast, only 381 counties have a greater than national representation of Hispanics, as do 117 counties for Asians, and 697 counties for blacks. It can certainly be argued that there has been a greater diffusion of minorities, especially Hispanics, across the counties. The vast majority of U.S. counties (2,990) have shown some increase in their Hispanic populations during the 1990s, and in about a quarter of all counties, that increase exceeded 1,000 persons over the past decade. Yet their overall gains are heavily concentrated in the core counties of immigrant metro areas, and in the West and Southwestern U.S. Just 100 of these core counties accounted for more than 70 percent of all the nation's Hispanic gains during the decade. The diffusion of Hispanics outward from these core areas, in terms of total numbers, is far less rapid than recent press accounts imply.

While there was some dispersal of immigrant Asian and Hispanic groups during the 1990s, the greater tendency was a continued concentration in established ports of entry. The eight metros with the largest Hispanic gains account for 46 percent of all Hispanic growth in the U.S. over the decade, now home to 51 percent of the total hispanic population. These gains were due to immigration and domestic migration, as well as the relatively young age and natural increase of the Hispanic population.

Indeed, a mere 30 of the nation's 276 metros accounted for fully 70 percent of all Hispanic growth. New to this list is Phoenix, which more than doubled its Hispanic population over the 1990s—thanks to direct immigration and a

UP AND COMING

Metropolitan areas with a Hispanic or Asian population of at least 50,000 in 2000, and a percent increase in the Hispanic or Asian population greater than 100 percent between 1990 and 2000.

HISPANIC POPULATION GROWTH METROPOLITAN AREA*	1990-2000 HISPANIC PERCENT INCREASE	2000 HISPANIC POPULATION
1. Greensboro–Winston-Salem–High Point, NC	**694%**	**62,210**
2. Charlotte–Gastonia–Rock Hill, NC-SC	**622%**	**77,092**
3. Raleigh–Durham–Chapel Hill, NC	**569%**	**72,580**
4. Atlanta, GA	**362%**	**268,851**
5. Las Vegas, NV-AZ	**262%**	**322,038**
6. Portland–Salem, OR-WA	**175%**	**196,638**
7. Orlando, FL	**170%**	**271,627**
8. Minneapolis–St. Paul, MN-WI	**162%**	**99,121**
9. Reno, NV	**145%**	**56,301**
10. Grand Rapids–Muskegon–Holland, MI	**136%**	**68,916**
11. Salt Lake City–Ogden, UT	**133%**	**144,600**
12. Phoenix–Mesa, AZ	**115%**	**817,012**
13. Oklahoma City, OK	**114%**	**72,998**
14. Dallas–Ft. Worth, TX	**113%**	**1,120,350**
15. West Palm Beach–Boca Raton, FL	**111%**	**140,675**
16. Seattle–Tacoma–Bremerton, WA	**108%**	**184,297**
17. Kansas City, MO-KS	**105%**	**92,910**
18. Providence–Warwick–Pawtucket, RI	**101%**	**88,411**
ASIAN POPULATION GROWTH METROPOLITAN AREA*	1990-2000 ASIAN PERCENT INCREASE	2000 ASIAN POPULATION
1. Las Vegas, NV-AZ	**286%**	**96,942**
2. Atlanta, GA	**200%**	**152,702**
3. Austin–San Marcos, TX	**175%**	**50,221**
4. Orlando, FL	**171%**	**54,314**
5. Tampa–St. Petersburg–Clearwater, FL	**149%**	**55,174**
6. Phoenix–Mesa, AZ	**149%**	**85,577**
7. Dallas–Ft. Worth, TX	**133%**	**219.891**
8. Portland–Salem, OR-WA	**119%**	**121,984**
9. Minneapolis–St. Paul, MN-WI	**118%**	**139,671**
10. Denver–Boulder–Greeley, CO	**115%**	**89.750**
11. Miami–Ft. Lauderdale, FL	**113%**	**86,106**
12. Detroit–Ann Arbor–Flint, MI	**111%**	**150,098**
13. Seattle–Tacoma–Bremerton, WA	**105%**	**358,255**
14. Salt Lake City–Ogden, UT	**103%**	**50,467**

* Metropolitan Area refers to CMSAs, MSAs, and (in New England) NECMAs, defined by the Office of Management and Budget.

Source: William H. Frey analysis of 1990 and 2000 U.S. Censuses

spillover from California. Las Vegas and Atlanta are also relative newcomers, which more than doubled and tripled their Hispanic populations respectively.

The concentrated gains among Asians in areas with existing Asian populations are even more apparent than with Hispanics (see chart, "Big Gainers"). The three Asian population juggernauts—New York, Los Angeles, and San Francisco—account for 37 percent of all Asian gains in the U.S. in the '90s. The top six areas account for almost half. Metros with fast-growing but smaller Asian populations include Dallas, which doubled its population, and Atlanta, where it tripled.

The New Ethnic Frontiers

There is some directed diffusion of Hispanics and Asians outward from these immigrant ports of entry. With rising employment opportunities in states such as Georgia, North Carolina, Nevada, Utah, and parts of the Midwest, new immigrant minorities have made pioneer-

BIG GAINERS

Metropolitan areas that had the largest gains in Hispanic and Asian populations between 1990 and 2000.

HISPANICS METROPOLITAN AREA*	1990-2000 HISPANIC GAINS	2000 HISPANIC POPULATION
1. Los Angeles–Riverside–Orange County, CA	**1,819,370**	**6,598,488**
2. New York–Northern New Jersey–Long Island, NY-NJ-CT-PA	**992,185**	**3,849,990**
3. Chicago–Gary–Kenosha, IL-IN-WI	**600,810**	**1,498,507**
4. Dallas–Ft. Worth, TX	**594,836**	**1,120,350**
5. Houston–Galveston–Brazoria, TX	**575,098**	**1,348,588**
6. Miami–Ft. Lauderdale, FL	**501,543**	**1,563,389**
7. Phoenix–Mesa, AZ	**437,452**	**817,012**
8. San Francisco–Oakland–San Jose, CA	**413,258**	**1,383,661**
9. San Diego, CA	**240,184**	**750,965**
10. Las Vegas, NV-AZ	**232,978**	**322,038**
ASIANS METROPOLITAN AREA*	1990-2000 ASIAN GAINS	2000 ASIAN POPULATION
1. New York–Northern New Jersey–Long Island, NY-NJ-CT-PA	**710,809**	**1,576,646**
2. Los Angeles–Riverside–Orange County, CA	**611,201**	**1,886,168**
3. San Francisco–Oakland–San Jose, CA	**554,326**	**1,446,563**
4. Washington–Baltimore, DC-MD-VA-WV	**212,350**	**454,702**
5. Seattle–Tacoma–Bremerton, WA	**183,134**	**358,255**
6. Chicago–Gary–Kenosha, IL-IN-WI	**179,537**	**428,819**
7. Boston–Worcester–Lawrence, MA-NH-ME-CT	**126,384**	**263,092**
8. Dallas–Ft. Worth, TX	**125,385**	**219,891**
9. Houston–Galveston–Brazoria, TX	**122,882**	**249,819**
10. San Diego, CA	**114,786**	**299,930**

* Metropolitan Area refers to CMSAs, MSAs, and (in New England) NECMAs, defined by the Office of Management and Budget.

Source: William H. Frey analysis of 1990 and 2000 U.S. Censuses

ing moves to these areas, establishing new minority frontiers. At the forefront are metros that house a minimum of 50,000 members of the minority, and have more than doubled that group's population over the 1990s. (see chart, "Up and Coming").

Hispanics have begun to make inroads into large and medium-sized metros in the Southeast and interior West—areas where growth is dominated largely by domestic migration, whites, and blacks. Atlanta, Charlotte, Raleigh-Durham, Greensboro, Orlando, and West Palm Beach are Southern metros with high rates of Hispanic gain. In the West, new Hispanic frontiers include Phoenix, Las Vegas, Portland, Salt Lake City, and Seattle. Several Midwest areas, including Minneapolis-St. Paul and Kansas City, are also on the list. Of course, the Hispanic shares of total population in most of these metros are quite small (with the exception of Phoenix and Las Vegas).

New frontier metros for Asians include many of the same metro areas. Additional areas for Asians include the high-tech university town of Austin, along with Tampa, Miami, and Detroit. Again, the fast growth and accumulation of sizeable Asian populations in these frontier metros do not translate into substantial Asian shares of the total population, but do portend a continued regional Asian growth.

Mini-Melting Pots

Only a handful of metros are racially diverse enough to be considered true melting pots. To qualify as such, a metro's white population must be less than the national average of 69 percent, and at least two minority groups must have a greater share of the population than their respective national averages. In metro Miami, for example, whites constitute only 36 percent of the population, while blacks and Hispanics account for 21 percent and 40 percent, respectively. These areas represent dominant primary or secondary destinations for two or more immigrant or minority groups. The list includes the country's largest immigrant gateway metros, Los Angeles, New York, Miami, Chicago, Dallas, Houston, Washington D.C., as well as 17 smaller metros located in California, Texas, and other Southwest states.

A NEW FACE

Twelve more metropolitan areas turned from majority white to majority minority between 1990 and 2000

METROPOLITAN AREA*	2000 METRO POPULATION	PERCENT WHITE	
		1990	2000
Houston–Galveston–Brazoria, TX (W)	**4,669,571**	**58.0%**	**48.0%**
Fresno, CA (H)	**922,516**	**51.8%**	**40.6%**
Albuquerque, NM (W)	**712,738**	**54.5%**	**47.7%**
Bakersfield, CA (W)	**661,645**	**62.7%**	**49.5%**
Stockton–Lodi, CA (W)	**563,598**	**58.8%**	**47.4%**
Salinas, CA (H)	**401,762**	**52.3%**	**40.3%**
Visalia–Tulare–Porterville, CA (H)	**368,021**	**54.6%**	**41.8%**
Merced, CA (H)	**210,554**	**54.2%**	**40.6%**
Yuma, AZ (H)	**160,026**	**54.4%**	**44.3%**
Albany, GA (B)	**120,822**	**52.9%**	**46.3%**
Sumter, SC (W)	**104,646**	**54.7%**	**49.4%**
Pine Bluff, AR (B)	**84,278**	**55.8%**	**48.0%**

(W) Whites outnumber all other populations; (H) Hispanics outnumber all other populations; (B) Blacks outnumber all other populations

* Metropolitan Area refers to CMSAs, MSAs, and (in New England) NECMAs, defined by the Office of Management and Budget.

Source: William H. Frey analysis of 1990 and 2000 U.S. Censuses

Two noteworthy additions to melting pot status are Las Vegas and Orlando. Las Vegas added significantly to its Hispanic and Asian populations, while Orlando saw increase for Hispanics and blacks. Despite large white gains in both areas, the white shares of their populations have declined dramatically (by 14 percent and 13 percent respectively) over the 1990s.

Some of these metros have "majority minority" populations where the white percentage is less than half of their total population: 22 of the nation's 276 metros have majority minorities, and 12 of these have graduated to this status since 1990 (see "A New Face"). The largest is Houston, which increased its Hispanic population by more than half a million over the decade, and its Asian and black populations by more than 100,000 each. Smaller metro areas in California and New Mexico achieved this status as a result of recent Hispanic gains.

Undoubtedly, the coming decade will see some additional "spilling-out" of the new immigrant minorities' second and third generations as their children enter the middle class and a national labor market. Clearly, the U.S. is not a single melting pot—where each minority spreads and blends evenly from coast to coast. Rather, the development of mini-melting pots, in the context of less diversity elsewhere, is creating locally unique racial demographic profiles within the nation that differ markedly from region to region.

---

* *This story treats racial groups, whites, blacks, Asians (including Native Hawaiians and other Pacific Islanders), and Native Americans (including Native Alaskans) as non-Hispanic members of those races, and treats all Hispanics as a separate single category. Further, because the 2000 census allowed respondents to select one or more races, the 2000 data presented here treats whites as those who selected only the white race, and treats blacks, Asians, and Native Americans as those who selected one or more race. As a result, a small number of persons in the latter three groups are included more than once in the 2000 tallies.*

William H. Frey is a demographer and Senior Fellow at the Milken Institute in Santa Monica, California, and on the faculty of the Population Studies Center, University of Michigan. He can be reached at www.frey-demographer.org.

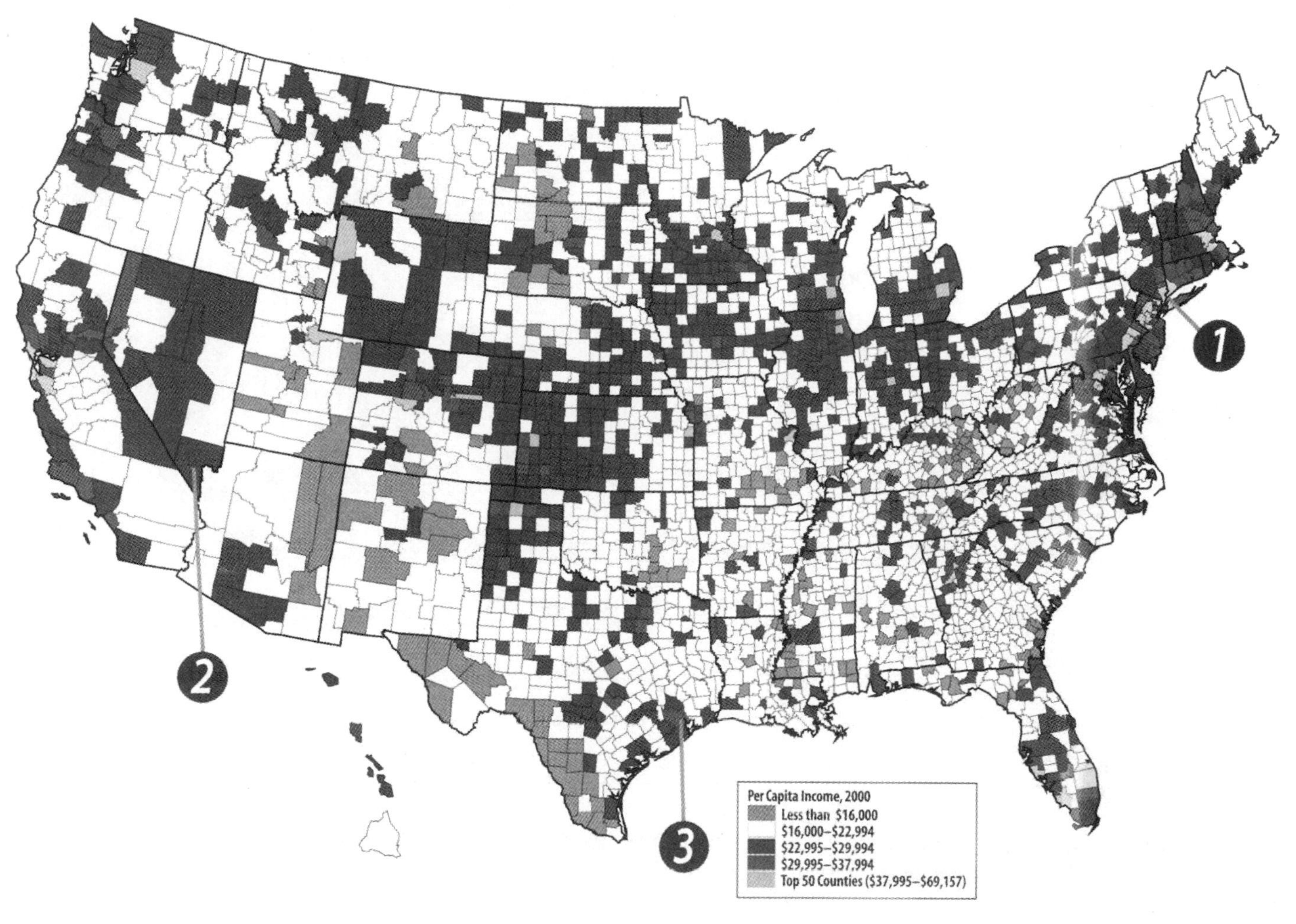

MAP: ARCVIEW GIS FROM ESRI

Counties With Cash

When you're hot, you're hot. When you're not—there's probably a reason.

BY JOHN FETTO

As April ushers in the tax season, it seemed like a good time to investigate where America's wealth is concentrated these days.

There are numerous ways to gauge wealth, from household income to median home value. But only one measure, per-capita income, indicates the amount of money available for each person to spend. Data provided by Washington, D.C.-based market research firm Woods & Poole Economics, Inc. was used to create our map that illustrates the distribution of per-capita income by county. The 50 counties with the highest per-capita income… range from $37,995 per person in Union County, New Jersey, to $69,157 in New York, New York (1). The national average is $28,309.

The heaviest concentrations of wealth are found in and around New York City,

ROLLING IN IT

Counties with the highest per-capita income in 2000 and projected income for 2010, in 1999 dollars.

COUNTY	PER CAPITA INCOME 2000	2010
New York, NY	$69,157	$99,088
Marin, CA	$54,608	$85,243
Pitkin, CO	$54,076	$79,455
Fairfield, CT	$53,474	$80,234
Somerset, NJ	$51,605	$81,320
Alexandria (independent city), VA	$50,752	$78,255
Westchester, NY	$50,402	$74,206
Morris, NJ	$49,640	$76,613
Bergen, NJ	$48,137	$72,053
Arlington, VA	$47,252	$71,679
Montgomery, MD	$46,911	$69,648
Teton, WY	$45,758	$65,623
San Francisco, CA	$45,694	$68,942
Montgomery, PA	$45,553	$67,748
Fairfax + Fairfax City + Falls Church, VA	$45,493	$69,378
Lake, IL	$45,218	$69,154
Nassau, NY	$45,176	$68,399
Oakland, MI	$44,767	$69,393
Nantucket, MA	$44,534	$66,055
San Mateo, CA	$43,884	$65,378

Source: Woods & Poole Economics Inc.

San Francisco, and Washington, D.C. In fact, 20 of the top 50 counties are clustered around one of these three metro areas—ten in New York City, five in San Francisco, and five in D.C. As our map shows, there is plenty of wealth scattered throughout the country, mostly in major metropolitan areas.

But not all major metros have a county in the money: Las Vegas, Miami, Houston, and Salt Lake City are four that don't make the cut.

What gives? Factors such as the percent of the population employed by the service sector, percent of retirees, household size, and urban landscape all play a role, says Martin Holdrich, senior economist at Woods & Poole. The economy of Las Vegas (2), for example, is driven by the service sector, which pays less than any other industry. "Unless, there is growth in the other sectors, Las Vegas counties will not be in the top 50," says Holdrich. Other cities affected by a high percentage of service workers are Reno, Honolulu, and Orlando.

Retirement counties also tend to rank lower on the wealth scale because typically, retiree incomes are low. "Retired persons do have income, but the flow of dollars going through their households annually is much lower than it was when they were working," says Holdrich. Phoenix, Tucson, Miami, and their surrounding counties are all affected in part by the retirement factor.

Another thing to consider in places like Phoenix, Tucson, and Miami is immigration. Immigrants tend to be younger and work in the service sector—a double whammy where income is concerned.

Immigrant households are also typically larger than those of nonimmigrants. "Income per capita is biased against places with large families," says Holdrich. That's also why you won't find Salt Lake City or many other Utah counties with large numbers of Mormon households near the top of the list, simply because they have larger-than-average households. In fact, we found that nine of the 20 lowest-ranking counties for per-capita income are among the top 20 counties with the most persons per household.

County size is important to consider when examining a map of income as well. Huge geographic areas, like Houston (3), incorporate vast disparities in income: from inner city to affluent suburbs, says Holdrich. Which is why you're less likely to see a county with high per-capita income in areas of the country with geographically large counties. Western counties' per-capita income tends to skew low because of their large size. Where counties are smaller, and wealth and poverty can be easily separated by a county line, per-capita income is up.

Just as there are metro areas that don't appear to have much wealth, there are non-metro areas that have loads of it, including seasonal escapes for the wealthy. Non-metro areas that score in the top 20 for per-capita income include Pitkin County, Colorado ($54,076), home to Aspen; Teton County, Wyoming ($45,758), Jackson Hole; and the island county of Nantucket, Massachusetts ($44,534).

Several upscale Florida communities appear near the top of the list as well. They are Sarasota County, Martin County, Collier County, and Indian River County.

Remember the old adage, it takes money to make money? Well, the richest counties are doing their best not to disprove that. In fact, very little will change with respect to wealth distribution in the next ten years.

In 2010, the only changes to our list of the ten wealthiest counties will be a little place-swapping here and there. Still, nobody will be packing up and moving off the list. The average per-capita income of the top ten is projected to increase by 51 percent between now and 2010. Now *that's* a raise.

Do We Still Need Skyscrapers?

The Industrial Revolution made skyscrapers possible. The Digital Revolution makes them (almost) obsolete

by William J. Mitchell

Our distant forebears could create remarkably tall structures by exploiting the compressive strength of stone and brick, but the masonry piles they constructed in this way contained little usable interior space. At 146 meters (480 feet), the Great Pyramid of Cheops is a vivid expression of the ruler's power but inside it is mostly solid rock; the net-to-gross floor area is terrible. On a square base of 230 meters, it encloses the King's Chamber, which is just five meters across. The 52-meter spiraling brick minaret of the Great Mosque of Samarra does not have any interior at all. And the 107-meter stone spires of Chartres Cathedral, though structurally sophisticated, enclose nothing but narrow shafts of empty space and cramped access stairs.

The Industrial Revolution eventually provided ways to open up the interiors of tall towers and put large numbers of people inside. Nineteenth-century architects found that they could achieve greatly improved ratios of open floor area to solid construction by using steel and reinforced concrete framing and thin curtain walls. They could employ mechanical elevators to provide rapid vertical circulation. And they could integrate increasingly sophisticated mechanical systems to heat, ventilate and cool growing amounts of interior space. In the 1870s and 1880s visionary New York and Chicago architects and engineers brought these elements together to produce the modern skyscraper. Among the earliest full-fledged examples were the Equitable Building (1868–70), the Western Union Building (1872–75) and the Tribune Building (1873–75) in New York City, and Burnham & Root's great Montauk Building (1882) in Chicago.

These newfangled architectural contraptions found a ready market because they satisfied industrial capitalism's growing need to bring armies of office workers together at locations where they could conveniently interact with one another gain access to files and other work materials, and be supervised by their bosses. Furthermore, tall buildings fitted perfectly into the emerging pattern of the commuter city, with its high-density central business district, ring of low-density bedroom suburbs and radial transportation systems for the daily return journey. This centralization drove up property values in the urban core and created a strong economic motivation to jam as much floor area as possible onto every available lot. So as the 20th century unfolded, and cities such as New York and Chicago grew, downtown skylines sprouted higher while the suburbs spread wider.

But there were natural limits to this upward extension of skyscrapers, just as there are constraints on the sizes of living organisms. Floor and wind loads, people, water and supplies must ultimately be transferred to the ground, so the higher you go, the more of the floor area must be occupied by structural supports, elevators and service ducts. At some point, it becomes uneconomical to add additional floors; the diminishing increment of usable floor area does not justify the increasing increment of cost.

Urban planning and design considerations constrain height as well. Tall buildings have some unwelcome effects at ground level; they cast long shadows, blot out the sky and sometimes create dangerous and unpleasant blasts of wind. And they generate pedestrian and automobile traffic that strains the capacity of surrounding streets. To control these effects, planning authorities typically impose limits on height and on the ratio of floor area to ground area. More subtly, they may apply formulas relating allowable height and bulk to street dimensions—frequently yielding the stepped-back and tapering forms that so strongly characterize the Manhattan skyline.

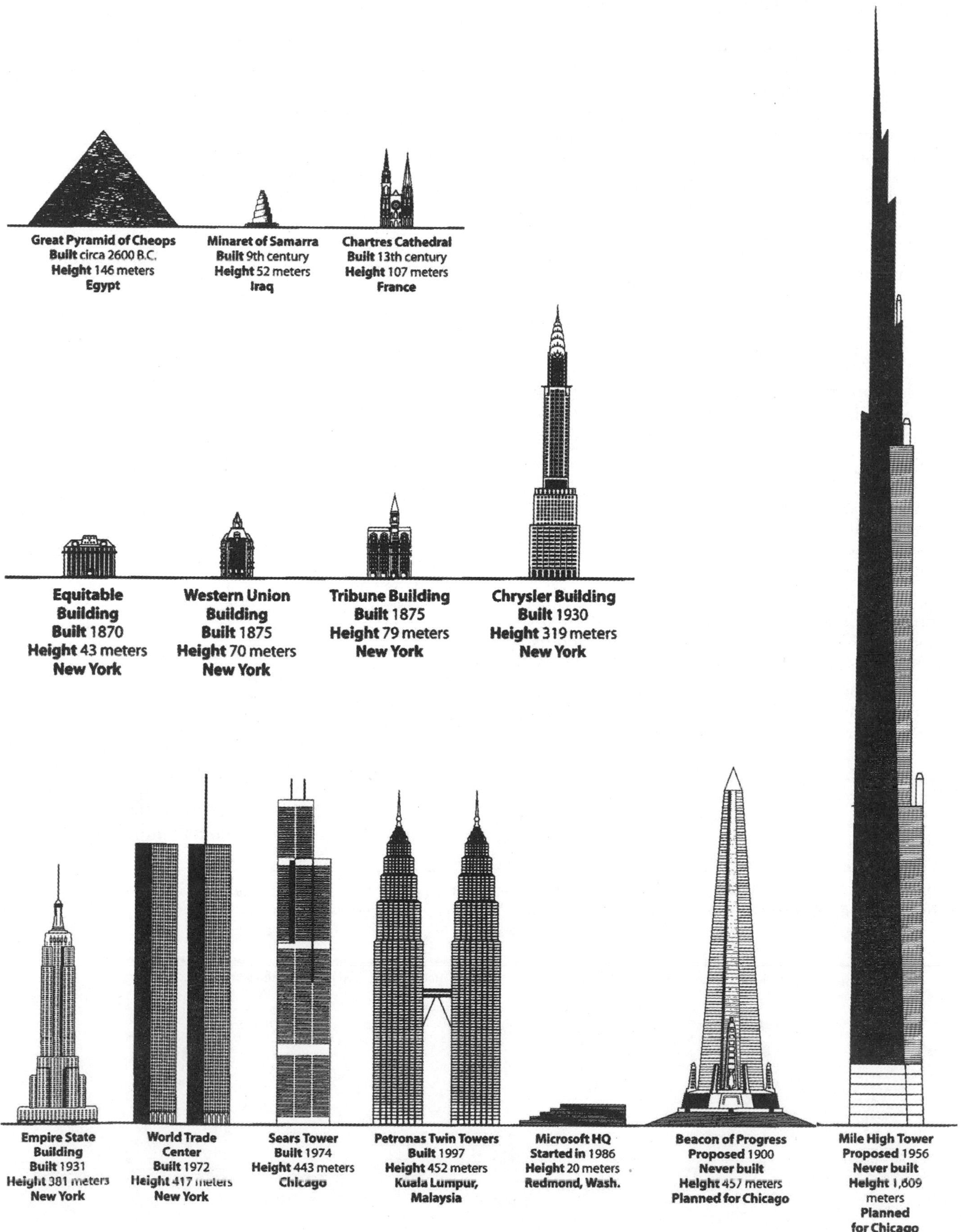
Great Pyramid of Cheops
Built circa 2600 B.C.
Height 146 meters
Egypt
Minaret of Samarra
Built 9th century
Height 52 meters
Iraq
Chartres Cathedral
Built 13th century
Height 107 meters
France
Equitable Building
Built 1870
Height 43 meters
New York
Western Union Building
Built 1875
Height 70 meters
New York
Tribune Building
Built 1875
Height 79 meters
New York
Chrysler Building
Built 1930
Height 319 meters
New York
Empire State Building
Built 1931
Height 381 meters
New York
World Trade Center
Built 1972
Height 417 meters
New York
Sears Tower
Built 1974
Height 443 meters
Chicago
Petronas Twin Towers
Built 1997
Height 452 meters
Kuala Lumpur, Malaysia
Microsoft HQ
Started in 1986
Height 20 meters
Redmond, Wash.
Beacon of Progress
Proposed 1900
Never built
Height 457 meters
Planned for Chicago
Mile High Tower
Proposed 1956
Never built
Height 1,609 meters
Planned for Chicago

The consequence of these various limits is that exceptionally tall buildings—those that really push the envelope—have always been expensive, rare and conspicuous. So organizations can effectively draw attention to themselves and express their power and prestige by finding ways to construct the loftiest skyscrapers in town, in the nation or maybe even in the world. They frequently find this worthwhile, even when it does not make much immediate practical sense.

There has, then, been an ongoing, century-long race for height. The Chrysler Building (319 meters) and the Empire State Building (381 meters) battled it out in New York in the late 1920s, adding radio antennas and even a dirigible mooring mast to gain the last few meters.

The contest heated up again in the 1960s and 1970s, with Lower Manhattan's World Trade Center twin towers (417 meters), Chicago's John Hancock tower (344 meters) and finally Chicago's gigantic Sears Tower (443 meters). More recently, Cesar Pelli's skybridge-linked Petronas Twin Towers (452 meters) in Kuala Lumpur have—for a while at least—taken the title of world's tallest building.

Along the way, there were some spectacular fantasy entrants as well. In 1900 Desiré Despradelle of the Massachusetts Institute of Technology proposed a 457-meter "Beacon of Progress" for the site of the Chicago World's Fair; like Malaysia's Petronas Towers of almost a century later, it was freighted with symbolism of a proud young nation's aspirations. Despradelle's enormous watercolor rendering hung for years in the M.I.T. design studio to inspire the students. Then, in 1956, Frank Lloyd Wright (not much more than five feet in his shoes and cape) topped it with a truly megalomaniac proposal for a 528-story, mile-high tower for the Chicago waterfront.

While this race has been running, though, the burgeoning Digital Revolution has been reducing the need to bring office workers together face-to-face, in expensive downtown locations. Efficient telecommunications have diminished the importance of centrality and correspondingly increased the attractiveness of less expensive suburban sites that are more convenient to the labor force. Digital storage and computer networks have increasingly supported decentralized remote access to data bases rather than reliance on centralized paper files. And businesses are discovering that their marketing and public-relations purposes may now be better served by slick World Wide Web pages on the Internet and Superbowl advertising spots than by investments in monumental architecture on expensive urban sites.

We now find, more and more, that powerful corporations occupy relatively unobtrusive, low- or medium-rise suburban office campuses rather than flashy downtown towers. In Detroit, Ford and Chrysler spread themselves amid the greenery in this way—though General Motors has bucked the trend by moving into the lakeside Renaissance Center. Nike's campus in Beaverton, Ore., is pretty hard to find, but www.nike.com is not. Microsoft and Netscape battle it out from Redmond, Wash., and Mountain View, Calif., respectively, and—though their logos, the look and feel of their interfaces, and their Web pages are familiar worldwide—few of their millions of customers know or care what the headquarters buildings look like. And—a particularly telling straw in the wind—Sears has moved its Chicago workforce from the great Loop tower that bears its name to a campus in far-suburban Hoffman Estates.

Does this mean that skyscrapers are now dinosaurs? Have they finally had their day? Not quite, as a visit to the fancy bar high atop Hong Kong's prestigious Peninsula Hotel will confirm. Here the washroom urinals are set against the clear plate-glass windows so that powerful men can gaze down on the city while they relieve themselves. Obviously this gesture would not have such satisfying effect on the ground floor. In the 21st century, as in the time of Cheops, there will undoubtedly be taller and taller buildings, built at great effort and often without real economic justification, because the rich and powerful will still sometimes find satisfaction in traditional ways of demonstrating that they're on top of the heap.

WILLIAM J. MITCHELL is dean of the School of Architecture and Planning at the Massachusetts Institute of Technology.

China Journal I

Henry Petroski

The Yangtze is the third longest river in the world. Originating from 5,800-meter-high Mount Tanggula on the Tibet Plateau, the Yangtze follows a sinuous west-to-east route for more than 6,000 kilometers before emptying into the East China Sea at Shanghai. The river has 3,600 tributaries and drains almost 2 million square kilometers, almost 19 percent of China's land area.

During flood season, the water level in the river can rise as much as 15 meters, affecting 15 million people and threatening 1.5 million hectares of cultivated land. Historic floods have been devastating. The flood of 1870 is still talked about along the middle reaches of the river, and the flood of 1954 inundated 3 million hectares of arable land and claimed 30,000 lives. Altogether in the 20th century, as many as half a million people may have died in the Yangtze's flood waters.

The Yangtze also has some of the most beautiful scenery in the world in the region known as the Three Gorges, with spectacular cliffs and steep mountains rising as high as 1,500 meters. Interspersed with gently rolling hills and long sloping riverbanks, the gorges have been compared in majesty to the Grand Canyon. Cruising the river through the Three Gorges is considered a classic travel experience, as each bend in the river reveals a new perspective on the marvels that geological change has wrought.

Making Choices

Balancing the desire to preserve the river in all its natural glory against that to tame it to control flooding, generate power and provide more reliable shipping conditions presents a classical dilemma involving engineering and society. When nationalist leader Sun Yat-Sen proposed a Three Gorges Dam in 1919, the ecological costs were overshadowed by the economic benefits for China. In the mid-1940s, a preliminary survey, along with planning and design efforts, was carried out by the U.S. Bureau of Reclamation under the direction of John Lucian Savage, designer of the Hoover and Grand Coulee dams. In his exploratory role, Savage became the first non-Chinese engineer to visit the Three Gorges with the thought of locating an appropriate dam site. Savage's work is the likely inspiration for John Hersey's novel, *A Single Pebble,* whose opening sentence is, "I became an engineer." In the story, the unnamed engineer travels up the Yangtze in a junk pulled by trackers in the ancient and, once, the only way to make the river journey upstream.

Chairman Mao Zedong was a staunch supporter of a Three Gorges Dam, which he felt would provide a forceful symbol of China's self-sufficiency and ability to develop its resources without Western aid. As early as 1953, Mao expressed his preference for a single large dam rather than a series of smaller ones, and he suggested that he would resign the chairmanship of the Communist Party in China to assist in the design of the project. Mao's poem about being at ease swimming across the turbulent Yangtze reflects on how all things change, like the swift river and the gorges through which it flows. He knows that Goddess, a prominent peak in the middle reaches of the Three Gorges, will marvel at the accomplishment of a dam.

In 1992, the Chinese government announced officially its determination to tame the Yangtze with what would be the world's largest hydroelectric dam, ultimately to be fitted with 26 generators rated at 700 megawatts each. The total of 18,200 megawatts is equivalent to the output of approximately 15 of the largest nuclear-power plants operating in the world today. Since one of China's most pressing environmental problems is pollution from burning fossil fuels, the prospect of a clean hydroelectric dam generating about 10 percent of the country's power is very appealing to the Chinese leadership. In addition to providing flood control and power generation, the dam will open up the Yangtze as far upriver as Chongqing to 10,000-metric-ton ships, providing an opportunity for China to develop container ports almost 2,000 kilometers inland. This purpose goes hand in hand with China's plan to soon become a full partner in world trade operations.

For all its practical benefits to China, the Three Gorges Dam project has been opposed by numerous groups both domestic and international. Especially vocal have been human-rights advocates, environmentalists and historians. Among the most persistent opposing voices has been Dai Qing, who was educated as an engineer but became disillusioned during the Cultural Revolution and finally turned to investigative journalism. Her 1989 book, *Yangtze! Yangtze!*, was highly critical of the idea of a Three

BOB SACHA/NATIONAL GEOGRAPHIC SOCIETY

Figure 1. Three Gorges Dam will contain the world's largest hydroelectric plant when completed, with generators expected to provide 10 percent of China's electricity. The impoundment will prevent flooding, yet the project is not without detractors on environmental grounds.

Gorges Dam and led to her temporary imprisonment. That book and her subsequent one, *The River Dragon Has Come!,* published in 1998, state the fundamental case against the project but seem to have had little, if any, effect on the progress of the dam.

When complete, Three Gorges Dam, which will stretch about 2 kilometers across the Yangtze at Sandouping, will be 185 meters high and will create a reservoir 600 kilometers long, reaching all the way to Chongqing. The filling of the reservoir will displace on the order of a million people, inundate almost 50,000 hectares of prime farmland, submerge archaeological treasures and forever alter the appearance of the Three Gorges.

The project has been described as "perhaps the largest, most expensive, and perhaps most hazardous hydroelectric project ever attempted." Vocal protesters and international politics have no doubt influenced the World Bank's refusal to finance the project. Bowing to pressure from environmental groups, the Clinton Administration opposed competitive financing through the Export-Import Bank, effectively discouraging American companies from participating. The Chinese government has nonetheless been resolute.

As in all large dam projects, choosing the site was of fundamental importance. Of 15 locations seriously considered, the final choice was made on the basis of geological foundation conditions and accessibility to construction equipment and materials. The chosen dam site is 28 kilometers upriver from Yichang, where the Yangtze runs wide between gently sloping banks that provide staging areas for the construction project. The geology in the area is ideal, in that it is underlain with solid granite for some 10 kilometers surrounding the dam site, providing a stable construction base.

The project was planned to be completed in three stages. Phase I, stretching from 1993 to 1997, consisted of building coffer dams within which the river bottom could be excavated and the foundation of the dam begun. A temporary ship lock was also constructed during this phase in order to allow shipping to pass the construction site throughout the project. Phase II, extending from 1998 to 2003, involves the construction of a good part of the dam proper. Concrete is being poured 24 hours a day to complete the spillway of the dam, the intake portions of the dam designed for the power generation and the initial stage of the power plant itself. At the end of Phase II, the reservoir will be filled and the dam will begin to generate power, which will produce revenue to fund the final phase of the project. Phase III, stretching from 2004 to 2009, will involve the completion of the dam across the river, including additional powerhouse units. According to the China Yangtze Three Gorges Project Development Corporation (CTGPC), the government-authorized entity created to own the project, construction is on schedule for the completion of the present phase in 2003.

[PHOTOGRAPH COURTESY OF ALAN R. MILLER, NEW MEXICO TECH.]

Figure 2. Yangtze River, although offering spectacular scenery, may have claimed a half-million lives during the 1900s in devastating floods.

A First-hand Perspective

I was invited recently to lead a civil engineering delegation from the United States to visit the Three Gorges Dam construction site and talk with Chinese engineers about the project. The delegation would have the opportunity to see first-hand the scale and technical nature of this gargantuan engineering project and to visit the areas along the Yangtze that will be permanently altered by the creation of the reservoir. The delegation would see the towns that will be submerged and from which so many people will be displaced. Our group would also have an opportunity to experience China in this time of rapid emergence as a full player on the world economic scene.

[PHOTOGRAPH COURTESY OF ALAN R. MILLER.]

Figure 3. Lock at Gezhouba Dam, completed in 1981, provides shipping access above Yichang.

Our delegation consisted of 40 engineers. They were mostly civil engineers, some with extensive experience in dam construction and power generation, but there were also a number of electrical and mechanical engineers, among others, as well as a geologist, reflecting the inherent interdisciplinary nature of large engineering projects. About 25 guests traveled with the delegation. Most were spouses of the delegates, but there were also a half-dozen professional sociologists who were interested in the relocation problems associated with the Three Gorges Project.

The conventional wisdom in the United States about the project is that it is technologically risky, environmentally unsound, sociologically devastating and economically unwise for China at this time. Thus, the overall view of the project that is held by most Americans is that it is ill-advised at best and a disaster in the making at worst. Different members of the delegation took different preconceptions with them to China, and some brought home altered perceptions.

The delegation assembled in Los Angeles in mid-November for a predeparture briefing. The 15-hour flight to Hong Kong was pleasant and uneventful, with most delegates getting a good night's sleep. A five-hour layover in Hong Kong gave some of us an opportunity to ride the new Airport Express into the city that is now one part of but still apart from China.

The world of difference between Hong Kong and the interior of China was emphasized by the fact that our flight from Hong Kong to Wuhan was classified as an international one. Wuhan created in 1950 out of the merger of three cities separated only by the Yangtze and Han rivers, a region rich in Chinese history. The consolidated city is located midway on a north-south line between Beijing and Canton and an east-west line between Shanghai and Chongqing. In contrast to the bright stainless-steel expansiveness of the new airport at Hong Kong, the dated one at Wuhan was tiny, dingy and drab. Wuhan, one of China's industrial cities, has a population of about 4 million. It was our point of entry into China's interior because it is on the Yangtze River and conveniently connected by a modern toll highway to Yichang, headquarters of the CTGPC and only 30 kilometers downstream from the construction site.

A Land of Contrasts

Although a straight shot on a new superhighway, the bus ride to Yichang took about four-and-a-half hours, so we spent the night in Wuhan. This important river port evokes 19th-century technology as much as Hong Kong does 21st. That is not to say that Wuhan is without its buses and cars, the increase of which throughout China is creating enormous traffic and pollution problems, or its better hotels complete with CNN on television. Rather, the enormous reliance of the people on muscle power harks back to a previous century. Myriad bicycles have their dedicated lanes, and they carry goods that in America would be found in pickup trucks and delivery vans. It is common to see bicyclists struggling up the slightest incline under a load of reinforcing steel or plastic pipe that extends several meters ahead of and behind the bike. Smaller loads, though not always smaller by much, are carried in bundles hung from the ends of bamboo poles balanced on the shoulders of bearers, who trek along among the bicycles.

The few hours we had in Wuhan were spent riding a bus to and from the Yellow Crane Tower, a restored ancient hilltop pagoda, perhaps the city's most famous tourist attraction. On the ride to and from the Yellow Crane Tower, which was apparently named after a mythic bird—there are no cranes colored yellow in China, our tour guide informed us—we crossed and recrossed a road-and-railroad bridge spanning the Yangtze. Through the haze with which we would become quite familiar, we could glimpse a newer cable-stayed crossing in the distance, one of the many newly constructed modern bridges we would encounter as we crisscrossed the country.

The next day, the bus ride to Yichang was through primitive farmland. In sharp contrast to the new cars and buses traveling the highway on which we rode, the farms showed no sign of mechanization. Those farmers who did not walk behind a water buffalo worked bent over in their fields. During harvest, farmers stay in the tents and tiny shacks that abound beside the fields. Clusters of small run-down farmhouses marked simple villages, with virtually all buildings oriented with their entrance facing south, in the tradition of much-grander Chinese houses. Although in the days of collective farming there was some machinery, our guide told us, that has not survived into the present era when smaller plots of land are worked by individual farmers. That is not to say that they own the land, however, for we were also told that the state owns all the land in China.

Since it was late fall, there were few crops in evidence. The clearly irregular fields followed the contours of irrigation ditches, and some worked-out fields were excavated deeper than their neighbors to allow for fish farming and lotus cultivation. Hubei province's great Jingbei Plain west of Wuhan is extraordinarily flat, and after several hours' riding we had become so accustomed to the flatness of the land that the sudden appearance of hills with terraced fields worked many of us out of a torpor.

The presence of hills soon yielded to mountains, which signaled our land approach to Xiling Gorge, the most downriver of the Three Gorges and thus often referred to as the third gorge. The twists and turns of the highway through the mountains caused the city of Yichang to appear as suddenly as new stretches of river would when we would sail through the gorges a few days hence. The most prominent building to first come into view in the city was the modern China Telecom Building, the city's tallest. It and the headquarters building of the CTGPC dominate the skyline of hilly Yichang, which has come to be known as "dam city" and "electricity city," in recognition of the many hydroelectric power plants in the area.

Our first technical visit was to Three Gorges University, a consortium of several institutions in the area that is the national center for teaching hydraulic and electrical engineering. At our meeting, we received an academic background briefing on the Three Gorges Dam project, which prepared us for our visit to the site the next day.

Before leaving the Yichang area, we visited the Gezhouba Dam, completed in 1981 and a prototype of sorts for the Three Gorges Dam. Located about 30 kilometers downstream from Sandouping, this hydroelectric dam has all the features of the larger structure. In particular, it has sediment-control gates, which by design when opened scour out accumulated sand and silt from behind the dam and distribute it in a controlled manner downstream. The issue of accumulating material behind the Three Gorges Dam is an objection raised by opponents, who argue that in time the reservoir will fill with silt and become unnavigable. Impounding silt behind the dam would also deprive the agricultural land downstream of natural replenishment. The reportedly successful operation of Gezhouba Dam, however, appears to have allayed immediate concerns about silt, at least among the engineers.

[PHOTOGRAPH COURTESY OF CATHERINE PETROSKI.]

Figure 4. Xiling Bridge crosses the Yangtze just downstream from the Three Gorges Dam site.

It was dark when we left Gezhouba Dam and boarded the buses for the ride to Sandouping, the base town for the Three Gorges Dam project. Since it was dark, we could not see the terrain through which we were riding, but the grades of the hills and the rock slopes visible in the bus's headlights made it clear that we were traveling through rough territory. The road was new, constructed in the past few years to serve the project site, and it led through a heavily guarded check station. At one point we passed through a tunnel estimated to be about two kilometers long, suggesting that the mountains above us were too high or steep to put a road over. After maybe 45 minutes of riding without seeing any significant number

[PHOTOGRAPH COURTESY OF CATHERINE PETROSKI.]

Figure 5. Ship locks for Three Gorges Dam have been carved out of solid granite.

of lights, we came upon Sandouping, a small town by Chinese standards but a bustling center beside the Yangtze. Our hotel was a relatively new high rise. From its windows we could see the outline of lights on the cables of a major suspension bridge, suggesting that we were beside the river.

In the daylight, we would learn that the graceful structure was the Xiling Bridge. On the way to the dam-construction site, we passed numerous warehouses and dormitories for workers. The latter, we were told, will be converted into tourist accommodations, since the recreational lake to be formed behind Three Gorges Dam is expected to bring large numbers of vacationers to this region. Dominating the route to the construction site was a large pit where granite is being crushed into pieces of aggregate for the concrete. A system of conveyor belts carries the stone over and along the road to the concrete plant.

The Meaning of Big

The construction site is so large, extending well over a kilometer out from the river bank and into the riverbed, that it is hard to encompass it in a single view. Perhaps the dominant first impression is the countless number of tall construction cranes, literally countless because they blend into each other and disappear behind each other. Our guide joked that we were now seeing a real yellow tower crane, as opposed to the mythical source of the name of the Yellow Crane Tower that we puzzled over in Wuhan.

The first stop on the site was at the location of the locks. Twin pairs of five locks are being carved out of solid granite and lined with concrete. They will carry 10,000-metric-ton ships and barges in stages through the difference in water level behind and in front of the dam. Viewed from near their bottom, the scale of this one aspect of the Three Gorges Project is enormous. I certainly have never seen anything like it, and I imagine that it rivals even the construction of the individually larger locks of the Panama Canal. Workers at the bottom of the manmade granite box canyons looked minuscule, and it seemed impossible that these locks were blasted out of the granite in only a few years's time. Our guide told us that the Chinese calligraphy atop a nearby promontory motivated the workers to keep at the task with "first-class management, high-quality workmanship, first-rate construction."

For American engineers, one notable feature of this Chinese construction site was the freedom with which we visitors were allowed to move among the piles of construction materials and debris. Such traipsing around is unheard of at construction sites in the U.S. Only a simple railing with wide openings separated us from a 30-meter-or-so fall into one of the ship-lock excavations, but neither the Chinese nor the visitors seemed to be bothered by their proximity to the precipice.

After spending some time at the locks, we reboarded our buses and were driven over to the dam proper, which we viewed head-on from its downriver side. The scale of this part of the project was even grander than that of the locks, for it rose higher into the air and stretched over a kilometer wide before us. Under construction to our left was the spillway, with one section of it raised to the dam's final height, giving a sense of how the completed structure will loom over this part of the river. To our right was the power-plants section, which will hold 14 hydraulic turbine generator units capable of generating 9,800 megawatts of power when the dam is completed. (The remaining 8,400-megawatt capacity of the dam's power plant will not be realized until the third phase of the project is completed and all potential generating capacity is in place.)

Behind us stood the batch plant, where concrete was being mixed constantly for the 24-hour a day work schedule. One of the major considerations in placing concrete in such a massive structure is how to dissipate the heat of hydration that is generated in the concrete. If the concrete experiences too much thermal expansion as it sets, cracks will develop when it cools and contracts. Taking the heat away in a controlled and timely manner obviates this unwanted behavior. At the Three Gorges Dam, the thermal problem is being handled in several ways. As with Hoover Dam, cooling pipes are being imbedded into the concrete to carry away some of the heat. The amount of undesirable heat is itself being eliminated at the source by mixing and placing the concrete at the lowest temperature possible. This is accomplished through cooling the aggregate by blowing cold air over it, by using ice water in the mixing process and by ensuring that no concrete comes out of the batch plant at over seven degrees Celsius. The measures appear to be working. So far only one significant crack has appeared in the part of the dam in place, and the Chinese engineers seem confident that it has been satisfactorily repaired.

After the dam itself and the tower cranes—red, white and yellow—the next most prominent feature of the construction site is the conveyor-belt system that rises up to great heights on temporary concrete columns. The conveyor system to deliver the concrete is a crucial component of the job, for the rate at which concrete is placed largely determines if the project can be kept on schedule. The unique Rotec conveyor system is one of the rare American presences in the project (Caterpillar and General Electric being others). Unfortunately, shortly before our visit to the site, there was an accident with one of the conveyors, killing some workers. Before that accident, we were told, the safety record of the project had been excellent. At the time of our visit, the conveyor system was not operating at the desired capacity, which irritated the Chinese, and local papers were carrying stories of a law suit against the conveyor company for breach of contract.

While at the construction site of the Three Gorges Dam, it is hard not be be awed by the enormity of the project and the confidence of engineers working to hold back the legendary Yangtze, building on their experience with Gezhouba Dam and the many other flood-control and hydroelectric projects completed throughout their country in recent decades. (A recent survey by the World Commission on Dams found that 46 percent of the world's 45,000 large dams are located in China. It also reported that, although they have contributed significantly to human development, dams have been the cause of considerable social and environmental damage.)

The convincing official arguments that the Chinese put forth about the multifarious good that the Three Gorges Dam will bring to their emerging economy impress visitors from a country that is what it is today in part because its engineers also tamed great and scenic rivers like the Colorado and the Snake. The preconceived opposition to the Chinese project as being merely irresponsible and antienvironmental that some members of our delegation brought with them from America was allayed as we stood before this monument-in-progress. For the time being, at least, we saw the Three Gorges Dam through Chinese eyes on Chinese ground. The next day we would board a riverboat to cruise past the dam site, up through the storied gorges and past their Goddess Peak, reflecting on the changes the world-class engineering project is bringing to the great Yangtze.

Henry Petroski is A. S. Vesic Professor of Civil Engineering and a professor of history at Duke University. Address: Box 90287, Durham, NC 27708-0287

UNIT 5

Population, Resources, and Socioeconomic Development

Unit Selections

Key Points to Consider

- How are you personally affected by the population explosion?
- Give examples of how economic development adversely affects the environment. How can such adverse effects be prevented?
- How do you feel about the occurrence of starvation in developing world regions?
- What might it be like to be a refugee?
- In what forms is colonialism present today?
- For how long are world systems sustainable?

Links: www.dushkin.com/online/
These sites are annotated in the World Wide Web pages.

African Studies WWW (U.Penn)
http://www.sas.upenn.edu/African_Studies/AS.html

Geography and Socioeconomic Development
http://www.ksg.harvard.edu/cid/andes/Documents/Background%20Papers/Geography& Socioeconomic%20Development.pdf

Human Rights and Humanitarian Assistance
http://www.pitt.edu/~ian/resource/human.htm

Hypertext and Ethnography
http://www.umanitoba.ca/faculties/arts/anthropology/tutor/aaa_presentation.new.html

Research and Reference (Library of Congress)
http://lcweb.loc.gov/rr/

Space Research Institute
http://arc.iki.rssi.ru/Welcome.html

World Population and Demographic Data
http://geography.about.com/cs/worldpopulation/

The final unit of this anthology includes discussions of several important problems facing humankind. Geographers are keenly aware of regional and global difficulties. It is hoped that their work with researchers from other academic disciplines and representatives of business and government will help bring about solutions to these serious problems.

Probably no single phenomenon has received as much attention in recent years as the so-called population explosion. World population continues to increase at unacceptably high rates. The problem is most severe in the less developed countries, where in some cases, populations are doubling in less than 20 years.

The human population of the world passed the 6 billion mark in 1999. It is anticipated that population increase will continue well into the twenty-first century, despite a slowing in the rate of population growth globally since the 1960s. The first article in this section deals with issues of population growth. The second reviews the devastation of AIDS in Africa. Then, declining petroleum reserves are discussed in a *Scientific American* article, and "Gray Dawn: The Global Aging Crisis" reviews the global increase in the number of elderly. Next, freshwater is considered as a scarce resource in "A Rare and Precious Resource." The following article makes a strong case for expanding forest cover to trap carbon dioxide. The plight of civil-war–ravaged Sudan is discussed next. Gerhard Heilig outlines changes in land use in China as that country shifts its economic focus. The last article, "Helping the World's Poorest," makes a plea for developed world assistance to the poorest countries.

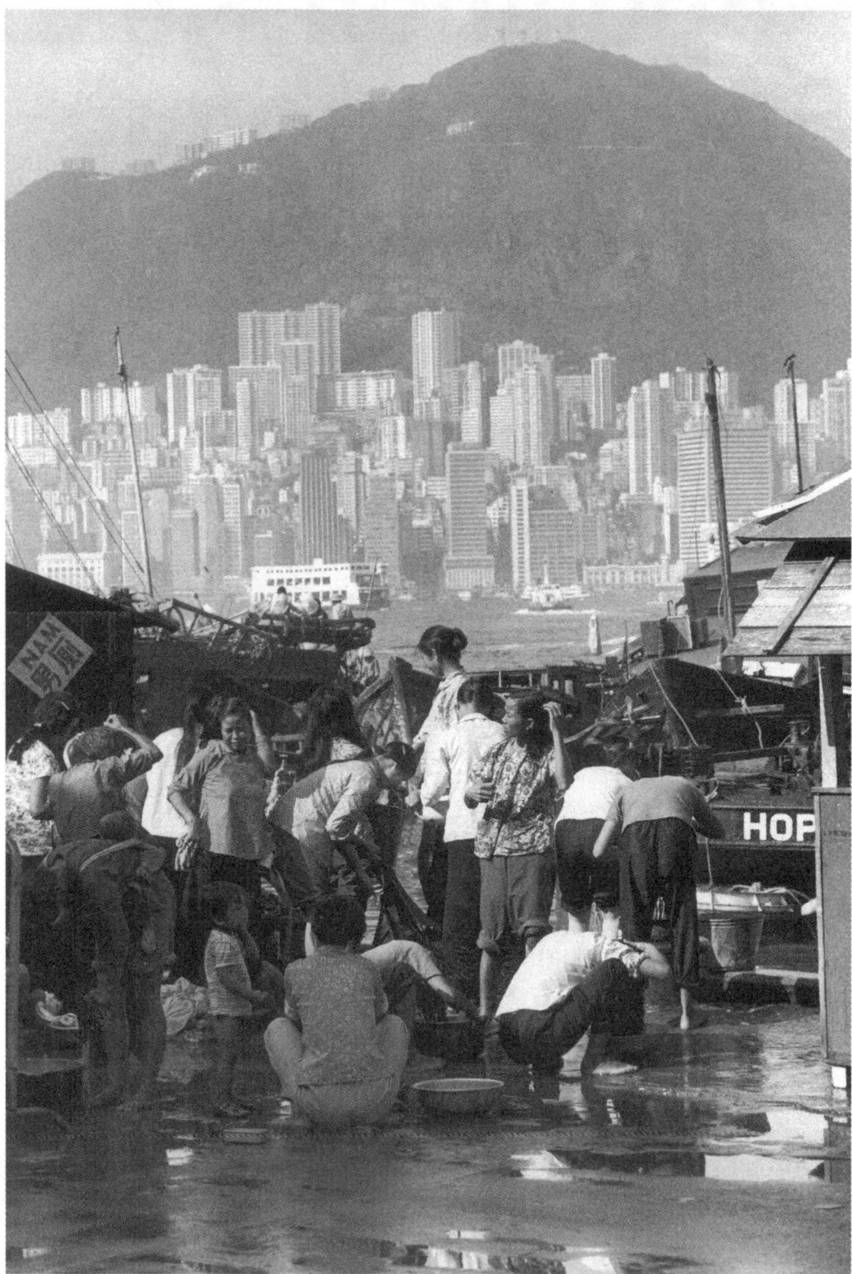

Before the Next Doubling

Nearly 6 billion people now inhabit the Earth—almost twice as many as in 1960. At some point over the course of the next century, the world's population could double again. But we don't have anything like a century to prevent that next doubling; we probably have less than a decade.

by Jennifer D. Mitchell

In 1971, when Bangladesh won independence from Pakistan, the two countries embarked on a kind of unintentional demographic experiment. The separation had produced two very similar populations: both contained some 66 million people and both were growing at about 3 percent a year. Both were overwhelmingly poor, rural, and Muslim. Both populations had similar views on the "ideal" family size (around four children); in both cases, that ideal was roughly two children smaller than the actual average family. And in keeping with the Islamic tendency to encourage large families, both generally disapproved of family planning.

But there was one critical difference. The Pakistani government, distracted by leadership crises and committed to conventional ideals of economic growth, wavered over the importance of family planning. The Bangladeshi government did not: as early as 1976, population growth had been declared the country's number one problem, and a national network was established to educate people about family planning and supply them with contraceptives. As a result, the proportion of couples using contraceptives rose from around 6 percent in 1976 to about 50 percent today, and fertility rates have dropped from well over six children per woman to just over three. Today, some 120 million people live in Bangladesh, while 140 million live in Pakistan—a difference of 20 million.

Bangladesh still faces enormous population pressures—by 2050, its population will probably have increased by nearly 100 million. But even so, that 20 million person "savings" is a colossal achievement, especially given local conditions. Bangladeshi officials had no hope of producing the classic "demographic transition," in which improvements in education, health care, and general living standards tend to push down the birth rate. Bangladesh was—and is—one of the poorest and most densely populated countries on earth. About the size of England and Wales, Bangladesh has twice as many people. Its per capita GDP is barely over $200. It has one doctor for every 12,500 people and nearly three-quarters of its adult population are illiterate. The national diet would be considered inadequate in any industrial country, and even at current levels of population growth, Bangladesh may be forced to rely increasingly on food imports.

All of these burdens would be substantially heavier than they already are, had it not been for the family planning program. To appreciate the Bangladeshi achievement, it's only necessary to look at Pakistan: those "additional" 20 million Pakistanis require at least 2.5 million more houses, about 4 million more tons of grain each year, millions more jobs, and significantly greater investments in health care—or a significantly greater burden of disease. Of the two nations, Pakistan has the more robust economy—its per capita GDP is twice that of Bangladesh. But the Pakistani economy is still primarily agricultural, and the size of the average farm is shrinking, in part because of the expanding population. Already, one fourth of the country's farms are under 1 hectare, the standard minimum size for economic viability, and Pakistan is looking increasingly towards the international grain markets to feed its people. In 1997, despite its third consecutive year of near-record harvests, Pakistan attempted to double its wheat imports but was not able to do so because it had exhausted its line of credit.

And Pakistan's extra burden will be compounded in the next generation. Pakistani women still bear an average of well over five children, so at the current birth rate, the 10 million or so extra couples would produce at least 50 million children. And these in turn could bear nearly 125 million children of their own. At its current fertility rate, Pakistan's population will double in just 24 years—that's more than twice as fast as Bangladesh's population is growing. H. E. Syeda Abida Hussain, Pakistan's Minister of Population Welfare, explains the problem bluntly: "If we achieve success in lowering our population growth substantially, Pakistan has a future. But if, God forbid, we should not—no future."

The Three Dimensions of the Population Explosion

Some version of Mrs. Abida's statement might apply to the world as a whole. About 5.9 billion people currently inhabit the Earth. By the middle of the next century, according to U.N. projections, the population will probably reach 9.4 billion—and all of the net increase is likely to occur in the developing world. (The total population of the industrial countries is expected to decline slightly over the next 50 years.) Nearly 60 percent of the increase will occur in Asia, which will grow from 3.4 billion people in 1995 to more than 5.4 billion in 2050. China's population will swell from 1.2 billion to 1.5 billion, while India's is projected to soar from 930 million to 1.53 billion. In the Middle East and North Africa, the population will probably more than double, and in sub-Saharan Africa, it will triple. By 2050, Nigeria alone is expected to have 339 million people—more than the entire continent of Africa had 35 years ago.

Despite the different demographic projections, no country will be immune to the effects of population growth. Of course, the countries with the highest growth rates are likely to feel the greatest immediate burdens—on their educational and public health systems, for instance, and on their forests, soils, and water as the struggle to grow more food intensifies. Already some 100 countries must rely on grain imports to some degree, and 1.3 billion of the world's people are living on the equivalent of $1 a day or less.

But the effects will ripple out from these "front-line" countries to encompass the world as a whole. Take the water predicament in the Middle East as an example. According to Tony Allan, a water expert at the University of London, the Middle East "ran out of water" in 1972, when its population stood at 122 million. At that point, Allan argues, the region had begun to draw more water out of its aquifers and rivers than the rains were replenishing. Yet today, the region's population is twice what it was in 1972 and still growing. To some degree, water management now determines political destiny. In Egypt, for example, President Hosni Mubarak has announced a $2 billion diversion project designed to pump water from the Nile River into an area that is now desert. The project—Mubarak calls it a "necessity imposed by population"—is designed to resettle some 3 million people outside the Nile flood plain, which is home to more than 90 percent of the country's population.

Elsewhere in the region, water demands are exacerbating international tensions; Jordan, Israel, and Syria, for instance, engage in uneasy competition for the waters of the Jordan River basin. Jordan's King Hussein once said that water was the only issue that could lead him to declare war on Israel. Of course, the United States and the western European countries are deeply involved in the region's antagonisms and have invested heavily in its fragile states. The western nations have no realistic hope of escaping involvement in future conflicts.

Yet the future need not be so grim. The experiences of countries like Bangladesh suggest that it is possible to build population policies that are a match for the threat. The first step is to understand the causes of population growth. John Bongaarts, vice president of the Population Council, a non-profit research group in New York City, has identified three basic factors. (See figure on the next page.)

Unmet demand for family planning. In the developing world, at least 120 million married women—and a large but undefined number of unmarried women—want more control over their pregnancies, but cannot get family planning services. This unmet demand will cause about one-third of the projected population growth in developing countries over the next 50 years, or an increase of about 1.2 billion people.

Desire for the large families. Another 20 percent of the projected growth over the next 50 years, or an increase of about 660 million people, will be caused by couples who may have access to family planning services, but who choose to have more than two children. (Roughly two children per family is the "replacement rate," at which a population could be expected to stabilize over the long term.)

Population momentum. By far the largest component of population growth is the least commonly understood. Nearly one-half of the increase projected for the next 50 years will occur simply because the next reproductive generation—the group of people currently entering puberty or younger—is so much larger than the current reproductive generation. Over the next 25 years, some 3 billion people—a number equal to the entire world population in 1960—will enter their reproductive years, but only about 1.8 billion will leave that phase of life. Assuming that the couples in this reproductive bulge begin to have children at a fairly early age, which is the global norm, the global population would still expand by 1.7 billion, even if all of those couples had only two children—the longterm replacement rate.

Meeting the Demand

Over the past three decades, the global percentage of couples using some form of family planning has increased dramatically—from less than 10 to more than 50 percent. But due to the growing population, the absolute number of women not using family planning is greater today than it was 30 years ago. Many of these women fall into that first category above—they want the services but for one reason or another, they cannot get them.

Sometimes the obstacle is a matter of policy: many governments ban or restrict valuable methods of contraception. In Japan, for instance, regulations discourage the use of birth control pills in favor of condoms, as a public health measure against sexually transmitted diseases. A study conducted in 1989 found that some 60 countries required a husband's permission before a woman can be sterilized; several required a husband's consent for all forms of birth control.

Elsewhere, the problems may be more logistical than legal. Many developing countries lack clinics and pharmacies in rural areas. In some rural areas of sub-Saharan Africa, it takes an average of two hours to reach the nearest contraceptive provider. And often contraceptives are too expensive for most people. Sometimes the products or services are of such poor quality that they are not simply ineffective, but dangerous. A woman who has been injured by a badly made or poorly inserted IUD may well be put off by contraception entirely.

In many countries, the best methods are simply unavailable. Sterilization is often the only available nontraditional option, or the only one that has gained wide acceptance. Globally, the procedure accounts for about 40 percent of contraceptive use and in some countries the fraction is much higher: in the Dominican Republic and India, for example, it stands at 69 percent. But women don't generally resort to sterilization until well into their childbearing years, and in some countries, the procedure isn't permitted until a woman reaches a certain age or bears a certain number of children. Sterilization is therefore no substitute for effective temporary methods like condoms, the pill, or IUDs.

There are often obstacles in the home as well. Women may be prevented from seeking family planning services by disapproving husbands or in-laws. In Pakistan, for example, 43 percent of husbands object to family planning. Frequently, such objections reflect a general social disapproval inculcated by religious or other deeply-rooted cultural values. And in many places, there is a crippling burden of ignorance: women simply may not know what family planning services are available or how to obtain them.

Yet there are many proven opportunities for progress, even in conditions that would appear to offer little room for it. In Bangladesh, for instance, contraception was never explicitly illegal, but many households follow the Muslim custom of *purdah*, which largely secludes women in their communities.

Population of Developing Countries, 1950--95, with Projected Growth to 2050

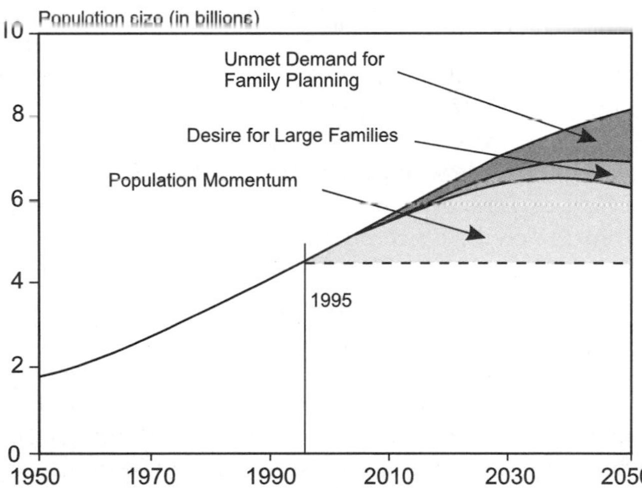

Source: U.N., World Population Prospects: The 1996 Revision (New York: October 1998); and John Bongaarts, "Population Policy Options in the Developing World," Science, 11 February 1994.

Since it's very difficult for such women to get to family planning clinics, the government brought family planning to them: some 30,000 female field workers go door-to-door to explain contraceptive methods and distribute supplies. Several other countries have adopted Bangladesh's approach. Ghana, for instance, has a similar system, in which field workers fan out from community centers. And even Pakistan now deploys 12,000 village-based workers, in an attempt to reform its family planning program, which still reaches only a quarter of the population.

Reducing the price of contraceptives can also trigger a substantial increase in use. In poor countries, contraceptives can be an extremely price-sensitive commodity even when they are very cheap. Bangladesh found this out the hard way in 1990, when officials increased contraceptive prices an average of 60 percent. (Under the increases, for example, the cheapest condoms cost about 1.25 U.S. cents per dozen.) Despite regular annual sales increases up to that point, the market slumped immediately: in 1991, condom sales fell by 29 percent and sales of the pill by 12 percent. The next year, prices were rolled back; sales rebounded and have grown steadily since then.

Additional research and development can help broaden the range of contraceptive options. Not all methods work for all couples, and the lack of a suitable method may block a substantial amount of demand. Some women, for instance, have side effects to the pill; others may not be able to use IUDs because of reproductive tract infections. The wider the range of available methods, the better the chance that a couple will use one of them.

Planning the Small Family

Simply providing family planning services to people who already want them won't be enough to arrest the population juggernaut. In many countries, large families are still the ideal. In Senegal, Cameroon, and Niger, for example, the average woman still wants six or seven children. A few countries have tried to legislate such desires away. In India, for example, the Ministry of Health and Family Welfare is interested in promoting a policy that would bar people who have more than two children from political careers, or deny them promotion if they work within the civil service bureaucracy. And China's well-known policy allows only one child per family.

But coercion is not only morally questionable—it's likely to be ineffective because of the backlash it invites. A better starting point for policy would be to try to understand why couples want large families in the first place. In many developing countries, having lots of children still seems perfectly rational: children are a source of security in old age and may be a vital part of the family economy. Even when they're very young, children's labor can make them an asset rather than a drain on family income. And in countries with high child mortality rates, many births may be viewed as necessary to compensate for the possible deaths (of course, the cumulative statistical effect of such a reaction is to *over*-compensate).

Religious or other cultural values may contribute to the big family ideal. In Pakistan, for instance, where 97 percent of the population is Muslim, a recent survey of married women found that almost 60 percent of them believed that the number of children they have is "up to God." Preference for sons is another widespread factor in the big family psychology: many large families have come about from a perceived need to bear at least one son. In India, for instance, many Hindus believe that they need a son to perform their last rites, or their souls will not be released from the cycle of births and rebirths. Lack of a son can mean abandonment in this life too. Many husbands desert wives who do not bear sons. Or if a husband dies, a son is often the key to a woman's security: 60 percent of Indian women over 60 are widows, and widows tend to rely on their sons for support. In some castes, a widow has no other option since social mores forbid her from returning to her birth village or joining a daughter's family. Understandably, the fear of abandonment prompts many Indian women to continue having children until they have a son. It is estimated that if son preference were eliminated in India, the fertility rate would decline by 8 percent from its current level of 3.5 children per woman.

Yet even deeply rooted beliefs are subject to reinterpretation. In Iran, another Muslim society, fertility rates have dropped from seven children per family to just over four in less than three decades. The trend is due in some measure to a change of heart among the government's religious authorities, who had become increasingly concerned about the likely effects of a population that was growing at more than 3 percent per year. In 1994, at the International Conference on Population and Development (ICPD) held in Cairo, the Iranian delegation released a "National Report on Population" which argued that according to the "quotations from prophet Mohammad... and verses of [the] holy Quran, what is standing at the top priority for the Muslims' community is the social welfare of Muslims." Family planning, therefore, "not only is not prohibited but is emphasized by religion."

Promotional campaigns can also change people's assumptions and behavior, if the campaigns fit into the local social context. Perhaps the most successful effort of this kind is in Thailand, where Mechai Viravidaiya, the founder of the Thai Population and Community Development Association, started a program that uses witty songs, demonstrations, and ads to encourage the use of contraceptives. The program has helped foster widespread awareness of family planning throughout Thai society. Teachers use population-related examples in their math classes; cab drivers even pass out condoms. Such efforts have paid off: in less than three decades, contraceptive use among married couples has risen from 8 to 75 percent and population growth has slowed from over 3 percent to about 1 percent—the same rate as in the United States.

Better media coverage may be another option. In Bangladesh, a recent study found that while local journalists recognize the importance of family planning, they do not understand population issues well enough to cover them effectively and objectively. The study, a collaboration between the University Research Corporation of Bangladesh and Johns Hopkins University in the United States, recommended five ways to improve coverage: develop easy-to-use information for journalists (press releases, wall charts, research summaries), offer training and workshops, present awards for population journalism, create a forum for communication between journalists and family planning professionals, and establish a population resource center or data bank.

Often, however, the demand for large families is so tightly linked to social conditions that the conditions themselves must be viewed as part of the problem. Of course, those conditions vary greatly from one society to the next, but there are some common points of leverage:

Reducing child mortality helps give parents more confidence in the future of the children they already have. Among the most effective ways of reducing mortality are child immunization programs, and the promotion of "birth spacing"—lengthening the time between births. (Children born less than a year and a half apart are twice as likely to die as those born two or more years apart.)

Improving the economic situation of women provides them with alternatives to child-bearing. In some countries, officials could reconsider policies or customs that limit women's job opportunities or other economic rights, such as the right to inherit property. Encouraging "micro-leaders" such as Bangladesh's Grameen Bank can also be an effective tactic. In Bangladesh, the Bank has made loans to well over a million villagers—mostly impoverished women—to help them start or expand small businesses.

Improving education tends to delay the average age of marriage and to further the two goals just mentioned. Compulsory school attendance for children undercuts the economic incentive for larger families by reducing the opportunities for child labor. And in just about every society, higher levels of education correlate strongly with small families.

Momentum: The Biggest Threat of All

The most important factor in population growth is the hardest to counter—and to understand. Population momentum can be easy to overlook because it isn't directly captured by the statistics that attract the most attention. The global growth rate, after all, is dropping: in the mid-1960s, it amounted to about a 2.2 percent annual increase; today the figure is 1.4 percent. The fertility rate is dropping too: in 1950, women bore an average of five children each; now they bear roughly three. But despite these continued declines, the absolute number of births won't taper off any time soon. According to U.S. Census Bureau estimates, some 130 million births will still occur annually for the next 25 years, because of the sheer number of women coming into their child-bearing years.

The effects of momentum can be seen readily in a country like Bangladesh, where more than 42 percent of the population is under 15 years old—a typical proportion for many poor countries. Some 82 percent of the population growth projected for Bangladesh over the next half century will be caused by momentum. In other words, even if from now on, every Bangladeshi couple were to have only two children, the country's population would still grow by 80 million by 2050 simply because the next reproductive generation is so enormous.

The key to reducing momentum is to delay as many births as possible. To understand why delay works, it's helpful to think of momentum as a kind of human accounting problem in which a large number of births in the near term won't be balanced by a corresponding number of deaths over the same period of time. One side of the population ledger will contain those 130 million annual births (not all of which are due to momentum, of course), while the other side will contain only about 50 million annual deaths. So to put the matter in a morbid light, the longer a substantial number of those births can be delayed, the longer the death side of the balance sheet will be when the births eventually occur. In developing countries, according to the Population Council's Bongaarts, an average 2.5-year delay in the age when a woman bears her first child would reduce population growth by over 10 percent.

One way to delay childbearing is to postpone the age of marriage. In Bangladesh, for instance, the median age of first marriage among women rose from 14.4 in 1951 to 18 in 1989, and the age at first birth followed suit. Simply raising the legal age of marriage may be a useful tactic in countries that permit marriage among the very young. Educational improvements, as already mentioned, tend to do the same thing. A survey of 23 developing countries found that the median age of marriage for women with secondary education exceeded that of women with no formal education by four years.

Another fundamental strategy for encouraging later childbirth is to help women break out of the "sterilization syndrome" by providing and promoting high-quality, temporary contraceptives. Sterilization might appear to be the ideal form of contraception because it's permanent. But precisely because it is permanent, women considering sterilization tend to have their children early, and then resort to it. A family planning program that relies heavily on sterilization may therefore be working at cross purposes with itself: when offered as a primary form of contraception, sterilization tends to promote early childbirth.

What Happened to the Cairo Pledges?

At the 1994 Cairo Conference, some 180 nations agreed on a 20-year reproductive health package to slow population growth. The agreement called for a progressive rise in annual funding over the life of the package; according to U.N. estimates, the annual price tag would come to about $17 billion by 2000 and $21.7 billion by 2015. Developing countries agreed to pay for two thirds of the program, while the developed countries were to pay for the rest. On a global scale, the package was fairly modest: the annual funding amounts to less than two weeks' worth of global military expenditures.

Today, developing country spending is largely on track with the Cairo agreement, but the developed countries are not keeping their part of the bargain. According to a recent study by the U.N. Population Fund (UNFPA), all forms of developed country assistance (direct foreign aid, loans from multilateral agencies, foundation grants, and so on) amounted to only $2 billion in 1995. That was a 24 percent increase over the previous year, but preliminary estimates indicate that support declined some 18 percent in 1996 and last year's funding levels were probably even lower than that.

The United States, the largest international donor to population programs, is not only failing to meet its Cairo commitments, but is toying with a policy that would undermine international family planning efforts as a whole. Many members of the U.S. Congress are seeking reimposition of the "Mexico City Policy" first enunciated by President Ronald Reagan at the 1984 U.N. population conference in Mexico City, and repealed by the Clinton administration in 1993. Essentially, a resurrected Mexico City Policy would extend the current U.S. ban on funding abortion services to a ban on funding any organization that:

- funds abortions directly, or
- has a partnership arrangement with an organization that funds abortions, or
- provides legal services that may facilitate abortions, or
- engages in any advocacy for the provision of abortions, or
- participates in any policy discussions about abortion, either in a domestic or international forum.

The ban would be triggered even if the relevant activities were paid for entirely with non-U.S. funds. Because of its draconian limits even on speech, the policy has been dubbed the "Global Gag Rule" by its critics, who fear that it could stifle, not just abortion services, but many family planning operations involved only incidentally with abortion. Although Mexico City proponents have not managed to enlist enough support to reinstate the policy, they have succeeded in reducing U.S. family planning aid from $547 million in 1995 to $385 million in 1997. They have also imposed an unprecedented set of restrictions that meter out the money at the rate of 8 percent of the annual budget per month—a tactic that *Washington Post* reporter Judy Mann calls "administrative strangulation."

If the current underfunding of the Cairo program persists, according to the UNFPA study, 96 million fewer couples will use modern contraceptives in 2000 than if commitments had been met. One-third to one-half of these couples will resort to less effective traditional birth control methods; the rest will not use any contraceptives at all. The result will be an additional 122 million unintended pregnancies. Over half of those pregnancies will end in births, and about 40 percent will end in abortions. (The funding shortfall is expected to produce 16 million more abortions in 2000 alone.) The unwanted pregnancies will kill about 65,000 women by 2000, and injure another 844,000.

Population funding is always vulnerable to the illusion that the falling growth rate means the problem is going away. Worldwide, the annual population increase had dropped from a high of 87 million in 1988 to 80 million today. But dismissing the problem with that statistic is like comforting someone stuck on a railway crossing with the news that an oncoming train has slowed from 87 to 80 kilometers an hour, while its weight has increased. It will now take 12.5 years instead of 11.5 years to add the next billion people to the world. But that billion will surely arrive—and so will at least one more billion. Will still more billions follow? That, in large measure, depends on what policymakers do now. Funding alone will not ensure that population stabilizes, but lack of funding will ensure that it does not.

The Next Doubling

In the wake of the Cairo conference, most population programs are broadening their focus to include improvements in education, women's health, and women's social status among their many goals. These goals are worthy in their own right and they will ultimately be necessary for bringing population under control. But global population growth has gathered so much momentum that it could simply overwhelm a development agenda. Many countries now have little choice but to tackle their population problem in as direct a fashion as possible—even if that means temporarily ignoring other social problems. Population growth is now a global social emergency. Even as officials in both developed and developing countries open up their program agendas, it is critical that they not neglect their single most effective tool for dealing with that emergency: direct expenditures on family planning.

The funding that is likely to be the most useful will be constant, rather than sporadic. A fluctuating level of commitment, like sporadic condom use, can end up missing its objective entirely. And wherever it's feasible, funding should be designed to develop self-sufficiency—as, for instance, with UNFPA's $1 million grant to Cuba, to build a factory for making birth control pills. The factory, which has the capacity to turn out 500 million tablets annually, might eventually even provide the country with a new export product. Self-sufficiency is likely to grow increasingly important as the fertility rate continues to decline. As Tom Merrick, senior population advisor at the World Bank explains, "while the need for contraceptives will not go away when the total fertility rate reaches two—the donors will."

Even in narrow, conventional economic terms, family planning offers one of the best development investments available. A study in Bangladesh showed that for each birth prevented, the government spends $62 and saves $615 on social services expenditures—nearly a tenfold return. The study estimated that the Bangladesh program prevents 890,000 births a year, for a net annual savings of $547 million. And that figure does not include savings resulting from lessened pressure on natural resources.

Over the past 40 years, the world's population has doubled. At some point in the latter half of the next century, today's population of 5.9 billion could double again. But because of the size of the next reproductive generation, we probably have only a relatively few years to stop that next doubling. To prevent all of the damage—ecological, economic, and social—that the next doubling is likely to cause, we must begin planning the global family with the same kind of urgency that we bring to matters of trade, say, or military security. Whether we realize it or not, our attempts to stabilize population—or our failure to act—will likely have consequences that far outweigh the implications of the military or commercial crisis of the moment. Slowing population growth is one of the greatest gifts we can offer future generations.

Jennifer D. Mitchell is a staff researcher at the Worldwatch Institute.

From *World Watch* magazine, January/February 1998, pp. 20–27.

SCIENCE AND TECHNOLOGY

A turning-point for AIDS?

The impact of the global AIDS epidemic has been catastrophic, but many of the remedies are obvious. It is now a question of actually doing something

DURBAN

WHEN Thabo Mbeki, South Africa's president, opened the world AIDS conference in Durban on July 9th, he was widely expected to admit that he had made a mistake. Mr Mbeki has been flirting with the ideas of a small but vociferous group of scientists who, flying in the face of all the evidence, maintain that AIDS is not caused by the human immunodeficiency virus (HIV). His speech at the opening ceremony would have been the ideal opportunity for a graceful climbdown. Instead, he blustered and prevaricated, pretending that there was a real division of opinion among scientists about the matter, and arguing that the commission that he has appointed to look into this non-existent division would resolve it.

AIDS is the most political disease around. People talk a lot about AIDS "exceptionalism", and in many ways it is exceptional. For a start, it is difficult to think of another disease that would have brought the host country's head of state out of his office to open a conference, confused though his ideas may be. It is also exceptional, in modern times, in the attitudes of the healthy towards the infected. Illness usually provokes sympathy. But in many parts of the world those who have HIV are treated rather as lepers were in biblical days. Indeed, Gugu Dlamini, a community activist in KwaZulu Natal, the South African province in which Durban lies, was stoned to death by her neighbours when she revealed that she had the virus. In many parts of the world, as Kevin De Cock, of America's Centres for Disease Control (CDC), pointed out to the conference, attitudes to AIDS can be summed up in four words: silence, stigma, discrimination and denial. Mr Mbeki himself is at least guilty of denial.

Nevertheless, the fact that this, the 13th such AIDS conference, was held in Africa shows that some progress is being made. The previous conference, in Geneva in 1998, claimed to be "bridging the gap" between the treatment of the disease in the rich and poor worlds. It did no such thing. This one set as its goal to "break the silence". It may have succeeded. What needed to be shouted from the rooftops was that, contrary to some popular views, AIDS is not primarily a disease of gay western men or of intravenous drug injectors. It is a disease of ordinary people leading ordinary lives, except that most of them happen to live in a continent, Africa, that the rich countries of the world find it easy to ignore.

In some places the problem is so bad that it is hard to know where to begin. According to United Nations estimates, 25m of the 34m infected people in the world live in Africa. In absolute terms, South Africa has the most cases (4m, or about 20% of the adult population), but several of its neighbours have even worse ratios. In Botswana, for example, 36% of the adult population is now infected with HIV. Barring some currently unimaginable treatment—unimaginable in both efficacy and cost—almost all of these people will die as a result.

The hydra-headed monster

And mere numbers are not the only issue. People talk, rhetorically, of waging war on diseases. In the case of AIDS, the rhetoric could be inverted, for the effects of the illness on human populations are similar to those of war. Most infectious diseases tend to kill infants and the old. AIDS, like war, kills those in the prime of life. Indeed, in one way it is worse than war. When armies fight, it is predominantly young men who are killed. AIDS kills young women, too.

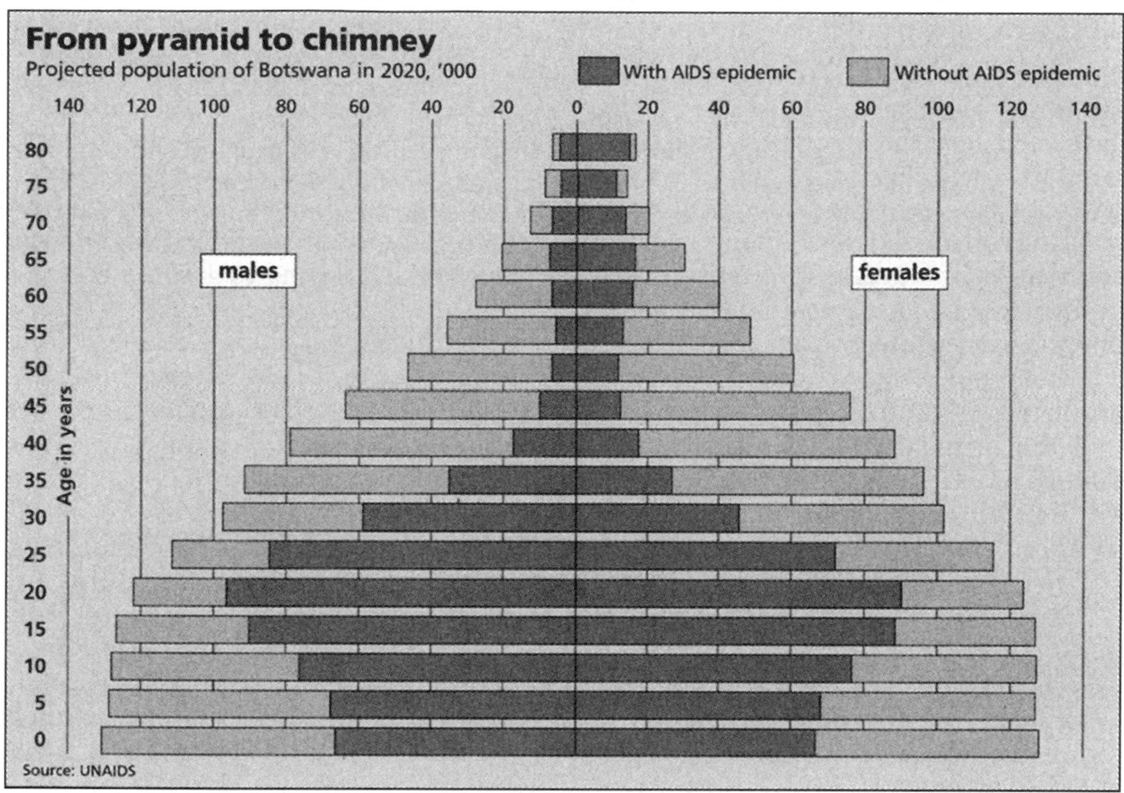

The result is social dislocation on a grand scale. As the diagram on the next page shows, the age-distribution of Botswana's population will change from the "pyramid" that is typical of countries with rapidly growing populations, to a "chimney-shaped" graph from which the young have been lopped out. Ten years from now, according to figures released at the conference by USAID, the American government's agency for international development, the life expectancy of somebody born in Botswana will have fallen to 29. In 20 years' time, the old will outnumber the middle-aged. Nor are things much better in other countries in southern Africa. In Zimbabwe and Namibia, two of Botswana's neighbours, life expectancy in 2010 will be 33. In South Africa it will be 35.

The destruction of young adults means that AIDS is creating orphans on an unprecedented scale. There are 11.2m of them, of whom 10.7m live in Africa. On top of that, vast numbers of children are infected as they are born. These are the exception to the usual rule that infants do not get the disease. Children are rarely infected in the womb, but they may acquire the virus from their mothers' vaginal fluids when they are born, or from breast milk. More than 5m children are reckoned to have been infected in this way. Almost 4m of them are already dead.

It sounds hopeless. And yet it isn't. Two African countries, Uganda and Senegal, seem to have worked out how to cope with the disease. Their contrasting experiences serve both as a warning and as a lesson to other countries in the world, particularly those in Asia that now have low infection rates and may be feeling complacently smug about them. The warning: act early, or you will be sorry. The lesson: it is, even so, never too late to act. Senegal began its anti-AIDS programme in 1986, before the virus had got a proper grip. It has managed to keep its infection rate below 2%. Uganda began its programme in the early 1990s, when 14% of the adult population was already infected. Now that figure is down to 8% and falling. In these two countries, the epidemic seems to have been stopped in its tracks.

As Roy Anderson, a noted epidemiologist from Oxford University, pointed out to the conference, stopping an epidemic requires one thing: that the average number of people infected by somebody who already has the disease be less than one. For a sexually transmitted disease, this average has three components: the "transmissibility" of the disease, the average rate that an infected person acquires new and uninfected partners, and the average length of time for which somebody is infectious.

Cutting off the hydra's heads

The easiest of these to tackle has been transmissibility. Surprisingly, perhaps, AIDS is not all that easily transmissible compared with other diseases. But there are three ways—one certain, one as yet a pious hope, and one the subject of some controversy—to reduce the rate of transmission between adults still further. The first is to use condoms. The second is to develop a microbicide that will kill the virus in the vagina. And the third is to treat other sexually transmitted diseases.

Both Senegal and Uganda have been strong on the use of condoms. In Senegal, for example, the annual number of condoms used rose from 800,000 in 1988 to 9m in 1997.

Nevertheless, it still takes a lot of encouragement to persuade people to use them. Partly, this is a question of discounting the future. For decades African lives have been shorter, on average, than those in the rest of the world. With AIDS, they are getting shorter still. A Botswanan who faces the prospect of death before his 30th birthday is likely to be more reckless than an American who can look forward to well over twice that lifespan; a short life might as well be a merry one.

There is also the question of who wears the condom. Until recently, there was no choice. Only male condoms were available. And women in many parts of Africa are in a weak negotiating position when it comes to insisting that a man put one on. The best way out of this is to alter the balance of power. That, in general, means more and better education, particularly for girls. This, too, has been an important component of the Senegalese and Ugandan anti-AIDS programmes. A stop-gap, though, is the female condom, a larger version of the device that fits inside the vagina, which is proving surprisingly popular among groups such as Nairobi prostitutes. But an even less intrusive—and to a man invisible—form of protection would be a vaginal microbicide that kills the virus before it can cross the vaginal wall.

Here, however, the news is bad. Much hope had been pinned on a substance called nonoxynol-9 (the spermicide used to coat condoms that are intended to prevent pregnancy rather than disease). Unfortunately, the results of a major United Nations trial announced at the conference have confirmed the suspicion that nonoxynol-9 does not work against HIV. So researchers have gone back to the drawing-board and are searching for suitable (and suitably cheap) substances among the cast-offs from anti-viral drugs used to treat AIDS in rich countries.

More equivocal is the value of treating other sexually transmitted diseases as a way of preventing the transmission of HIV. Clearly, such treatment is a good thing in its own right. But a study carried out a few years ago at Mwanza, Tanzania, suggested that it also stymies HIV. That would not be surprising, since the vaginal lesions that other venereal diseases produce should make excellent entry points for the virus. Yet a more recent study at Rakai, Uganda, suggests that other venereal diseases make no difference; the matter is now a subject of much debate.

Sex is not the only way that HIV is transmitted. Infected mothers can give it to their children. But here, too, transmissibility can be reduced dramatically.

A first way of doing this is to test pregnant women to see if they have the virus. If they do, they are unlikely to pass it on to the fetus in the womb, but they are quite likely to do so in the act of giving birth. According to figures presented to the conference by Ruth Nduati, of the University of Nairobi, up to 40% of children born to untreated infected women catch AIDS this way. But that number can be reduced drastically—to around 20%—by giving infected pregnant women a short course of an antiviral drug just before they give birth.

Until recently, the preferred drug was AZT. Many African governments balked at using this because, although it is cheap by western standards, it can stretch African health budgets to breaking point. However, recent studies carried out in Kenya and South Africa have shown that an even cheaper drug called nevirapine will do just as well. A course of this costs $4, still a fair whack for an impoverished country, but worth it both for the life of a child and for the cost-saving of not having to treat that child's subsequent illness.

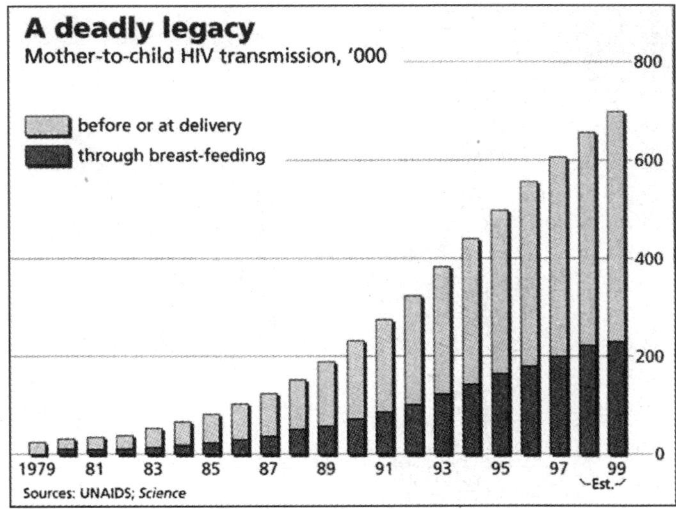

Once safely born, the child of an infected mother is still not out of the woods. This is because it can be infected via its mother's milk. Oddly, this is a more intractable problem than transmission at birth. Nobody knows (because nobody has tried to find out) if carrying on with AZT or nevirapine would keep a mother's milk virus-free. But the cost would be prohibitive anyway. The only alternative is not to breast-feed.

That may sound easy, but it is not. First, the formula milk that could substitute for breast milk costs money. Second, unless clean water is available to mix with it, the result is likely to be a diarrhoeal disease that may kill the child anyway. And third, by failing to breast-feed, a mother in many parts of Africa is in effect announcing that she has the virus, and thus exposing herself to both stigma and discrimination. Not breast-feeding is, nevertheless, an effective addition to pre-natal antiviral drugs. According to Dr Nduati, combining both methods can bring the infection rate below 8%.

The second of Dr Anderson's criteria, the rate of acquisition of new and uninfected partners, is critical to the speed with which AIDS spreads, but is also far harder to tackle. The reasons why AIDS has spread faster in some places than in others are extremely complicated. But one important factor is so-called disassortative mating.

As far as is known, all AIDS epidemics start with the spread of the disease in one or more small, high-risk groups. These groups include prostitutes and their clients, male homosexuals and injecting drug users. The rate at which an epidemic spreads to lower-risk groups depends a great deal on whether different groups mate mainly among themselves (assortative mating) or whether they mate a lot with other people (disassortative mating). The more disassortative mating there is, the faster the virus will spread.

Sub-Saharan Africa and the Caribbean (the second-worst affected part of the world) have particularly high levels of disassortative mating between young girls and older men. And in an area where AIDS is already highly prevalent, older men are a high-risk group; they are far more likely to have picked up the virus than younger ones. This helps to explain why the rate of infection is higher in young African women than it is in young African men.

Inter-generational churning may thus, according to Dr Anderson's models, go a long way towards explaining why Africa and the Caribbean have the highest levels of HIV infection in the world. And it suggests that, as with condom use, a critical part of any anti-AIDS campaign should be to give women more power. In many cases, young women are coerced or bribed into relationships with older men. This would diminish if girls were better educated—not least because they would then find it easier to earn a living.

The partial explanation for Africa's plight that disassortative mating provides should not, however, bring false comfort in other areas. Dr Anderson's models suggest that lower levels of disassortative mating cannot stop an epidemic, they merely postpone it. Those countries, such as Ukraine, where HIV is spreading rapidly through a high-risk group (in Ukraine's case, injecting drug users), need to act now, even if the necessary action, such as handing out clean needles, is politically distasteful. Countries such as India, where lower-risk groups are starting to show up in the statistics, and where the prevalence rates in some states are already above 2%, needed to act yesterday, and to aim their message more widely. The example of Senegal (and, indeed, the strongly worded, morally neutral advertising campaigns conducted in many western countries in the 1980s), shows the value of early action as surely as do Dr Anderson's models.

To tackle the third element of those models—the length of time that somebody is infectious—really requires a vaccine. Drugs can reduce it to some extent, by bringing people's viral load down to the point where they will not pass on the disease. But effective therapies are currently expensive and, despite the widespread demands at the conference for special arrangements that would lower their price in poor countries, are unlikely to become cheap enough for routine use there for some time. On top of that, if drugs are used carelessly, resistant strains of the virus can emerge, rendering the therapies useless. A study by the CDC, published to coincide with the conference, showed resistant strains in the blood of three-quarters of the participants in a United Nations AIDS drug-access programme in Uganda.

The search for a vaccine

Vaccines are not immune to the emergence of resistant strains. But they are one-shot treatments and so are not subject to the whims of patient compliance with complex drug regimes. Non-compliance is the main cause of the emergence of resistant strains, since the erratic consumption of a particular drug allows populations of resistant viruses to evolve and build up.

In total, 21 clinical trials of vaccines are happening around the world, but only five are taking place in poor countries, and only two are so-called phase 3 trials that show whether a vaccine will work effectively in the real world. Preliminary results from these two trials, which are being conducted by an American company called VaxGen, are expected next year. They are eagerly awaited, for even a partially effective vaccine could have a significant impact on the virus's spread. A calculation by America's National Institutes of Health shows that, over the course of a decade, a 60%-effective vaccine introduced now would stop nearly twice as many infections as a 90%-effective one introduced five years hence.

Even then, there is the question of cost. This is being addressed by the International AIDS Vaccine Initiative (IAVI), a New York-based charity. IAVI, according to its boss Seth Berkley, acts like a venture-capital firm. At the moment, that capital amounts to about $100m, gathered from various governments and foundations. IAVI provides small firms with seed money to develop new products, but instead of demanding a share of the equity in return, it requires that the eventual product, if any, should be sold at a low profit margin—about 10%. If a sponsored firm breaks this arrangement, IAVI can give the relevant patents to anybody it chooses. At the moment, IAVI has four such partnerships, and it chose the conference to announce that one—a collaboration with the Universities of Oxford and Nairobi—has just received regulatory approval and will start trials in September.

None of these things alone will be enough to stop the epidemic in its tracks, but in combination they may succeed. And one last lesson from Dr Anderson's equations is not to give up just because a policy does not seem to be working. Those equations predict that applying a lot of effort to an established epidemic will have little initial effect. Then, suddenly, infection rates will drop fast. The message is: "hang in there". AIDS may be exceptional, but it is not that exceptional. Good science and sensible public policy can defeat it. There is at least a glimmer of hope.

The End of Cheap Oil

Global production of conventional oil will begin to decline sooner than most people think, probably within 10 years

by Colin J. Campbell and Jean H. Laherrère

In 1973 and 1979 a pair of sudden price increases rudely awakened the industrial world to its dependence on cheap crude oil. Prices first tripled in response to an Arab embargo and then nearly doubled again when Iran dethroned its Shah, sending the major economies sputtering into recession. Many analysts warned that these crises proved that the world would soon run out of oil. Yet they were wrong.

Their dire predictions were emotional and political reactions; even at the time, oil experts knew that they had no scientific basis. Just a few years earlier oil explorers had discovered enormous new oil provinces on the north slope of Alaska and below the North Sea off the coast of Europe. By 1973 the world had consumed, according to many experts' best estimates, only about one eighth of its endowment of readily accessible crude oil (so-called conventional oil). The five Middle Eastern members of the Organization of Petroleum Exporting Countries (OPEC) were able to hike prices not because oil was growing scarce but because they had managed to corner 36 percent of the market. Later, when demand sagged, and the flow of fresh Alaskan and North Sea oil weakened OPEC's economic stranglehold, prices collapsed.

The next oil crunch will not be so temporary. Our analysis of the discovery and production of oil fields around the world suggests that within the next decade, the supply of conventional oil will be unable to keep up with demand. This conclusion contradicts the picture one gets from oil industry reports, which boasted of 1,020 billion barrels of oil (Gbo) in "proved" reserves at the start of 1998. Dividing that figure by the current production rate of about 23.6 Gbo a year might suggest that crude oil could remain plentiful and cheap for 43 more years—probably longer, because official charts show reserves growing.

Unfortunately, this appraisal makes three critical errors. First, it relies on distorted estimates of reserves. A second mistake is to pretend that production will remain constant. Third and most important, conventional wisdom erroneously assumes that the last bucket of oil can be pumped from the ground just as quickly as the barrels of oil gushing from wells today. In fact, the rate at which any well—or any country—can produce oil always rises to a maximum and then, when about half the oil is gone, begins falling gradually back to zero.

COURTESY OF THE SOCIETY OF EXPLORATION GEOPHYSICISTS

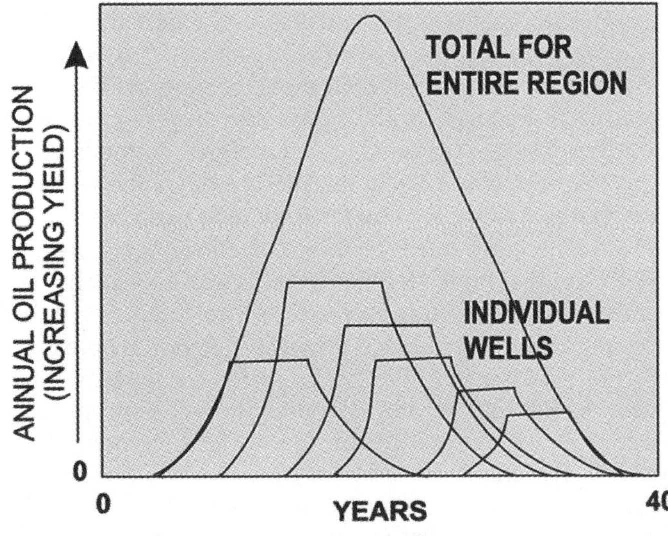

JENNIFER C. CHRISTIANSEN; LAURIE GRACE

FLOW OF OIL starts to fall from any large region when about half the crude is gone. Adding the output of fields of various sizes and ages (bottom curves at right) usually yields a bell-shaped production curve for the region as a whole. M. King Hubbert (top), a geologist with Shell Oil, exploited this fact in 1956 to predict correctly that oil from the lower 48 American states would peak around 1969.

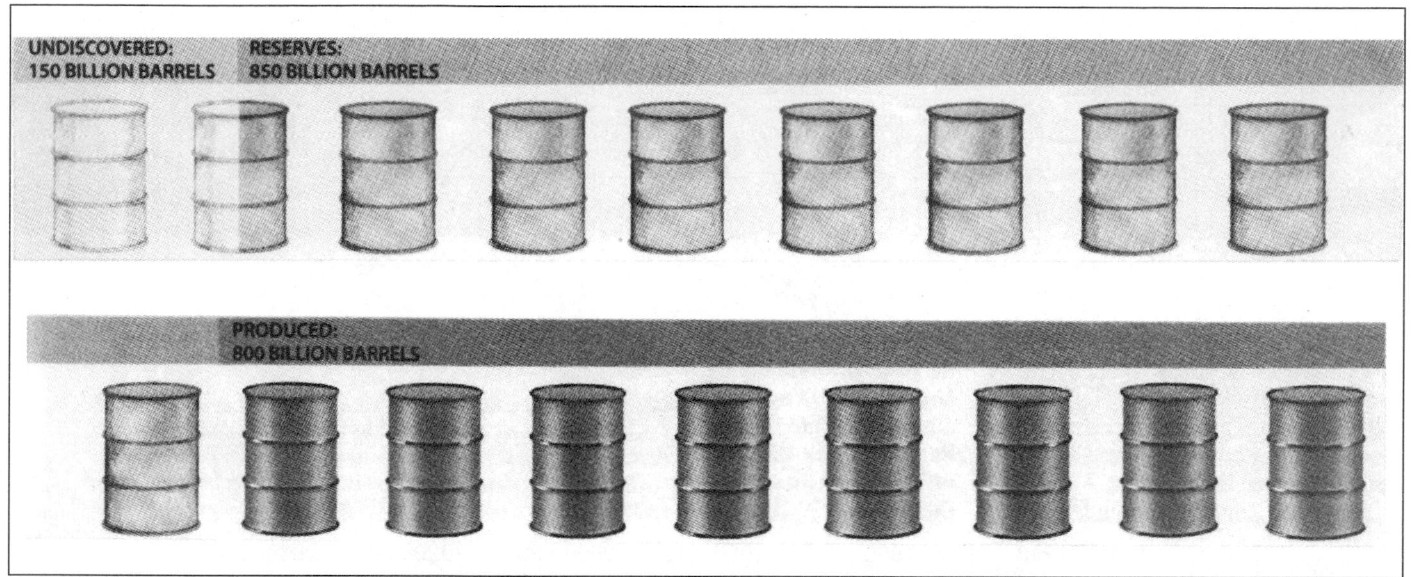

EARTH'S CONVENTIONAL CRUDE OIL is almost half gone. Reserves (defined here as the amount as likely as not to come out of known fields) and future discoveries together will provide little more than what has already been burned.

From an economic perspective, when the world runs completely out of oil is thus not directly relevant: what matters is when production begins to taper off. Beyond that point, prices will rise unless demand declines commensurately. Using several different techniques to estimate the current reserves of conventional oil and the amount still left to be discovered, we conclude that the decline will begin before 2010.

Digging for the True Numbers

We have spent most of our careers exploring for oil, studying reserve figures and estimating the amount of oil left to discover, first while employed at major oil companies and later as independent consultants. Over the years, we have come to appreciate that the relevant statistics are far more complicated than they first appear.

Consider, for example, three vital numbers needed to project future oil production. The first is the tally of how much oil has been extracted to date, a figure known as cumulative production. The second is an estimate of reserves, the amount that companies can pump out of known oil fields before having to abandon them. Finally, one must have an educated guess at the quantity of conventional oil that remains to be discovered and exploited. Together they add up to ultimate recovery, the total number of barrels that will have been extracted when production ceases many decades from now.

The obvious way to gather these numbers is to look them up in any of several publications. That approach works well enough for cumulative production statistics because companies meter the oil as it flows from their wells. The record of production is not perfect (for example, the two billion barrels of Kuwaiti oil wastefully burned by Iraq in 1991 is usually not included in official statistics), but errors are relatively easy to spot and rectify. Most experts agree that the industry had removed just over 800 Gbo from the earth at the end of 1997.

Getting good estimates of reserves is much harder, however. Almost all the publicly available statistics are taken from surveys conducted by the *Oil and Gas Journal* and *World Oil*. Each year these two trade journals query oil firms and governments around the world. They then publish whatever production and reserve numbers they receive but are not able to verify them.

The results, which are often accepted uncritically, contain systematic errors. For one, many of the reported figures are unrealistic. Estimating reserves is an inexact science to begin with, so petroleum engineers assign a probability to their assessments. For example, if, as geologists estimate, there is a 90 percent chance that the Oseberg field in Norway contains 700 million barrels of recoverable oil but only a 10 percent chance that it will yield 2,500 million more barrels, then the lower figure should be cited as the so-called P90 estimate (P90 for "probability 90 percent") and the higher as the P10 reserves.

In practice, companies and countries are often deliberately vague about the likelihood of the reserves they report, preferring instead to publicize whichever figure, within a P10 to P90 range, best suits them. Exaggerated estimates can, for instance, raise the price of an oil company's stock.

The members of OPEC have faced an even greater temptation to inflate their reports because the higher their reserves, the more oil they are allowed to export. National companies, which have exclusive oil rights in the main OPEC countries, need not (and do not) release detailed statistics on each field that could be used to verify the country's total reserves. There is thus good reason to suspect that when, during the late 1980s, six of the 11 OPEC nations increased their reserve figures by colossal amounts, ranging from 42 to 197 percent, they did so only to boost their export quotas.

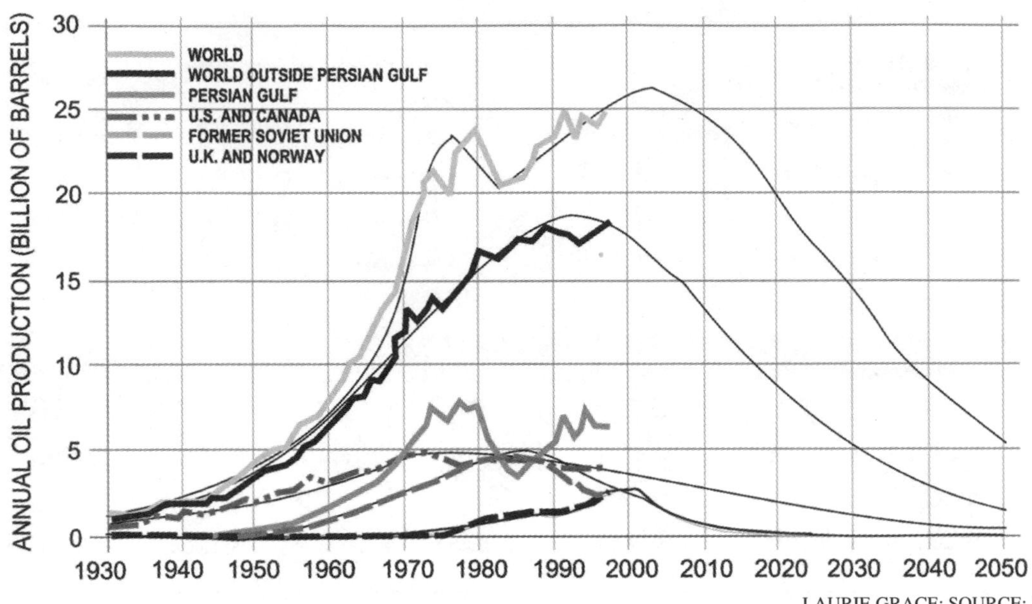

LAURIE GRACE; SOURCE: JEAN H. LAHERRRE

GLOBAL PRODUCTION OF OIL, both conventional and unconventional, recovered after falling in 1973 and 1979. But a more permanent decline is less than 10 years away, according to the authors' model, based in part on multiple Hubbert curves (thin lines). U.S. and Canadian oil topped out in 1972; production in the former Soviet Union has fallen 45 percent since 1987. A crest in the oil produced outside the Persian Gulf region now appears imminent.

Previous OPEC estimates, inherited from private companies before governments took them over, had probably been conservative, P90 numbers. So some upward revision was warranted. But no major new discoveries or technological breakthroughs justified the addition of a staggering 287 Gbo. That increase is more than all the oil ever discovered in the U.S.—plus 40 percent. Non-OPEC countries, of course, are not above fudging their numbers either: 59 nations stated in 1997 that their reserves were unchanged from 1996. Because reserves naturally drop as old fields are drained and jump when new fields are discovered, perfectly stable numbers year after year are implausible.

Unproved Reserves

Another source of systematic error in the commonly accepted statistics is that the definition of reserves varies widely from region to region. In the U.S., the Securities and Exchange Commission allows companies to call reserves "proved" only if the oil lies near a producing well and there is "reasonable certainty" that it can be recovered profitably at current oil prices, using existing technology. So a proved reserve estimate in the U.S. is roughly equal to a P90 estimate.

Regulators in most other countries do not enforce particular oil-reserve definitions. For many years, the former Soviet countries have routinely released wildly optimistic figures—essentially P10 reserves. Yet analysts have often misinterpreted these as estimates of "proved" reserves. *World Oil* reckoned reserves in the former Soviet Union amounted to 190 Gbo in 1996, whereas the *Oil and Gas Journal* put the number at 57 Gbo. This large discrepancy shows just how elastic these numbers can be.

Using only P90 estimates is not the answer, because adding what is 90 percent likely for each field, as is done in the U.S., does not in fact yield what is 90 percent likely for a country or the entire planet. On the contrary, summing many P90 reserve estimates always understates the amount of proved oil in a region. The only correct way to total up reserve numbers is to add the mean, or average, estimates of oil in each field. In practice, the median estimate, often called "proved and probable," or P50 reserves, is more widely used and is good enough. The P50 value is the number of barrels of oil that are as likely as not to come out of a well during its lifetime, assuming prices remain within a limited range. Errors in P50 estimates tend to cancel one another out.

We were able to work around many of the problems plaguing estimates of conventional reserves by using a large body of statistics maintained by Petroconsultants in Geneva. This information, assembled over 40 years from myriad sources, covers some 18,000 oil fields worldwide. It, too, contains some dubious reports, but we did our best to correct these sporadic errors.

According to our calculations, the world had at the end of 1996 approximately 850 Gbo of conventional oil in P50 reserves—substantially less than the 1,019 Gbo reported in the *Oil and Gas Journal* and the 1,160 Gbo estimated by *World Oil*. The difference is actually greater than it appears because our value represents the amount most likely to come out of known oil fields, whereas the larger number is supposedly a cautious estimate of proved reserves.

For the purposes of calculating when oil production will crest, even more critical than the size of the world's reserves is the size of ultimate recovery—all the cheap oil there is to be had. In order to estimate that, we need to know whether, and how fast, reserves are moving up or down. It is here that the official statistics become dangerously misleading.

How Much Oil Is Left to Find?

We combined several techniques to conclude that about 1,000 billion barrels of conventional oil remain to be produced. First, we extrapolated published production figures for older oil fields that have begun to decline. The Thistle field off the coast of Britain, for example, will yield about 420 million barrels (*a*). Second, we plotted the amount of oil discovered so far in some regions against the cumulative number of exploratory wells drilled there. Because larger fields tend to be found first—they are simply too large to miss—the curve rises rapidly and then flattens, eventually reaching a theoretical maximum: for Africa, 192 Gbo. But the time and cost of exploration impose a more practical limit of perhaps 165 Gbo (*b*). Third, we analyzed the distribution of oil-field sizes in the Gulf of Mexico and other provinces. Ranked according to size and then graphed on a logarithmic scale, the fields tend to fall along a parabola that grows predictably over time. (*c*). (Interestingly, galaxies, urban populations and other natural agglomerations also seem to fall along such parabolas.) Finally, we checked our estimates by matching our projections for oil production in large areas, such as the world outside the Persian Gulf region, to the rise and fall of oil discovery in those places decades earlier (*d*).

—*C.J.C. and J.H.L.*

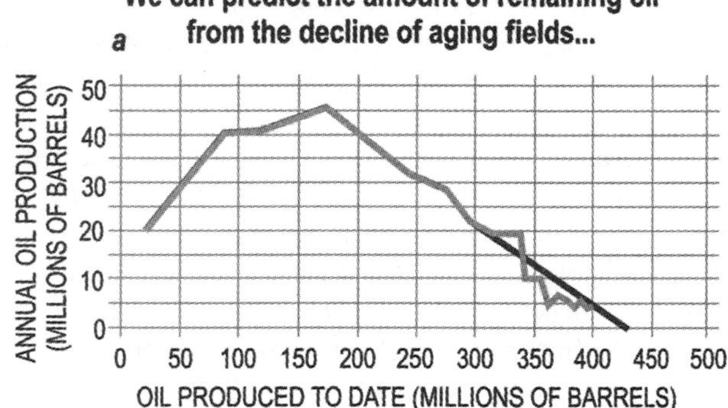

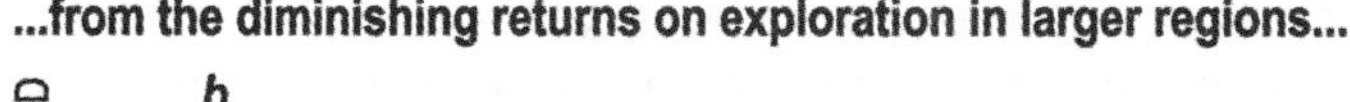

...from the diminishing returns on exploration in larger regions...

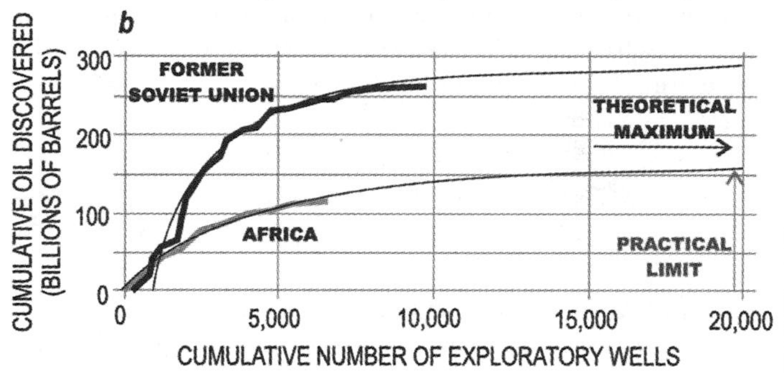

...by extrapolating the size of new fields into the future...

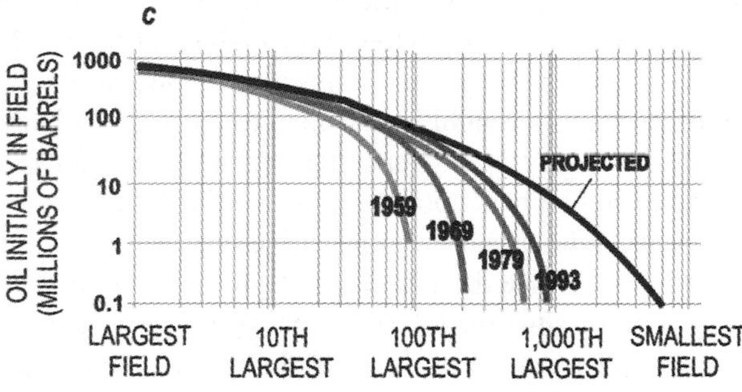

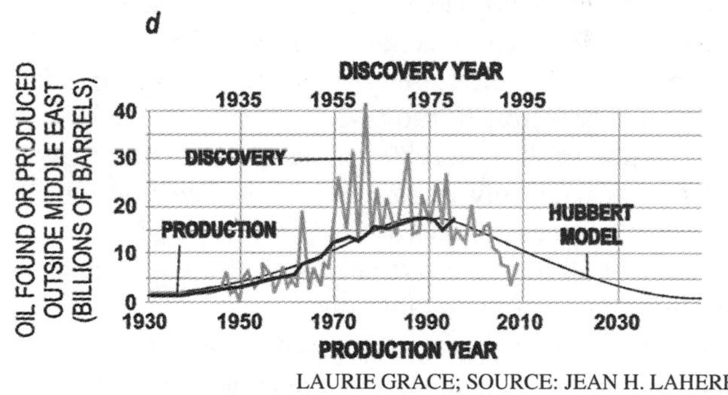

LAURIE GRACE; SOURCE: JEAN H. LAHERRRE

Diminishing Returns

According to most accounts, world oil reserves have marched steadily upward over the past 20 years. Extending that apparent trend into the future, one could easily conclude, as the U.S. Energy Information Administration has, that oil production will continue to rise unhindered for decades to come, increasing almost two thirds by 2020.

Such growth is an illusion. About 80 percent of the oil produced today flows from fields that were found before 1973, and the great majority of them are declining. In the 1990s oil companies have discovered an average of seven Gbo a year; last year they drained more than three times as much. Yet official figures indicated that proved reserves did not fall by 16 Gbo, as one would expect—rather they expanded by 11 Gbo. One reason is that several dozen governments opted not to report declines in their reserves, perhaps to enhance their political cachet and their ability to obtain loans. A more important cause of the expansion lies in revisions: oil companies replaced earlier estimates of the reserves left in many fields with higher numbers. For most purposes, such amendments are harmless, but they seriously distort forecasts extrapolated from published reports.

To judge accurately how much oil explorers will uncover in the future, one has to backdate every revision to the year in which the field was first discovered—not to the year in which a company or country corrected an earlier estimate. Doing so reveals that global discovery peaked in the early 1960s and has been falling steadily ever since. By extending the trend to zero, we can make a good guess at how much oil the industry will ultimately find.

We have used other methods to estimate the ultimate recovery of conventional oil for each country [*see box*, "Earth's Conventional Crude Oil"] and we calculate that the oil industry will be able to recover only about another 1,000 billion barrels of conventional oil. This number, though great, is little more than the 800 billion barrels that have already been extracted.

It is important to realize that spending more money on oil exploration will not change this situation. After the price of crude hit all-time highs in the early 1980s, explorers developed new technology for finding and recovering oil, and they scoured the world for new fields. They found few: the discovery rate continued its decline uninterrupted. There is only so much crude oil in the world, and the industry has found about 90 percent of it.

Predicting the Inevitable

Predicting when oil production will stop rising is relatively straightforward once one has a good estimate of how much oil there is left to produce. We simply apply a refinement of a technique first published in 1956 by M. King Hubbert. Hubbert observed that in any large region, unrestrained extraction of a finite resource rises along a bell-shaped curve that peaks when about half the resource is gone. To demonstrate his theory, Hubbert fitted a bell curve to production statistics and projected that crude oil production in the lower 48 U.S. states would rise for 13 more years, then crest in 1969, give or take a year. He was right: production peaked in 1970 and has continued to follow Hubbert curves with only minor deviations. The flow of oil from several other regions, such as the former Soviet Union and the collection of all oil producers outside the Middle East, also follows Hubbert curves quite faithfully.

The global picture is more complicated, because the Middle East members of OPEC deliberately reined back their oil exports in the 1970s, while other nations continued producing at full capacity. Our analysis reveals that a number of the largest producers, including Norway and the U.K., will reach their peaks around the turn of the millennium unless they sharply curtail production. By 2002 or so the world will rely on Middle East nations, particularly five near the Persian Gulf (Iran, Iraq, Kuwait, Saudi Arabia and the United Arab Emirates), to fill in the gap between dwindling supply and growing demand. But once approximately 900 Gbo have been consumed, production must soon begin to fall. Barring a global recession, it seems most likely that world production of conventional oil will peak during the first decade of the 21st century.

Perhaps surprisingly, that prediction does not shift much even if our estimates are a few hundred billion barrels high or low. Craig Bond Hatfield of the University of Toledo, for example, has conducted his own analysis based on a 1991 estimate by the U.S. Geological Survey of 1,550 Gbo remaining—55 percent higher than our figure. Yet he similarly concludes that the world will hit maximum oil production within the next 15 years. John D. Edwards of the University of Colorado published last August one of the most optimistic recent estimates of oil remaining: 2,036 Gbo. (Edwards concedes that the industry has only a 5 percent chance of attaining that very high goal.) Even so, his calculations suggest that conventional oil will top out in 2020.

Smoothing the Peak

Factors other than major economic changes could speed or delay the point at which oil production begins to decline. Three in particular have often led economists and academic geologists to dismiss concerns about future oil production with naive optimism.

First, some argue, huge deposits of oil may lie undetected in far-off corners of the globe. In fact, that is very unlikely. Exploration has pushed the frontiers back so far that only extremely deep water and polar regions remain to be fully tested, and even their prospects are now reasonably well understood. Theoretical advances in geochemistry and geophysics have made it possible to map productive and prospective fields with impressive accuracy. As a result, large tracts can be condemned as barren. Much of the deepwater realm, for example, has been shown to be absolutely nonprospective for geologic reasons.

What about the much touted Caspian Sea deposits? Our models project that oil production from that region will grow until around 2010. We agree with analysts at the USGS World Oil Assessment program and elsewhere who rank the total resources there as roughly equivalent to those of the North Sea—that is, perhaps 50 Gbo but certainly not several hundreds of billions as sometimes reported in the media.

A second common rejoinder is that new technologies have steadily increased the fraction of oil that can be recovered from fields in a basin—the so-called recovery factor. In the 1960s oil companies assumed as a rule of thumb that only 30 percent of the oil in a field was typically recoverable; now they bank on an average of 40 or 50 percent. That progress will continue and will extend global reserves for many years to come, the argument runs.

Of course, advanced technologies will buy a bit more time before production starts to fall [see "Oil Production in the 21st Century," by Roger N. Anderson*]. But most of the apparent improvement in recovery factors is an artifact of reporting. As oil fields grow old, their owners often deploy newer technology to slow their decline. The falloff also allows engineers to gauge the size of the field more accurately and to correct previous underestimation—in particular P90 estimates that by definition were 90 percent likely to be exceeded.

Another reason not to pin too much hope on better recovery is that oil companies routinely count on technological progress when they compute their reserve estimates. In truth, advanced technologies can offer little help in draining the largest basins of oil, those onshore in the Middle East where the oil needs no assistance to gush from the ground.

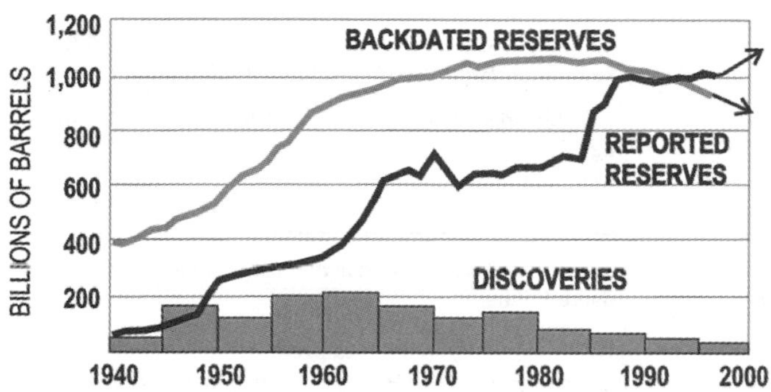

LAURIE GRACE; SOURCE: PETROCONSULTANTS, *OIL AND GAS JOURNAL* AND U.S. GEOLOGICAL SURVEY

GROWTH IN OIL RESERVES since 1980 is an illusion caused by belated corrections to oil-field estimates. Back-dating the revisions to the year in which the fields were discovered reveals that reserves have been falling because of a steady decline in newfound oil (bottom bars).

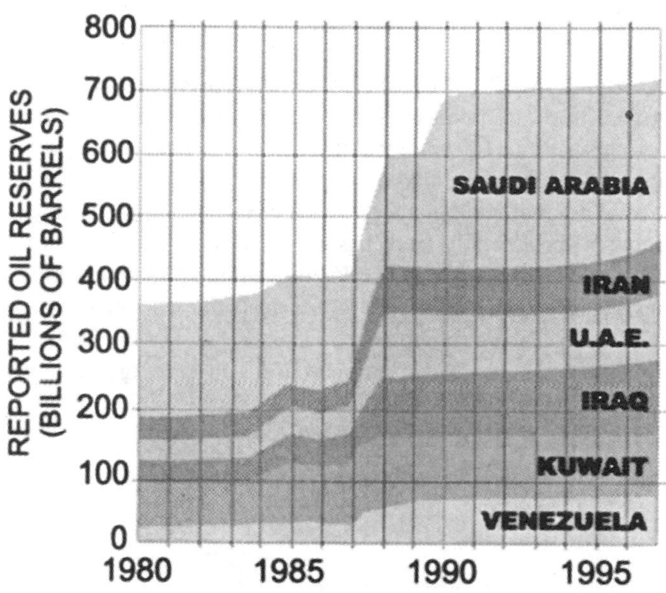

LAURIE GRACE; SOURCE: *OIL AND GAS JOURNAL*

SUSPICIOUS JUMP in reserves reported by six OPEC members added 300 billion barrels of oil to official reserve tallies yet followed no major discovery of new fields.

Last, economists like to point out that the world contains enormous caches of unconventional oil that can substitute for crude oil as soon as the price rises high enough to make them profitable. There is no question that the resources are ample: the Orinoco oil belt in Venezuela has been assessed to contain a staggering 1.2 trillion barrels of the sludge known as heavy oil. Tar sands and shale deposits in Canada and the former Soviet Union may contain the equivalent of more than 300 billion barrels of oil [see "Mining for Oil," by Richard L. George*]. Theoretically, these unconventional oil reserves could quench the world's thirst for liquid fuels as conventional oil passes its prime. But the industry will be hard-pressed for the time and money needed to ramp up production of unconventional oil quickly enough.

Such substitutes for crude oil might also exact a high environmental price. Tar sands typically emerge from strip mines. Extracting oil from these sands and shales creates air pollution. The Orinoco sludge contains heavy metals and sulfur that must be removed. So governments may restrict these industries from growing as fast as they could. In view of these potential obstacles, our skeptical estimate is that only 700 Gbo will be produced from unconventional reserves over the next 60 years.

On the Down Side

Meanwhile global demand for oil is currently rising at more than 2 percent a year. Since 1985, energy use is up about 30 percent in Latin America, 40 percent in Africa and 50 percent in Asia. The Energy Information Administration forecasts that worldwide demand for oil will increase 60 percent (to about 40 Gbo a year) by 2020.

The switch from growth to decline in oil production will thus almost certainly create economic and political tension. Unless alternatives to crude oil quickly prove themselves, the market share of the OPEC states in the Middle East will rise rapidly. Within two years, these nations' share of the global oil business will pass 30 percent, nearing the level reached during the oil price shocks of the 1970s. By 2010 their share will quite probably hit 50 percent.

The world could thus see radical increases in oil prices. That alone might be sufficient to curb demand, flattening production for perhaps 10 years. (Demand fell more than 10 percent after the 1979 shock and took 17 years to recover.) But by 2010 or so, many Middle Eastern nations will themselves be past the midpoint. World production will then have to fall.

With sufficient preparation, however, the transition to the post-oil economy need not be traumatic. If advanced methods of producing liquid fuels from natural gas can be made profitable and scaled up quickly, gas could become the next source of transportation fuel [see "Liquid Fuels from Natural Gas," by Safaa A. Fouda*]. Safer nuclear power, cheaper renewable energy, and oil conservation programs could all help postpone the inevitable decline of conventional oil.

Countries should begin planning and investing now. In November a panel of energy experts appointed by President Bill Clinton strongly urged the administration to increase funding for energy research by $1 billion over the next five years. That is a small step in the right direction, one that must be followed by giant leaps from the private sector.

The world is not running out of oil—at least not yet. What our society does face, and soon, is the end of the abundant and cheap oil on which all industrial nations depend.

The Authors

COLIN J. CAMPBELL and JEAN H. LAHERRÈRE have each worked in the oil industry for more than 40 years. After completing his Ph.D. in geology at the University of Oxford, Campbell worked for Texaco as an exploration geologist and then at Amoco as chief geologist for Ecuador. His decade-long study of global oil-production trends has led to two books and numerous papers. Laherrère's early work on seismic refraction surveys contributed to the discovery of Africa's largest oil field. At Total, a French oil company, he supervised exploration techniques worldwide. Both Campbell and Laherrère are currently associated with Petroconsultants in Geneva.

Further Reading

UPDATED HUBBERT CURVES ANALYZE WORLD OIL SUPPLY. L. F. Ivanhoe in *World Oil*, Vol. 217, No. 11, pages 91–94; November 1996.

THE COMING OIL CRISIS. Colin J. Campbell. Multi-Science Publishing and Petroconsultants, Brentwood, England, 1997.

OIL BACK ON THE GLOBAL AGENDA. Craig Bond Hatfield in *Nature*, Vol. 387, page 121; May 8, 1997.

Editor's note: All of the articles mentioned in this article can be found in *Scientific American,* March 1998.

Gray Dawn: The Global Aging Crisis

Peter G. Peterson

DAUNTING DEMOGRAPHICS

THE LIST of major global hazards in the next century has grown long and familiar. It includes the proliferation of nuclear, biological, and chemical weapons, other types of high-tech terrorism, deadly super-viruses, extreme climate change, the financial, economic, and political aftershocks of globalization, and the violent ethnic explosions waiting to be detonated in today's unsteady new democracies. Yet there is a less-understood challenge—the graying of the developed world's population—that may actually do more to reshape our collective future than any of the above.

Over the next several decades, countries in the developed world will experience an unprecedented growth in the number of their elderly and an unprecedented decline in the number of their youth. The timing and magnitude of this demographic transformation have already been determined. Next century's elderly have already been born and can be counted—and their cost to retirement benefit systems can be projected.

Unlike with global warming, there can be little debate over whether or when global aging will manifest itself. And unlike with other challenges, even the struggle to preserve and strengthen unsteady new democracies, the costs of global aging will be far beyond the means of even the world's wealthiest nations—unless retirement benefit systems are radically reformed. Failure to do so, to prepare early and boldly enough, will spark economic crises that will dwarf the recent meltdowns in Asia and Russia.

How we confront global aging will have vast economic consequences costing quadrillions of dollars over the next century. Indeed, it will greatly influence how we manage, and can afford to manage, the other major challenges that will face us in the future.

For this and other reasons, global aging will become not just the transcendent economic issue of the 21st century, but the transcendent political issue as well. It will dominate and daunt the public-policy agendas of developed countries and force the renegotiation of their social contracts. It will also reshape foreign policy strategies and the geopolitical order.

The United States has a massive challenge ahead of it. The broad outlines can already be seen in the emerging debate over Social Security and Medicare reform. But ominous as the fiscal stakes are in the United States, they loom even larger in Japan and Europe, where populations are aging even faster, birthrates are lower, the influx of young immigrants from developing countries is smaller, public pension benefits are more generous, and private pension systems are weaker.

Aging has become a truly global challenge, and must therefore be given high priority on the global policy agenda. A gray dawn fast approaches. It is time to take an unflinching look at the shape of things to come.

The Floridization of the developed world. Been to Florida lately? You may not have realized it, but the vast concentration of seniors there—nearly 19 percent of the population—represents humanity's future. Today's Florida is a demographic benchmark that every developed nation will soon pass. Italy will hit the mark as early as 2003, followed by Japan in 2005 and Germany in 2006. France and Britain will pass present-day Florida around 2016; the United States and Canada in 2021 and 2023.

Societies much older than any we have ever known. Global life expectancy has grown more in the last fifty years than over the previous five thousand. Until the Industrial Revolution, people aged 65 and over never amounted to more than 2 or 3 percent of the population. In today's developed world, they amount to 14 percent. By the year 2030, they will reach 25 percent and be closing in on 30 in some countries.

An unprecedented economic burden on working-age people. Early in the next century, working-age populations in most developed countries will shrink. Between 2000 and 2010, Japan, for example, will suffer a 25 percent drop in the number of workers under age 30. Today the ratio of working taxpayers to nonworking pensioners in the developed world is around 3:1. By 2030, absent reform, this ratio will fall to 1.5:1, and in some countries, such as Germany and Italy, it will drop all the way down to 1:1 or even lower. While the longevity revolution represents a miraculous triumph of modern medicine and the extra years of life will surely be treasured by the elderly and their families, pension plans and other retirement benefit programs were not designed to provide these billions of extra years of payouts.

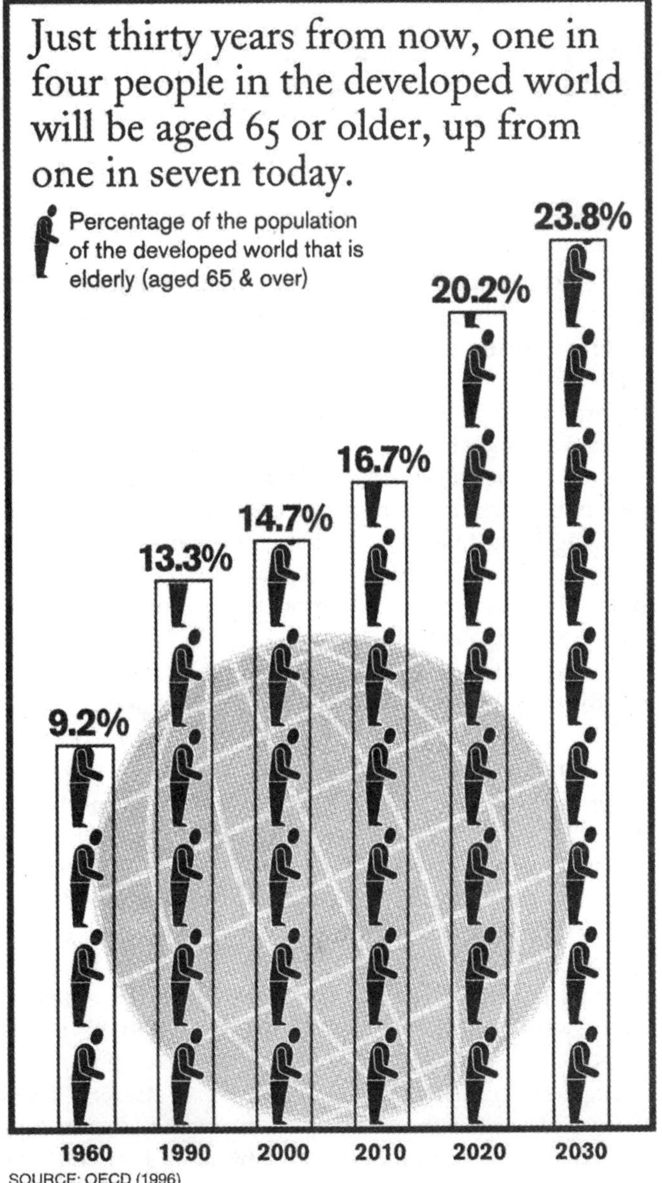

The aging of the aged: the number of "old old" will grow much faster than the number of "young old." The United Nations projects that by 2050, the number of people aged 65 to 84 worldwide will grow from 400 million to 1.3 billion (a threefold increase), while the number of people aged 85 and over will grow from 26 million to 175 million (a sixfold increase)—and the number aged 100 and over from 135,000 to 2.2 million (a sixteenfold increase). The "old old" consume far more health care than the "young old"—about two to three times as much. For nursing-home care, the ratio is roughly 20:1. Yet little of this cost is figured in the official projections of future public expenditures.

Falling birthrates will intensify the global aging trend. As life spans increase, fewer babies are being born. As recently as the late 1960s, the worldwide total fertility rate (that is, the average number of lifetime births per woman) stood at about 5.0, well within the historical range. Then came a behavioral revolution, driven by growing affluence, urbanization, feminism, rising female participation in the workforce, new birth control technologies, and legalized abortion. The result: an unprecedented and unexpected decline in the global fertility rate to about 2.7—a drop fast approaching the replacement rate of 2.1 (the rate required merely to maintain a constant population). In the developed world alone, the average fertility rate has plummeted to 1.6. Since 1995, Japan has had fewer births annually than in any year since 1899. In Germany; where the rate has fallen to 1.3, fewer babies are born each year than in Nepal, which has a population only one-quarter as large.

A shrinking population in an aging developed world. Unless their fertility rates rebound, the total populations of western Europe and Japan will shrink to about one-half of their current size before the end of the next century. In 1950, 7 of the 12 most populous nations were in the developed world: the United States, Russia, Japan, Germany, France, Italy, and the United Kingdom. The United Nations projects that by 2050, only the United States will remain on the list. Nigeria, Pakistan, Ethiopia, Congo, Mexico, and the Philippines will replace the others. But since developing countries are also experiencing a drop in fertility, many are now actually aging faster than the typical developed country. In France, for example, it took over a century for the elderly to grow from 7 to 14 percent of the population. South Korea, Taiwan, Singapore, and China are projected to traverse that distance in only 25 years.

From worker shortage to rising immigration pressure. Perhaps the most predictable consequence of the gap in fertility and population growth rates between developed and developing countries will be the rising demand for immigrant workers in older and wealthier societies facing labor shortages. Immigrants are typically young and tend to bring with them the family practices of their native culture—including higher fertility rates. In many European countries, non-European foreigners already make up roughly 10 percent of the population. This includes 10 million to 13 million Muslims, nearly all of whom are working-age or younger. In Germany, foreigners will make up 30 percent of the total population by 2030, and over half the population of major cities like Munich and Frankfurt. Global aging and attendant labor shortages will therefore ensure that immigration remains a major issue in developed countries for decades to come. Culture wars could erupt over the balkanization of language and religion; electorates could divide along ethnic lines; and émigré leaders could sway foreign policy.

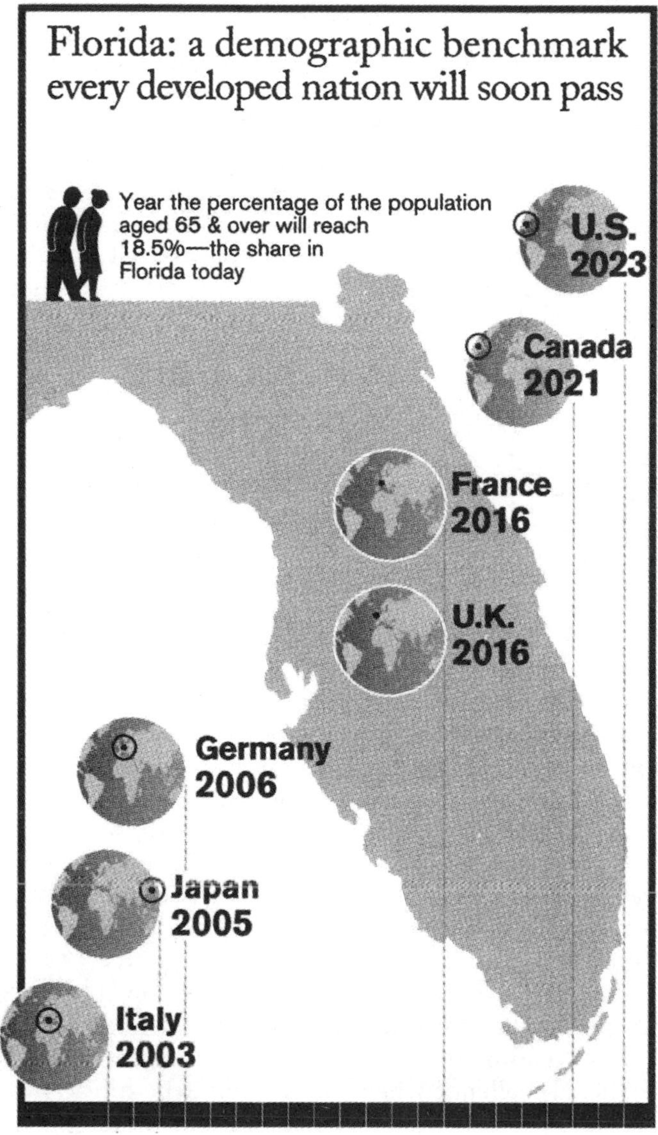

SOURCE: OECD (1996); author's calculations

GRAYING MEANS PAYING

OFFICIAL PROJECTIONS suggest that within 30 years, developed countries will have to spend at least an extra 9 to 16 percent of GDP simply to meet their old-age benefit promises. The unfunded liabilities for pensions (that is, benefits already earned by today's workers for which nothing has been saved) are already almost $35 trillion. Add in health care, and the total jumps to at least twice as much. At minimum, the global aging issue thus represents, to paraphrase the old quiz show, a $64 trillion question hanging over the developed world's future.

To pay for promised benefits through increased taxation is unfeasible. Doing so would raise the total tax burden by an unthinkable 25 to 40 percent of every worker's taxable wages—in countries where payroll tax rates sometimes already exceed 40 percent. To finance the costs of these benefits by borrowing would be just as disastrous. Governments would run unprecedented deficits that would quickly consume the savings of the developed world.

And the $64 trillion estimate is probably low. It likely underestimates future growth in longevity and health care costs and ignores the negative effects on the economy of more borrowing, higher interest rates, more taxes, less savings, and lower rates of productivity and wage growth.

There are only a handful of exceptions to these nightmarish forecasts. In Australia, total public retirement costs as a share of GDP are expected to rise only slightly, and they may even decline in Britain and Ireland. This fiscal good fortune is not due to any special demographic trend, but to timely policy reforms—including tight limits on public health spending, modest pension benefit formulas, and new personally owned savings programs that allow future public benefits to shrink as a share of average wages. This approach may yet be emulated elsewhere.

Failure to respond to the aging challenge will destabilize the global economy, straining financial and political institutions around the world. Consider Japan, which today runs a large current account surplus making up well over half the capital exports of all the surplus nations combined. Then imagine a scenario in which Japan leaves its retirement programs and fiscal policies on autopilot. Thirty years from now, under this scenario, Japan will be importing massive amounts of capital to prevent its domestic economy from collapsing under the weight of benefit outlays. This will require a huge reversal in global capital flows. To get some idea of the potential volatility, note that over the next decade, Japan's annual pension deficit is projected to grow to roughly 3 times the size of its recent and massive capital exports to the United States; by 2030, the annual deficit is expected to be 15 times as large. Such reversals will cause wildly fluctuating interest and exchange rates, which may in turn short-circuit financial institutions and trigger a serious market crash.

As they age, some nations will do little to change course, while others may succeed in boosting their national savings rate, at least temporarily, through a combination of fiscal restraint and household thrift. Yet this too could result in a volatile disequilibrium in supply and demand for global capital. Such imbalance could wreak havoc with international institutions such as the European Union.

In recent years, the EU has focused on monetary union, launched a single currency (the euro), promoted cross-border labor mobility, and struggled to harmonize fiscal, monetary, and trade policies. European leaders expect to have their hands full smoothing out differences between members of the Economic and Monetary Union (EMU)—from the timing of their business cycles to the diversity of their credit institutions and political cultures. For this reason, they established official public debt and deficit criteria (three percent of GDP for EMU membership) in order to discourage maverick nations from placing undue economic burdens on fellow members. But the EU has yet to face up to the biggest challenge to its future viability: the likelihood of varying national responses to the fiscal pressures of demographic aging. Indeed, the EU does not even include unfunded pension liabilities in the official EMU debt and deficit criteria—which is like measuring icebergs without looking beneath the water line.

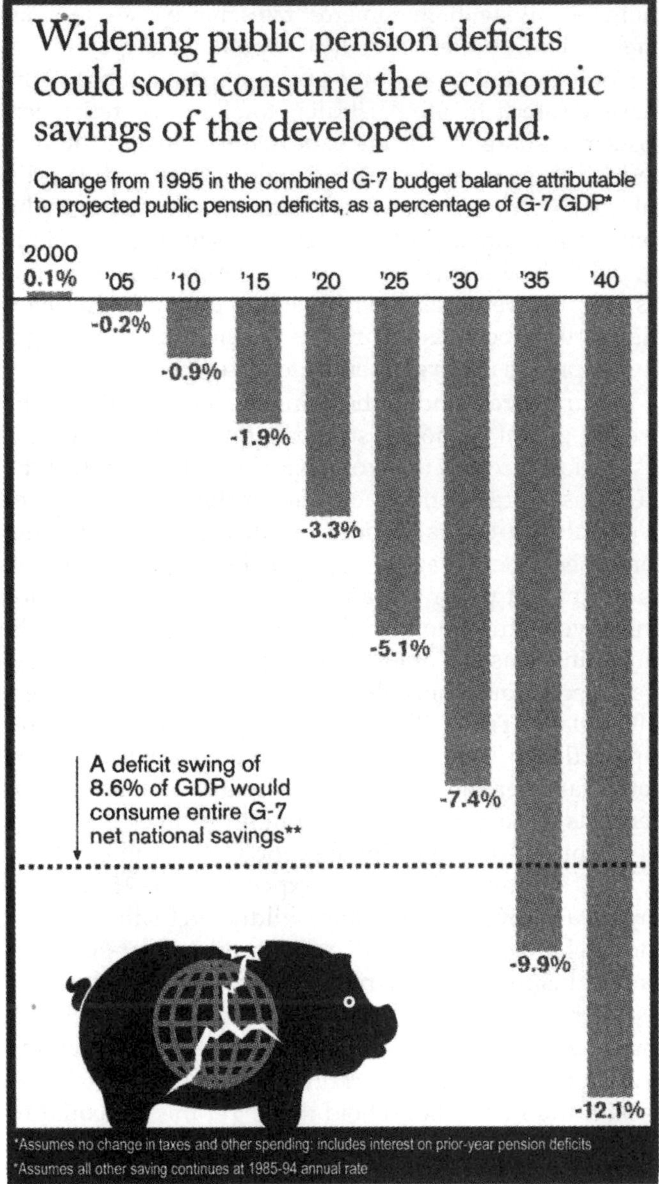

SOURCE: OECD (1996); author's calculations

When these liabilities come due and move from "off the books" to "on the books," the EU will, under current constraints, be required to penalize EMU members that exceed the three percent deficit cap. As a recent IMF report concludes, "over time it will become increasingly difficult for most countries to meet the deficit ceiling without comprehensive social security reform." The EU could, of course, retain members by raising the deficit limit. But once the floodgates are opened, national differences in fiscal policy may mean that EMU members rack up deficits at different rates. The European Central Bank, the euro, and a half-century of progress toward European unity could be lost as a result.

The total projected cost of the age wave is so staggering that we might reasonably conclude it could never be paid. After all, these numbers are projections, not predictions. They tell us what is likely to happen if current policy remains unchanged, not whether it is likely or even possible for this condition to hold. In all probability, economies would implode and governments would collapse before the projections ever materialize. But this is exactly why we must focus on these projections, for they call attention to the paramount question: Will we change course sooner, when we still have time to control our destiny and reach a more sustainable path? Or later, after unsustainable economic damage and political and social trauma cause a wrenching upheaval?

A GRAYING NEW WORLD ORDER

WHILE THE fiscal and economic consequences of global aging deserve serious discussion, other important consequences must also be examined. At the top of the list is the impact of the age wave on foreign policy and international security.

Will the developed world be able to maintain its security commitments? One need not be a Nobel laureate in economics to understand that a country's GDP growth is the product of workforce and productivity growth. If workforces shrink rapidly, GDP may drop as well, since labor productivity may not rise fast enough to compensate for the loss of workers. At least some developed countries are therefore likely to experience a long-term decline in total production of goods and services—that is, in real GDP.

Economists correctly focus on the developed world's GDP per capita, which can rise even as its workforce and total GDP shrink. But anything with a fixed cost becomes a national challenge when that cost has to be spread over a smaller population and funded out of shrinking revenues. National defense is the classic example. The West already faces grave threats from rogue states armed with biological and chemical arsenals, terrorists capable of hacking into vulnerable computer systems, and proliferating nuclear weapons. None of these external dangers will shrink to accommodate our declining workforce or GDP.

Leading developed countries will no doubt need to spend as much or more on defense and international investments as they do today. But the age wave will put immense pressure on governments to cut back. Falling birthrates, together with a rising demand for young workers, will also inevitably mean smaller armies. And how many parents will allow their only child to go off to war?

With fewer soldiers, total capability can be maintained only by large increases in technology and weaponry. But boosting military productivity creates a Catch-22. For how will governments get the budget resources to pay for high-tech weaponry if the senior-weighted electorate demands more money for high-tech medicine? Even if military capital is successfully substituted for military labor, the deployment options may be dangerously limited. Developed nations facing a threat may feel they have only two extreme (but relatively inexpensive) choices: a low-level response (antiterrorist strikes and cruise-missile diplomacy) or a high-level response (an all-out attack with strategic weapons).

Will Young/Old become the next North/South fault line? Historically, the richest industrial powers have been growing, capital-exporting, philanthropic giants that project their power and mores around the world. The richest industrial powers of the future may be none of these things. Instead, they may be demographically imploding, capital-importing, fiscally starving neutrals who twist and turn to avoid expensive international entanglements. A quarter-century from now, will the divide between today's "rich" and "poor" nations be better described as a divide between growth and decline, surplus and deficit, expansion and retreat, future and past? By the mid-2020s, will the contrast between North and South be better described as a contrast between Young and Old?

If today's largest low-income societies, especially China, set up fully funded retirement systems to prepare for their own future aging, they may well produce ever larger capital surpluses. As a result, today's great powers could someday depend on these surpluses to keep themselves financially afloat. But how should we expect these new suppliers of capital to use their newly acquired leverage? Will they turn the tables in international diplomacy? Will the Chinese, for example, someday demand that the United States shore up its Medicare system the way Americans once demanded that China reform its human rights policies as a condition for foreign assistance?

As Samuel Huntington recently put it, "the juxtaposition of a rapidly growing people of one culture and a slowly growing or stagnant people of another culture generates pressure for economic and/or political adjustments in both societies." Countries where populations are still exploding rank high on any list of potential trouble spots, whereas the countries most likely to lose population—and to see a weakening of their commitment to expensive defense and global security programs—are the staunchest friends of liberal democracy.

In many parts of the developing world, the total fertility rate remains very high (7.3 in the Gaza Strip versus 2.7 in Israel), most people are very young (49 percent under age 15 in Uganda), and the population is growing very rapidly (doubling every 26 years in Iran). These areas also tend to be the poorest, most rapidly urbanizing, most institutionally unstable—and most likely to fall under the sway of rogue leadership. They are the same societies that spawned most of the military strongmen and terrorists who have bedeviled the United States and Europe in recent decades. The Pentagon's long-term planners predict that outbreaks of regional anarchy will occur more frequently early in the next century. To pinpoint when and where, they track what they call "youth bulges" in the world's poorest urban centers.

Is demography destiny, after all? Is the rapidly aging developed world fated to decline? Must it cede leadership to younger and faster-growing societies? For the answer to be no, the developed world must redefine that role around a new mission. And what better way to do so than to show the younger, yet more tradition-bound, societies—which will soon age in their turn—how a world dominated by the old can still accommodate the young.

WHOSE WATCH IS IT, ANYWAY?

FROM PRIVATE discussions with leaders of major economies, I can attest that they are well briefed on the stunning demographic trends that lie ahead. But so far they have responded with paralysis rather than action. Hardly any country is doing what it should to prepare. Margaret Thatcher confesses that she repeatedly tried to raise the aging issue at G-7 summit meetings. Yet her fellow leaders stalled. "Of course aging is a profound challenge," they replied, "but it doesn't hit until early in the next century—after my watch."

Americans often fault their leaders for not acknowledging long-term problems and for not facing up to silent and slow-motion challenges. But denial is not a peculiarly American syndrome. In 1995, Silvio Berlusconi's *Forza Italia* government was buffeted by a number of political storms, all of which it weathered—except for pension reform, which shattered the coalition. That same year, the Dutch parliament was forced to repeal a recent cut in retirement benefits after a strong Pension Party, backed by the elderly, emerged from nowhere to punish the reformers. In 1996, the French government's modest proposal to trim pensions triggered strikes and even riots. A year later the Socialists overturned the ruling government at the polls.

Each country's response, or nonresponse, is colored by its political and cultural institutions. In Europe, where the welfare state is more expansive, voters can hardly imagine that the promises made by previous generations of politicians can no longer be kept. They therefore support leaders, unions, and party coalitions that make generous unfunded pensions the very cornerstone of social democracy. In the United States, the problem has less to do with welfare-state dependence than the uniquely American notion that every citizen has personally earned and is therefore entitled to whatever benefits government happens to have promised.

How governments ultimately prepare for global aging will also depend on how global aging itself reshapes politics. Already some of the largest and most strident interest groups in the United States are those that claim to speak for senior citizens, such as the American Association of Retired Persons, with its 33 million members, 1,700 paid employees, ten times that many trained volunteers, and an annual budget of $5.5 billion.

Senior power is rising in Europe, where it manifests itself less through independent senior organizations than in labor unions and (often union-affiliated) political parties that formally adopt pro-retiree platforms. Could age-based political parties be the wave of the future? In Russia, although the Communist resurgence is usually ascribed to nationalism and nostalgia, a demographic bias is at work as well. The Communists have repositioned themselves as the party of retirees, who are aggrieved by how runaway inflation has slashed the real value of their pensions. In the 1995 Duma elections, over half of those aged 55 and older voted Communist, versus only ten percent of those under age 40.

Commenting on how the old seem to trump the young at every turn, Lee Kuan Yew once proposed that each taxpaying worker be given two votes to balance the lobbying clout of each retired elder. No nation, not even Singapore, is likely to enact Lee's suggestion. But the question must be asked: With ever more electoral power flowing into the hands of elders, what can motivate political leaders to act on behalf of the long-term future of the young?

A handful of basic strategies, all of them difficult, might enable countries to overcome the economic and political challenges of an aging society: extending work lives and postponing retirement; enlarging the workforce through immigration and increased labor force participation; encouraging higher fertility and investing more in the education and productivity of future workers; strengthening intergenerational bonds of responsibility within families; and targeting government-paid benefits to those most in need while encouraging and even requiring workers to save for their own retirements. All of these strategies unfortunately touch raw nerves—by amending existing social contracts, by violating cultural expectations, or by offending entrenched ideologies.

TOWARD A SUMMIT ON GLOBAL AGING

ALL COUNTRIES would be well served by collective deliberation over the choices that lie ahead. For that reason I propose a Summit on Global Aging. Few venues are as well covered by the media as a global summit. Leaders have been willing to convene summits to discuss global warming. Why not global aging, which will hit us sooner and with greater certainty? By calling attention to what is at stake, a global aging summit could shift the public discussion into fast forward. That alone would be a major contribution. The summit process would also help provide an international framework for voter education, collective burden-sharing, and global leadership. Once national constituencies begin to grasp the magnitude of the global aging challenge, they will be more inclined to take reform seriously. Once governments get into the habit of cooperating on what in fact is a global challenge, individual leaders will not need to incur the economic and political risks of acting alone.

This summit should launch a new multilateral initiative to lend the global aging agenda a visible institutional presence: an Agency on Global Aging. Such an agency would examine how developed countries should reform their retirement systems and how developing countries should properly set them up in the first place. Perhaps the most basic question is how to weigh the interests and well-being of one generation against the next. Then there is the issue of defining the safety-net standard of social adequacy. Is there a minimum level of retirement income that should be the right of every citizen? To what extent should retirement security be left to people's own resources? When should government pick up the pieces, and how can it do so without discouraging responsible behavior? Should government compel people in advance to make better life choices, say, by enacting a mandatory savings program?

Another critical task is to integrate research about the age wave's timing, magnitude, and location. Fiscal projections should be based on assumptions that are both globally consistent and—when it comes to longevity, fertility, and health care costs—more realistic than those now in use. Still to be determined: Which countries will be hit earliest and hardest? What might happen to interest rates, exchange rates, and cross-border capital flows under various political and fiscal scenarios?

But this is not all the proposed agency could do. It could continue to build global awareness, publish a high-visibility annual report that would update these calculations, and ensure that the various regular multilateral summits (from the G-7 to ASEAN and APEC) keep global aging high on their discussion agendas. It could give coherent voice to the need for timely policy reform around the world, hold up as models whatever major steps have been taken to reduce unfunded liabilities, help design funded benefit programs, and promote generational equity. On these and many other issues, nations have much to learn from each other, just as those who favor mandatory funded pension plans are already benefiting from the examples of Chile, Britain, Austria, and Singapore.

Global aging could trigger a crisis that engulfs the world economy. This crisis may even threaten democracy itself. By making tough choices now world leaders would demonstrate that they genuinely care about the future, that they understand this unique opportunity for young and old nations to work together, and that they comprehend the price of freedom. The gray dawn approaches. We must establish new ways of thinking and new institutions to help us prepare for a much older world.

PETER G. PETERSON is the author of *Gray Dawn: How the Coming Age Wave Will Transform America—and the World*. He is Chairman of The Blackstone Group, a private investment bank, Chairman of The Institute for International Economics, Deputy Chairman of The Federal Reserve Bank of New York, Co-founder and President of The Concord Coalition, and Chairman of The Council on Foreign Relations.

A rare and precious resource

Fresh water is a scarce commodity. Since it's impossible to increase supply, demand and waste must be reduced. But how?

Houria Tazi Sadeq*

Water is a bond between human beings and nature. It is ever-present in our daily lives and in our imaginations. Since the beginning of time, it has shaped extraordinary social institutions, and access to it has provoked many conflicts.

But most of the world's people, who have never gone short of water, take its availability for granted. Industrialists, farmers and ordinary consumers blithely go on wasting it. These days, though, supplies are diminishing while demand is soaring. Everyone knows that the time has come for attitudes to change.

Few people are aware of the true extent of fresh water scarcity. Many are fooled by the huge expanses of blue that feature on maps of the world. They do not know that 97.5 per cent of the planet's water is salty—and that most of the world's fresh water—the remaining 2.5 per cent—is unusable: 70 per cent of it is frozen in the icecaps of Antarctica and Greenland and almost all the rest exists in the form of soil humidity or in water tables which are too deep to be tapped. In all, barely one per cent of fresh water—0.007 per cent of all the water in the world, is easily accessible.

Sharper vision

Desalinization, state of the art irrigation systems, techniques to harvest fog—technological solutions like these are widely hailed as the answer to water scarcity. But in searching for the "miracle" solution, hydrologists and policy-makers often lose sight of the question: how can we use and safeguard this vital resource? UNESCO's International Hydrological Programme (IHP) takes an interdisciplinary approach to this question. On the one hand, IHP brings together scientists from 150 countries to develop global and regional assessments of water supplies and, for example, inventories of groundwater contamination. At the same time, the programme focuses on the cultural and socio-economic factors involved in effective policy-making. For example, groundwater supplies in Gaza (Palestinian Authority) are coming under serious strain, partly because of new business investment in the area. IHP has a two-pronged approach. First, train and help local hydrologists accurately assess the supplies. Second, work with government officials to set up a licensing system for pumping groundwater.

By joining forces with the World Water Council, an international think-tank on hydrological issues, IHP is now hosting one of the most ambitious projects in the field: World Water Vision. Hundreds of thousands of hydrologists, policy-makers, farmers, business leaders and ordinary citizens will take part in public consultations to develop regional scenarios as to how key issues like contamination will evolve in the next 25 years.

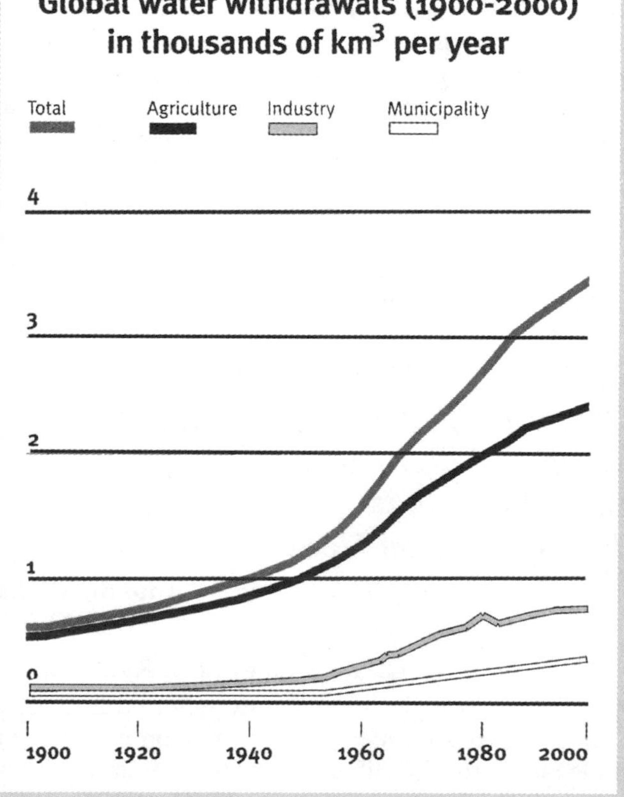

- A person can survive for about a month without food, but only about a week without water.
- About 70 per cent of human skin consists of water.
- Women and children in most developing regions travel an average of 10 to 15 kilometres each day to get water.
- Some 34,000 people die a day from water-related diseases like diarrhoea and parasitic worms. This is the equivalent to casualties from 100 jumbo jets crashing every day!
- A person needs five litres of water a day for drinking and cooking and another 25 litres for personal hygiene.
- The average Canadian family uses 350 litres of water a day. In Africa, the average is 20 liters and in Europe, 165 litres.
- A dairy cow needs to drink about four litres of water a day to produce one litre of milk.
- A tomato is about 95 per cent water.
- About 9,400 litres of water are used to make four car tires.
- A bout 1.4 billion litres of water are needed to produce a day's supply of the world's newsprint.

Sources: International Development Initiative of McGill University, Canada; Saint Paul Water Utility, Minnesota, USA

Lack of access to safe water and basic sanitation, by region, 1990–1996 (percent)

Region	People without access to safe water	People without access to basic sanitation
Arab States	**21**	**30**
Sub-Saharan Africa	**48**	**55**
South-East Asia and the Pacific	**35**	**45**
Latin America and the Caribbean	**23**	**29**
East Asia	**32**	**73**
East Asia (excluding China)	**13**	**–**
South Asia	**18**	**64**
Developing countries	**29**	**58**
Least developed countries	**43**	**64**

Source: *Human Development Report 1998*, New York, UNDP

Periods of complete renewal of the earth's water resources

Kinds of water	Period of renewal
Biological water	**several hours**
Atmospheric water	**8 days**
Water in river channels	**16 days**
Soil moisture	**1 year**
Water in swamps	**5 years**
Water storages in lakes	**17 years**
Groundwater	**1400 years**
Mountain glaciers	**1600 years**
World ocean	**2500 years**
Polar ice floes	**9700 years**

Source: *World Water Balance and Water Resources of the Earth*, Gidrometeoizdat, Leningrad, 1974 (in Russian)

Over the past century, population growth and human activity have caused this precious resource to dwindle. Between 1900 and 1995, world demand for water increased more than sixfold—compared with a threefold increase in world population. The ratio between the stock of fresh water and world population seems to show that in overall terms there is enough water to go round. But in the most vulnerable regions, an estimated 460 million people (8 per cent of the world's population) are short of water, and another quarter of the planet's inhabitants are heading for the same fate. Experts say that if nothing is done, two-thirds of humanity will suffer from a moderate to severe lack of water by the year 2025.

The water from the fountain glides,
flows and dreams as,
almost dumb, it
licks the mossy stone.

Antonio Machado
(1875–1939), Spain

Inequalities in the availability of water—sometimes even within a single country—are reflected in huge differences in consumption levels. A person living in rural Madagascar uses 10 litres a day, the minimum for survival, while a French person uses 150 litres and an American as many as 425.

Scarcity is just one part of the problem. Water quality is also declining alarmingly. In some areas, contamination levels are so high that water can no longer be used even for industrial purposes. There are many reasons for this—untreated sewage, chemical waste, fuel leakages, dumped garbage, contamination of soil by chemicals used by farmers. The worldwide extent of such pollution is hard to assess because data are lacking for several countries. But some figures give an idea of the problem. It is thought for example that 90 per cent of waste water in developing countries is released without any kind of treatment.

Things are especially bad in cities, where water demand is exploding. For the first time in human history, there will soon be more people living in cities than in the

A thirsty planet

We now have less than half the amount of water available per capita than we did 50 years ago. In 1950, world reserves, (after accounting for agricultural, industrial and domestic uses) amounted to 16.8 thousand cubic metres per person. Today, global reserves have dropped to 7.3 thousand cubic metres and are expected to fall to 4.8 thousand in just 25 years.

Scientists have developed many ways of measuring supplies and evaluating water scarcity. In the maps at right, "catastrophic" levels mean that reserves are unlikely to sustain a population in the event of a crisis like drought. Low supplies refer to levels which put in danger industrial development or ability to feed a population.

Just 50 years ago, not a country in the world faced catastrophic water supply levels. Today, about 35 per cent of the population lives under these conditions. By 2025, about two-thirds will have to cope with low if not catastrophic reserves. In contrast, "water rich" regions and countries—such as northern Europe, Canada, almost everywhere in South America, Central Africa, the Far East and Oceania—will continue to enjoy ample reserves.

The sharp declines reflect the soaring water demands of growing populations, agricultural needs and industrialization. In addition, nature has been far from even-handed. More than 40 per cent of the water in rivers, reservoirs and lakes is concentrated in just six countries: Brazil, Russia, Canada, the United States, China and India. Meanwhile just two per cent of river, reservoir and lake water is found in about 40 per cent of the world's land mass.

As a result, in 2025 Europe and the United States will have half the per capita reserves they did in 1950, while Asia and Latin America will have just a quarter of what they previously enjoyed. But the real drama is likely to hit Africa and the Middle East, where available supplies by 2025 may be only an eighth of what they were in 1950.

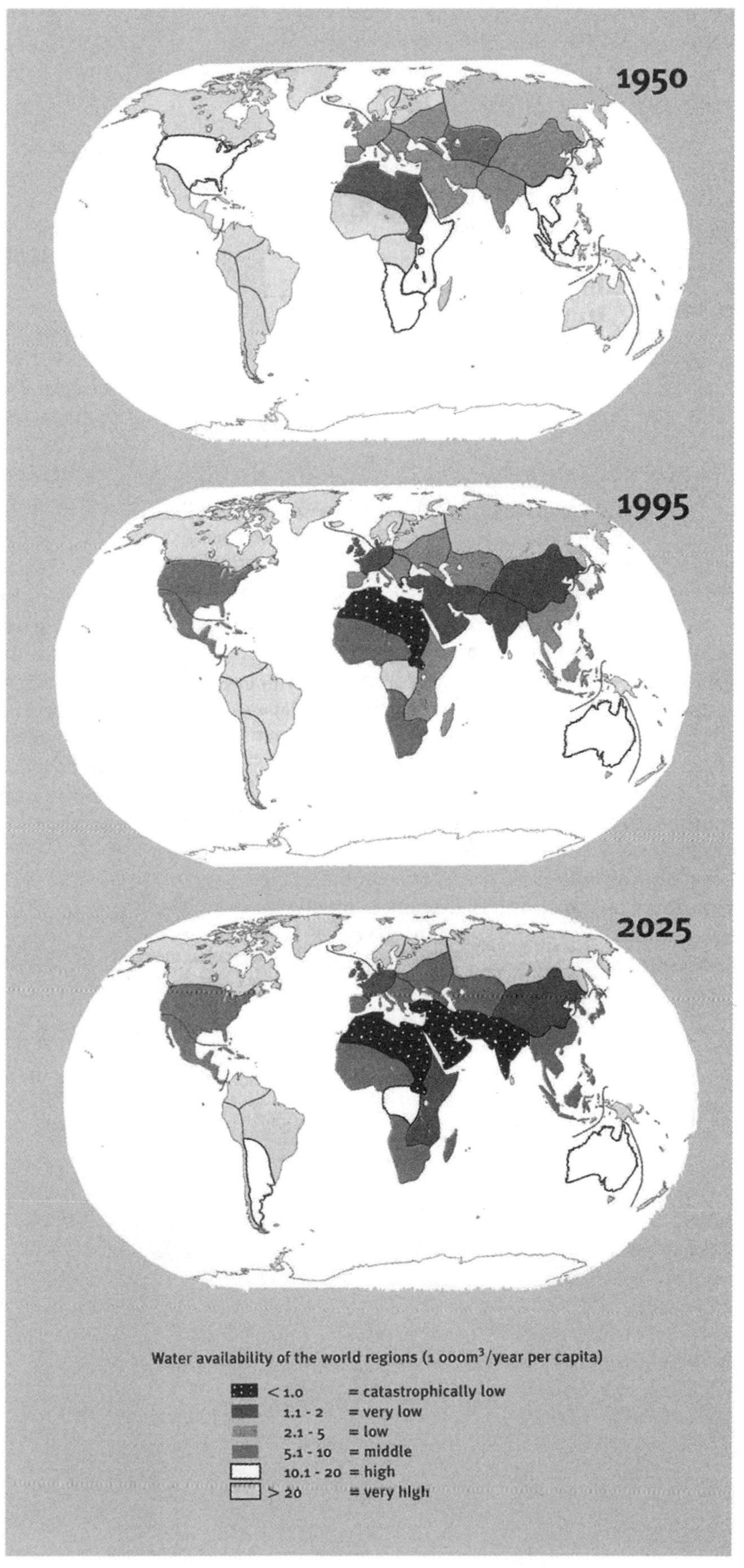

countryside and so water consumption will continue to increase. Soaring urbanization will sharpen the rivalry between the different kinds of water users.

Curbing the explosion in demand

Today, farming uses 69 per cent of the water consumed in the world, industry 23 per cent and households 8 per cent. In developing countries, agriculture uses as much as 80 per cent. The needs of city-dwellers, industry and tourists are expected to increase rapidly, at least as much as the need to produce more farm products to feed the planet. The problem of increasing water supply has long been seen as a technical one, calling for technical solutions such as building more dams and desalination plants. Wild ideas like towing chunks of icebergs from the poles have even been mooted.

But today, technical solutions are reaching their limits. Economic and socio-ecological arguments are levelled against building new dams, for example: dams are costing more and more because the best sites have already been used, and they take millions of people out of their environment and upset ecosystems. As a result, twice as many dams were built on average between 1951 and 1977 than during the past decade, according to the US environmental research body Worldwatch Institute.

Hydrologists and engineers have less and less room for manoeuvre, but a new consensus with new actors is taking shape. Since supply can no longer be expanded—or only at prohibitive cost for many countries—the explosion in demand must be curbed along with wasteful practices. An estimated 60 per cent of the water used in irrigation is lost through inefficient systems, for example.

Economists have plunged into the debate on water and made quite a few waves. To obtain "rational use" of water, i.e. avoiding waste and maintaining quality, they say consumers must be made to pay for it. Out of the question, reply those in favour of free water, which some cultures regard as "a gift from heaven." And what about the poor, ask the champions of human rights and the right to water? Other important and prickly questions being asked by decisionmakers are how to calculate the "real price" of water and who should organize its sale.

The state as mediator

The principle of free water is being challenged. For many people, water has become a commodity to be bought and sold. But management of this shared resource cannot be left exclusively to market forces. Many elements of civil society—NGOs, researchers, community groups—are campaigning for the cultural and social aspects of water management to be taken into account.

Even the World Bank, the main advocate of water privatization, is cautious on this point. It recognizes the value of the partnerships between the public and private sectors which have sprung up in recent years. Only the state seems to be in a position to ensure that practices are fair and to mediate between the parties involved—consumer groups, private firms and public bodies. At any rate, water regulation and management systems need to be based on other than purely financial criteria. If they aren't, hundreds of millions of people will have no access to it.

---

*Moroccan jurist, president of the Maghreb–Machrek Water Union, vice-president of the International Water Secretariat

Reprinted with permission from *The Unesco Courier*, February 1999, pp. 18–21.

Forest 'Sinks' as a Tool for Climate-Change Policymaking

A Look at the Advantages and Challenges

Forests can trap or "sink" large amounts of atmospheric carbon, believed to be a primary cause of global warming. Scientists are now looking at this natural process as a low-cost mitigation strategy that will buy humanity a few decades to make more fundamental changes. But as a policy tool, forest sinks pose implementation challenges that will require planning and diplomacy to resolve.

By Roger A. Sedjo

The degree to which natural processes can mitigate the build-up of atmospheric carbon has generated considerable debate among the countries that have been drafting the detailed rules to implement the Kyoto Protocol, the international climate change treaty. While the Kyoto process may now collapse following the withdrawal of support by the United States, the concept of forest sinks offers advantages that are likely to make it important in any successor policy to address climate change. Since President Bush has also moved away from support of caps on carbon dioxide (CO_2) emissions because of his concerns about energy supply, this could mean that sinks are all the more important, particularly in the early phases of any long-term comprehensive carbon mitigation plan.

The fundamental science of carbon sinks is well understood—biological growth binds carbon in the cells of trees and other plants while releasing oxygen into the atmosphere, through the process of photosynthesis. Ecosystems with greater biomass divert more carbon dioxide (CO_2) from Earth's atmosphere and sequester it; forests in particular can absorb large amounts of carbon. Under the Kyoto Protocol, a forest is a carbon sink and a new or expanded forest is allowed to generate credits for removing carbon from the atmosphere.

The most recent round of Kyoto Protocol negotiations, held last November in The Hague, came to a standstill in part because a compromise over carbon sinks failed. American and European negotiators could not reach agreement on the extent to which carbon captured in biological sinks would be given credit in meeting country carbon-reduction targets as agreed to earlier at Kyoto.

At first glance, the idea of providing carbon credits for forest sinks sounds easy to implement, but a number of questions have been raised:

- Should existing forests count?
- Is there an agreed measure of absorption?
- How long will it take for a newly planted forest to start absorbing CO_2, and at what rate?
- Should a country receive CO_2 credits if it develops forests in a country other than its own?
- What are the politics of sinks?
- What are the economics of sinks?

Some experts claim that there seem to be no precise answers to these and other questions about forest sinks. (It's important to point out that a substantial amount of carbon is sequestered in the oceans as well as modest amounts in soil.) So, in the context of strategy to control climate change, how important is the sink issue and what compromises may be necessary to prevent sinks from fouling up the grand design?

Let us address these questions one at a time.

Should existing forests count?

In general, the view is that existing forests have inadvertently served as sinks and thus should not count under the Kyoto Protocol. However, there may be some exceptions to this rule. For example, it may be sensible to provide carbon credits for protecting forests that would otherwise be converted to other uses, such as agriculture. In many cases, the value of the carbon credits would exceed the value of the land in nonforest uses. In addition, if existing forests continue to grow and sequester additional carbon, particularly as a result of forest management, then one can argue that credits should be provided for the additional carbon. This is sometimes referred to as a "baseline" problem—deciding which measures are considered over and above what would have happened anyway.

Is there an agreed measure of absorption?

Yes. The amount of carbon held in the forest depends on the amount of dry biomass there. Most developed countries have fairly accurate forest inventories that can provide the baseline for estimating the forest biomass. About 50% of the dry weight of the biomass will be carbon. Different tree and plant species have different densities, but these differences are well known, and forest biomass is easy to estimate by using sampling techniques.

How long will it take for a newly planted forest to start absorbing CO_2, and at what rate?

The rate of carbon absorption depends on the amount of dry biomass in the forest. Trees typically grow slowly at first, then at an increasing rate until growth begins to level off as they approach maturity. The growth pattern depends on species, climatic conditions, soil fertility, and other factors. In some parts of the world, certain species grow quickly and can accumulate substantial biomass in less than a decade.

Should a country receive CO2 credits if it develops forests in a country other than its own?

Forest growth is much more rapid in some regions than in others. Resource conservation would dictate that most of the carbon-sequestering forests should be located in regions where carbon can be absorbed efficiently. Thus, it is sensible for one country to invest in the forests of another—with permission, of course—as a way to earn carbon credits. Additionally, such an approach may transfer large amounts of capital from developed countries to developing countries, thus promoting their economic development.

What are the politics of sinks?

Forest sinks appear to offer the potential of low-cost carbon absorption. However, not all countries are equally blessed with these resources. Much of Europe consists of even-aged growth in what are called "regulated" forests. The expected potential for additional forest growth to absorb carbon is limited. In fact, many observers argue that European forests are likely to experience some decline over the early decades of the twenty-first century. Thus, it is not surprising that European countries would resist the inclusion of forest sinks for carbon monitoring under the Kyoto Protocol.

By contrast, many countries outside of Europe, including the United States, expect their stock of managed forests to increase during the first decades of the twenty-first century. The United States, Australia, Canada, and Japan are keen to use forest sinks to meet any climate treaty obligations. Many environmental groups appear to believe that meeting carbon targets should be painful and thus view forest sinks as insufficiently austere. However, other environmental groups view carbon credits from forests as offering the potential to help protect tropical forests from destruction and from forestland conversion to agricultural and other uses.

What are the economics of forest sinks?

Most studies indicate that the costs associated with sinks appear to be modest compared with the costs of making the necessary changes in the energy sector. Forest sinks often have other associated benefits, such as erosion reduction, watershed protection, and biodiversity protection of existing native forests. However, their potential to offset carbon emissions is limited. At best, the potential of forests and other terrestrial systems that act as carbon sinks to offset emissions is probably not more than one-third of current net emissions.

Additionally, as the volume of forest sinks increases across the globe, their costs will rise and their additional potential will decline. Thus, perhaps the best way to view sinks is as a temporary low-cost mitigation strategy that can buy humanity three to five decades to make more fundamental adjustments.

Looking Ahead

Carbon sinks appear to offer substantial potential to assist humankind in addressing the challenge posed by climate change but they are more than forest ecosystems, however. Grasslands, wetlands, and agriculture all offer the potential to absorb carbon. Although grasslands do not build up a large aboveground mass like forests do, they are effective in the sequestration of carbon into the soil. Wetlands, too, hold large amounts of carbon in storage. Agricultural lands can contribute to carbon absorption if proper management is followed. No-tillage agriculture offers the potential to restore large volumes of carbon to agricultural soils and thus contribute to the absorption of carbon from the atmosphere.

Forests appear to offer the greatest potential because they can absorb large volumes of carbon both above and below the ground. Furthermore, the measurement and monitoring of aboveground forest carbon is reasonably simple. The condition of the forest can readily be ascertained visually and with standard forest inventorying procedures, which have been used for decades—indeed, centuries. Carbon can be estimated from the standard forest inventories with only modest additional data requirements. Furthermore, if payments are made for carbon absorbed in the forest biomass, they typically do not reflect the true values because the forest soils also sequester carbon.

As a policy tool, forest sinks pose some distinct challenges. Suppose that a huge reforestation effort is driven by the desire to absorb carbon and that many of these trees would also be suitable as timber. Timber producers, which annually plant an estimated several million hectares of trees for industrial wood purposes, are going to reconsider their tree-growing investments. After all, with all of these new forests being created, the outlook for future timber prices must appear to be bleak. Thus, many timber producers may decide to reduce their own investments in timber growing. The net effect will be to offset some of the increased planting for carbon purposes with the reduction in industrial forest-growing investments. This reduction—that is, the impacts that are precipitated by carbon-absorbing forest projects but are external to those projects—is called *leakage*.

A second form of leakage is associated with protecting threatened forests, as often is proposed for the tropics. Suppose that a particularly valuable forest is threatened with conversion to agriculture. Intervention may be able to save this forest and thus claim credits for the carbon that is prevented from being emitted. However, such an action might simply deflect the deforestation pressure from one forest to another, with no net reduction in carbon emissions.

It should be noted that leakage is not unique to forest sinks. Potential leakage is pervasive throughout many of the proposed climate remedies. Consider the proposal to tax carbon emissions from fossil fuels in developed countries as a way to provide financial incentives to assist developed countries in meeting their emission reduction targets. Such a policy would increase energy prices in the developed world and energy-intensive industries would have incentives to move to the developing world, where no emission targets or carbon taxes exist, and hence energy is cheaper. The net effect could be the transfer of emissions from developed countries to developing countries without a significant reduction in global emissions. This leakage in the energy sector could be substantial and could have significant implications for the world economy.

Can such an outcome be avoided for both carbon sinks and energy? Yes, but it would require implementing similar rules across countries so that leakage is not created through circumvention outside a project or outside a particular country. One step would be to allow sink credits only on a country's net carbon sink increases, and debits for net sink reduction.

Overall, forest sinks have the potential to play a valuable role in carbon sequestration. Although sinks are only a partial solution anticipated global warming, they do appear to have the potential to sequester 10 to 20% of the anticipated build-up of atmospheric carbon over the next 50 years. Furthermore, sinks can accomplish the task at relatively low costs compared to many other approaches.

Roger A. Sedjo is a senior fellow in RFF's Energy and Natural Resources Division, director of RFF's Forest Economics and Policy Program.

Trying to save Sudan

A faith-based bloc wants to halt Africa's longest-running war

BY MICHAEL SATCHELL

It was question time for the seventh graders from Mills E. Godwin Middle School in Dale City, Va., who were visiting Capitol Hill as guests of their congressman, Republican Rep. Frank Wolf. Along with fellow human-rights activists, Wolf has spent over a decade trying to raise public concern about a conflict in one of Africa's most remote and dangerous regions, only to be ignored, patronized, and dismissed—told by Clinton administration Secretary of State Madeleine Albright that the issue was "not marketable to the American people." So Wolf couldn't help but be encouraged by the first student question: "What is the United States going to do about Sudan?"

Sudan? It is the battleground for Africa's longest and bloodiest civil war, in which the Islamic Arab government in Khartoum is crushing black Christian rebels in the south. But the conflict has hardly ranked among the U.S. government's—or the American public's—peacemaking priorities. It could be considered a case of reverse CNN effect: No television pictures, and thus little outcry over an 18-year war that has cost more than 2 million lives, created some 4.4 million refugees, and been marked by slavery, mass rape, and deliberate starvation. The devastation of the Dinka and Nuer tribes has been so severe that the U.S. Holocaust Memorial Museum last year issued its first "genocide warning" for any nation beyond Europe.

Pariah nation. Still, Albright had a point. In the realpolitik of U.S. foreign policymaking, there has not been an effective domestic constituency for making Sudan a priority. Now, though, a remarkable alliance is taking shape. The emotional touchstones: slavery, religious persecution, and civilian atrocities. Leading the broadly ecumenical coalition are African-American churches and white Christian evangelicals, among them the Rev. Franklin Graham—a Bush confidante who is the son of the Rev. Billy Graham. His ministry runs a hospital in southern Sudan that has been bombed nine times by government forces. The bipartisan Sudan coalition also includes key lawmakers, civil rights organizations, feminist alliances, and labor unions. Its goal is to make Sudan a pariah nation by using many of the same tactics that forced South Africa to end apartheid. The strategy ranges from stockholder divestment campaigns and closing off U.S. capital markets to companies helping Khartoum develop its newfound oil wealth, to street demonstrations and civil disobedience. "Slavery in Sudan is just as paramount a concern as apartheid was in South Africa," says Kweisi Mfume, head of the NAACP.

The Clinton administration, angry at Sudan's support of terrorists, isolated and bombed Khartoum but did little to try to end the war. The Sudan coalition wants President Bush to spearhead an international peace effort, pressure the United Nations Security Council to intervene with sanctions or a peacekeeping force, and appoint a special envoy whom the Sudanese can't ignore, such as former Vice President Al Gore or former Secretary of State James Baker. They also want the administration to begin shipping food, medicine, and other aid directly to the south.

While President Bush has shown little enthusiasm for involvement in regional conflicts lacking direct American interests, there are early signs of White House attention to Sudan. The president has twice cited religious persecution there. Secretary of State Colin Powell and White House political adviser Karl Rove have put Sudan on their agendas. Ending the war will be a priority, Powell declared after a March brainstorming session, adding: "There is perhaps no greater tragedy on the face of the Earth."

That kind of talk resonates on Capitol Hill, where growing support for the Sudan campaign crosses the ideological spectrum from the 37-member Congressional Black Caucus to conservatives such as Jesse Helms, chairman of the Senate Foreign Relations Committee, and House Majority Leader Dick Armey, who calls the civil war "a nightmare of unspeakable proportions." Emotional testimony at congressional hearings on chattel slavery in Sudan—Helms was reduced to tears during one session—is fueling the determination to end it. Tens of thousands of black southerners have been kidnapped in raids by government soldiers and their Arab militias and carried north into bondage. Western Christian groups, buying freedom at an average $35 a head, have repatriated some 42,000 captives.

Beyond slavery, there is a new impetus to end the strife. The discovery in the past several years of some 2 billion barrels of oil reserves has dramatically escalated the conflict from a guerrilla brush war to a scorched-earth offensive by heavily mechanized government troops. Most of the oil lies in the southern lands of the Dinka and Nuer, and the Khartoum government is brutally depopulating large areas around oil zones to protect them from possible rebel attacks.

Burned alive. Human rights and aid workers report tens of thousands are being forced from their homes by aerial bombing and strafing, and by soldiers razing entire villages, destroying food stocks, and committing atrocities. In and around the town of Bentiu, reports Amnesty International, "male villagers were killed in mass executions; women and children were nailed to trees with iron spikes ...soldiers slit the throats of children." In February, an aid worker traveling south of Bentiu counted 23 destroyed villages and quotes survivors as saying that those who couldn't flee—the elderly, sick, and very young—were burned alive by the troops.

Thanks to massive investment by foreign oil companies, Sudan's revenues from oil exports have leaped from zero in 1998 to an estimated $585 million last year with production expected to double in two years. Sudan's main oil developers include Canadian, French, Austrian, Swedish, Chinese, and Malaysian companies.

Members of the Sudan coalition want President Bush to pressure Sudan's oil partners to suspend operations until there is a peace settlement. Citing the Clinton administration's inaction in the 1994 Rwandan genocide that claimed up to 600,000 lives, they view Sudan as a litmus test for the new administration's concern for religious persecution and human rights.

Concern alone won't bring a swift end to Africa's most intractable conflict. "The odds of any kind of rapid success are minuscule," says a State Department official. Still, the Sudan peace lobby hopes its burgeoning campaign is a start.

China's changing land

Population, food demand and land use in China

Gerhard K. Heilig

China's land-use changes directly affect the country's capacity to generate sufficient food supplies. Losses of arable land due to natural disasters, agricultural restructuring, and infrastructure expansion might lead to food production deficits in the future.

China's food prospects, however, are also of geostrategic and geopolitical relevance to the West. Food deficits in China might destabilize the country and jeopardize the process of economic and political reform. Despite China's strong commitment to self-sufficiency, the country may become a major importer of (feed) grain. This is of great economic interest to large grain exporters such as the United States, France, or Australia.

There is also the danger that climate change might affect China's vegetation cover—especially the large grasslands, which are important for the country's livestock production. An increased frequency of catastrophic weather events could trigger massive floods or extended droughts that would affect major agricultural areas in various parts of China. These trends pose serious risks for the country's future food security.

What are the major trends in China's land-use changes?

There are few places in the world where people have changed the land so intensively, and over such a long period, as in China. The Loess Plateau of Northern China, for instance, was completely deforested in pre-industrial times. The Chinese started systematic land reclamation and irrigation schemes, converting large areas of natural land into rice paddies, as far back as the early Han Dynasty, in the fourth and third centuries BC. This process, which was scientifically planned and coordinated by subsequent dynastic bureaucracies, reached its first climax in the 11th and 12th centuries. Another period of massive land modification followed in the second half of the 18th and first half of the 19th century.

The LUC project, however, deals with a more recent phase—approximately since the foundation of the People's Republic of China in 1949—and in particular the period since economic reforms began in 1978. Although there has been widespread speculation in the scientific literature about losses of cultivated land in China due to pollution and urban expansion, very little hard data was available when the LUC project started. Through its collaboration with Chinese partners and other sources, LUC has received highly detailed land-use and land-cover data for China. This information includes statistical data, mapped information and remote sensing data. Table 1 presents some results from LUC's analyses of the most recent trends, based on new surveys from the Chinese State Land Administration:

- Conversion of cropland into horticulture was the most important factor in land-use change in China in recent years. Between 1988 and 1995 farmers converted some 1.2 million hectares (ha) of cropland into horticulture. This conversion is a positive trend, indicating a growing market orientation of Chinese agriculture.
- Manifold construction activities (roads, settlements, industry and mining) diminished China's cultivated land by 980,000 ha between 1988 and 1995.
- The third most important type of land-use change was reforestation, diverting almost 970,000 ha of previously cultivated land.
- Between 1988 and 1995, China also lost some 850,000 ha due to natural disasters–mainly flooding and droughts.

These data clearly indicate that anthropogenic factors are mainly responsible for recent land-use changes in China. The growing demand for meat, fish, fruit, and vegetables

Table 1:
Increase, decrease and net-change of cultivated land in China by region 1988—1995 (in hectares).

	Increase				Decrease Conversion						
	Recla-mation	Drain-age	Re-use of aban-doned land	Conv. from agricul-tural land	Con-struct. (1)	to horti-culture	to forest land	to grass-land	to fish-ponds	Disas-ters	Net-Change
North	289.733	18.233	106,028	41,080	-229.825	-298.595	-111.895	-41.255	-7.979	-105,535	-340.020
North-east	396.867	21.991	39.957	25.852	-109,662	-87.417	-156.501	-90.631	-9.426	-250.871	-219.842
East	43.250	21.147	34.284	44.628	-242.824	-178.677	-24.765	-1.416	-45.624	-29.328	-379.324
Central	79.943	7.665	13.159	26.529	-91.802	-101.858	-111.782	-2.689	-61.519	-41.456	-283.771
South	320.001	22.686	18.870	96.681	-117.023	-116.966	-81.465	-10.361	-87.096	-56.534	-11.206
South-west	358.704	8.687	40.260	90.450	-92.583	-114.235	-161.770	-93.864	-7.902	-132.915	-105.169
Plateau	28.044	980	3.135	3.935	-7.927	-163	-363	-11.874	-1	-486	15.281
North-west	681.902	19.798	93.428	84.270	-88.588	-325.316	-321.214	-296.605	-6.322	-239.252	-397.900
TOTAL	2.198.444	121.177	349.121	413.465	-980.235	-1.223.229	-969.756	-548.694	-225.868	-856.377	-1.721.951

Source: State Land Administration, Statistical Information on the Land of China in 1995. Beijing, 1996. And equivalent reports for 1988 to 1994.

Note: (1) "Construction" includes all kinds of infrastructure, industrial areas and residential areas. In the original data tables this category includes all construction by state-owned units (cities, towns, mining and factories, railways, highways, water reservoirs, public buildings) and constructions by rural communities (rural roads, township and village enterprises, rural water reservoirs, offices, education and sanitation, rural private resident housing).

drives much of the agricultural restructuring, such as conversion to horticultural land and fishponds. Environmental programs are promoting reforestation, and the expansion of infrastructure is a function of rapid economic development and urbanization.

What are important drivers of land-use change in China?

Proximate determinants, such as those discussed above, are just the last step in a chain of causation that triggers land-use change in China. There are, however, three fundamental factors behind these trends:

- Population growth. Most recent projections from the United Nations Population Division (see Figure 1) assume that China's population will increase to some 1.49 billion people by 2025 and then slowly decline to 1.48 by 2050.
- Income growth. By all measures, China had spectacular economic growth rates in recent years. The number of people in poverty declined by some 200 million.
- Urbanization. Although China still has a large agricultural population, most experts predict a rapid increase in the number and size of towns and cities in the future. This urbanization is associated with changes in labor-force participation and lifestyle.

Population growth increases the demand for food and thus leads to intensification of agriculture and expansion of cultivated land. However, as the LUC analysis shows, there is a high error range in projecting China's population for more than 20 to 30 years. Its huge initial size amplifies even very small changes in fertility and mortality. For instance, between estimates made in 1994 and 1998, the United Nations Population Division had to revise its population projection for China for the year 2050 by 128 million. This uncertainty is unavoidable, and must be taken into account in predicting food demand and other population-related changes.

There is also considerable uncertainty concerning China's future economic development. Current trends indicate that China will experience a rapid transition from

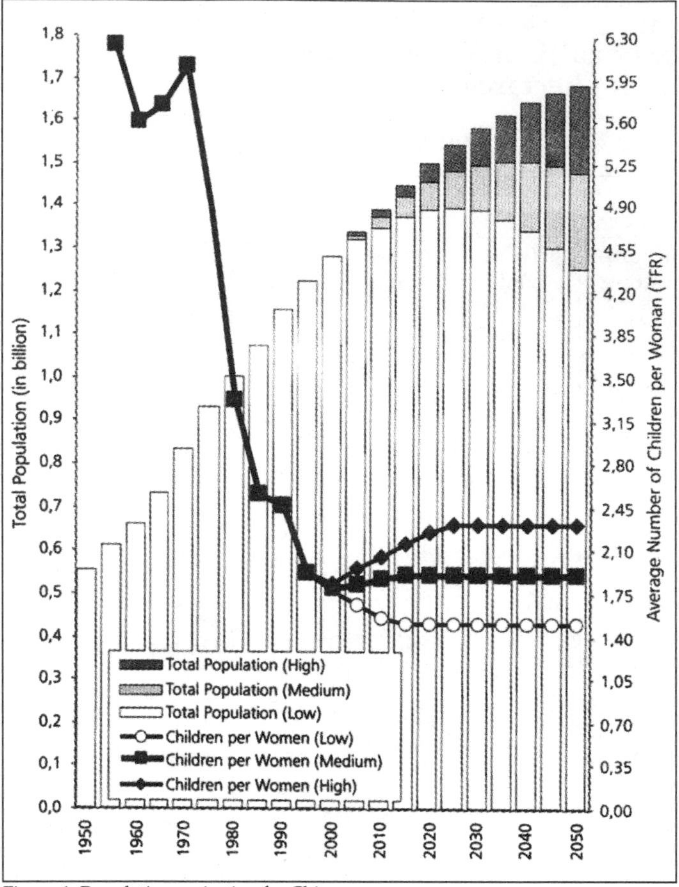

Figure 1: Population projection for China

an agricultural to an industrial and service society. This would lead to expansion of infrastructure and areas of settlement, encroaching on valuable cropland, especially around urban-industrial agglomerations in coastal provinces.

An increase of productivity in both industry and agriculture could also lead to massive unemployment—particularly among the agricultural population. China already has an excess agricultural labor force of at least 120 million, which will increase the potential for rural-urban migration. Policy measures could probably slow down urbanization to some extent, but most projections assume a massive increase in urban population from the current 370 million to 800 million people. All these trends would—directly or indirectly—influence land use in China. With growing income and urban lifestyle, for instance, Chinese consumers will further change their diet (see Figure 2).

According to FAO estimates, there was already a massive increase in the domestic supply of meat from 6.6 to 47.9 million metric tons between the mid-1960s and the mid-1990s—with a significant effect on crop production patterns. The harvest of maize (the major feed crop) increased from 25 to 113 million tons between the mid-1960s and mid-1990s. Use of cereals for feeding animals grew from 12 million tons in 1964–66 to 107 million tons in 1994–96. Similar trends can be observed with other food commodities. Between the mid-1960s and mid-1990s, China's vegetable production increased from 37.9 to 182.7 million tons, and the production of fish increased from 3.3 to 24.3 million tons. These consumer-driven changes in agricultural production caused most of the land-use change in China during the last few decades.

Some general observations resulting from LUC's research

LUC's various models and analyses indicate that China is certainly facing a critical phase of its development during the next three decades. In that period, the demographic momentum will inevitably lead to further population growth, in the order of some 260 million people. Their demand for food, water, and shelter will greatly increase pressure on China's land and water resources. The country's urbanization and economic development will amplify this pressure. Without effective control of pollution and farmland loss, China faces serious problems of land degradation and productivity decline that might threaten the country's food security.

The LUC project has analyzed how global climate change might affect natural vegetation, agriculture, and water management systems in China. This is essential for a long-term water and land resource strategy. China will only be able to cope with its serious problems of flooding and drought if it takes into account the interactions between human and natural factors. For instance, flood damage has increased in recent years because farmers moved into areas that should have been reserved for flood control. The serious water deficit in downstream areas of the Yellow River is amplified by a massive increase in (rather inefficient) agricultural water consumption upstream. As the LUC analysis on *Human Impact on Yellow River Water Management* (IIASA IR 98-016) has shown. China will need intense water management activities to secure a reliable water supply.

Despite recent progress, great data deficits and uncertainties still exist concerning both biophysical and socioeconomic conditions and trends. While LUC was able—with the help of Chinese colleagues—to improve, cross-check, and update several (georeferenced) data sets on China (climate, soils, water, cultivated land, grassland, natural vegetation, population, etc.), project staff still see the need for additional sources of information. In particular, remote sensing data could improve land-use analyses and planning for certain regions. Due to the rapid change in China, available statistical or mapped data are not always up to date. For instance, the conversion of arable land due to infrastructure expansion and urban sprawl in recent years could be analyzed more accurately with satellite images.

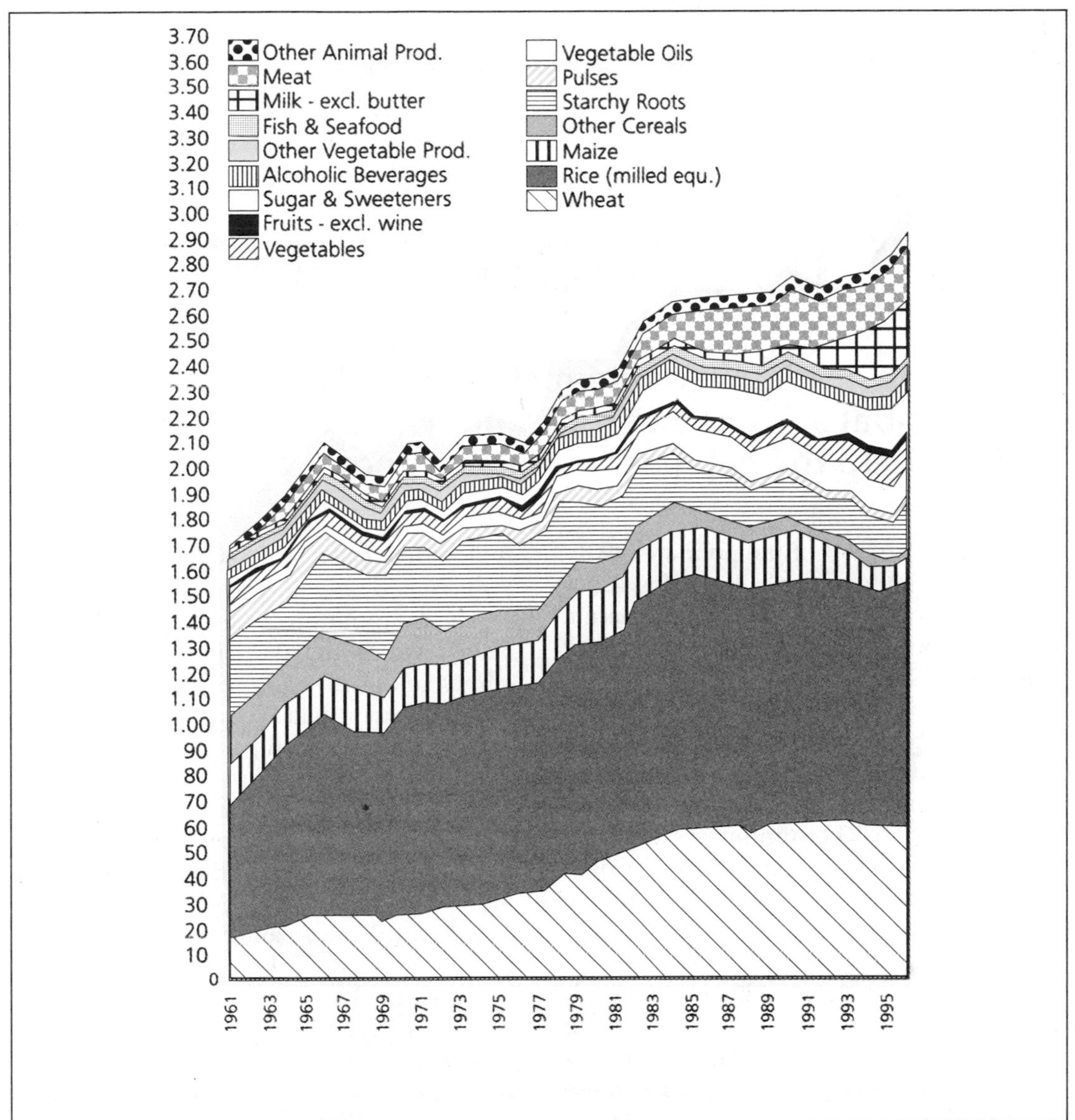

Figure 2: Per capita food consumption by commodity.

Helping the world's poorest

Jeffrey Sachs, a top academic economist, argues that rich countries must mobilise global science and technology to address the specific problems which help to keep poor countries poor

IN OUR Gilded Age, the poorest of the poor are nearly invisible. Seven hundred million people live in the 42 so-called Highly Indebted Poor Countries (HIPCs), where a combination of extreme poverty and financial insolvency marks them for a special kind of despair and economic isolation. They escape our notice almost entirely, unless war or an exotic disease breaks out, or yet another programme with the International Monetary Fund (IMF) is signed. The Cologne Summit of the G8 in June was a welcome exception to this neglect. The summiteers acknowledged the plight of these countries, offered further debt relief and stressed the need for a greater emphasis by the international community on social programmes to help alleviate human suffering.

The G8 proposals should be seen as a beginning: inadequate to the problem, but at least a good-faith prod to something more useful. We urgently need new creativity and a new partnership between rich and poor if these 700m people (projected to rise to 1.5 billion by 2030), as well as the extremely poor in other parts of the world (especially South Asia), are to enjoy a chance for human betterment. Even outright debt forgiveness, far beyond the G8's stingy offer, is only a step in the right direction. Even the call to the IMF and World Bank to be more sensitive to social conditions is merely an indicative nod.

A much more important challenge, as yet mainly unrecognised, is that of mobilising global science and technology to address the crises of public health, agricultural productivity, environmental degradation and demographic stress confronting these countries. In part this will require that the wealthy governments enable the grossly underfinanced and underempowered United Nations institutions to become vibrant and active partners of human development. The failure of the United States to pay its UN dues is surely the world's most significant default on international obligations, far more egregious than any defaults by impoverished HIPCs. The broader American neglect of the UN agencies that assist impoverished countries in public health, science, agriculture and the environment must surely rank as another amazingly misguided aspect of current American development policies.

The conditions in many HIPCs are worsening dramatically, even as global science and technology create new surges of wealth and well-being in the richer countries. The problem is that, for myriad reasons, the technological gains in wealthy countries do not readily diffuse to the poorest ones. Some barriers are political and economic. New technologies will not take hold in poor societies if investors fear for their property rights, or even for their lives, in corrupt or conflict-ridden societies. *The Economist's* response to the Cologne Summit ("Helping the Third World", June 26th) is right to stress that aid without policy reform is easily wasted. But the barriers to development are often more subtle than the current emphasis on "good governance" in debtor countries suggests.

Research and development of new technologies are overwhelmingly directed at rich-country problems. To the extent that the poor face distinctive challenges, science and technology must be directed purposefully towards them. In today's global set-up, that rarely happens. Advances in science and technology not only lie at the core of long-term economic growth, but flourish on an intricate mix of social institutions—public and private, national and international.

Currently, the international system fails to meet the scientific and technological needs of the world's poorest. Even when the right institutions exist—say, the World Health Organisation to deal with pressing public health disasters facing the poorest countries—they are generally starved for funds, authority and even access to the key negotiations between poor-country governments and the Fund at which important development strategies get hammered out.

The ecology of underdevelopment

If it were true that the poor were just like the rich but with less money, the global situation would be vastly easier

Different ecologies

1995	HIPCs* (42)	Rich countries (30)
GDP per person, PPP$†	1,187	18,818
Life expectancy at birth, years†	51.5	76.9
Population by ecozones, % in:		
tropical	55.6	0.7
dry	17.6	3.7
temperate and snow	12.5	92.6
highland	14.0	2.5

Source: J. Sachs *Highly indebted poor countries †Unweighted averages

than it is. As it happens, the poor live in different ecological zones, face different health conditions and must overcome agronomic limitations that are very different from those of rich countries. Those differences, indeed, are often a fundamental cause of persisting poverty.

Let us compare the 30 highest-income countries in the world with the 42 HIPCs (see table above). The rich countries overwhelmingly lie in the world's temperate zones. Not every country in those bands is rich, but a good rule of thumb is that temperate-zone economies are either rich, formerly socialist (and hence currently poor), or geographically isolated (such as Afghanistan and Mongolia). Around 93% of the combined population of the 30 highest-income countries lives in temperate and snow zones. The HIPCs by contrast, include 39 tropical or desert societies. There are only three in a substantially temperate climate, and those three are landlocked and therefore geographically isolated (Laos, Malawi and Zambia).

Not only life but also death differs between temperate and tropical zones. Individuals in temperate zones almost everywhere enjoy a life expectancy of 70 years or more. In the tropics, however, life expectancy is generally much shorter. One big reason is that populations are burdened by diseases such as malaria, hookworm, sleeping sickness and schistosomiasis, whose transmission generally depends on a warm climate. (Winter may be the greatest public-health intervention in the world.) Life expectancy in the HIPCs averages just 51 years, reflecting the interacting effects of tropical disease and poverty. The economic evidence strongly suggests that short life expectancy is not just a result of poverty, but is also a powerful cause of impoverishment.

All the rich-country research on rich-country ailments, such as cardiovascular diseases and cancer, will not solve the problems of malaria. Nor will the biotechnology advances for temperate-zone crops easily transfer to the conditions of tropical agriculture. To address the special conditions of the HIPCs, we must first understand their unique problems, and then use our ingenuity and co-operative spirit to create new methods of overcoming them.

Modern society and prosperity rest on the foundation of modern science. Global capitalism is, of course, a set of social institutions—of property rights, legal and political systems, international agreements, transnational corporations, educational establishments, and public and private research institutions—but the prosperity that results from these institutions has its roots in the development and applications of new science-based technologies. In the past 50 years, these have included technologies built on solid-state physics, which gave rise to the information-technology revolution, and on genetics, which have fostered breakthroughs in health and agricultural productivity.

Science at the ecological divide

In this context, it is worth noting that the inequalities of income across the globe are actually exceeded by the inequalities of scientific output and technological innovation. The chart below shows the remarkable dominance of rich countries in scientific publications and, even more notably, in patents filed in Europe and the United States.

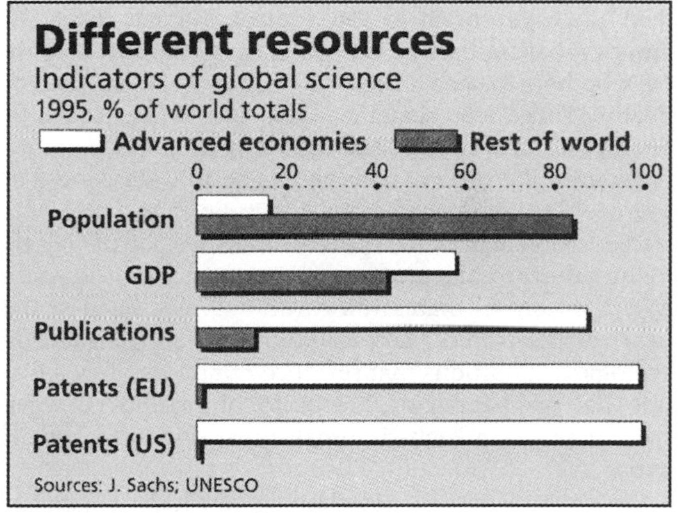

Sources: J. Sachs; UNESCO

The role of the developing world in one sense is much greater than the chart indicates. Many of the scientific and technological breakthroughs are made by poor-country scientists working in rich-country laboratories. Indian and Chinese engineers account for a significant proportion of Silicon Valley's workforce, for example. The basic point, then, holds even more strongly: global science is directed by the rich countries and for the rich-country markets, even to the extent of mobilising much of the scientific potential of the poorer countries.

The imbalance of global science reflects several forces. First, of course, science follows the market. This is especially true in an age when technological leaps require expensive scientific equipment and well-provisioned research laboratories. Second, scientific advance tends to have increasing returns to scale: adding more scientists to a community does not diminish individual marginal productivity but tends to increase it. Therein lies the origin of university science departments, regional agglomerations such as Silicon Valley and Route 128, and mega-laboratories at leading high-technology firms including Merck, Microsoft and Monsanto. And third, science requires a partnership between the public and private sectors. Free-market ideologues notwithstanding, there is scarcely one technology of significance that was not nurtured through public as well as private care.

If technologies easily crossed the ecological divide, the implications would be less dramatic than they are. Some technologies, certainly those involving the computer and other ways of managing information, do indeed cross over, and give great hopes of spurring technological capacity in the poorest countries. Others—especially in the life sciences but also in the use of energy, building techniques, new materials and the like—are prone to "ecological specificity". The result is a profound imbalance in the global production of knowledge: probably the most powerful engine of divergence in global well-being between the rich and the poor.

Consider malaria. The disease kills more than 1m people a year, and perhaps as many as 2.5m. The disease is so heavily concentrated in the poorest tropical countries, and overwhelmingly in sub-Saharan Africa, that nobody even bothers to keep an accurate count of clinical cases or deaths. Those who remember that richer places such as Spain, Italy, Greece and the southern United States once harboured the disease may be misled into thinking that the problem is one of social institutions to control its transmission. In fact, the sporadic transmission of malaria in the sub-tropical regions of the rich countries was vastly easier to control than is its chronic transmission in the heart of the tropics. Tropical countries are plagued by ecological conditions that produce hundreds of infective bites per year per person. Mosquito control does not work well, if at all, in such circumstances. It is in any event expensive.

Recent advances in biotechnology, including mapping the genome of the malaria parasite, point to a possible malaria vaccine. One would think that this would be high on the agendas of both the international community and private pharmaceutical firms. It is not. A Wellcome Trust study a few years ago found that only around $80m a year was spent on malaria research, and only a small fraction of that on vaccines.

The big vaccine producers, such as Merck, Rhône-Poulenc's Pasteur-Mérieux-Connaught and SmithKline Beecham, have much of the in-house science but not the bottom-line motivation. They strongly believe that there is no market in malaria. Even if they spend the hundreds of millions, or perhaps billions, of dollars to do the R&D and come up with an effective vaccine, they believe, with reason, that their product would just be grabbed by international agencies or private-sector copycats. The hijackers will argue, plausibly, that the poor deserve to have the vaccine at low prices—enough to cover production costs but not the preceding R&D expenditures.

The malaria problem reflects, in microcosm, a vast range of problems facing the HIPCs in health, agriculture and environmental management. They are profound, accessible to science and utterly neglected. A hundred IMF missions or World Bank health-sector loans cannot produce a malaria vaccine. No individual country borrowing from the Fund or the World Bank will ever have the means or incentive to produce the global public good of a malaria vaccine. The root of the problem is a much more complex market failure: private investors and scientists doubt that malaria research will be rewarded financially. Creativity is needed to bridge the huge gulfs between human needs, scientific effort and market returns.

Promise a market

The following approach might work. Rich countries would make a firm pledge to purchase an effective malaria vaccine for Africa's 25m newborn children each year if such a vaccine is developed. They would even state, based on appropriate and clear scientific standards, that they would guarantee a minimum purchase price—say, $10 per dose—for a vaccine that meets minimum conditions of efficacy, and perhaps raise the price for a better one. The recipient countries might also be asked to pledge a part of the cost, depending on their incomes. But nothing need be spent by any government until the vaccine actually exists.

Even without a vast public-sector effort, such a pledge could galvanise the world of private-sector pharmaceutical and biotechnology firms. Malaria vaccine research would suddenly become hot. Within a few years, a breakthrough of profound benefit to the poorest countries would be likely. The costs in foreign aid would be small: a few hundred million dollars a year to tame a killer of millions of children. Such a vaccine would rank among the most effective public-health interventions conceivable. And, if science did not deliver, rich countries would end up paying nothing at all.

Malaria imposes a fearsome burden on poor countries, the AIDS epidemic an even weightier load. Two-thirds of the world's 33m individuals infected with the HIV virus are sub-Saharan Africans, according to a UN estimate in 1998, and the figure is rising. About 95% of worldwide HIV cases are in the developing world. Once again, science is stopping at the ecological divide.

Rich countries are controlling the epidemic through novel drug treatments that are too expensive, by orders of magnitude, for the poorest countries. Vaccine research, which could provide a cost-effective method of prevention, is dramatically underfunded. The vaccine research that is being done focuses on the specific viral strains prevalent in the United States and Europe, not on those which bedevil Africa and Asia. As in the case of malaria, the potential developers of vaccines consider the poor-country market to be no market at all. The same, one should note, is true for a third worldwide killer. Tuberculosis is still taking the lives of more than 2m poor people a year and, like malaria and AIDS, would probably be susceptible to a vaccine, if anyone cared to invest in the effort.

The poorer countries are not necessarily sitting still as their citizenry dies of AIDS. South Africa is on the verge of authorising the manufacture of AIDS medicines by South African pharmaceutical companies, despite patents held by American and European firms. The South African government says that, if rich-country firms will not supply the drugs to the South African market at affordable prices (ones that are high enough to meet marginal production costs but do not include the patent-generated monopoly profits that the drug companies claim as their return for R&D), then it will simply allow its own firms to manufacture the drugs, patent or no. In a world in which science is a rich-country prerogative while the poor continue to die, the niceties of intellectual property rights are likely to prove less compelling than social realities.

There is no shortage of complexities ahead. The world needs to reconsider the question of property rights before patent rights allow rich-country multinationals in effect to own the genetic codes of the very foodstuffs on which the world depends, and even the human genome itself. The world also needs to reconsider the role of institutions such as the World Health Organisation and the Food and Agriculture Organisation. These UN bodies should play a vital role in identifying global priorities in health and agriculture, and also in mobilising private-sector R&D towards globally desired goals. There is no escape from such public-private collaboration. It is notable, for example, that Monsanto, a life-sciences multinational based in St Louis, Missouri, has a research and development budget that is more than twice the R&D budget of the entire worldwide network of public-sector tropical research institutes. Monsanto's research, of course, is overwhelmingly directed towards temperate-zone agriculture.

People, food and the environment

Public health is one of the two distinctive crises of the tropics. The other is the production of food. Poor tropical countries are already incapable of securing an adequate level of nutrition, or paying for necessary food imports out of their own export earnings. The HIPC population is expected to more than double by 2030. Around one-third of all children under the age of five in these countries are malnourished and physically stunted, with profound consequences throughout their lives.

As with malaria, poor food productivity in the tropics is not merely a problem of poor social organisation (for example, exploiting farmers through controls on food prices). Using current technologies and seed types, the tropics are inherently less productive in annual food crops such as wheat (essentially a temperate-zone crop), rice and maize. Most agriculture in the equatorial tropics is of very low productivity, reflecting the fragility of most tropical soils at high temperatures combined with heavy rainfall. High productivity in the rainforest ecozone is possible only in small parts of the tropics, generally on volcanic soils (on the island of Java, in Indonesia, for example). In the wet-dry tropics, such as the vast savannahs of Africa, agriculture is hindered by the terrible burdens of unpredictable and highly variable water supplies. Drought and resulting famine have killed millions of peasant families in the past generation alone.

Scientific advances again offer great hope. Biotechnology could mobilise genetic engineering to breed hardier plants that are more resistant to drought and less sensitive to pests. Such genetic engineering is stymied at every point, however. It is met with doubts in the rich countries (where people do not have to worry about their next meal); it requires a new scientific and policy framework in the poor countries; and it must somehow generate market incentives for the big life-sciences firms to turn their research towards tropical foodstuffs, in co-operation with tropical research centres. Calestous Juma, one of the world's authorities on biotechnology in Africa, stresses that there are dozens, or perhaps hundreds, of underused foodstuffs that are well adapted to the tropics and could be improved through directed biotechnology research. Such R&D is now all but lacking in the poorest countries.

The situation of much of the tropical world is, in fact, deteriorating, not only because of increased population but also because of long-term trends in climate. As the rich countries fill the atmosphere with increasing concentrations of carbon, it looks ever more likely that the poor tropical countries will bear much of the resulting burden.

Anthropogenic global warming, caused by the growth in atmospheric carbon, may actually benefit agriculture in high-latitude zones, such as Canada, Russia and the northern United States, by extending the growing season and improving photosynthesis through a process known as carbon fertilisation. It is likely to lower tropical food productivity, however, both because of increased heat stress on plants and because the carbon fertilisation effect appears to be smaller in tropical ecozones. Global warming is also contributing to the increased severity of tropical climatic disturbances, such as the "one-in-a-century" El Niño that hit the tropical world in 1997–98, and the "one-in-a-century" Hurricane Mitch that devastated Honduras and Nicaragua a year ago. Once-in-a-century weather events seem to be arriving with disturbing frequency.

The United States feels aggrieved that poor countries are not signing the convention on climatic change. The truth is that these poor tropical countries should be calling for outright compensation from America and other rich countries for the climatic damages that are being imposed on them. The global climate-change debate will be stalled until it is acknowledged in the United States and Europe that the temperate-zone economies are likely to impose heavy burdens on the already impoverished tropics.

New hope in a new millennium

The situation of the HIPCs has become intolerable, especially at a time when the rich countries are bursting with new wealth and scientific prowess. The time has arrived for a fundamental re-thinking of the strategy for co-operation between rich and poor, with the avowed aim of helping the poorest of the poor back on to their own feet to join the race for human betterment. Four steps could change the shape of our global community.

First, rich and poor need to learn to talk together. As a start, the world's democracies, rich and poor, should join in a quest for common action. Once again the rich G8 met in 1999 without the presence of the developing world. This rich-country summit should be the last of its kind. A G16 for the new millennium should include old and new democracies such as Brazil, India, South Korea, Nigeria, Poland and South Africa.

Second, rich and poor countries should direct their urgent attention to the mobilisation of science and technology for poor-country problems. The rich countries should understand that the IMF and World Bank are by themselves not equipped for that challenge. The specialised UN agencies have a great role to play, especially if they also act as a bridge between the activities of advanced-country and developing-country scientific centres. They will be able to play that role, however, only after the United States pays its debts to the UN and ends its unthinking hostility to the UN system.

We will also need new and creative institutional alliances. A Millennium Vaccine Fund, which guaranteed future markets for malaria, tuberculosis and AIDS vaccines, would be the right place to start. The vaccine-fund approach is administratively straightforward, desperately needed and within our technological reach. Similar efforts to merge public and private science activities will be needed in agricultural biotechnology.

Third, just as knowledge is becoming the undisputed centrepiece of global prosperity (and lack of it, the core of human impoverishment), the global regime on intellectual property rights requires a new look. The United States prevailed upon the world to toughen patent codes and cut down on intellectual piracy. But now transnational corporations and rich-country institutions are patenting everything from the human genome to rainforest biodiversity. The poor will be ripped off unless some sense and equity are introduced into this runaway process.

Moreover, the system of intellectual property rights must balance the need to provide incentives for innovation against the need of poor countries to get the results of innovation. The current struggle over AIDS medicines in South Africa is but an early warning shot in a much larger struggle over access to the fruits of human knowledge. The issue of setting global rules for the uses and development of new technologies—especially the controversial biotechnologies—will again require global co-operation, not the strong-arming of the few rich countries.

Fourth, and perhaps toughest of all, we need a serious discussion about long-term finance for the international public goods necessary for HIPC countries to break through to prosperity. The rich countries are willing to talk about every aspect except money: money to develop new malaria, tuberculosis and AIDS vaccines; money to spur biotechnology research in food-scarce regions; money to help tropical countries adjust to climate changes imposed on them by the richer countries. The World Bank makes mostly loans, and loans to individual countries at that. It does not finance global public goods. America has systematically squeezed the budgets of UN agencies, including such vital ones as the World Health Organisation.

We will need, in the end, to put real resources in support of our hopes. A global tax on carbon-emitting fossil fuels might be the way to begin. Even a very small tax, less than that which is needed to correct humanity's climate-deforming overuse of fossil fuels, would finance a greatly enhanced supply of global public goods. No better time to start than as the new millennium begins.

Jeffrey Sachs is director of the Centre for International Development and professor of international trade at Harvard University. A prolific writer, he has also advised the governments of many developing and East European countries.

Index

T

U

V

W

Y

Z

Test Your Knowledge Form

We encourage you to photocopy and use this page as a tool to assess how the articles in *Annual Editions* expand on the information in your textbook. By reflecting on the articles you will gain enhanced text information. You can also access this useful form on a product's book support Web site at *http://www.dushkin.com/online/*.

NAME: DATE:

TITLE AND NUMBER OF ARTICLE:

BRIEFLY STATE THE MAIN IDEA OF THIS ARTICLE:

LIST THREE IMPORTANT FACTS THAT THE AUTHOR USES TO SUPPORT THE MAIN IDEA:

WHAT INFORMATION OR IDEAS DISCUSSED IN THIS ARTICLE ARE ALSO DISCUSSED IN YOUR TEXTBOOK OR OTHER READINGS THAT YOU HAVE DONE? LIST THE TEXTBOOK CHAPTERS AND PAGE NUMBERS:

LIST ANY EXAMPLES OF BIAS OR FAULTY REASONING THAT YOU FOUND IN THE ARTICLE:

LIST ANY NEW TERMS/CONCEPTS THAT WERE DISCUSSED IN THE ARTICLE, AND WRITE A SHORT DEFINITION:

We Want Your Advice

ANNUAL EDITIONS revisions depend on two major opinion sources: one is our Advisory Board, listed in the front of this volume, which works with us in scanning the thousands of articles published in the public press each year; the other is you—the person a ctu-ally using the book. Please help us and the users of the next edition by completing the prepaid article rating form on this page and returning it to us. Thank you for your help!

ANNUAL EDITIONS: Geography 02/03

ARTICLE RATING FORM

Here is an opportunity for you to have direct input into the next revision of this volume. We would like you to rate each of the articles listed below, using the following scale:

1. **Excellent: should definitely be retained**
2. **Above average: should probably be retained**
3. **Below average: should probably be deleted**
4. **Poor: should definitely be deleted**

Your ratings will play a vital part in the next revision. Please mail this prepaid form to us as soon as possible. Thanks for your help!

RATING	ARTICLE
______	1. Rediscovering the Importance of Geography
______	2. The Geography of Poverty and Wealth
______	3. The Four Traditions of Geography
______	4. Teaching Geography's Four Traditions With Poetry
______	5. The American Geographies
______	6. Human Domination of Earth's Ecosystems
______	7. Sculpting the Earth From Inside Out
______	8. Nuclear Power: A Renaissance That May Not Come
______	9. A Broken Heartland
______	10. Global Warming: The Contrarian View
______	11. The Future of Our Forests
______	12. Restoring Life to the 'Dead Zone': How a Sound Farm Policy Could Save Our Oceans
______	13. Texas and Water: Pay Up or Dry Up
______	14. Beyond the Valley of the Dammed
______	15. The Himba and the Dam
______	16. Past and Present Land Use and Land Cover in the USA
______	17. Operation Desert Sprawl
______	18. A Modest Proposal to Stop Global Warming
______	19. A Greener, or Browner, Mexico?
______	20. The Rise of the Region State
______	21. Continental Divide
______	22. Beyond the Kremlin's Walls
______	23. The Delicate Balkan Balance
______	24. A Continent in Peril
______	25. AIDS Has Arrived in India and China
______	26. Greenville: From Back Country to Forefront
______	27. Underwater Refuge
______	28. The Rio Grande: Beloved River Faces Rough Waters Ahead
______	29. Does It Matter Where You Are?
______	30. Transportation and Urban Growth: The Shaping of the American Metropolis
______	31. GIS Technology Reigns Supreme in Ellis Island Case
______	32. Mapping the Outcrop
______	33. Gaining Perspective
______	34. Census 2000: Micro Melting Pots
______	35. Counties With Cash
______	36. Do We Still Need Skyscrapers?
______	37. China Journal I
______	38. Before the Next Doubling
______	39. A Turning-Point for AIDS?
______	40. The End of Cheap Oil
______	41. Gray Dawn: The Global Aging Crisis
______	42. A Rare and Precious Resource
______	43. Forest 'Sinks' as a Tool for Climate-Change Policymaking: A Look at the Advantages and Challenges
______	44. Trying to Save Sudan
______	45. China's Changing Land: Population, Food Demand and Land Use in China
______	46. Helping the World's Poorest

(Continued on next page)

BUSINESS REPLY MAIL
FIRST-CLASS MAIL PERMIT NO. 84 GUILFORD CT
POSTAGE WILL BE PAID BY ADDRESSEE

McGraw-Hill/Dushkin
530 Old Whitfield Street
Guilford, Ct 06437-9989

ABOUT YOU

Name ______________________ Date ______

Are you a teacher? ❒ A student? ❒
Your school's name ______________________

Department ______________________

Address ______ City ______ State ______ Zip ______

School telephone # ______________________

YOUR COMMENTS ARE IMPORTANT TO US!

Please fill in the following information:
For which course did you use this book? ______________________

Did you use a text with this ANNUAL EDITION? ❒ yes ❒ no
What was the title of the text? ______________________

What are your general reactions to the *Annual Editions* concept? ______________________

Have you read any pertinent articles recently that you think should be included in the next edition? Explain. ______________________

Are there any articles that you feel should be replaced in the next edition? Why? ______________________

Are there any World Wide Web sites that you feel should be included in the next edition? Please annotate. ______________________

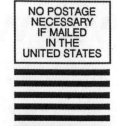

May we contact you for editorial input? ❒ yes ❒ no
May we quote your comments? ❒ yes ❒ no